PROFESSIONAL
LEARNING COMMUNITIES
BY DESIGN

PROFESSIONAL
LEARNING COMMUNITIES
BY DESIGN

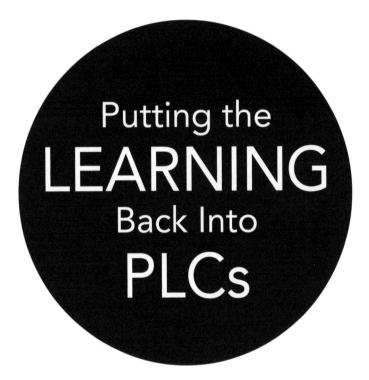

Putting the
LEARNING
Back Into
PLCs

LOIS BROWN EASTON
Foreword by Shirley Hord

A Joint Publication

CORWIN
A SAGE Company

learningforward

CORWIN
A SAGE Company

FOR INFORMATION:

Corwin
A SAGE Company
2455 Teller Road
Thousand Oaks, California 91320
(800) 233-9936
Fax: (800) 417-2466
www.corwin.com

SAGE Ltd.
1 Oliver's Yard
55 City Road
London EC1Y 1SP
United Kingdom

SAGE India Pvt. Ltd.
B 1/I 1 Mohan Cooperative
Industrial Area
Mathura Road, New Delhi 110 044
India

SAGE Asia-Pacific Pte. Ltd.
33 Pekin Street #02-01
Far East Square
Singapore 048763

Acquisitions Editor: Dan Alpert
Associate Editor: Megan Bedell
Editorial Assistant: Sarah Bartlett
Production Editor: Amy Schroller
Copy Editor: Matthew Adams
Typesetter: C&M Digitals (P) Ltd.
Proofreaders: Theresa Kay, Sally Jaskold,
                & Charlotte J. Waisner
Indexer: Molly Hall
Cover Designer: Michael Dubowe
Permissions Editor: Karen Ehrmann

Copyright © 2011 by Corwin

Printed in the United States of America

Library of Congress Cataloging-in-Publication Data

Easton, Lois Brown.

Professional learning communities by design: putting the learning back into PLCs/Lois Brown Easton.

p. cm.
Includes bibliographical references and index.

ISBN 978-1-4129-8711-0 (pbk.)

1. Professional learning communities. 2. Teachers—In-service training. 3. School improvement programs. 4. Remedial teaching. I. Title.

LB1731.E158 2011
370.71—dc23   2011023673

This book is printed on acid-free paper.

11 12 13 14 15 10 9 8 7 6 5 4 3 2 1

Contents

Table of Discussions

Table of Resources Included on Companion CD

Chapter 1

Chapter 2

Foreword

School improvement to improve the quality of classroom teaching

School improvement to meet the requirements of the 21st century

School improvement to ensure every student learns well

While the verses may differ, the refrain remains the same: reform our schools!

Many schools are successfully meeting the needs of a broad range of students who come to school from widely varying family backgrounds, family cultures and traditions; homes of non-English–speaking parents, resulting in multiple languages in a classroom; students who come from all levels of our social and economic platforms—in a word, to form an amazing array of individuals, with significant differences in capacities, to experience an instructional program that will benefit the learning needs of each. Many other schools are unsuccessfully meeting these challenges, while the profession as well as the press and the public want results that indicate each child is learning well.

HOW TO MOVE THIS INTENTION INTO REALITY?

The Process

The *improvement of our schools* seldom results from mandates issued from some higher authority: the superintendent or some other district office coordinator/director, the principal, or grade-level team leader or academic subject matter department head—the recipient typically, teachers. Such "directives" might be adopted, but the likelihood of more than superficial implementation is slight.

Engaging staff, including the implementers, in the study of multiple sources of student data to ascertain where students are performing well, and celebrating those outcomes, is a first step. Revisiting the data to identify areas where performance is poor warrants careful scrutiny. Thoughtful and reflective work is encouraged here in order to discover possible explanations for the less-than-desirable performance of the students.

As a result of the staff's identification and specification work, a focus for immediate, and possibly long-term, attention is made. A decision is taken about what is not working and will be deleted. Plus a commitment is made to find a solution or "new way"—a *change*—that has the potential for increased results and introduce it into the school. What has become very clear is that change (its adoption and implementation) cannot occur without the provision of ongoing and long-term learning for the professionals who will deliver the "new way."

Enter: The Professional Learning Community

The premise, the purpose, the promise of the Professional Learning Community (PLC) is the learning of the professionals of the staff—in schools, those certified, responsible, and accountable for delivering an effective instructional program for all students.

Most of our citizens would volunteer that we have schools for the purpose of student learning. They may debate what students should learn, or how, or when, but there is consensus that schools are for student learning. Research tells us that the most significant factor in whether students learn well is quality teaching. Note that it is not just teach*er* quality, but teach*ing* quality, for many factors within the school, in addition to the teachers, contribute to the quality of the teaching.

How can teaching quality be increased or enhanced? Through continuous professional learning, is a unanimous response. What makes abundant good sense for the professionals' learning is the setting or environment of an effective PLC. This setting is one in which a self-organizing group of people come together to explore students' work, to assess the quality of that work, and make shared decisions about what to do when student performance is poor. Because the community shares leadership and its concomitant power, authority, and decision making, this is messy work. Staff members are learning how to become a community of professional learners while they are doing the work.

Such communities have been a long time in development. In the early years of this country, schools were modestly organized around some mother's fireplace where the Bible was likely the only "textbook" for reading. As teaching became recognized for the important role it played, teachers' colleges were organized and built, course work prescribed, and credits or degrees awarded. At graduation, teachers found their life's work occurring in the "egg crate" school house where there was no professional and little personal interaction between and among the teaching staff.

In current school settings where the idea of PLC is being introduced into their faculties, teachers have the opportunity to meet together—a significant change! It would appear from the number of schools that describe their PLC as a "time to meet" (period) the time to meet *is* the innovation and the purpose of the PLC. Given little guidance and no expectations of what to do in this meeting time, not much happens.

A second typical description of PLC is the community's focus on collaborative work. It is possible, of course, that such collaboration can have substantial results, but whether or not it prepares the fifth-grade team to do a more successful job of teaching long division tomorrow to their poorly performing students is not very likely. Collaboration *is* the means, or a skill needed to be able to work and learn together productively; it is not the end.

It would seem sensible that educators would derive some rather clear understandings of the three words of the PLC label: *professionals* are those certified or licensed to do an established system of work; *community* is a group of individuals who share common goals; and, these professionals meet in their community to focus on *learning*. Rather than an understanding that the learning is meant to be adult learning that is directly related to the needs of students, one wonders, given the widespread attention now being directed to student learning, if the understanding that is gained from professional learning community is learning for students. Student learning is the ultimate goal—but it is achieved through adults who learn how to become more effective. The attention on adult learning is sorely missing in many PLC settings.

Despite the abundance of information and resources committed to professional learning, we have much to learn about how to create and maintain effective communities of professional learners. These communities are comprised of continuous learners, who seek thoughtfully and consistently to learn how to provide students with higher quality teaching so that students are more successful learners.

Lois Easton's story of and commentary on the PLC developing at Glen Haven Middle School helps us do just that, as do the resources provided with this extremely beneficial book.

Shirley Hord

Acknowledgments

The author would like to thank Dan Alpert, Managing Editor of Corwin, and Joellen Killion, Deputy Executive Director of Learning Forward (formerly National Staff Development Council) for their vision and wisdom, high expectations, and encouragement.

She would also like to thank the many reviewers of both a very early version of this book and a later version. The contributions of the following reviewers are gratefully acknowledged:

R. Daniel Cunningham, Jr., Executive Director
        of EXCELerator Solutions
The College Board
District and Student Services
Reston, VA

Linda C. Diaz, Director
Title I and Professional Development
Monroe County School District
Key West, FL

Joan Irwin, Professional Development Consultant
Newark, DE

Nancy Kellogg, Education Consultant
Center for Learning and Teaching in the West
Boulder, CO

Terri Patterson, Executive Director of Elementary
        Education and Professional Development
Waco ISD
Waco, TX

Claudia J. Thompson, Executive Director of
        Curriculum and Professional Development
Peninsula School District
Gig Harbor, WA

About the Author

 **Lois Easton** works as a consultant, coach, and author. She is particularly interested in learning designs—for adults and for students. She recently retired as Director of Professional Development at Eagle Rock School and Professional Development Center, Estes Park, Colorado. A project of the American Honda Education Corporation, Eagle Rock School is a year-round, tuition-free, residential high school for students who have not experienced success in traditional academic settings. The school provides educators who visit the Professional Development Center with experiences in innovative education. As director, Easton designed and administered the professional development program for preservice and student teachers; practicing teachers and administrators; university and college students, both graduate and undergraduate; and researchers. She designed and administered an internship program for 12 young educators per year and an alternative licensure program accredited by the Colorado Department of Education.

Easton was director of Re:Learning Systems at the Education Commission of the States (ECS) from 1992 to 1994. Re:Learning was a partnership between the Coalition of Essential Schools (CES) at Brown University in Providence, Rhode Island, and ECS. The Coalition focuses on school-level restructuring based on the research on American high schools that Dr. Ted Sizer and others performed in the 1980s. ECS, an interstate compact that works with state policy makers to improve the quality of education throughout the country, partnered with CES in Re:Learning to orient reform efforts from "schoolhouse to statehouse" and to effect reform systemwide. Easton was director of the systemic side of the reform.

Prior to that, Easton served in the Arizona Department of Education as English/Language Arts Coordinator, establishing the role in the School Improvement Unit and directing the development of the Language Arts Essential Skills, the state's first standards-based curriculum framework. She became Director of Curriculum and Instruction, and then, as Director of Curriculum and Assessment Planning, designed and implemented the Arizona Student Assessment Program (ASAP), which focused on systemic reform on the basis of curriculum standards aligned with state performance assessments.

A middle school English teacher for 15 years, Easton earned her PhD at the University of Arizona. Her dissertation was a policy analysis of the ASAP. She has held state and national offices, particularly in language arts organizations. She was president of the Arizona English Teachers Association and was elected to the Secondary Steering Committee of the National Council of Teachers of English. She was cochair of the 2001 Conference of the National Staff Development Council in Denver. She is serving a 3-year term as copresident of the Colorado Staff Development Council (now Learning Forward Colorado).

Easton has been a frequent presenter at conferences (she is a senior consultant for Learning Forward) and a contributor to educational journals, such as *Educational Leadership*, *The Journal of Staff Development*, and the *Phi Delta Kappan*. Her book *The Other Side of Curriculum: Lessons From Learners* was published by Heinemann in 2001. She is editor of a book published by the National Staff Development Council in August 2004, *Powerful Designs for Professional Learning*, which was issued in its second edition in 2008. Corwin published her third book, *Engaging the Disengaged: How Schools Can Help Struggling Students Succeed*, in 2008. This book won the Educational Book of the Year Award from Kappa Delta Gamma in 2009. ASCD published her fourth book, *Protocols for Professional Learning*, in 2009.

Introduction

Design. The word is almost magical. It conjures buildings such as Gaudi's masterpiece the Sagrada Família in Barcelona, the music of the Bs (Bach, Beethoven, Brahms, Bartok, Beatles), the poetry of Neruda, the silhouette of *David*, Monet's *Water Lilies*. These have *design* in terms of their coherence.

As designs, they emerged from the passion, purposes, environment, and life experiences of their designers, as well as the media with which they were working. What might have been chaos became coherent. The stone found its sculpture, the notes their music, the syllables their pattern. What was messy found order.

Design. As a verb, the word has another meaning. It refers to the effort of planning, making something happen "the way it should." It connotes control, often from outside the environment, as people devise steps ("The Seven Steps to . . .") or a formula ("If you do *X*, *Y* will happen"). The implication is that there is a right way to work toward a right outcome (and, conversely, a wrong way and a wrong outcome).

PLCs By Design. In this book, *design* refers to the process of finding coherence, what works in a particular environment. It is about purpose and what furthers purpose. Design is not engineered nor imposed from the outside. It is neither a formula nor a set of foolproof steps. Design is open to opportunity. So, if you're looking for a magic formula for creating PLCs that are guaranteed to lead to improved student learning, this is not the book for you. If you are looking for guidelines toward coherence and achievement of purpose; if you are willing to study the messiness of real life; if you are interested in distilling lessons from learning and apply those lessons to your own environment, as they fit—this is the book for you.

Professional Learning Communities. Humans have a need to make meaning, connect, and grow (Wheatley & Kellner-Rogers, 1996, p. 36), so we create organizations. We are, mostly, disappointed in the organizations we create. Wheatley suggests that we may have the best intentions in mind and, at first, our organizations may achieve those intentions: "We see a need. We join with others. We find the necessary information or resources. We respond creatively, quickly. We create a solution that works" (p. 37).

What goes wrong? We interfere with the most natural of organizations—a "self-organizing" organization—and "build rigid structures incapable of responding. We box ourselves in behind hard boundaries . . ." (p. 37). Our analytic culture forces us to try to control each another. So, we invent sure-fire steps or magical formulae; we mechanize what is natural. Often, these steps or formulae are imposed from the outside, insensitive to our own passion, purposes, environment, and life experiences.

Steps and formulae are beguiling. It is too hard to "dare to describe the true fuzziness, the unexpected turns, the bursts of creative insight" that are part of self-organizing organizations (p. 37). It is better to "pretend that we were in control every step of the way" (p. 37). We prefer to talk about "executing plans" rather than reveling in surprises (p. 37).

Professional Learning Communities (PLCs) are a good example of a good idea that might go bad. They startled the education world in the 1990s—at once seeming both promising and commonsensical: "Of course! Learning communities of educators! In a learning institution. Why not?" The first PLCs were probably stellar examples of self-organizing organizations, started by people who saw a need, joined with others, and found what they needed to respond creatively (p. 37).

Some PLCs remain self-organizing and vibrant. Some early PLCs have disappeared in disappointment, however. Some have become regulated. And, some never had the chance to self-organize. They emerged according to someone else's dictate, a result of easy-to-follow steps and uncompromising principles. The whole concept of PLC today is under fire. To many, *PLC* is just another name for "business as usual."

The premise of this book is that PLCs *as a concept* are still worthy and, as school-based organizations, can make a difference for students. However, PLCs need to be self-organizing. They need to be created and find coherence as self-organizing organizations according to purpose, passion, and environment.

I am not proposing anarchy. In fact, self-organization guarantees that anarchy won't last long. I am not proposing that we cede to chaos. I am proposing that we examine PLCs from the point of view of the muck of messiness that shapes itself into coherence. While I'm not going to offer prescriptions in this book, I am going to offer insights and "lessons learned" about the way PLCs develop, structure themselves, mature, and sustain themselves.

Structure emerges from self-organization. Wheatley maintains, "We work with what is available and encourage forms to come forth. We foster tinkering and discovery. We help create connections. We nourish with information. We stay clear about what we want to accomplish. We remember that people self-organize and trust them to do so" (p. 38). Instead of providing specific steps, we "provide what [people] need to do to begin their work" (p. 38). The structure springs "from the process of doing the work. These structures will be useful but temporary" (p. 38).

We do not "do to" people; we help people "do for themselves most of what in the past has been done to them" so that they can "design what is necessary to do the work. They agree on behaviors and relationships that make sense to them" (p. 38).

What do we most need to be self-organizing? We need to be learners. We need to learn.

Learning. The middle word, the **central** word, in *PLC* is *learning*. Although the other words are important—educators are professional and community is important—it is **learning** that helps us self-organize to achieve coherence and purpose. Wheatley notes that "fuzzy, messy, continuously exploring systems bent on discovering what works are far more practical and successful than our attempts at efficiency" (p. 25). We must be mindful, attentive to "what's available" and "what's possible" (p. 25). Learning means that we "slosh around in the mess, involve many individuals, encourage discoveries, and move quickly past mistakes" (p. 25). We must be "learning all the time, engaging everyone in finding what works" (p. 25).

The middle word in PLC is also, I think, the most central to understanding PLCs and the one that, if activated, prevents PLCs from descending into disappointment. Failed PLCs provide just one more reason educational cynics look upon educational innovation with "This too shall pass" or "Been there, done that" or "Didn't work then, won't work now."

Learning is a matter, first, of consciousness. It requires paying attention. It requires deciding what to notice. It demands a pace slow enough for people to reflect and process with others what is happening. Learning occurs when people ask, "What are we learning from this?" "Why is this learning important to us? Why does it matter?" "What are we going to do about what we are learning?"

The Other Two Words in PLC. The words *professional* and *community* in *PLC* deserve some attention. President Bill Clinton stated in 1998, "Teaching is the essential profession, the one that makes all other professions possible" (p. 1). One of the aspects of a profession is that it has a knowledge base and ways to act upon and expand that knowledge base. Doctors have a knowledge base, which they act upon when they diagnose and prescribe. Lawyers have a knowledge base, which they act upon when they file briefs. CPAs have a hefty knowledge base in terms of tax codes.

Educators have a knowledge base, too. For, example, the 1998 publication by the American Psychological Association, *How Students Learn: Reforming Schools Through Learner-Centered Education* (edited by Nadine M. Lambert and Barbara L. McCombs) is a compendium of what is known about how young people learn and how educators can help them learn. A similar resource is *How People Learn: Brain, Mind, Experience, and School*, published in 2000 by the National Research Council.

Doctors expand their knowledge base through professional learning (associations, conferences, journals) and practices (internships and rounds). Lawyers network with others in groups with strings of names that usually challenge their receptionists, research precedent, and study cases. CPAs keep current with tax classes each year.

Unfortunately, educators do not regularly act upon nor expand their knowledge base in education as much as other professionals do. In "A Knowledge Base for the Teaching Profession: What Would It Look Like and How Can We Get One?" James Hiebert, Ronald Gallimore, and James W. Stigleruch (2002) bemoan the chasm between research and practice. In terms of expanding the knowledge base, they see a new role for professional development that is "long-term, school-based, collaborative, focused on students' learning, and linked to curricula" (p. 3). They are not talking about traditional professional development, however, sometimes known as "sit 'n' git," "drive-by," "sage-on-the-stage" or "seagull style" (the seagull flies in, drops a load, and moves on). They are talking about professional learning.

Characteristics of Professional Learning. In *Powerful Designs for Professional Learning* (2008a, pp. 3–4), I described 12 qualities of powerful professional learning, characteristics that distinguish it from professional development:

1. **Powerful professional learning arises from and returns benefits to the real world of teaching and learning**. This is more important than it sounds. Often the superintendent or principal who wants to start the school year off right hires a speaker. Sometimes a committee chooses the person. But usually staff are clear that not much change is expected as a result of the speech. It may also be clear that the speaker knows very little about the school or district or their

needs and may be giving a generic speech, perhaps one that has gone well in other venues. After such speakers have bowed to the applause, folded up their notes and disengaged their technology, nothing much does change in the real world of teaching and learning—unless the school engages in professional learning activities related to what they have heard.

2. **Powerful professional learning requires the collection, analysis and presentation of real data**—from student work and teacher practice. Test scores matter but so do other representations of achievement, demographics, perceptions, and programs and practices that operate in the school. All these, according to Victoria Bernhardt (2008) are important to collect . . . before, during, and after professional learning experiences. Before, they help educators decide for themselves what they need to learn. During, they help educators monitor changes happening in classrooms and schools, adjusting as necessary. After, they provide evidence of improvement and suggest next steps.

3. **Powerful professional learning begins with what will really help young people learn**, engages those involved in helping them learn, and has an effect on the classrooms (and schools, districts, even states) where those students and their teachers learn. Educators who engage in powerful professional learning first work to understand how a school or district can improve learning for all children, using data as well as their own skills, knowledge, and experiences.

4. **Powerful professional learning results in application in the classroom**. Throughout the professional learning experience (which may be continuous), the focus remains on what is happening with learners (both student and adult) in the classroom, school, and district. During their learning, educators return to the learning environment to do the following:

   - Try out a new technique with learners;
   - Set up a research process to obtain data;
   - Receive feedback from students and coaches and mentors;
   - Reflect on what they are learning;
   - Confer with others about what is being learned;
   - Report results; and
   - Modify what they are doing and repeat these processes.

   They may also plan next steps.

5. **Powerful professional learning experiences may not formally** *end*; they may simply evolve into other powerful forms as participants raise more questions or want to try another strategy. Powerful professional learning usually leads to the desire to make continued improvement. It may even change an institution into a learning community.

6. **Powerful professional learning honors the professionalism, expertise, experiences, and skills of staff**. When administrators rely on outsiders, they may communicate the message that those within a school or district lack expertise. Although this can sometimes be the case, with powerful professional learning experiences school and district staff can develop their own expertise. During the process, educators identify content needs that fit the

context of their environment and select powerful professional learning strate-gies that will help them learn; they also identify the people who can lead the learning, people who might very well be in the school or district itself.

A culture becomes a continuous learning community when educators are asked to apply their skills and professionalism to improve student learning—and when they recognize the skills and professionalism everyone else brings to the improvement process.

7. **Powerful professional learning is content-rich** because the content is the school or district itself . . . its staff . . . its learners. This is content that mat-ters to the people engaged in the experience.

8. **Powerful professional learning is collaborative or has collaborative aspects to it**. Educators learn from each other, enriching their own profes-sional lives and the culture of the school or district. They build a shared vision of a school or district, and—contrasting that with realities—they work on what matters and help each other make changes. They set goals, help each other meet these goals and hold themselves and other accountable.

9. **Powerful professional learning establishes a culture of quality**. Powerful professional learning encourages discussion about what quality looks like, in terms of the work educators and their students do.

10. **Powerful professional learning results in "buy-in" because it utilizes the talent within**. Those who are going to implement change will be more likely to do so if they are involved in the design of the change through powerful professional learning. An aphorism speaks to this phenomenon: *Them's as does the doin' does the decidin'*.

11. **Powerful professional learning slows the pace of schooling**, providing time for the inquiry and reflection that promote learning and application. Educators seldom pause in their hectic schedules to make sense of what is going on. They just keep going. Powerful professional learning is a gift to educators who sel-dom have a chance to reflect on their own teaching and learning.

12. **Powerful professional learning designs provide the activities that make professional learning communities (PLCs) more than just a structure**. Without meaningful learning activities that occur during PLC time, PLCs may go the way of so many other structures, such as block scheduling and small schools, that were instituted without enough attention to what teach-ers and students do that would take advantage of those structures.

This book is about growing professional learning communities and, therefore, becoming more professional.

Community. Many groups call themselves communities, whether they are one or not. *Community*, in the strictest sense, means people with something in common—which may be no more than the fact that they belong to the same group!

Names for other groups help us discern the differences. For example, an organiza-tion is not necessarily a community. Both may have common purposes, but the main difference may lie with who sets the common purpose. In an organization (or, as a type of organization, a business), which is often structured as a hierarchy, the bosses (or a board or trustees) set the purpose. In fact, the purpose usually comes first in an organization ("We are organizing to save the whales"; "Our business is fixing computers"). The hierarchy dictates that others join the organization or are employed by the business in order to achieve that purpose. In an effort to achieve conviviality, the bosses may declare that the organization is a community, but the inequality that is necessary for a business may lurk just under the surface of *bonhomie*.

A community is more likely to determine its purpose together, with each member of the community wielding as much power as another. In fact, the "first order of business" in a community might be to determine purpose. Wheatley calls this process one of finding identity. "Who are we? What do we want to work on?"

Associations seem to be "organization lite"; that is, they are more loosely connected than organizations. Clubs and societies seem more oriented toward the social aspects of being together—that is, we are together because we share interests (think golf), enjoy being together and may have no other purpose. Unions and alliances suggest politically oriented organizations with an agenda of protection or change.

One type of group—a guild—comes close to community for me. In a guild, people engaged in the same work share their knowledge and understanding. A guild usually features apprentices, who are new to the work, and masters, who are experienced. In a typical guild, the masters share with apprentices what they have learned. In a community, the sharing is not one-way—from master to apprentice. It is two-way, multiple ways, universal. Also, in community, learning is not static, a thing to be passed on from generation to generation. It is renewable, as members of community contribute to its regeneration each time they learn and share learning. In fact, putting the word *learning* with *community* is what matters. A community is a type of organization that helps humans make meaning, connect, learn, and grow.

ABOUT THIS BOOK

This book is more description than prescription. As you read it, you will follow the story of a school, Glen Haven Middle School, from its first steps toward becoming a PLC through its first year of engagement in the process. You might think of this description as an extended case study. You will not find any prescriptive rules or steps. You will, however, find commentary about what is happening at Glen Haven at various points during the year, ideas that you might consider in your own environment. You will also find tools to use to explore those ideas. These are on the CD that accompanies this book.

The story of Glen Haven gives rise to the commentary, not vice-versa. Glen Haven does not serve as an afterthought example to the ideas. The ideas arise from the story. What the faculty and staff encounter along the way to becoming a PLC leads to discussion.

Thus, the content of the book emerges from the joining together of people at Glen Haven Middle School. As Wheatley says, "Emergence is the surprising capacity we discover only when we join together" (p. 67). "We can never predict what will emerge" (p. 66). You may chafe at what happens at Glen Haven—it isn't what you would have done. You may rail, "Why did they do that?" or, more likely, "Why *didn't* they do that?" For example, the Glen Haven Middle School PLC decides to focus on writing. The data show they should have been more concerned about learning in mathematics. As it turns out, although the need was there in terms of mathematics, the English department had more capacity.

You may think, "Someone should have set them on the right course. Where was the expert? Where were the gurus?" Of course, as Wheatley maintains, we cannot really direct a system from the outside; "we can only disturb it. As external agents we provide only small impulses of information. We can nudge, titillate, or provoke one another into some new ways of seeing. But we can never give anyone an instruction and expect him or her to follow it precisely. We can never assume that anyone else sees the world as we do" (p. 49). So, our steps, our process, our principles may not be the right ones or, if followed, may not lead to the outcome a school needs to move forward.

You may also wonder why we can't just bottle what one successful PLC does and have a budding PLC drink from that bottle Alice-style (but look what happened to her!). Despite exhortations from policy makers, we can't just "go to scale" by replicating what one school has done. Wheatley illuminates this problem: "If a system appears that works well, our dilemmas in understanding it through traditional analysis only intensify. The success of this system results from conditions and relationship that are unique and entangled. How can we ever learn enough about them to recreate such success? Emergent phenomena cannot be recreated. They cannot be transferred. We live in a world that we cannot plan for, control, or replicate" (p. 74).

What can we do? We can pay attention to our own learning. We can ask ourselves questions related to events at Glen Haven Middle School. We can look closely at our own schools and their processes. We can discuss some of the commentaries on Glen Haven's story—how they apply in our own situations.

Why A Story? Most of what is in this book is based on a story. I chose a story format because I believe stories are powerful—in fact, I have included them in other books I have written (*The Other Side of Curriculum: Lessons From Learners*, *Powerful Designs for Professional Learning*, and *Engaging the Disengaged: How Schools Can Help Struggling Students Succeed*). Stories are memorable, sometimes prompting us to recall facts and details that have faded over time.

John Kotter, an expert on leadership at the Harvard Business School, who has written extensively on how organizations change (*Leading Change*, 1996) wrote, "Over the years I have become convinced that we learn best—and change—from hearing stories that strike a chord within us."

Another business leader, Tom Peters, wrote, "He/she who has the best/most compelling most resonant story wins" (2010, p. 70). I don't really want to win, but I want to be sure something in this book resonates with you enough that you think about and share your ideas with your colleagues and take steps toward realizing your purpose.

According to Terrance Gargiulo in *The Power of Stories in Communication & Management* (2009), story-based communications are implicit, evocative, and emergent. Meaning is "encoded in packets of compelling and memorable nuggets" (p. 4). These story nuggets are "more emotional in nature," and "meant to trigger people's experiences, personal associations, and linkages" (p. 4). Typical ways of communicating do not have the same power, tending to be explicit, logical, and controlled.

Tom Atlee, founder, codirector, and research director of the nonprofit Co-Intelligence Institute, brings us another perspective: "Story, as a pattern, is a powerful way of organizing and sharing individual experience and exploring and co-creating shared realities" (Atlee, 2007, p. 1).

Futurist John B. Mahaffie asserts, "Access to information is not enough. Information has to have meaning to truly break through to people's understanding.

We are all capable of making intellectual connections to information—understanding it factually. But <u>stories</u> can get through to people by emotional connections to deliver meaning much more strongly. So ultimately we are "story learners" (2009, p. 1).

Frankly, I could not have written this book without stories. They are textural, full of possibility, and go where they need to go.

That said, Glen Haven Middle School is not a real school (at least, not one I know of). Despite what an early reviewer claimed about this book being a documentary, it is not. Glen Haven Middle School is a composite of a number of schools I've worked with over the past two decades. The experiences that the characters have are experiences I've had or have learned about from others in the course of my work. The processes that GHMS staff experience in order to figure out their PLC are messy and real. The conflicts and problems are messy and real. The solutions emerged from the particulars of their problems—and might not actually be the solutions I would have chosen. I admit that, sometimes, I was surprised by what happened at Glen Haven Middle School as the story progressed.

Even though they are not "real," you'll discover a handy cast of characters after this introduction. Even though the events did not really happen, at least on the dates noted in the narrative, you'll also find a calendar of events for Glen Haven's year of discovery.

Organization. Mostly, the material in this book is organized chronologically, from June of one year to August of the next year. The story of Glen Haven proceeds in snippets in each chapter, followed by my commentary on what happened during each piece of narrative. This means that the commentary does not proceed in any predictable, controlled way. It appears according to what is important to Glen Haven's work at a particular moment. And, since you've read this Introduction, you know that the content of the commentaries does not occur linearly, according to anyone's formula for starting a PLC.

You'll also notice that the commentary floats from 30,000 to 2 feet and back again. In other words, sometimes the commentary settles on a "big idea" at 30,000 feet. At other times, it is barely off the ground, addressing techniques of facilitation, for example. Sometimes, it's in between. It addresses whatever seems important to address in terms of the Glen Haven story.

The chapter titles suggest a somewhat linear process for starting, growing, and sustaining a PLC. Because of the story structure of this book, I follow each chapter title with a Victorian age writing convention like this one from Chapter 1:

In which a dream and a conference inspire; in which the Investigative Team discovers its purpose and unites around professional learning and Professional Learning Communities (PLCs) for Glen Haven Middle School to help all students succeed; in which they invent and recruit for a Design Team.

Dickens used a variety on this convention in *Oliver Twist*: "Oliver, being offered another place, makes his first entry into public life" (Chapter 4). I hope these serve as an advance organizer for you and also pique your interest.

Throughout the book, there are references to "resources" on the CD that comes with the book. You can easily access these, download them, and use them as actual resources or as slides in a PowerPoint® or in any other way you desire. You'll find a list of resources in each chapter, organized by the chapter number and the resource number on the CD, such as Resource 3.1, which refers to Chapter 3, Resource 1.

At the end of each chapter, you'll encounter three questions that are your invitation to participate in the work of Glen Haven . . . in your own environment and with your own colleagues. They are an invitation to learn from this book. You are first asked WHAT you learned from the chapter. One of the characters in the book reflects on what he/she learned, giving you an example of what I mean by learning. You are next asked SO WHAT in relationship to your learning. Again, one of the characters provides an example, this time about why the learning is important and what it means to him or her. SO WHAT is the vehicle for the question, "Why does this learning matter to me?" Finally, you are asked NOW WHAT. What will you do about this learning? Your response may be as simple as sharing your learning with a colleague, "doing lunch," so to speak. Again, one of the characters reflects on what he/she will do in terms of the learning.

I hope you find these three questions helpful in making your own meaning from these chapters.

Chapter by Chapter. These titles will guide you if you'd like to browse through the book rather than read chapters in sequence. The Dickensian convention under each title will provide a little more detail and, perhaps, lure you into the chapter.

CHAPTER 1 SETTING THE STAGE FOR PLCS (JUNE AND JULY)

See page 8.

CHAPTER 2 FINDING INITIAL STRUCTURES (AUGUST)

In which Design Team members learn more than they ever thought they would about each other. In which they look at Glen Haven's readiness for professional learning, and plan the first PLC event. In which they learn the differences between presenting and facilitating.

CHAPTER 3 PURSUING THE NEED TO KNOW; MAKING SENSE OF WHAT WE KNOW (AUGUST–OCTOBER)

In which the Design Team debriefs the previous day's all-faculty PLC meeting with joy and fear; in which a Data Specialty Team is formed and collects—what else?—data, and the whole faculty analyzes these data, arriving at 5 goals for themselves.

CHAPTER 4 FINDING PROCESSES FOR WORKING TOGETHER (NOVEMBER AND DECEMBER)

*In which the Design Team meets to consider what they had wrought so far. The Design Team and the Data Specialty Team get into it! Also, the PLC understands and appreciates individual differences and learns to work together better, and various specialty teams collect more data from and about students. In which it was a miracle **anything** got done with all the vacations and holidays!*

CHAPTER 5 APPRECIATING NEW DATA, DISCOVERING DIVERGENCE (JANUARY–MARCH)

In which five new specialty teams form to learn more about students, parents, community members, and the district. In which the PLC labors mightily to make sense of the new data and in which they focus on struggling students. In which the Design Team gets unsettling news.

CHAPTER 6 GRAPPLING WITH CHANGE, PURSUING PROMISING PROCESSES (MARCH AND APRIL)

In which the Design Team learns about developmental and needs-based reactions to change and in which the English Department takes off on its own: an all-staff writing assessment and a experience in using a tuning protocol with student work. Also, in which the Design Team considers a conundrum.

CHAPTER 7 EXPANDING CONTEXT, FOCUSING ON THE FUTURE (MAY AND JUNE)

*In which more data hits Glen Haven Middle School (and the whole district) between the eyes. In which the Design Team plans the next PLC during which the whole PLC takes stock and looks toward the future. In which the whole staff debates **IT** (but not Information Technology) and focuses on what to do during the summer.*

CHAPTER 8 EXPLORING LEADERSHIP AND TAKING ACTION (JUNE–AUGUST)

In which the Design Team faces reality and in which faculty members participate in summer learning experiences. In which Josie compares Glen Haven Middle School's work with the PLC work in another school. In which the Design Team thinks ahead to fall and the second PLC year.

CHAPTER 9 LOOKING AHEAD, FACING CHALLENGES (JUNE–AUGUST)

In which several staff members engage in invigorating professional learning, and the Design Team works with the district to identify a new principal, and participates in hiring new staff members. In which the Design Team learns from the interview process and considers some challenges for the next year, including de-privatizing their classrooms, raising the level of intensity to an epidemic, and seeking deeper discussion.

GLEN HAVEN MIDDLE SCHOOL

Staff Roster

* = **Investigative Team**   DSP = **Data Specialty Team**
+ = **First Design Team**

Role	Name	Assignment
FRONT OFFICE:		
Principal	Josie Bermudez*+DSP	"Head Learner"
Assistant Principal	Andrew Loyer (Andy)	Management
Instructional Coach	Rosalind Best (Roz)+	Curriculum/instruction assessment; professional development
Administrative Assistant	Jacquelyn Patterson	Office
COUNSELORS:		
Counselor 1	Forrest Long+	6th grade + ½ 7th grade
Counselor 2	Lorena Soltar	½ 7th grade + 8th grade
LIBRARY MEDIA:		
Library Media Specialist	Alice Rodas (Allie) DSP	Head of library/media
Library Media Aide	Fran Gallucci	Admin assistant
Technology Aide	Douglas Donohue (Doug)	Technology (lib & staff)
SPECIAL EDUCATION		
Self-contained classroom	Jane Reid	15 students
Pull-out/Immersion	Fatima Hoyle	150 students
INSTRUCTIONAL STAFF		
Math 1	Margie Lyons	6th-grade core; 7th- & 8th-grade math
Math 2	Burt Reilly	6th-grade core; 7th- & 8th-grade math
Math 3	Anthony Mevoli (Andy)+DSP	6th-grade core; 7th- & 8th-grade math
Math 4	Libby Gandy	6th-grade core; 7th- & 8th-grade math
Math 5	Julianne Blake (Juli)	6th-grade core; 7th- & 8th-grade math
Math/Science 1	Eva Teller	6th-grade core; 7th- & 8th-grade science

(Continued)

(Continued)

Role	Name	Assignment
Math/Science 2	Pamela Rosario	6th-grade core; 7th- & 8th-grade science
Math/Science 3	Lan He Bin	6th-grade core; 7th- & 8th-grade science
Science 1	Sanjay Mishra	6th-grade core
Science 2	Kelly Bosco*+	7th- & 8th-grade science
Science 3	Carol Tanner	7th- & 8th-grade science
Lang Arts 1	Kathleen Meehan (Kay)	6th-grade core
Lang Arts 2	Roberta Beckel (Robbie)*	7th- & 8th-grade lang arts
Lang Arts 3	Aaron Dombroski*+	7th- & 8th-grade lang arts
Lang Arts 4	Anita Solazzo	7th- & 8th-grade lang arts
Lang Arts 5	K. D. Weg DSP	7th- & 8th-grade lang arts
Lang Arts 6	Benjamin LaSala (Ben)	7th- & 8th-grade lang arts
Social Studies 1	Jon Miller	6th-grade core
Social Studies 2	Ariel Aboud+	7th- & 8th-grade social studies
Social Studies 3	Sue Tanaka	7th- & 8th-grade social studies
Social Studies 4	Eric Gomez	7th- & 8th-grade social studies
Social Studies 5	Frank Kemmerer	7th- & 8th-grade social studies
Social Studies 6	Jennifer Hasan	7th- & 8th-grade social studies
Technology 1	Carl Chiapetta	6th-grade core
Technology 2	Renee Lawrence	7th- & 8th-grade electives
Band/Orchestra 1	Dinh Tuan DSP	6th-grade explore
Band/Orchestra 2	Kyrah Williams	7th- & 8th-grade electives
Choir 1	Amy Arredondo	6th-grade core
Choir 2	Myrna Soriano	7th- & 8th-grade electives
Art/Woodshop 1	Daniel Lee	6th-grade core
Art/Woodshop 2	Russ Bern	7th- & 8th-grade electives
Fitness & Health 1	Daniel Joss	6th-grade core
Fitness & Health 2	Tasha Peart*+DSP	7th- & 8th-grade electives

Role	Name	Assignment
Fitness & Health 3	Grace Nugent	7th- & 8th-grade electives
Intro to For Lang: Sp	Bobbie DeSantis	6th-grade core
Spanish I & II	Lynn Romero	7th- & 8th-grade electives
Intro to For Lang: Fr	Maria Zimnis	6th-grade core
French I & II	Allan Yarrow	7th- & 8th-grade electives
AIDES		
Aide 1	Tiffany Wilde	6th grade & focus for 6th
Aide 2	Dorotea Gibbon (Dottie)+	Mathematics & focus for 6th
Aide 3	Lindy Tukel	Science & focus for 6th
Aide 4	Gwen Pate	Lang arts & focus for 6th
Aide 5	Judith Maestas (Judy) DSP	Social studies & focus for 6th
Aide 6	Maree Ferraro	Special ed & focus for 6th

CALENDAR FOR GHMS

Schedules:

- <u>Design Team</u> meets approximately every 2 weeks for two periods, rotating
- <u>A Faculty Meeting</u> is held every other Tuesday after last class (unless repurposed by principal)
- <u>District Professional Development Days</u> are held as scheduled by district (unless repurposed by principal with district approval); twice a year these are for grading and planning
- <u>Early Release</u> is for 3 hours once a month, usually on a Wednesday; these may be used for Professional Learning Community events

June (Prior to Year 1)

Sunday	Monday	Tuesday	Wednesday	Thursday	Friday	Saturday
						1
2	3	4	5	6	7	8
9	10	11	12	13	14	15

(Continued)

(Continued)

Sunday	Monday	Tuesday	Wednesday	Thursday	Friday	Saturday
16	17	18	19	20—Josie's dream; 3 teachers return from conference	21—Josie and 3 teachers meet: the Investigative Team is born	22
23	24	25	26	27	28	29
30						

JULY SCHOOL YEAR 1

Sunday	Monday	Tuesday	Wednesday	Thursday	Friday	Saturday
	1	2	3	4	5—Investigative Team meets; designs Design Team	6
7	8	9	10	11	12	13
14	15	16	17	18	19	20
21	22	23	24	25—Investigative Team plans first Design Team meeting	26	27
28	29	30	31			

AUGUST SCHOOL YEAR 1

Sunday	Monday	Tuesday	Wednesday	Thursday	Friday	Saturday
				1	2	3
4	5—First Design Team meeting	6	7	8	9	10
11	12	13	14—Teachers return	15—First PLC meeting	16—Design Team debriefs	17

(Continued)

(Continued)

Sunday	Monday	Tuesday	Wednesday	Thursday	Friday	Saturday
18	19—District PD	20—Work in classrooms	21—Students return & classes start	22—Design Team meets in PM	23	24
25	26	27	28	29	30	31

SEPTEMBER SCHOOL YEAR 1

Sunday	Monday	Tuesday	Wednesday	Thursday	Friday	Saturday
1	2—Labor Day Holiday	3—Faculty Meeting	4	5—Design Team meets in AM	6	7
8	9	10	11	12	13	14
15	16	17—Faculty Meeting	18—Early release; PLC practices data analysis	19—Design Team meets in PM	20—Data Specialty Team meets at lunch	21
22	23	24	25	26	27—Data Specialty Team meets at lunch	28
29	30					

OCTOBER SCHOOL YEAR 1

Sunday	Monday	Tuesday	Wednesday	Thursday	Friday	Saturday
		1—Faculty Meeting repurposed for Data Specialty Team	2	3—Design Team meets in AM	4—Data Specialty Team meets at lunch	5
6	7	8	9	10	11—Data Specialty Team meets at lunch	12
13	14	15—Faculty Meeting	16—Early release; PLC engages in artifact hunt	17—Design Team meets in PM	18	19

(Continued)

(Continued)

Sunday	Monday	Tuesday	Wednesday	Thursday	Friday	Saturday
20	21—Data Specialty Team has PM subs; Data Dessert for parents & community	22	23	24	25	26
27	28	29—Faculty Meeting	30—District PD Day used for data analysis	31—Design Team meets—AM		

NOVEMBER SCHOOL YEAR 1

Sunday	Monday	Tuesday	Wednesday	Thursday	Friday	Saturday
					1	2
3	4—Data Specialty Team meets at lunch	5	6	7	8	9
10	11—Veteran's Day Holiday	12—Faculty Meeting	13—Early Release; Design and Data Specialty Teams meet	14—Design Team meets—PM	15	16
17	18	19	20	21	22	23
24	25	26—Faculty meeting repurposed so Design and Data Specialty Team can meet	27—Holiday	28—Holiday	29—Holiday	30

DECEMBER SCHOOL YEAR 1

Sunday	Monday	Tuesday	Wednesday	Thursday	Friday	Saturday
1	2	3	4	5—Design Team meets AM	6	7
8	9	10—Faculty Meeting	11	12	13	14
15	16	17—Design Team and Data Specialty Team meet to have a dialogue about 5 goals	18—Early Release (learning preferences and 5 goals)	19—Design Team meets PM	20	21
22	23—Holiday	24—Holiday	25—Holiday	26—Holiday	27—Holiday	28
29	30—Holiday	31—Holiday				

JANUARY SCHOOL YEAR 1

Sunday	Monday	Tuesday	Wednesday	Thursday	Friday	Saturday
			1—Holiday	2—Holiday	3—Holiday	4
5	6—District PD day (AM for district and PM for five school specialty teams)	7—Faculty meeting	8	9—Design Team "gives" subs to five specialty teams for 3 hours in AM	10	11
12	13	14	15	16	17	18
19	20—MLK Day (school out)	21—Faculty Meeting repurposed so five specialty teams can meet	22—Early Release Day (used for data sorting and identifying key learnings)	23—Design Team "gives" subs to five specialty teams for 3 hours in PM	24	25
26	27	28	29	30	31	

FEBRUARY SCHOOL YEAR 1

Sunday	Monday	Tuesday	Wednesday	Thursday	Friday	Saturday
						1
2	3	4—Faculty Meeting	5	6—Design Team meets AM	7	8
9	10	11	12—Early Release Day (for looking at additional data)	13	14	15
16	17—President's Day (school out)	18—District PD Day	19	20—Design Team meets PM	21	22
23	24	25—Faculty Meeting	26	27	28	

MARCH SCHOOL YEAR 1

Sunday	Monday	Tuesday	Wednesday	Thursday	Friday	Saturday
						1
2	3	4	5	6—Design Team meets AM (CBAM)	7	8
9	10	11—Faculty Meeting	12	13	14	15
16	17	18	19—Early Release (writing assessment)	20—Design Team meets (results of CBAM) PM	21	22
23	24	25—Faculty Meeting	26	27	28	29
30	31					

APRIL SCHOOL YEAR 1

Sunday	Monday	Tuesday	Wednesday	Thursday	Friday	Saturday
		1	2	3—Spring Break	4—Spring Break	5
6	7	8—Faculty Meeting	9	10—Design Team meets AM	11	12
13	14	15	16—Early Release (revisit goals + summer plans)	17	18	19
20	21—Testing	22—Testing	23—Testing	24—Testing	25—Testing	26
27	28	29—Faculty Meeting	30			

MAY SCHOOL YEAR 1

Sunday	Monday	Tuesday	Wednesday	Thursday	Friday	Saturday
				1—Design Team meets PM	2	3
4	5	6	7—District PD (graduation rates)	8	9	10
11	12	13—Faculty Meeting	14—Early Release Day	15—Design Team meets AM	16	17
18	19	20	21	22	23	24
25	26	27	28	29—Design Team meets	30	31

JUNE SCHOOL YEAR 1

Sunday	Monday	Tuesday	Wednesday	Thursday	Friday	Saturday
1	2	3—Last Faculty Meeting of Year	4	5—Design Team meets	6—Students Dismissed	7
8	9—District PD	10—District PD	11—Teachers Dismissed	12—Design Team meets re. principal search process	13—Principal Search	14
15	16—Writing Project; Paper screening: principal	17—Writing Project	18—Writing Project Action Research Team meets	19—Writing Project; Phone interviews: principal	20—Writing Project; Phone interviews: principal	21
22	23—Writing Project	24—Writing Project	25—Writing Project Action Research Team meets	26—Writing Project; Site Interviews: Principal;	27—Writing Project; Site Interviews: Principal	28
29	30—Writing Project; Site Interviews: Principal					

JULY SCHOOL YEAR 2

Sunday	Monday	Tuesday	Wednesday	Thursday	Friday	Saturday
		1—Writing Project	2—Writing Project	3—Writing Project	4 Holiday	5
6	7—Lesson Study	8—Lesson Study	9—Lesson Study Action Research Team meets	10—Lesson Study	11—Lesson Study	12
13	14	15	16	17—	18	19
20	21	22	23—Action Research Team meets	24—Design Team meets	25	26
27	28	29	30	31		

AUGUST SCHOOL YEAR 2

Sunday	Monday	Tuesday	Wednesday	Thursday	Friday	Saturday
					1	2
3	4	5	6	7—Design Team meets	8	9
10	11	12	13	14	15	16
17	18—Teachers Return	19—District PD	20—PLC meets	21—Design Team meets; Work in schools	22—Work in schools	23
24	25—School starts	26—Faculty meeting	27	28	29	30
31						

PROFILE OF GLEN HAVEN MIDDLE SCHOOL

General:

School Name: Glen Haven Middle School (GHMS)

District Name: Glen Haven School District (GHSD), one of three districts in an urban area in the Midwest

Size of District: 12,013 students (capacity 12,650)

Schools:

- One high school—4 grades (9–12)
  - **Glen Haven High School**—3,711 students (capacity 4,000)
    (GHMS was the high school until 1978 when the current facility was built)
- Two middle schools—3 grades (6–8)
  - **Glen Haven Middle School**—875 students (capacity 900)
    (built in 1950s; in 1978 became junior high school grades 7–9; in 1995 became a middle school grades 6–8; three stories red brick, with offices, gym, auditorium, and multiple room on first floor; added temporary buildings in 2007)
  - **E. M. Ross Middle School**—2,833 students (capacity 3,000)
    (opened in 1995)
- Four elementary schools—7 grades (preK–5)
  - **Garden Lane Elementary School**—951 students (capacity 1,000) (opened in 1977).

- o **Orchard Elementary School**—1,404 students (capacity 1,500) (opened in 1998)
- o **Penwick Elementary School**—1,483 students (capacity 1,500) (opened in 1983)
- o **Rosemont Elementary School**—706 students (capacity 900)

  (oldest elementary school, built 1941; was originally the only school in district; became K–8 in 1963; then K–5 in 1995)

Feeder Pattern: Rosemont and Garden Lane feed into Glen Haven Middle School; GHMS feeds into GHHS

1

Setting the Stage for PLCs (June and July)

In which a dream and a conference inspire; in which the Investigative Team discovers its purpose and unites around professional learning and Professional Learning Communities (PLCs) for Glen Haven Middle School (GHMS) to help all students succeed; in which they invent and recruit for a Design Team.

Josie awoke early that morning in June. She had been dreaming again, and she felt the sheen of sweat on her face. Same dream, just a different time of year. Students were bulky in their coats and scarves. Taking up more room in the hallway, they were pushing against each other as they hurried to . . . where? what? The halls were definitely those of GHMS where she was principal—refurbished from their high school days in bright colors, buffed green linoleum atop the original—and still creaky—oak plank floors.

In fact, Josie heard nothing at all in her dream—no flat metallic sound of locker doors being slammed, no high- and low-pitched voices typical of tweens, nothing. And then, this morning, she noticed that students in her dream were without faces. Beneath their hoodies, nothing. When they turned toward her, almost in slow motion in that hall, they were faceless. That's when she awoke.

This dream had been building over the last couple of months, but never before had she seen nothing where there should have been eager faces—eyebrows launched, eyes reflecting the fluorescent lights, mouths open as students smiled and called to each other, freckles, even pimples. Nothing.

Dreams about school were nothing new to Josie; as a teacher she used to wake up to find herself sitting straight up in bed, teaching a lesson. It would be a real lesson, something she planned to teach that day and was, for some reason, rehearsing at 3 a.m.

Later that day, three teachers from Glen Haven returned from a conference in Dallas. They had given up some summer vacation time to go to this conference and were entirely delighted with their decision. They had something to share with Josie.

Kelly, Tasha, and Aaron had bonded as teachers, all three entering Glen Haven Middle School at the same time, 5 years ago. Their bond was more than a phenomenon of the calendar, however. They shared compatible views of students—how they learn and how teachers can best reach them, especially struggling students. Though Kelly taught science, he and Tasha, a physical education teacher, and Aaron, an English teacher, hung out together, meeting in the science lab for lunch and celebrating TGIF at a local bar and grill. Their conversation bored their significant others—it was always about teaching and learning, why one student seemed to be learning in science but not English, about how to engage a group of students in their health and fitness class, about teaching strategies one of them had read about in a professional journal, about a new assessment technique one of them was trying.

Aaron texted Josie the day the trio returned from the conference—the day Josie had awakened suddenly from what she called her "faceless" dream. They wanted to meet with her. The next day, Josie met them at a small coffeehouse near the university. They could hardly contain their enthusiasm—the conference they had just returned from was all about professional learning and PLCs. Josie listened as they described how professional learning was different from professional development (see Resource 1.1). She took notes on the definition of a PLC as well as some of its characteristics (see Resource 1.2). Then she shared her dream with her colleagues.

"I think I'm anxious," she said as she ended her description of the dream. "I looked at this year's test scores . . . and they're about the same—OK in English language arts, absolutely rotten in math. So many of our students aren't doing what they could. There's all this potential—empty—like the faces in my dream."

Aaron ventured, "Maybe we can do better in terms of test scores, but that's not what concerns me. I'm worried about the struggling students, the ones that are on the edge of learning."

"Well," Tasha said, "I'm worried about the way our demographics have changed and how we're not doing anything different from what we did 5 years ago. Are we still serving all kids well?"

"And," Kelly said, "I'm really worried more about their learning than their test scores. I don't think test scores tell us whether or not they've learning anything."

Josie was quiet for a moment and then spoke up: "I agree with everything you have said. These are things that have been on my mind too. So. . . ."

"So," Kelly continued, "I think we need to look at ourselves, as learners. What do we know and need to know? How can we learn what we need to know in order to help all kids learn?"

"That's what the conference was all about," Aaron said, "and we think we should have Professional Learning Communities and engage in professional learning."

"Whoa," Josie said. "That's a big step. Could we start smaller, just a few of us, doing something manageable?"

Investigative Team Members:

Josie Bermudez, Principal

Kelly Bosco, Science, Seventh and Eighth Grades

Tasha Peart, Fitness and Health, Seventh and Eighth Grades

Aaron Dobroski, Language Arts, Seventh and Eighth Grades

"We can start small and gradually, but we need to have the big picture in mind," Tasha said.

"We're talking about changing the culture of our school," Kelly said.

"From an institution to a learning community," Aaron added.

"I like the idea," Josie reminded them. "In fact, it's not really a new idea. It's been around since, well, the 50s at least, with Quality Circles." (See Resource 1.3.)

"So, let's start Quality Circles with the whole school in the fall," Tasha said. "We can't just keep doing what we're doing. And, the only way we can change is to become learners, too."

"Let's start them—whatever we call them," Josie affirmed, "but let's not start them with the whole school in the fall. I think

that having the four of us make a decision about something that affects the whole school is not fair to the rest of the faculty. They may not be interested in 'professional learning.'" She sipped her iced tea. "And, we need to take this to the district level—it's not in the strategic plan. What about funding? What about time?"

Aaron let her questions sit a minute and then said, "Why don't we investigate PLCs and professional learning then? Why don't we sound out our colleagues? Can you find out how the district views PLCs, Josie?"

"Sure," Josie said. "Let's think about this summer as an 'investigative' summer." She paused and then said, "The last thing I want to do is mandate something new. We all have enough on our plates as it is. And, no one is taking anything off them."

The others acknowledged the accuracy of her statement with slight smiles. "But, we can do some research, right? We don't have to plunge into this. We don't want to 'do' this to others. I mean, we don't want to decide to do PLCs without involving the rest of the staff . . . because they'll be doing them. I mean, that's one of the principles of PLCs, that 'them's as does the doin' does the decidin'!"

"Say again?!"

"Oh, it's an aphorism, a saying," Aaron explained. "We heard it at our conference. Basically it means that those who are going to do the work need to have some say in how the work is done: 'Them's as does the doin' does the decidin'!"

They laughed and then divided up the work. Josie would confer with administrators at the district level. Aaron, Tasha, and Kelly would work up a short description of professional learning and PLCs, along with a survey. They would e-mail the description to the whole staff and put the survey online (see Resources 1.1, 1.2, and 1.5). "We might not get everyone to respond to the survey because it's the beginning of summer break, but let's see what we can get." The group decided to meet 2 weeks later to share information.

Let's take a closer look at some of the topics that came up for the GHMS Investigative Team.

A HISTORY OF PLCS

PLCs are not new; they have a distinguished history, going back at least to W. Edwards Deming (see Resource 1.3). Best known for his work in Japan after World War II, Deming focused on creating a quality culture in the workplace. He was asked by Ford Motor Company in the United States to address its falling sales in the 1980s, both as a quality and a management issue. In 1993, Deming published *The New Economics for Industry, Government, Education,* which included his System of Profound Knowledge and 14 Points for Management, one of which focused on making everyone in an organization responsible for quality. Quality circles derived from his formula PDCA (Plan, Do, Check, Act) and his focus on results, emerging first in industry and migrating into education. In schools, quality circles are cross-level groups of faculty who identify, analyze, and solve problems; they may be led by an administrator or a peer but become self-managing as they mature. They are deeply involved in the improvement of the organization for the benefit of students and may involve students.

In the 1980s and 1990s, Peter Senge's five disciplines included team work (e.g., Senge, 1990), and schools in the Coalition of Essential Schools formed Critical

Friends Groups. Kruse, Seashore Louis, and Bryk (1994) wrote about school-level teams early, but Shirley Hord is possibly the first to use the term "Professional Learning Community" or "PLC" in her 1997 work.

IMPORTANCE OF INVOLVING THE INVOLVED

"Buy-in" is a chief concern at all levels of a system when change is contemplated. Superintendents worry about whether the board, parents, and the community will buy-in to an implementation plan for a policy from the "state." Assistant superintendents worry about whether principals and teachers will buy-in to another curriculum revision or a change in assessment. Principals worry that teachers won't buy-in to a new—and perhaps completely worthwhile—program from the "head shed."

There should be a thesaurus of phrases educators use to respond to something they need to buy in to: "been there, done that"; "this, too, will pass"; "flavor of the month/year"; "what will 'they' take off our plate?" and "ho-hum." *Buy-in* may be a five-letter word, but to some it's really a four-letter word, an expletive describing the straw that broke the camel's back.

In truth, buy-in *can* describe something underhanded: "We (whoever 'we' is in the system) have made a decision, and we want 'you' (whoever 'you' is in the system) to like it, so we have decided to roll out our initiative in a favorable way, a way that will ensure that you like what is being done to you."

In some places, buy-in is more about marketing or propaganda than it is about improving learning for all students. It's about "spin."

Buy-in becomes a nonissue when those who will be affected by an initiative are involved in determining the process and product from the start. The sooner the better. Of course, real participation in creating change is messy; it's much easier to dictate change from the top (and plan a buy-in strategy). People engaged in creating real change are going to have points of view and differences of opinion. These options might make for a better outcome, but they always take more time and patience than an initiative created by a powerful individual or a small, select committee. The only problem with dictated reform is that those who are supposed to be "doin'" the work may subconsciously (even consciously) sabotage it, even if the buy-in strategies for that reform would win a gold star from Madison Avenue.

The best questions educators can use to avoid the need for buy-in are, "Who should be here? Who else should be here? Whose voices do we need to hear?" Josie, Aaron, Tasha, and Kelly pulled back from their initial impulse to just *do* professional learning and PLCs. They named themselves the Investigative Team rather than the Leadership Team. Later in this chapter you'll read how the Investigative Team decides to include more of their colleagues through a Design Team. You'll discover how both teams access others' voices through e-mail, online surveys, and other means. The Investigative Team, including Principal Josie Bermudez, understood the need to get more teachers involved from the start.

Interestingly enough, in most schools the one voice that is *not* sought when schools are changed is the voice of students. Of all people who should be involved in a reform initiative, students are least included. They (and their parents and community members) are the consumers. Try to imagine a major corporation saying,

"We don't need to hear from our consumers about our product. We'll improve it the way we want to, without their input." Watch how Glen Haven Middle School enlists students in the reform effort.

IMPORTANCE OF MEETING IN THE MIDDLE

Reform initiatives are often classified as "top-down" or "bottom-up." Top-down initiatives come from those whose rank is generally understood as higher than the teachers and staff in a school. In most states top-down reform might track like this:

State Superintendent & State Board of Education

State Department of Education

District Superintendents & Assistant Superintendents

School Principals

School Faculty & Staff (noncertificated)

A reform starting anywhere above the faculty and staff level can be considered top-down.

Top-down reform can occur from the level of the federal government as well, with funding requirements. States (and districts) that want federal monies to run their schools need to adhere to the stipulations of an RFP (request for proposal). In the past few decades, federal programs such as the Elementary and Secondary Education Act (ESEA) and Title I School Improvement Grants have dictated school improvement efforts. Recently, No Child Left Behind (NCLB), Race to the Top, Investing in Innovation, and other programs have had significant influence on what schools, districts, and states do.

Bottom-up reforms (sometimes called "grassroots" reform) turn this diagram on its head:

State Superintendent & State Board of Education

State Department of Education

District Superintendent & Assistant Superintendents

School Principal

School Teachers & School Staff (noncertificated)

Few reforms are strictly bottom-up. Bottom-up reform suggests that practitioners dictate policy, a rarity in the real world. One example of an organization that tried to instigate bottom-up reform is the Coalition of Essential Schools (Sizer, 1985) through its Re:Learning Initiative. On the basis of research on high schools in the 1980s and a set of nine (now 10) principles about making schools—especially high schools—more conducive to learning for students, faculty and staff in a set of schools decided to join forces; they became the Coalition of Essential Schools. No one person could determine that a school would join the Coalition; it took a "yes" vote from 80%

to 90% of school personnel. Eventually, members of the Coalition, which was focused on the school level, realized that district and state policy support was needed. A set of mechanisms, including a district summer retreat, for districts addressed the need at that level. States were encouraged by Coalition schools to join a "schoolhouse to statehouse" reform called Re:Learning. The purpose of Re:Learning was to help schools deal with state policy—either to reshape it in critical ways or to enable the schools to get waivers.

As Re:Learning developed, it became clear that it was not just a bottom-up reform. It began to be simultaneously a top-down and bottom-up effort. States signed on to Re:Learning to support schools in the state that were involved in the Coalition. State policy makers worked through Re:Learning to implement state reforms.

Actually, Re:Learning was rather short-lived, and the district piece was not sufficiently emphasized. The Coalition continues today, but Re:Learning ceased operation in 1994.

The best way to think about top-down and bottom-up reform is to consider how the "top" and "bottom" can be coupled so that a state and its district have what they need (often in the form of accountability) and schools have the room to maneuver within the reform to fit the needs of teachers, students, and community. According to Michael Fullan (1994), "Neither top-down nor bottom-up strategies for educational reform work. What is required is a more sophisticated blend of the two" (p. 1). He added, "What works is simultaneous school-district co-development reflecting both top-down and bottom-up initiatives" (p. 13). This type of coupling has been characterized as simultaneously loose and tight by business gurus Peters and Waterman (2004, p. 318). The "tight" part might be an expectation, such as forming school-based professional learning communities, with the "loose" part being school- and district-level decisions about what and how to implement PLCs.

The PLC initiative at Glen Haven Middle School at first seems bottom-up. What the Investigative Team didn't know is that state and district policy makers were already exploring the value of PLCs. In fact, like a lot of states, the state in which GHMS operated would soon mandate that schools have PLCs of some kind, leaving the details up to districts and schools. PLCs would be simultaneously top-down and bottom-up, at least for Glen Haven, which "jumped the gun" in terms of school-based professional learning; GHMS's PLC became a model of school implementation for state and district policy makers. The eventual State Board of Education rule was quite loose: "Schools should engage in professional learning by forming PLCs." It was tight in the sense that there was no way out of the rule. It was loose because it allowed schools to choose a variety of implementation strategies.

Simultaneously top-down and bottom-up reform, as well as "loose-tight" policies at the state and district levels, are important ways to achieve buy-in naturally. "Them's as does the doin' does the decidin'" is much more than the simple homily it seems. It is an important key to school-based change that has an effect on student learning.

THE IMPORTANCE OF REINVENTING THE WHEEL

Sometimes people claim that there's no point in reinventing the wheel, and in some cases, that is true, especially for "tame" problems (Garmston & Wellman, 1999) that lead straight to solutions. But for "wicked" problems, reinventing the wheel is important, even critical, to the success of the solution. The problems we encounter in education are usually wicked, not simple, linear problems. They are "tenacious and nonlinear. They contain unpredictable barriers and recur, folding back on themselves. . . . Existing ways of thinking cannot handle wicked problems. Individuals and groups require new mental models for problem finding and problem approaches" (Garmston & Wellman, 1999, p. 223):

Tame Problems	Wicked Problems
An algorithm exists.	Known algorithms are inadequate.
Can be worked "inside the box."	Require new mental models.
Lend themselves to action research.	Are dynamical, producing emergent phenomena within systems and subsystems.
Direct and discernible cause-and-effect relationships are apparent.	Have a fractal nature [repeating patterns].
Interactions may be complex but are not dynamical.	Recur, folding back on themselves and amplify with each iteration.
Properties of the system maintain their identity before, during, and after interactions.	Contain values conflicts rooted in self-sealing logic [not open to discussion]. (Garmston & Wellman, 1999, p. 225)

Garmston, R., & Wellman, B. (1999). *The adaptive school: A sourcebook for developing collaborative groups.* Christopher-Gordon Publishers, p. 225. Used by Permission From Christopher-Gordon Publishers.

Here are examples of wicked problems related to developing and implementing standards (Garmston & Wellman, 1999, p. 224):

curriculum development   district culture

curriculum alignment   school culture

reporting practices   professional responsibilities

assessment development   data collection

assessment alignment   equity of resources

organizational development   instructional practices

professional development   parent expectations

accountability   principal evaluations

special education   teacher evaluations

Garmston, R., & Wellman, B. (1999). *The adaptive school: A sourcebook for developing collaborative groups.* Christopher-Gordon Publishers, p. 224. Used by Permission From Christopher-Gordon Publishers.

With wicked problems, states, districts, and schools cannot just adopt what someone else has done (the wheel). The wheel, mounted on an entirely different vehicle, may simply not work (although it may have worked quite well on the original vehicle). The size and composition of the new vehicle—its motor, transmission, brakes, and frame—require designing a completely different wheel, although based on the concept of "wheel" as it existed on the original vehicle.

States and districts that decide to pilot a new initiative with just a few schools, hoping that other schools can learn from the pilot schools and simply adopt the initiative, might find themselves disappointed. The same can be said in terms of depending on "lighthouse" models, or demonstration schools to drive a reform to scale. To change metaphors a bit, expecting other schools to succeed in a piloted initiative is a little like expecting that a size *S* t-shirt will fit a size *XL* quarterback. The reverse is also true: The size *XL* t-shirt might fit the size *S* kicker, but not well.

Going through at least some of the process of invention ensures that

- the context shapes the implementation (size 10 for a size 10);
- those implementing the reform know not only the *what* of the reform but the *why* and the *how*;
- when the implementers encounter a wicked (or even a tame) problem, they have a good idea of how to address it, having gone through the process of inventing their own wheels (applying the reform to their own environment); and
- members of a school *own* the initiative; it's not something from that model school in the next county.

The thing to remember about reinventing the wheel is that implementation may succeed or fail based on how well educators really understand what they're doing and why. They must think deeply, and sometimes, such thinking requires going through origination of a process or practice.

Pilots, lighthouse schools, and demonstration sites have their role, however. Other states, districts, and schools can examine how another state, district, or school is implementing a reform—what works and what doesn't—and take those conditions under consideration in trying to implement the reform themselves. But each state, district, and school trying to implement a reform needs to customize the reform to its own context, its own environment. Each needs to go through some kind of process to understand the logic models, premises, or assumptions embedded in the reform. Each needs to go through the design stage with these key questions in mind:

- Why do we need to engage in this reform? What do our data tell us? What needs will be addressed if we install this initiative?
- How are our context, environment, and culture different from the originating state/district/school?
- What will this reform look like in our state/district/school? How will its silhouette in our state, district/school differ from its original silhouette?
- What will *we* do to implement this reform? Who needs to be involved in the process? Who else? Whose voice do we especially need to ensure successful implementation?
- What are our own particular challenges in terms of implementation? How will we address them?
- What indicators will tell us it is working?

Actually, the issue of reinventing the wheel (or not) comes down to a letter. Ad**o**ption does not work; ad**a**p(ta)tion does. Sometimes, even adaptation doesn't work, and educators may need to originate a solution.

Josie met with Tasha, Aaron, and Kelly 2 weeks later. They joined her on her back patio and sipped iced tea. They stirred their tea and nibbled on cookies, talked about the hot weather, and shared the latest from their families. Finally, Josie said, "Well. . . ."

"Well," Kelly began, "92% of the faculty went online and completed the surveys."

"Really!" Josie exclaimed. "Wow, that's great!"

"People want more information," Kelly said, "but mostly they're interested."

"They seem to realize the need. We cannot just continue doing what we're doing and get any better. We need to become learners ourselves," Tasha added.

"Well, I've got good news, too, " said Josie. "You probably know Stephanie Hodges, the assistant superintendent for curriculum? She's also in charge of professional development, and she has convinced the superintendent and the board that Glen Haven School District needs to have PLCs and engage in professional learning."

"Oh-oh," said Tasha. "Does that mean we're required to do them?"

"No, although you should know that folks at the state Department of Education are contemplating mandating them," Josie said. "We're jumping the gun and, perhaps, we can be helpful to other schools when they invent PLCs for themselves—not only here, in this district, but also around the state. We're the scouts, out exploring the territory."

"I like that," Tasha said. "We don't want the district or state to tell us what to do about our own learning. We want to base what we do and how we do it on what we need."

"Agreed," Josie said. "I think that's one of the premises Stephanie would like us to focus on—school-based PLCs. How to start and sustain them. I don't think she has any other agenda except to have us report what we've done and what we've learned."

"That's great," Aaron said.

"She even has a little money to help us out," Josie said, to a round of applause from the others.

"Where do we start?" Aaron asked. Kelly was prepared. He distributed a packet of ideas he'd gotten at the conference about research on PLCs (Resource 1.4) and organizing for PLCs (Resource 1.6, Resource 1.7, and Resource 1.8). The group read them silently and then discussed the most relevant points.

Then, Tasha, eager to get to business, said, "I think we need to get a couple of other staff members to help us design what's next. I think we need someone from the sixth-grade team. They seem to be working exceptionally well together."

"And someone from electives. Also a math teacher."

Josie said, "I think we have money to pay each of you a stipend."

"Let's call this new group the Design Team," Tasha said, "just to be clear that we're not the absolute leaders, you know, the ones in charge who know and do everything."

"Let's not call us the leadership team," Aaron confirmed. "It's important that we start out on the right foot, what we call things. We," he said, gesturing around the table, " might just be called the investigators."

"Or the instigators?" Tasha said. "Or the rabble-rousers? Or the troublemakers?"

"Guilty as charged," Aaron laughed.

"How about like Channel 9?" Kelly asked. "The GHMS Investigative Team?"

Another toast of iced tea glasses, and the Investigative Team was born.

"I think we might be the ones who ask the others to participate," Tasha said. "Not you. Is that okay, Josie?"

"You bet. From what I've read, my role should be to serve as a peer, not as a leader, the leader. I mean, we all should be leaders in this, so I'm fine with your contacting the other teachers. Who do you think you'll contact?"

Tasha, Aaron, and Kelly listed the teachers who had expressed greater interest than the others.

"What about choosing someone who is not as enthusiastic, you know, just to represent that point of view?" Josie asked.

"I'm not sure that's a good idea at this early stage," Aaron said. "I think we need to begin with people who are really interested."

"OK," Josie said. "If we're the scouts, let's look for pioneers, the first to settle a territory. How do we get them involved and what do we do at the first meeting of the Design Team?"

Kelly responded to the second question, "I think they should go through almost the same dialogue we went through. They need to understand how we got to the decision to try PLCs and professional learning."

"Even my 'faceless' dream?" Josie asked.

"Even your dream," Kelly said. "By the way, have you had any more of those dreams?"

"Actually, no," Josie said and raised her iced tea glass to toast the others.

"That's a good sign," Aaron spoke for all of them.

"Let's talk more about this Design Team," Tasha said. "Who should be invited to join it?"

Let's explore a few ideas related to what the Investigative Team has done so far.

POSITIVE DEVIANCE

Tasha didn't know it at the time, but she really hit on a good idea when she suggested inviting someone from the sixth-grade team because "they seem to be working exceptionally well together." The theory of positive deviance—which, contrary to how it sounds, is actually quite a good thing—is simple. Rather than start something brand new, look for where a prototype of what you want has already been successful in your environment. The sixth-grade team had clearly been functioning as a team—and was, therefore, a source of positive deviance in a school culture that otherwise did not function as a team. The sixth-grade team was successful enough that others in the school had noted their progress. Why not start with them, figure out what they were doing, and ask them to teach the rest of the faculty? We'll see whether, indeed, GHMS can access the successes of the sixth-grade team.

You'll find some key components of positive deviance in Resource 1.9.

DESIGN TEAM: PART 1

The decision to form a design team was a good one, but as the investigators talked, they realized there were several issues to consider: appointment versus volunteer members, members who are representative or not, exclusive versus inclusive membership, leadership, and how the design team would get its work done.

<u>Appointed or Volunteer?</u> The investigators deliberated at length about how to grow the team. In the end, they decided not to appoint people. Appointment confers status, they decided. It may seem to those not appointed that they are not "in" with whoever is in power. Appointment sets up an "us" and "them" barrier, factionalizing faculty.

On the other hand, asking for volunteers is, well, asking for *volunteers*. Volunteers choose to participate and may even choose whether to attend meetings or whether to get work done. A volunteer can unvolunteer more easily than an appointed member.

"Still," Tasha said, "the work will go better if people want to do it, if they volunteer for it."

Representative or Not? The conventional way to organize school committees is to have representatives from each grade or subject. In this way, it is thought, everyone has a voice and everyone gets the information—usually. Representation does not always work as well as it should. Moreover, representation leads to partisanship. The English teacher says to the science teacher, "Well, we can't do that in our department." Or, the third-grade teacher says to the fifth-grade teacher, "We need to save that unit for third grade; Jim has a dynamite unit on that topic." The broader good—the whole school and all its students and staff—may be unreachable as people defend their territories.

After some deliberation, the GHMS Investigative Team was still uncertain about representation. "I would rather have people really excited about what we're doing and not feeling obligated to protect the interests of those teaching a particular subject or grade," Josie ventured, and the others agreed. Still, they were afraid about being unbalanced: "What if it's all math people," Aaron asked, "especially if we're going to do data? No one from the English department will want to do data!"

At the end of this discussion, the Investigative Team leaned toward nonrepresentative Design Team members.

Exclusive or Inclusive? The Design Team role is a hard one. Faculty might see the Design Team as exclusive, the "inner circle," even the principal's "pets." There's less stress if members of the team volunteer. There's even less stress if the team is nonrepresentational. Exclusivity is no longer an issue if the size of the team can vary according to interest, with some members providing continuity.

A fully open team is risky. What if turnover is so high that no one holds the history of the work and can recommend decisions with precedent in mind (although precedent shouldn't limit decision making)? What if everyone dropped out? (That would certainly be an indicator of something amiss in terms of the initiative!) On the other hand, what if current members show no signs of wanting to leave? (Is that an indicator that something's going right with the initiative?) What if more and more people keep joining the team, until it's so big it's unwieldy?

Aaron spoke for the others when he concluded, "We should be inclusive rather than exclusive, even if that gets messy."

Leadership. Principals and assistant principals may declare that they will *not* be the leader of a task force, committee, or team, but eyes inevitably turn toward this person when meetings start or decisions need to be made. Sitting in the corner, rather than at the head, foot, or middle of the table doesn't help much. Disguises do not help. The hierarchical tradition of most schools and districts makes it difficult for some educators to deny obeisance to titular leadership.

Principals often find that it takes supreme effort, restraint, and persistence to avoid leading meetings or rendering opinions that may be construed as decisions. Eventually, many principals cave in and lead meetings or venture opinions.

One of the best ways to change leadership notions is through open discussion, perhaps based on an article such as *Leader and Learner*, by Stephanie Hirsh and Shirley Hord, which is included on the CD as Resource 1.10.

One tack principals can take is to partner with a teacher to plan and facilitate meetings and leave it up to the teacher to begin and end the meeting. Another is to participate as a "regular" educator with others in distributed leadership tasks (such as preparing an agenda, finding a room, facilitating an activity, bringing closure). Another strategy is silence, patient silence, waiting for others to say what they would say themselves—this almost always happens.

Teachers rise to the occasion when asked to take on leadership roles, although they may not want to commit to being *the* leader. They are more likely to be comfortable sharing the role (cofacilitating a meeting) or leading one element of a meeting (such as preparing the agenda).

The more leadership is shared, the more sustainable an effort is likely to be. When one leader leaves, the other leaders are accustomed to the task and step forward. The more leadership is shared, the more vital the effort is likely to be, energized by everyone's ideas, not just the leader's. The more leadership is shared, the more efficacious a faculty feels, not doing what someone else bids them do to improve learning for all, but contributing significantly to the ideas and the work itself.

Resource 1.11 describes various aspects of leadership in terms of assets that all members of a group bring to collaborative work. Resource 1.12 describes the many leadership jobs that need to be shared by a collaborative team.

"Could we take a moment to read the article ourselves?" Aaron asked.

"Good idea," Tasha said. "Shall we use the protocol we used at the conference: Three Levels of Text?" They read the article quickly, looking, as the protocol bade them do, for a sentence that meant the most to them, a phrase that spoke to them, and a single word that captured the gist of the article. After everyone had finished reading and finding parts of the text to share, they read aloud and pointed out in the article, one at a time, the sentences, phrases, and words they had chosen. Then, when everyone had gotten a chance to speak, they held a general discussion of the meaning of the article and its relevance to their own work.

You'll find a copy of the protocol as Resource 1.13. You'll also find out more about protocols in Chapter 6.

"I think we need to be sure that Design Team members read this article about leadership," Josie noted. "It was certainly helpful for us to use the protocol to guide our discussion."

"And, to hear from people who are usually too shy to participate," Aaron said, with a nod to Tasha who, in fact, showed little, if any, inclination to be shy.

"We definitely should have the Design Team read the article using the protocol and also invite them to think about their leadership assets and the roles that are needed in a Design Team and PLC," Kelly added.

Getting the Work Done. Overcommitment is one problem for school teams and committees.[1] Exhaustion results. The people who volunteer again and again are likely to volunteer to be part of a design team on such an important initiative. How can they be protected and still contribute and feel useful and worthy?

One of two results occurs with design teams as they work. Either they try to do all the work and do, indeed, become exhausted; or they delegate so much work, and in such an official fashion, that they are seen as the bosses. Neither is desirable.

Moving from knowing to doing is one of the hardest things for a team to do. In teamwork, knowing is often disguised as planning, and it feels enough like doing that some teams plan, refine, and plan again, but never take action. This phenomenon is not limited to what happens in schools. Jeffrey Pfeffer and Robert Sutton, who wrote *The Knowing-Doing Gap: How Smart Companies Turn Knowledge Into Action* (2000), noted that "one of the great mysteries in organizational management" is "why knowledge of what needs to be done frequently fails to result in action or behavior consistent with that knowledge. We came to call this the knowing-doing problem" (quoted in Sparks, 2004, p. 1).

What's the solution? Pfeffer and Sutton (2000) suggest that the relationship be reversed: "Embed more of the process of acquiring new knowledge in the actual doing of the task. . ." (quoted in Sparks, 2004, p. 2). Rather than perpetually planning, educators might begin to do what needs to be done, learning as they go. Dennis Sparks, "itinerant teacher" and former executive director of the National Staff Development Council (now known as Learning Forward), promotes "sustained job-embedded professional learning and the creation of school cultures that promote reflection, clear communication, and dialogue about the assumptions that underlie improvements in student learning" (Sparks, 2004, p. 2). He's talking about PLCs and the professional learning characteristic of the best of them when educators take action to improve their own schools.

The shadows had moved from one side of Josie's backyard to the other by the time they finished their discussion of design teams and leadership. "Ahhh," Josie said, "this is such a sweet time in summer, the time of the shadows."

"I think we've got it," Aaron commented as he finished writing on the third piece of chart paper. (Who else but educators have chart paper, markers, and masking tape in their basements?) The Investigative Team had decided to profile the Design Team for the whole faculty, acknowledging that the characteristics of the Design Team might change when other faculty members volunteer to serve on it. They decided the following:

- *The Design Team will consist of volunteers who agree to serve at least 3 months (for continuity).*
- *The Design Team will be open to others (who agree to serve 3 months).*
- *People can leave the Design Team if they have served 3 months.*
- *The work will be nonrepresentational; that is, the focus will be on the whole school, not departments or grade levels.*
- *The Design Team focus will be on keeping the big picture in view and making sure the details harmonize with the big picture.*
- *The Design Team will also focus on listening and communicating—listening first, and then communicating in person, through e-mail or other technological means. "Who else needs to know? Who else and who else?" will become a mantra.*

---

[1] I do not consider overcommitment as "burnout." Burnout occurs when people keep doing something without having control over a situation, as when teachers are required to follow scripted lesson plans.

- *Leadership will be distributed among the Design Team, with two people planning and leading each meeting—one who did so for the previous meeting and one who is new. Other leadership tasks will be distributed among all members. The principal will share these leadership tasks and, in addition, serve as the liaison to the district.*
- *The Design Team will not do all the work, but it will do some of it and then look for others whose interests and qualifications make them appropriate for the task. These people will be asked to volunteer for the work. They will become a specialty team (such as a data team).*
- *The whole school will be a PLC, led by the Design Team. Either the Design Team or the PLC can identify needs, but the Design Team will study how to meet those needs and present strategies to the PLC.*

"We'll put out another e-mail," Kelly said, "letting people know what we're going to do next and inviting them to be part of the Design Team."

"It might be good to enclose the article I shared with you on the principal and PLCs," Josie said.

"Perhaps also the leadership assets piece and the jobs piece to let people know what kinds of things they might be doing," Kelly commented.

"So," Tasha said, standing up, "let's do it!" She thrust her hand into the middle of the group, and the others piled on their hands, just like Little League baseball.

As they pulled apart, Josie whispered, "Go, team. . . ."

DESIGN TEAM: PART 2

As it turned out, the Design Team became a permanent fixture at GHMS. As planned, all faculty and staff members were members of the GHMS PLC, and some faculty and staff worked on specialty teams as the year progressed. One specialty team, for example, focused on designing a survey for parents, community members, faculty and staff, and students. Other specialty teams emerged as the Design Team and the whole faculty worked together during the first year. And, interestingly enough, there were always one or two people (or more) who were interested in these special tasks. In a way, these specialized groups served as mini-PLCs. In fact, some of the specialty teams continued to work together, generally, organically, as mini-PLCs, simply because they liked doing so. Not everyone was on a specialty team (or mini-PLC), but everyone was part of the schoolwide PLC.

ORGANIZING A PLC

There are many ways of organizing PLCs. There is no one *right* way. In fact, educators in every school starting PLCs will need to determine the best structure for that school's context. See Resource 1.6 for a variety of ways to structure PLCs. See Resource 1.7 for a variety of ways schools can start PLCs.

During the year, the GHMS Design Team started out with nine members (including Josie, who stayed on the team), with a new member midyear. One member asked to leave the Design Team at the end of the year, but several others wanted to join it in its second year.

The faculty as a whole, and Design Team members in particular, were pleased with the way the Design Team was structured. They were glad that the positions were volunteer, nonexclusive, and nonrepresentative. Faculty members not on the Design Team felt comfortable enough about the design team concept to razz its members. They offered mock salutes as Design Team members approached. At one point, with a great deal of hilarity on everyone's part, the faculty threatened to stage a coup. The impermanent specialty teams were also a hit because no one minded volunteering for something that had an end to it, and people with specific interests found a way to contribute.

Josie found time for the Design Team to work during the school day by hiring regular substitutes for them every 2 weeks—2 hours in the morning or afternoon so they wouldn't consistently miss certain classes. Design Team members were reluctant to leave their classrooms but more confident in doing so because they had the same sub each time they were doing Design Team work.

A design team of five is about right for a faculty of about 40 people; a smaller school might want three, a larger school as many as nine or 10. What's important is deciding whether the design team is appointed or volunteer, representative or not. It's also important that the design team neither appear to be nor operate as an exclusive group.

It's also important to consider whether to involve noncertificated staff, such as classroom assistants, lunchroom workers, and secretaries. The GHMS Design Team decided to do so, but only one instructional assistant volunteered. Sometimes, noncertificated staff members have responsibilities that make it hard for them to participate in the work. And sometimes noncertificated staff feel as if the issues under consideration are outside their purview. Still, largely, the GHMS Design Team was glad it had included noncertificated staff members; above all, their decision resulted in a more cohesive, focused staff. Inclusion of noncertificated staff also honored these important members of the community.

At GHMS, surprisingly, a second level team unofficially formed—the keenly interested. They were the first to check a graffiti board the Design Team started in the hallway leading to faculty restrooms, the first to respond to e-mail and voicemail. They were vocal in the meetings. This group also fluctuated widely and refused to be official. As an informal second-tier team, this group provided a good feedback loop for the design team.

POLLYANNA?

Do not be misled here—not everything at GHMS was hunky-dory. You'll be reading in the following chapters how the Design Team and the PLC as a whole encountered problems and didn't always solve them. They didn't always learn from the problems and their possible solutions, either. Some of their problems were people problems. For example, they had their share of people who

- were negative no matter what the issue was (the "yabbuts"),
- dominated the discussion,
- advocated for their own ideas rather than engaging through inquiry,
- remained uninvolved,
- criticized but never stepped forward to help the group improve, or
- clung to the past.

You know the list. One of the smartest moves the Design Team made was to learn more about facilitation from Stephanie Hodges, the assistant superintendent. However, they also had systemic problems, such as

- having meeting times preempted by something else (usually characterized as an "emergency");
- being expected to show results before they had really gotten going;
- being expected to have clarity about what they were doing while they were still figuring it out themselves;
- a union that wanted to restrict the time the Design Team and the specialty teams spent out of contract time; and
- multiple priorities, including "flavor of the month" district initiatives (they really should have negotiated protection from these from the district at the start).

Aaron wrote a memo inviting members of the faculty and staff to consider being part of the Design Team; he circulated it among others on the Investigative Team for review and then e-mailed it, along with the profile of the Design Team. By the middle of July, five people had responded positively—they wanted to be part of the Design Team.

Tasha invited the Investigative Team to join her at the end of July to plan the first meeting of the Design Team. The team started with a champagne toast: "Death to the Investigative Team. Long live the Design Team."

As they worked on designing the first Design Team meeting, they realized that they wanted the Design Team to go through much the same process they had (reinventing the wheel, anyone?). They formulated this agenda:

Activity	Reasons	Materials Needed
Welcome and introductions	People may not know each other well	Some interesting way of introducing themselves: Pocket Partners? (See Resource 1.15 for this and other ways to start meetings)
Reasons for being part of the Design Team	What motivated them	None (oral activity—no need to chart)
Setting norms	Helpful in the long run for groups	Handout of possible norms (see Resource 1.14 for possible norms)
Defining "Design Team"	People need to have a common definition	3 × 5 cards and a modified Delphi process (see Resource 1.16 for a description of the Delphi process)
Describing the GHMS Design Team	Modification of the profile of the design team Discussion of professional learning Discussion of PLCs	Examples and nonexamples for professional learning (see Resource 1.17 for a resource to use for this activity) Creating a metaphor or acrostic poem for PLC
Barriers and boosters	Determining how the faculty might relate to the Design Team	Force-field analysis (see Resource 1.18 for information about force-field analysis)
Planning the first PLC meeting	Josie has commandeered the first district staff development day for the school's use!!!!	This chart for the Design Team

Activity	Reasons	Materials Needed
	People will want to know, based on e-mails they have received; they'll have lots of questions, maybe some concerns	
Next steps	We need to divide the tasks	Chart
Closure	We need to check norms and we need to close out the meeting	Closure activity???

Kelly concluded their last meeting as the Investigative Team with an activity he had learned at the conference that summer: Best Hopes and Worst Fears (Bob Chadwick, Beyond Conflict to Consensus, *2002). The Investigative Team's Best Hopes were quite similar: hope that the work would be worthwhile. Their Worst Fears were also similar: a fear that this effort would amount to nothing ("This too shall pass," "Been there, done that," and "Fear that this is the 'Flavor of the Month'").*

Tasha asked, "Why do we characterize attempts to change schools so cynically?" The other three laughed, but the four of them made a quick list:

- *The reform comes from outside the school; it's not school-based.*
- *The change is not about what we do in the classroom, with students.*
- *Someone from outside mandates the change.*
- *There's not enough support (time and money).*
- *Nothing goes away, and the new reform has to be added to the plate.*
- *The new reform doesn't fit with other reforms.*
- *Another reform is "just over the horizon."*
- *We've seen too many changes like this.*

Aaron responded, "What could we do to prevent these worst fears from happening?" The list was similar to the list above, but backwards:

- *Make sure it is school-based, not mandated from the outside.*
- *Make sure it is focused on what happens in the classroom.*
- *Make sure there are lots of choices for school-based decision making about the change.*
- *Make sure there are sufficient resources.*
- *Make sure that either something goes away or that the change fits with other things the school wants to do.*
- *Hold off on creating new reforms for a year or 2 (and make sure the PLC reform is the basis for anything new).*

Finally, Tasha said, "Let's do this with the Design Team. That would be a great way to end our first meeting."

NORMS

Some educators joke about norms, "Who's this Norm guy, anyway? Why do we need to pay attention to him?" Not particularly funny if your name happens to be Norm! The Investigative Team had no norms (or agreements on behavior); the group never felt the need to establish any because it saw itself as temporary, an *ad hoc* group in place only until a more permanent structure could be determined. When things go smoothly, groups do not think they need norms. When problems arise, it often feels too late to establish norms, a bit like closing the barn door after the horse escapes. Sometimes, groups feel too sophisticated to think about norms: "We're all adults here. We know how to behave!" Feeling "beyond norms" is in itself an indicator that a group may actually need norms. The declaration may signal an assumption that not everyone shares but no one dares contradict.

Most groups working on school change need established, practiced, and maintained norms (remember "wicked problems"?), without which a group may falter, experience trauma, and, eventually, fail.

Bruce Tuckman in 1965 developed an easy-to-remember set of stages of group development: Forming, Storming, Norming, and Performing (reprinted from Hord, Roussin, & Sommers, 2010) Here's a brief description of each stage:

Forming. According to Hord, Roussin, and Sommers, "the team meets and learns about the opportunity and challenges, and then agrees on goals and begins to tackle tasks." This is an easy stage. Group members are particularly amicable, wanting to like and be liked. They don't know enough about the work they are supposed to do to fight.

Storming. At this stage, "different ideas compete for consideration. The team addresses issues such as what problems they are really supposed to solve, how they will function independently and together, and what leadership model they will accept." This is a critical stage, "necessary to the growth of the team," but, unfortunately, some teams never move beyond it. Individuals need to grow out of advocacy for their own ideas and into acknowledgement of others' ideas. As Hord, Roussin, and Sommers describe it, "the groups . . . resolve their differences and group members will be able to participate with one another more comfortably and they won't feel that they are being judged in any way and will therefore share their own opinions and views." Some groups disintegrate at this stage.

A set of norms can help a group move out of storming to the next stage, especially if these norms are thoroughly understood, accepted at the beginning of each meeting, practiced, and evaluated at the end of each meeting. One norm, often omitted, describes what group members will do if someone violates a norm.

Norming. It is at this point that norms either prove valuable or, if missing, need to be developed. According to Hord, Roussin, and Sommers, "Team members adjust their behavior to each other as they develop work habits that make teamwork seem more natural and fluid. Team members often work through this stage by agreeing on rules, values, professional behavior, shared methods, working tools, and even taboos."

Performing. This is the "doing" stage. Team members are able to move beyond ideas and plans into taking action. Not all teams get to this stage, but those that do

> are able to function as a unit as they find ways to get the job done smoothly and effectively without inappropriate conflict or the need for external facilitation. Team members have become interdependent. By this time they are motivated and knowledgeable. The team members are now competent,

autonomous, and able to handle the decision-making process without supervision. Dissent is expected and allowed as long as it is channeled through means acceptable to the team.

It's important to remember that all groups have norms—that is, ways individuals behave with each other. When these are unstated, they allow for all kinds of behavior—productive and unproductive. When they are intentional (and understood, agreed upon, practiced, and evaluated), they can lead to action. Norming is an important group process—for all groups, even those as small as the Investigative Team—if groups are to accomplish difficult actions within a system that might be resistant (and most systems are). If the Investigative Team were to continue its work, it would need to establish and abide by norms.

Resource 1.15 provides as set of "starter" norms which a group can use as the basis for discussion of norms more specific to the group's work.

YOUR TURN: WHAT ARE YOU LEARNING?

Each of the chapters in this book ends with this trio of questions: *What Are You Learning? So What? Now What?* This processing tool is adapted from the work of Lipton and Wellman (2004).

In this section of each chapter, you'll read how a GHMS staff member processed what happened during the events in the chapter in terms of learning, and then you'll be invited to do the same. You may want to respond individually, and then—if you're lucky enough to be reading this book with others—discuss your answers with your colleagues. This trio of questions will help you think about what you've learned, why your learning is important in terms of the work you do, and some steps you might take to actualize the learning.

Tasha reminisced about that summer: "I learned so much! I guess the most important thing I learned is that things come together and work out. Josie was clearly prepared for us to learn about professional learning communities; she'd urged us to go to the conference. We were ready to learn about them. When we all got together, we were ready to do something. And, it seems like the faculty were ready, too. Most of them were ready to go."

What have you learned from this chapter?

SO WHAT?

Tasha continued, "Readiness seems important to me, but I don't think you wait until people are ready. If you did, nothing would happen. I think you establish some aspect of culture that helps people be ready for something to happen. You do what Josie did in terms of listening and sharing leadership roles. You talk about professional learning. Then—boom!—you're ready to go!"

What does your learning mean to you in your own environment?

NOW WHAT?

"Well," Tasha said, "We did some things because of our learning. The Investigative Team, for example, reading that article, thinking about the profile that would work for the Design Team. We acted because we were, somehow, ready."

What immediate first steps would you take to act upon an important learning from this chapter? A first step can be as simple as talking about your learning with colleagues. What outcomes would you want to see as result of your first step(s)?

RESOURCES FOR CHAPTER 1

1.1 Professional Learning and Professional Development

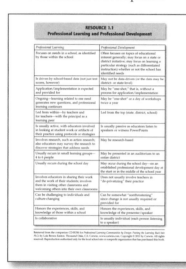

1.2 Definition and Characteristics of PLCs

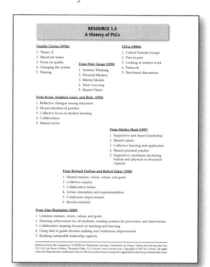

1.3 A History of PLCs

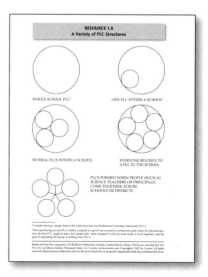

1.4 Some Research Related to PLCs

1.5 Survey of Faculty

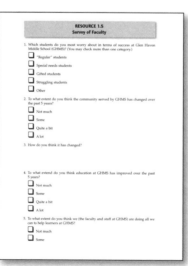

1.6 A Variety of PLC Structures

1.7 Starting PLCs

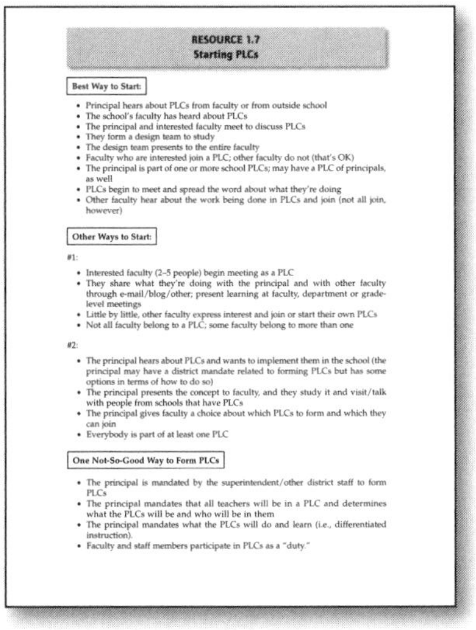
RESOURCE 1.7
Starting PLCs

Best Way to Start:

- Principal hears about PLCs from faculty or from outside school
- The school's faculty has heard about PLCs
- The principal and interested faculty meet to discuss PLCs
- They form a design team to study
- The design team presents to the entire faculty
- Faculty who are interested join a PLC; other faculty do not (that's OK)
- The principal is part of one or more school PLCs; may have a PLC of principals, as well
- PLCs begin to meet and spread the word about what they're doing
- Other faculty hear about the work being done in PLCs and join (not all join, however)

Other Ways to Start:

#1:

- Interested faculty (2–5 people) begin meeting as a PLC
- They share what they're doing with the principal and with other faculty through e-mail/blog/other; present learning at faculty, department or grade-level meetings
- Little by little, other faculty express interest and join or start their own PLCs
- Not all faculty belong to a PLC; some faculty belong to more than one

#2:

- The principal hears about PLCs and wants to implement them in the school (the principal may have a district mandate related to forming PLCs but has some options in terms of how to do so)
- The principal presents the concept to faculty, and they study it and visit/talk with people from schools that have PLCs
- The principal gives faculty a choice about which PLCs to form and which they can join
- Everybody is part of at least one PLC

One Not-So-Good Way to Form PLCs

- The principal is mandated by the superintendent/other district staff to form PLCs
- The principal mandates that all teachers will be in a PLC and determines what the PLCs will be and who will be in them
- The principal mandates what the PLCs will do and learn (i.e., differentiated instruction).
- Faculty and staff members participate in PLCs as a "duty."

1.8 Comparing PLCs to Business as Usual

RESOURCE 1.8
Comparing PLCs to Business as Usual

Professional Learning Communities (PLCs)	*Business as Usual*
A different way of "doing business" in schools	A new name for "business as usual"—the latest educational fad
People meeting together to focus on their own and each other's professional learning	People meeting together to focus on an agenda (busyness, business, announcements, etc.); accomplish tasks; learn something new from an outside expert
A variety of people meeting together	The usual groups: whole faculty, grade-level teams, subject-area disciplines, department meetings (although these *CAN* become PLCs)
Focus on new ways of meeting	Use of agendas (same old, same old)
Egalitarian (peer-to-peer)	Hierarchical (principal/department chair in charge, etc.)
Supportive, collegial, collaborative	Task-/decision-driven
Work driven by data about students/staff	Work driven by agenda of tasks to be done, decisions to be made
Variety of tools (protocols, lesson study, Standards in Practice)	Agenda or one-shot workshops; presentations
Subsequent work important: reflecting and debriefing; visiting other classrooms, schools; creating lessons and units and studying them	Ends when agenda is accomplished or when workshop is over
Action-oriented in terms of implementing new strategies; getting feedback and modifying strategies; conducting action research, etc.	Action-oriented in terms of accomplishing agenda, completing tasks, or making decisions or completing workshop
Study-oriented—classroom realities; books, articles to study; action research; data analysis	Agenda- or presentation-oriented
Helpful: coaching mentoring, follow-up; feedback; reflection	One-shot; abandonment in terms of workshop follow-up; isolating
Principal as colearner	Principal as manager, leader
Dialogue	Decision making; debate; discussion
Collective inquiry	Preset agenda, workshop topic
Continuous	One-shot deals (meetings or workshops)
Student focus	Focus on management items or focus on outside expertise in workshops
Systemic change	Incremental change

Retrieved from the companion CD-ROM for *Professional Learning Communities by Design: Putting the Learning Back Into PLCs* by Lois Brown Easton. Thousand Oaks, CA: Corwin, www.corwin.com. Copyright © 2011 by Corwin. All rights reserved. Reproduction authorized only for the local school site or nonprofit organization that has purchased this book.

1.9 Positive Deviance

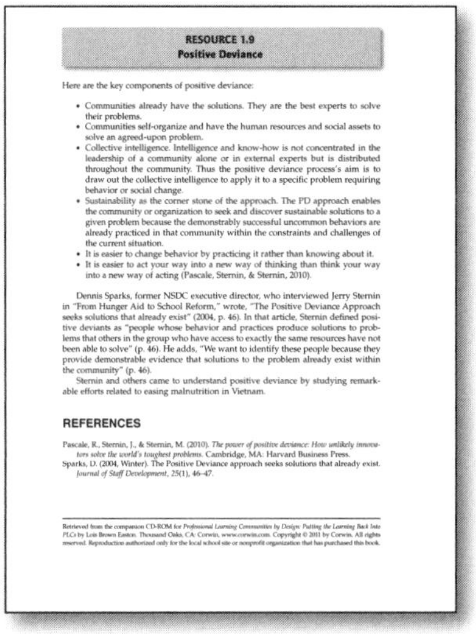
RESOURCE 1.9
Positive Deviance

Here are the key components of positive deviance:

- Communities already have the solutions. They are the best experts to solve their problems.
- Communities self-organize and have the human resources and social assets to solve an agreed-upon problem.
- Collective intelligence. Intelligence and know-how is not concentrated in the leadership of a community alone or in external experts but is distributed throughout the community. Thus the positive deviance process's aim is to draw out the collective intelligence to apply it to a specific problem requiring behavior or social change.
- Sustainability as the corner stone of the approach. The PD approach enables the community or organization to seek and discover sustainable solutions to a given problem because the demonstrably successful uncommon behaviors are already practiced in that community within the constraints and challenges of the current situation.
- It is easier to change behavior by practicing it rather than knowing about it.
- It is easier to act your way into a new way of thinking than think your way into a new way of acting (Pascale, Sternin, & Sternin, 2010).

Dennis Sparks, former NSDC executive director, who interviewed Jerry Sternin in "From Hunger Aid to School Reform," wrote, "The Positive Deviance Approach seeks solutions that already exist" (2004, p. 46). In that article, Sternin defined positive deviants as "people whose behavior and practices produce solutions to problems that others in the group who have access to exactly the same resources have not been able to solve" (p. 46). He adds, "We want to identify these people because they provide demonstrable evidence that solutions to the problem already exist within the community" (p. 46).

Sternin and others came to understand positive deviance by studying remarkable efforts related to easing malnutrition in Vietnam.

REFERENCES

Pascale, R., Sternin, J., & Sternin, M. (2010). *The power of positive deviance: How unlikely innovators solve the world's toughest problems.* Cambridge, MA: Harvard Business Press.
Sparks, D. (2004, Winter). The Positive Deviance approach seeks solutions that already exist. *Journal of Staff Development, 25*(1), 46–47.

Retrieved from the companion CD-ROM for *Professional Learning Communities by Design: Putting the Learning Back Into PLCs* by Lois Brown Easton. Thousand Oaks, CA: Corwin, www.corwin.com. Copyright © 2011 by Corwin. All rights reserved. Reproduction authorized only for the local school site or nonprofit organization that has purchased this book.

1.10 Article: *Leader and Learner*

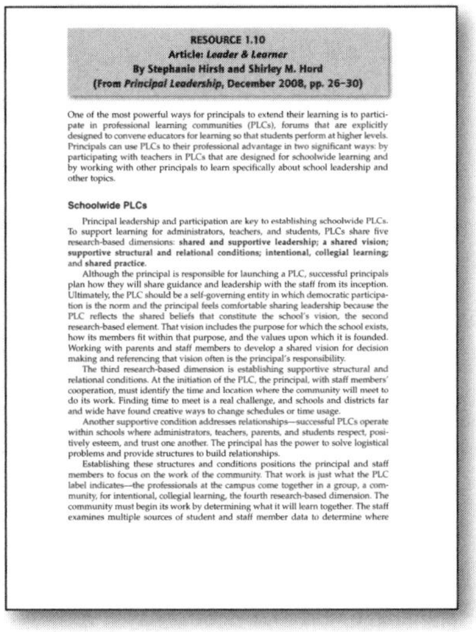
RESOURCE 1.10
Article: *Leader & Learner*
By Stephanie Hirsh and Shirley M. Hord
(From *Principal Leadership*, December 2008, pp. 26–30)

One of the most powerful ways for principals to extend their learning is to participate in professional learning communities (PLCs), forums that are explicitly designed to convene educators for learning so that students perform at higher levels. Principals can use PLCs to their professional advantage in two significant ways: by participating with teachers in PLCs that are designed for schoolwide learning and by working with other principals to learn specifically about school leadership and other topics.

Schoolwide PLCs

Principal leadership and participation are key to establishing schoolwide PLCs. To support learning for administrators, teachers, and students, PLCs share five research-based dimensions: **shared and supportive leadership; a shared vision; supportive structural and relational conditions; intentional, collegial learning;** and **shared practice**.

Although the principal is responsible for launching a PLC, successful principals plan how they will share guidance and leadership with the staff from its inception. Ultimately, the PLC should be a self-governing entity in which democratic participation is the norm and the principal feels comfortable sharing leadership because the PLC reflects the shared beliefs that constitute the school's vision, the second research-based element. That vision includes the purpose for which the school exists, how its members fit within that purpose, and the values upon which it is founded. Working with parents and staff members to develop a shared vision for decision making and referencing that vision often is the principal's responsibility.

The third research-based dimension is establishing supportive structural and relational conditions. At the initiation of the PLC, the principal, with staff members' cooperation, must identify the time and location where the community will meet to do its work. Finding time to meet is a real challenge, and schools and districts far and wide have found creative ways to change schedules or time usage.

Another supportive condition addresses relationships—successful PLCs operate within schools where administrators, teachers, parents, and students respect, positively esteem, and trust one another. The principal has the power to solve logistical problems and provide structures to build relationships.

Establishing these structures and conditions positions the principal and staff members to focus on the work of the community. That work is just what the PLC label indicates—the professionals at the campus come together in a group, a community, for intentional, collegial learning, the fourth research-based dimension. The community must begin its work by determining what it will learn together. The staff examines multiple sources of student and staff member data to determine where

1.11 Leadership Assets

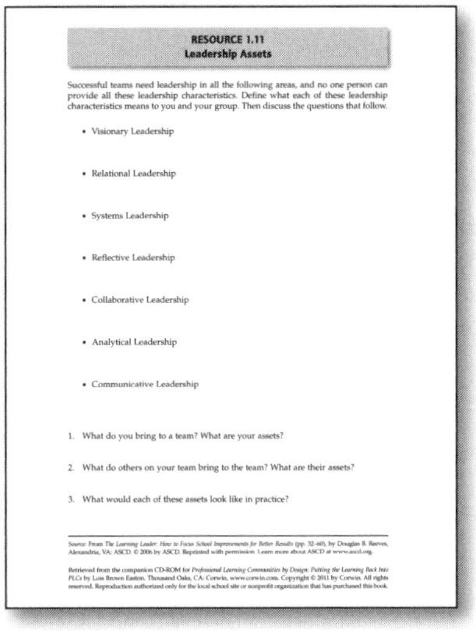
RESOURCE 1.11
Leadership Assets

Successful teams need leadership in all the following areas, and no one person can provide all these leadership characteristics. Define what each of these leadership characteristics means to you and your group. Then discuss the questions that follow.

- Visionary Leadership
- Relational Leadership
- Systems Leadership
- Reflective Leadership
- Collaborative Leadership
- Analytical Leadership
- Communicative Leadership

1. What do you bring to a team? What are your assets?
2. What do others on your team bring to the team? What are their assets?
3. What would each of these assets look like in practice?

Source: From *The Learning Leader: How to Focus School Improvements for Better Results* (pp. 32–60), by Douglas B. Reeves, Alexandria, VA: ASCD. © 2006 by ASCD. Reprinted with permission. Learn more about ASCD at www.ascd.org.

Retrieved from the companion CD-ROM for *Professional Learning Communities by Design: Putting the Learning Back Into PLCs* by Lois Brown Easton. Thousand Oaks, CA: Corwin, www.corwin.com. Copyright © 2011 by Corwin. All rights reserved. Reproduction authorized only for the local school site or nonprofit organization that has purchased this book.

1.12 Leadership Jobs

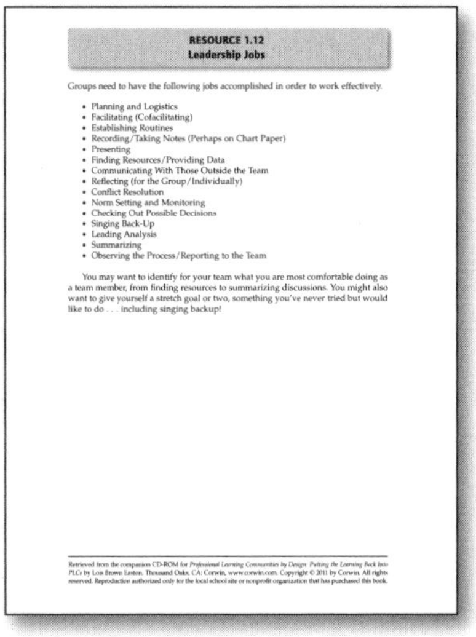
RESOURCE 1.12
Leadership Jobs

Groups need to have the following jobs accomplished in order to work effectively.

- Planning and Logistics
- Facilitating (Cofacilitating)
- Establishing Routines
- Recording/Taking Notes (Perhaps on Chart Paper)
- Presenting
- Finding Resources/Providing Data
- Communicating With Those Outside the Team
- Reflecting (for the Group/Individually)
- Conflict Resolution
- Norm Setting and Monitoring
- Checking Out Possible Decisions
- Singing Back-Up
- Leading Analysis
- Summarizing
- Observing the Process/Reporting to the Team

You may want to identify for your team what you are most comfortable doing as a team member, from finding resources to summarizing discussions. You might also want to give yourself a stretch goal or two, something you've never tried but would like to do . . . including singing backup!

Retrieved from the companion CD-ROM for *Professional Learning Communities by Design: Putting the Learning Back Into PLCs* by Lois Brown Easton. Thousand Oaks, CA: Corwin, www.corwin.com. Copyright © 2011 by Corwin. All rights reserved. Reproduction authorized only for the local school site or nonprofit organization that has purchased this book.

1.13 Three Levels of Text Protocol

1.14 Starter Norms

1.15 Pocket Partners and Other Ways to Begin Meetings

1.16 The Delphi Process

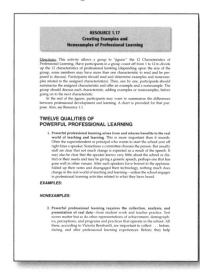

1.17 Creating Examples and Nonexamples of Professional Learning

1.18 Force-Field Analysis

2

Finding Initial Structures (August)

In which Design Team members learn more than they ever thought they would about each other. In which they look at Glen Haven's readiness for professional learning and plan the first PLC event. In which they learn the differences between presenting and facilitating.

Even though the air-conditioning was on high, the August heat penetrated the library media center at Glen Haven Middle School (GHMS). Coffee and tea were well iced, and even though it was only halfway through the morning, more than one person had a paper fan going. "It'll get cool," Josie reassured the rest of the staff when she sat down at the donut-shaped table, "it just hasn't been on much this summer." The donut-shaped table was perfect—there was no head of the table and everyone could see everyone else—and Aaron, Tasha, and Kelly sat at what would have been corners if the table had been square, leaving room between them for the rest of the Design Team.

As planned, they started the meeting with what Aaron said was a "crazy way" of introducing themselves. It might have been crazy, but both the new and transitioning members of the Design Team enjoyed it. Aaron Dobroski shared three things from his pocket (the keys to his new hybrid car, a picture of his spouse, and a rather dirty "binky" he'd rescued from the floor where his 6-month-old had tossed it) with Dottie (Dorotea Gibbon, classroom aide), who shared her grandchildren's pictures, the keys to her ancient Honda Civic (235,000 miles on it!), and a pen for writing her memoirs. Josie, sitting next to Forrest Long, one of the two counselors, introduced him by displaying the picture of him on his snowboard, his Sierra Club membership card, and his library card. Forrest introduced her by displaying from her purse a set of pencils (none of which was sharpened) held tight with red rubber band, her iPhone with games on it, and the key to her bicycle

> **Investigative Team Members:**
>
> Josie Bermudez, Principal
>
> Kelly Bosco, Science, Seventh and Eighth Grades
>
> Tasha Peart, Fitness and Health, Seventh and Eighth Grades
>
> Aaron Dobroski, Language Arts, Seventh and Eighth Grades

lock. Kelly Bosco introduced Roz (Rosalind Best), the school's new instructional coach, through the pack of gum in her purse (with reference to the piece in her mouth), her favorite credit card, and a picture of her cousin, a well-known actor. In turn, Roz introduced Kelly with a poem:

In his pocket a grocery list

Milk and bread—that was the gist.

A picture of his spouse

Standing in front of their house.

And, two lint-covered cough drops,

Smelling better than his socks!

After an extended groan from the group, Tasha introduced both Andy Mevoli (mathematics for the Sixth-Grade Core) and Robbie Beckel (language arts) along with herself. The contents of Andy's pocket yielded a rather used piece of chalk ("Been in there about 5 years," explained Andy), his expired driver's license, and a laminated dollar bill from his first job. Robbie's purse held a love note from her spouse, a picture of her horse, and a pair of reading glasses ("It's all those essays I have to read," she said).

Tasha displayed a copy of her Masters of Education diploma ("That was in your purse?" Aaron asked. "Well, sure!" Tasha responded, "you'd carry it around, too, if you'd had to work for it like I did!") and two pictures of her young children.

First Design Team

Josie Bermudez, Principal

Kelly Bosco, Science, Grades 7 and 8

Tasha Peart, Fitness and Health, Grades 7 and 8

Aaron Dobroski, Language Arts, Grades 7 and 8

Dottie Gibbon, Aide

Forrest Long, Counselor

Roz Best - School Coach

Andy Mevoli - Mathematics, Grade 6 Core and Grades 7 and 8

Robbie Beckel - Language Arts, Grades 7 and 8

"Are we done?" Andy asked when they had finished their pocket partner activity. "Great meeting. That wasn't too bad!"

Another couple of chuckles at his suggestion that the meeting might be over, and then Aaron shared an agenda with them. "We thought it would be good to have you go through a process similar to the process we went through when we first started to talk about professional learning and PLCs." And so the four members of the Investigative Team shared why they were interested in both and then invited the new members of the Design Team to share their interests. Unsurprisingly, the five new members voiced reasons similar to those the Investigative Team had shared at their first meeting. At the end, Aaron commented, "Well, our verses are a little different, but our chorus is the same: 'For the students.'"

Tasha suggested that the group consider norms for their work. She shared the starter norms on Resource 1.15, including the norms for collaboration (Garmston & Wellman, 1999). She led the group in some discussion of what these norms looked like in practice ("What would we hear and say? What would we do?") and when absent ("What actions would be the opposite of this norm?"). The group agreed to three points:

1. *Let's adhere to these norms unless we have reason to change them.*

2. *Let's refer to them at the beginning of each meeting ("Remember our norms? Anyone want to change them? Everybody agree to follow them?").*

3. *Let's check them at the end of each meeting ("How did we do? Any violations? Any changes we need to make in them?").*

Using the description of the Design Team that the Investigative Team had circulated and nearly fifty 3 × 5 cards (which they recycled), the Design Team employed the Delphi process (Resource 1.16) to come up with a definition of itself. First each person completed three cards, putting one key word to define the Design Team on each one. Then they considered all six cards in pairs, coming up with three. In groups of four, they consolidated their definitions until—as whole group—they agreed upon this definition:

The GHMS Design Team is a volunteer group, flexible in terms of membership and neither representative nor exclusive, whose major task is guiding the work of the school's PLC.

The members agreed that they could propose changes to the definition anytime, especially after they heard from the whole faculty and staff later in the month; they also agreed not to alter the statements that the Investigative Team had written to describe the Design Team until after that meeting.

After a short break, they dug into the information they had about professional learning and PLCs (Resources 1.1, 1.2, 1.3, 1.4, 1.6, 1.7, and 1.8). After a short discussion of what had "struck" them— what was most important to them in terms of all their reading—Tasha asked them to work together to create a metaphor to represent their understanding.

See Resource 2.1 for this and other ways of processing information. Their metaphors are in the box.

> ### Investigative Team Metaphors for PLCs
>
> Professional learning is like learning how to ride a bike. You can't just read about it; you have to get on the bike and get better and better at what you do.
>
> PLCs are like tossed salads. All the freshest vegetables (ideas) go into it, and the dressing is handmade (school-based). It is mixed well in a quality bowl (the school), each bite (each learning experience) tastes great, and all the students thrive.
>
> PLCs are like fitness clubs. When you first join, you are out-of-shape, and it's a struggle just to step onto the treadmill! Little by little, with lots of encouragement and some helpful information, you get better and better. You might even join a class so you can work out with others. After a year, you're really in shape.

"You know," Dottie said, "We need to do exactly this with the whole faculty. We need to get on the same page about all these things."

"Right," Roz said, "and I think we need to get into planning that meeting. It's what, only 2 weeks away?"

"Before we do that," Kelly said, "we did something else we would like to share. We looked at Glen Haven Middle School in terms of its readiness for work as a PLC—its context for professional learning. We charted barriers and boosters, forces for and against professional learning and PLCs. Here." He distributed a copy of what the Investigative Team had done and the Design Team studied it for a few minutes, sipping iced tea and coffee, and some members asked clarifying questions.

"We could change this now," Roz commented, "but I'm OK with it as it is. I suggest we validate these or change them with the entire faculty in our first PLC." Roz clearly wanted to get to planning the agenda.

"And," said Forrest, "we'll want to work on how we can build on the boosters and address the barriers."

"Just one more thing," Tasha said. "I'm realizing that context is really important. I've been investigating some of the

resources we were given at our conference this summer. I went online at www.learningforward.org and found some standards for professional learning. One of them is context. I also checked out a book we were given that has a good section on context and some surveys we might use. I think we should take one of the surveys, just to see where Glen Haven Middle School is in terms of readiness for this work."

"Online," Aaron said, "put it online." After the first Design Team meeting, Tasha did exactly that and attached some additional material from Learning Forward (formerly National Staff Development Council [NSDC]).

Here are some thoughts on the first part of the Design Team meeting.

MIRRORING

You may have wondered why the Investigative Team was so insistent on repeating its own experiences with the Design Team, and why the Design Team is so determined that the PLC will do so, too. What's the point of mirroring activities? What's the point of this redundancy? It certainly will take time to repeat Design Team activities at the first PLC meeting. Why can't the PLC just continue where the Design Team left off? Some of the answers to these questions have to do with the benefits of reinventing the wheel, which you read about in Chapter 1.

Another reason for redundancy is transparency. People are naturally suspicious if they think that something has been decided and is being presented to them as a *fait accompli*, even if the outcome makes sense to them. Another reason is intellectual and emotional processing. What one group does to reach a conclusion has been done through some level of processing, which results in a conclusion that makes sense and feels right. When the conclusion is presented to a group, without that processing, it may not make sense and it probably won't feel right.

Often one group will also figure out how to achieve "buy-in" so that the next group will like what they've concluded, even though they haven't been involved in the process. Your first encountered buy-in as a negative concept in Chapter 1.

THE IMPORTANCE OF PROCESSING

So far, GHMS staff members have engaged in several processing strategies. Processing is an important part of learning. Adults learn, according to Jack Mezirow in *Transformative Dimensions of Adult Learning* (1991), "through cues and symbolic models and through language" (p. 4). His model of adult learning requires reflection. Adults assess the premises they have heard in new information or a new experience according to the cognitive structures they have stored, which he calls "meaning schemes." These schemes are "made up of specific knowledge, beliefs, value judgments, and feelings" (p. 5) rather like schema (for which the singular is *schemata*, which is "an organized representation of an event that may serve as a prototype, norm, or context" [p. 10]). As we reflect (or process), we test what we've heard or seen against what we know. We may elaborate, create or transform our "meaning schemes." And, this is real learning. We remember. "Remembering appears to involve recognizing an object or event that previously had meaning and either strengthened or transformed an existing meaning perspective or a specific meaning scheme or schemes" (p. 6). If we don't process something, we are likely to forget it: "The event is no longer recognizable."

As if that weren't a strong enough argument for adult processing activities, we might also look at other theories of adult learning. Again, Mezirow helps us: "Information processing theory holds that what we learn and recall is . . . an active totality that we organize through the various processing mechanisms" (p. 9). A contextual theory maintains "what is learned and remembered depends on the various contexts of the event—psychological, social, cultural, and physical" (p. 9).

Because they are important to adult learning and, therefore, learning in PLCs, throughout this book you will encounter a number of processing activities. Some of these activities are serious and straightforward; some are more lighthearted, even fun. Resource 2.1 provides a few processing activities.

CONTEXT AND TWO OTHER ASPECTS OF PROFESSIONAL LEARNING

Tasha's curiosity took her to the website of Learning Forward, which describes professional learning in terms of three categories: context, process, and content. As this book was going to press, Learning Forward had engaged educators around the world at all levels of education in the task of redefining standards related to these three categories. Check www.learningforward.org for an update on their work.

She learned that *context* generally refers to how schools organize into learning communities and how they are guided by skillful leaders and provided resources for their work to improve school.

Process generally refers to how learning communities use data and research to evaluate and guide what they do to improve schools for all students. Process also refers to using learning strategies appropriate for adults in a school, especially those that stimulate collaboration.

Content standards generally refer to how educators provide quality teaching and learning experiences equitably for students, enlisting the support of community and families.

These are summarized in the Learning Forward purpose statement: "Every educator engages in effective professional learning every day so every student achieves." This purpose statement (or vision) surprised her (as it may you): "Every educator? Every day?" she wondered. But, why not? As the Bill and Melinda Gates Foundation declared, "Evidence shows clearly what most people know intuitively: teachers matter more to student learning than anything else inside a school." What helps teachers become effective? Their preparation programs and professional learning while they are teaching. Learning Forward's six "E" vision statement is right on target.

CONTEXT: A CONTINUUM

Tasha continued to investigate context and discovered that context is not a destination; it's a process. In terms of professional learning, a school never reaches *There* or stalls near *Not There*; it is sometimes in the middle and sometimes in more than one place at the same time, according to different qualities of context. Context is a school's environment, the culture of the school, a culture that can be described as more or less ready for professional learning and PLCs:

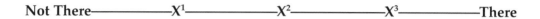

Not There————————X^1————————X^2————————X^3————————**There**

Schools cannot wait for their context for professional learning and PLCs to be perfect; it never will be. Instead, schools need to understand where their culture is, in terms of professional learning and PLCs, and build from there, relying on the tools and strategies of professional learning to move them further along the continuum. In other words, as schools engage in appropriate professional learning—no matter where they are when they begin their engagement—they will ready themselves for more—and deeper—professional learning.

ASSESSING CONTEXT

Several surveys help educators assess their context for professional learning.

Survey #1: The first survey, shown in Resource 2.2, assesses context through three lenses:

- What happens in effective learning communities?
- What kind of leadership is needed?
- What kinds of resources are needed?

These lenses relate to NSDC's (now LearningForward's) 2001 description of the context standards, which are being revised as this book goes to press. Still, these lenses are helpful for understanding context.

Survey #2: A second survey, Resource 2.3, provides a way for examining what a school culture needs in order to engage in school improvement. This survey is based on the work of Margery Ginsberg (2003, 2004, 2008), who maintains that a context supporting professional learning and focusing on school improvement has the following characteristics:

1. a shared language for teaching and learning,

2. ongoing, collaborative adult learning,

3. use of conventional and creative data,

4. advocacy at every level, and

5. a school or district signature.

You can learn more about these characteristics by examining the survey itself.

Survey #3: A third survey is actually a rubric that can be used as a survey instrument. It is based on a systems approach. This way of assessing a school's context "broadens the examination of context to include the school as a system as well as its place within a variety of other systems: districts and organizations such as teacher centers that support schools" (Easton, 2008a, p. 11).

A systems approach to change helps us check our tendency to draw cause-effect relationships between some kind of intervention in education (such as PLCs) and student achievement. Direct cause-effect relationships between professional learning and student achievement are very hard to draw because of all the factors that influence student achievement. For example, we may notice that student achievement begins to go up 2 years after school faculty and staff began to work in PLCs. There may very well be a relationship between the two events, but there may be other reasons for the increase in student achievement—some related to the school itself (a change in the daily schedule, a new textbook series), others related to the district (a policy change, a new superintendent), still others related to a regional service center (training literacy coaches for each school), or, finally, those related to the state (a change in law or policy, funding for a new project). We can certainly correlate the effectiveness of PLCs with increased student achievement—and researchers have done so—but we cannot isolate the link.

On the other hand, to support professional learning, PLCs, and increased student achievement, all of these parts of the system need to change. For example, as they learn something new, teachers need to change their own practices to help students learn better. Schools may need to change to allow teachers to learn and modify their own practices (setting aside time for adult learning and arranging for coaches, for example). Districts may need to make some changes in terms of aligning their teacher evaluation system to reflect professional learning. States may need to modify a funding stream to provide for professional learning related to a new initiative.

Roles throughout the system also need to change. Students' roles may change as they think of their teachers as learners. They may need to become accustomed to extra adults in their classrooms; they may be surveyed or interviewed about what they need as learners; they may even have their work shared among teachers. Parents and community members may need to change in terms of what they consider teacher learning—rather than a number of established days on the district calendar, teacher learning may involve early release or late start days, for example. They may hear from their offspring that teachers have coaches or that teachers are doing research . . . and wonder what these mean in terms of student learning.

What's needed in terms of systems goes beyond understanding what adults need; people throughout a system need to take an active role to support adult learning. Figure 2.1 (and Resource 2.4) helps people think about how a system might change to support professional learning (Easton, 2008a, CD Resource 1.4).

You probably noticed something called KASAB in Figure 2.1. KASAB is an acronym for deconstructing standards and objectives: What do people (students and adults) need to **K**now? What **A**ttitude do they need about their learning? What **S**kills do they need? What **A**spirations should they have regarding their learning? What **B**ehaviors should they exhibit? Joellen Killion (2008, p. 197), who created this way of looking at standards and objectives, has compressed the acronym to KASB by uniting **A**ttitude and **A**spirations. You will find a summary of KASB as Resource 2.5.

Figure 2.1 A Template for Systems Change Indicators

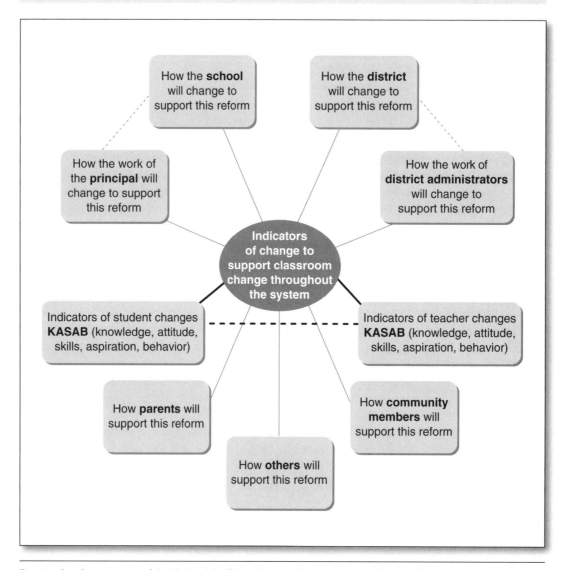

Survey #3 (Resource 2.6) pulls together on a 4-point scale many of the characteristics of a professional learning community:

- Time and how it is used
- Appropriate learning activities
- Space/location
- Leadership and governance
- Data collection and use
- Evaluation of professional learning
- Role changes
- Cultural changes
- Resources

I hope you'll find the descriptions of the characteristics in rubric form helpful. Pay particular attention to the descriptions of a "4" on each of the characteristics.

Survey #4: A fourth instrument (Resource 2.7) goes at context from another point of view. Getting right down to the guts of PLCs, it asks educators to rate the appeal of various characteristics of PLCs. I created this survey on the basis of set of descriptors developed by NSDC (now Learning Forward) and the New Jersey Department of Education in a document called *Collaborative Professional Learning in School and Beyond: A Tool Kit for New Jersey Educators* (Killion, 2009). Some descriptors originally came from the South Carolina State Department of Education.

This survey is fun to take because it is so obvious. I ask survey takers to put an X by any descriptor that appeals to them; they, naturally, mark many of the items. A scoring guide lets survey takers rate themselves based on the number of Xs they made. Of course, the scoring guide is rigged so that most people find they are "Gung ho! Get outta my way. My initials are PLC."

This survey is also a way to help people understand exactly what might happen in PLCs as well as what their roles might be.

Tasha had selected the rubric (Survey #3, Resource 2.6) and turned it into a survey, which she put online. "Take the survey as soon as possible," Tasha said, "and I'll get the results to you before our first PLC meeting. It'll be interesting to see our perceptions of Glen Haven. We may want to have everyone do the survey." (You'll find Design Team survey results in Resource 2.8.)

"So, now we can get on to planning the PLC meeting, right?" Roz asked, a bit plaintively this time.

"Actually," Forrest said with a clearing of this throat. He hadn't spoken much during this meeting. "Actually, I'm a little concerned. It seems like we're jumping into this too quickly. I'm not 100% sure we need PLCs. Why should we disrupt the whole faculty if they're not needed? And, it seems to me that we need to make sure we can do PLCs before we engage the whole faculty in what might be a wild goose chase."

"Jumping the gun." Aaron said, but not as a question.

"Putting the cart before the horse," Robbie ventured.

"Yes," Forrest said. "Whatever those sayings really mean. Why do we need PLCs? I'm not saying we don't; I'm just not sure why. And, if we do, just exactly how are we going to get PLCs done? How will we find the time? How will we organize? What structure will we have? Who's going to lead this?"

"I think the 'why' question is especially appropriate," Josie said. "It's interesting to me that that's the first reaction the Investigative Team had to PLCs. Remember, way back when we first talked about them?" She turned to Kelly, Tasha, and Aaron. "I told you about my dream and how I'd seen all these faceless students in it—potential, but empty. I mentioned test scores, but that's not really what was most important to me."

"I remember saying that I really worried about struggling students," Aaron said.

"The ones that are on the edge of learning," Tasha finished his thought for him. "I'll never forget the way you put it—'on the edge of learning.' I think I said something about how our neighborhood has changed, how our kids are different, but how we haven't changed the school much, if at all."

Kelly spoke up. "I do think about those test scores, but I think more about whether or not students are learning, really learning."

Josie finished their reflection, "So we said we've got to do something, and we had all heard about how effective school-based professional learning communities are in terms of helping schools improve."

"We didn't exactly check with you on why you might be interested in improving the school, did we?" Tasha asked, looking around the table. "We asked you about why you might be interested in professional

learning and PLCs, but we didn't get to why you might be interested. Professional learning and PLCs are possible solutions to problems—the means to an end but not the end in themselves."

"Well," Aaron said, "I remember commenting that our verses are a little different but we sing the same chorus, 'For the students.'"

"Course correction," Tasha said. "I don't think we can continue with what we might do until we're crystal clear about why."

"It'll take us off schedule, take a little more time to discover why we need to make changes," Kelly warned.

Forrest said, "I think we have to make sure we all have powerful reasons for engaging in professional learning and PLCs . . . and I think that we'll need to be sure the whole faculty has powerful reasons before we start PLCs."

"So, how can we do that?" Roz asked.

"We could look at how well we are meeting the vision and mission of the school," Aaron ventured.

"What vision and mission?" Robbie asked.

"The one in the staff handbook," Aaron stated.

"Never read that!" Tasha declared. "I'll bet most of us don't even know we have a vision or a mission."

MISSION, VISION, AND OTHER WAYS TO DISCOVER PURPOSE

Tasha is right. Many schools have mission and/or vision statements tucked away somewhere or engraved on a plaque hanging in the front hallway, right outside the principal's office. In many schools, few faculty members, fewer community members, almost no parents, and no students know it's there or consult it. Sometimes, no one can find a school's vision or mission statement.

Yet faculties as a whole or in groups, task forces, or committees probably spent quite a long time crafting those statements. Perhaps a principal wrote a vision statement and "ran it by" faculty or a committee. Perhaps the district required that schools echo the district's mission or vision, and so no one really worked on it at the school level.

Some mission and vision statements are highly distinctive and capture a school's unique focus on what those in the school believe and do, as well as how they position themselves for the future. Some are entirely bland and work as well in a school across town, across the state, even across the country. Some have been wordsmithed to death so that they are meaningless but offensive to no one. And then, sometimes, it's hard to tell a mission from a vision statement; some faculties spend an inordinate amount of time trying to distinguish between the two. Finally, some vision and mission statements become meaningless if the business of school requires little reference of them in terms of policy and practice.

The place to look for mission and vision is in what actually happens in a school. What is important about written mission and vision statements if they exist is congruence between what is stated and practiced. A school can have written mission or vision statements but little or no understanding of what these mean in practice. Other schools can *lack* a written mission or vision statement but have a common understanding of the right things to do terms of policy and practice. Still other schools can have—or lack—written mission or vision statements, and their faculties can think they have a shared understanding of what to do—but the truth is that policies and practices are not congruent (or, worse, sometimes congruent and sometimes not so).

The strongest schools have congruence between what they say and what they do—a "walking-their-talk" kind of congruence. Weaker schools lack congruence, especially in terms of the ability of people to understand and act upon beliefs. Self-deception results when schools have a written mission or vision, but no one understands what the words mean or how they apply to policy and practice.

Let's look at a few hypothetical (and simplified) cases:

Case 1:   Mission = Everyone is a learner.

The principal sets up workshops for teachers but does not attend them, except to introduce the speaker and take attendance.

Case 2:   No vision or mission statement. No written philosophy or set of beliefs.

The faculty believes that the school is student-centered.

Lecture is the most common teaching technique.

Case 3:   Vision: All students will graduate as citizens ready to partake in the democratic process.

The assistant principal decides that a club to support a candidate who is running for a state government position is inappropriate and disallows it.

Case 4:   No vision or mission statement. No written philosophy or set of beliefs.

Faculty members consider themselves collaborative.

The principal refers decisions that affect faculty members to those who are going to be affected by the decision.

Case 5:   The school has a written mission and vision statement.

No one knows what it is or where to find it.
Decisions are made without reference to the mission or vision (partly because no one can find it!).

Parents ask what the school stands for.

Although many school reformers advocate for the careful construction of a mission or vision statement, I believe understanding purposes and articulating beliefs are more important. Purposes and beliefs tend to be more to the point, descriptive, and detailed. "We can't let our students fail" is a robust purpose, but hardly the stuff of a mission or vision statement. Purpose answers a series of important questions:

1. "Are we doing the best we can in terms of educating young people?"

2. If not, "What do we need to change or improve?"

3. Next, "Why do we believe these changes will result in an affirmative answer to the question, 'Are we doing the best we can in terms of educating young people?'"

4. Ultimately, "How can we make needed changes or improvements?"

Purpose usually arises from disruptions in the system (things that aren't going as well as they should) or disequilibrium (changes or fluctuations that get our attention). Please note: No system, including a school, can avoid disruptions or disequilibrium; in

For more information about equilibrium and disequilibrium, see Margaret Wheatley's chapter "Change Stability and Renewal: The Paradoxes of Self-Organizing Systems" in *Leadership and the New Science: Learning About Organization From an Orderly Universe*, 1992, 1994, San Francisco: Berrett-Koehler Publishers, Inc.

fact, these are needed to push and prod schools into improvement. Equilibrium—when everyone can slap their hands together and declare, "It all works now. We're done. No more change"—is not really possible because the contexts for learning change.

One of the best ways to get people to identify purposes is to have them talk about what's bothering them about what's happening in their schools. Suzanne Bailey, a systems thinker, used to ask, "Where's the pain in the system?" to get at purpose (personal communication). Purpose is what the Investigative Team declared when they heard about the possibilities of PLCs.

You can use a simple chart to help people arrive at purposes based on problems they have identified. Please note that you are not looking for solutions, just identification of purposes. You'll find a blank chart in Resource 2.9. Begin with Questions #1 and #2 above. Corral some evidence related to what's not working. Reframe the statement about what's not working into a purpose. You may find that, once they've identified problems, people want to jump to solutions. If necessary, capture these on sticky notes and put them in a "Solutions Parking Lot," but help people be content with simply restating the problems as purposes for the work they might do together.

Here's how the Design Team clarified purposes for improving learning in Glen Haven.

What's Not Working as Well as It Could?	Evidence	Purposes
Students aren't engaged.	They don't pay attention in class. They don't do classwork. They don't do homework. They don't appear to like what they are doing.	Discover how to help students become engaged in their own learning.
Students do not write well.	Their writing in English classes is immature. They do not write much in other curriculum areas. They hate to write. They don't see any purpose in writing or making their writing better.	Discover how to help students value writing—their own and others'—and improve it so that they can communicate for a variety of purposes with a variety of readers.
Students don't "belong" to the school; they just endure it.	A lot of students do not fit in. They are teased or bullied. They have few relationships. This is a somewhat recent phenomenon.	Figure out a way to help students appreciate their opportunities in school.
Parents are not involved in the school.	They don't come to PTO meetings. They don't come for parent conferences. They don't volunteer at the school. Teachers are not sure if they support what students are doing.	Come to an understanding about what parents think about the school and their students within it and what they and their students need from the school.

The Design Team could have generated more purposes, but for the time being, they settled for these four problems and noticed that all of the purposes were about learning—their own learning. This is not unusual; most schools discover that their problems lead to purposes related to learning that people need to do. So, it's no surprise when a school looks for a structure for learning: a PLC.

The Glen Haven Design Team knew their purposes might grow when the whole faculty engaged in this process at the first PLC meeting. They also knew that they might need to broaden purposes or subsume specific purposes under a category, such as "communicate effectively through a variety of means, including writing." So, they knew they were not finished with purpose-setting.

The important thing about purpose is that people speak their purposes with passion. They say, "I really worry about students who don't seem to have friends or belong to any group." They exclaim, "They can't write, not even a single sentence that is clear." They weep, "They just don't get math. They do the formulas and the work, but they have no idea how exciting math is." Passion keeps a group going when the work gets hard.

Eventually, purpose may evolve into mission: *Our mission is to ensure that every student, supported both at home and at school, finds an important role at Glen Haven Middle School.* But don't start the process by engineering a mission. It's too hard. The process of crafting a mission can also be interminable, captivating to those who are interested but insufferably boring to those who aren't. People want to get to the real work, and identifying what's not working—something about which they are passionate—will help get them going and continue to engage.

Another way of getting to the real work is through beliefs or values (I don't distinguish between the two). Paired, purposes and beliefs are powerful. Together, they directly answer the question, "Why are we doing this?"

Belief statements can be short and sweet. They are usually concrete enough to lend themselves to policy and practice implications. They can be referenced easily: "How does this decision conform to our beliefs or values?" They can be considered—as they should—at the beginning of each year: "Do we still believe these things? What effect will these beliefs or values have on our work this year?" They can be considered during the year and at the end of the year, "Are we still acting according to our beliefs and values?" The important thing about beliefs and values is that they are developed through implications.

Values from the Young Women's Leadership Charter School, Chicago

"We value equitable access to resources and opportunities for every student.

"We value the contribution a single-sex education makes to educating the whole woman and promoting her leadership.

"We value inquiry, self-reflection, critical thinking, problem-solving and real world experience.

"We value the diversity in our school community.

"We value parents and families as partners.

"We value integrity, honesty and perseverance.

"We value professionalism in education through reflection, collaboration and shared leadership."

(http://www.ywlcs.org)

Here's an example of some belief statements and their implications:

Beliefs/Values	Implications
We believe in the worth of all members of the school community.	Our discipline policy is not a set of rules; instead it is a set of behaviors we think all school members should exhibit in community. We express positive expectations of students in classes in terms of what they can do personally, socially, and intellectually. We share our expectations of our selves.
We believe that learning is both a social and individual process of constructing meaning.	We keep lectures to a minimum and encourage students to learn in groups and express their learning both individually and as part of a group. We encourage students to find their own relevance/meaning in what they learn.
We believe that "belonging" is a very important aspect of learning, for both adults and students.	We have a variety of ways—including advisories and teams—that help students belong to at least one subgroup. We have a variety of ways, such as service, that help students belong to the school as a whole. We have a variety of ways, such as PLCs, so adults can work together to learn.

The development of belief or value statements can also provide an easy avenue to mission or vision statements, if these are required. Take a look at the set of value statements in the box. These are from the Young Women's Leadership Charter School in Chicago. You can probably see how these belief statements lead to a mission or vision statement (although it's not clear which came first). Here's the school's mission: "The Young Women's Leadership Charter School of Chicago inspires urban girls to engage in rigorous college preparatory learning in a small school focused on math, science and technology that nurtures their self-confidence and challenges them to achieve." This mission is distinctive among school mission statements and clearly identifies the focus of the school. The vision does the same: "All young women have the skills, tools and opportunities to develop as ethical leaders shaping their lives and the world." The implications of the belief statements, the mission, and the vision pilot the school's policies and practices.

What's most important about purpose, belief, mission, and vision—no matter how they're stated—is how they're used. They need to be referenced in terms of decision making and clear enough that they point to one decision over another. They need to be incorporated in some way into the life of the entire community—perhaps as the subject for student-led gatherings. New faculty and students need to learn them. Everyone needs to be able to say, "Oh, our school would never do that! It's against our philosophy!" or "That's what makes us so special, our beliefs about students."

"What was your other question, Forrest?" Josie asked.

"I just want to know how we're going to do PLCs? If there's no possibility of doing them, why go there? Why disrupt the school?" Forrest responded.

WHY, WHAT, AND HOW

Forrest brought up a chicken-and-egg problem regarding making change. Which comes first? Do people want to know **what** the change will be (or what the structure for change will be) first? Do they want to explore **why** change is needed? Do they want to know **how** the change will be made? (I know. There are three aspects to change and only two aspects to chickens and eggs.) The answer, by the way, is "Yes. Yes we want to know all these things, simultaneously." The answer is also that some people have preferences—they need to know the details before they can proceed. Or they need to get the big picture. Or they need to understand why change is important. What a job facilitating change is!

> TED is a small nonprofit that started out in 1984 as a conference bringing together people from three worlds: Technology, Entertainment, Design.

Conventionally, leaders present the **what** first—"This is what we need to do." It could be the fad *du jour* or a federal mandate, a good idea, or someone's way to the top. Simon Sinek addressed a triad of approaches (why, what and how) to change in a TED lecture in 2009. The title of his book captures his premise: *Start With Why: How Great Leaders Inspire Everyone to Take Action* (2009b). He studied leaders who have "had the greatest influence in the world that they all think, act, and communicate in the exact same way—and it's the complete opposite of what everyone else does. Sinek calls this powerful idea The Golden Circle, and it provides a framework upon which organizations can be built, movements can be lead, and people can be inspired. And it all starts with WHY."

So, Forrest's first request, related to **why**, was exactly what Sinek and others who have focused on powerful change, would recommend as a first step. But, let's go to his second question related to logistics or **how**.

HOW

Josie was able to put her hands on a document she received at a conference related to professional learning. She ran to her office and made copies for the Design Team. Here is what she found:

LOGISTICS OF PLCs (STRUCTURES, GOVERNANCE, AND RESOURCES)

(Adapted from Easton, 2008a, pp. 16–19)

Structures in Learning Communities

In addition to having a belief that everyone is a learner, schools that are professional learning communities structure time, size, and space so that adults as well as students can engage in learning.

Time. Setting aside time for professional learning is not enough; the *type* of time teachers have for learning is as important. Faculties need regular, embedded, continuous time of sufficient length to engage with each other. They need more than one-shot workshops or presentations. They need school and district administrators who "count" (for recertification or salary increases) learning experiences that do not fit the one-shot workshop or presentation model.

What faculties do with their time is important. The nature of PLC activities indicates how well time to learn is used. How is time "filled up"? By what? What is a school's schedule? How are the activities labeled?

Take a look at some differences among schools and districts: At one school, the schedule every Wednesday might include 60 minutes of collaborative professional learning for every adult. During the hour of adult learning time, students work on service projects with community mentors while adults focus on their own learning. Then, students and adults join each other for conventional or block classes. PLC activity is embedded in the school day.

In another school, meetings might occupy prominent and permanent positions on the schedule: weekly faculty meetings, department meetings and grade-level meetings. These activities might really be *meetings* in terms of agendas featuring announcements and reports, items for discussion and decision. So, PLCs meet during lunch, common planning periods, or after school (on contract time, or not). Lunch, common planning periods, after school: These are not ideal times for a PLC to meet. Lunch is usually fraught with responsibilities, such as "duty." Common planning periods might not bring the right people together for a PLC or other responsibilities, such as curriculum review, might interfere with PLC activities. After-school meetings require lots of caffeine, preferably in the form of chocolate! In other words, teachers are exhausted after a full day of work. These PLC slots are not embedded.

In another school up the block, there may be no mention of meetings (perhaps these meetings occur through the Internet and voicemail?), but in their place faculty gather for professional learning in PLCs. Thus, meetings are not the featured activity; PLCs are.

In one school, grade-level PLCs cover for each other so that their colleagues can meet during the day . . . and, in return, are covered when they meet. So, the fourth-grade PLC covers when the third-grade PLC meets, and vice versa. The math teachers at a nearby high school plan joint mathematics and science classes so that science teachers can meet during one period once a month, and are able to meet with coverage later that month. In another school, a set of substitutes rotates from grade level to grade level to cover for grade-level PLCs. In a high school, the same thing happens for each subject-area PLC.

In one district, the yearly calendar might include professional development days four times a year. During these days, individuals select from a number of workshops offered by the district or use these days for planning and grading purposes. Another district lists after-school and Saturday workshops and mentions appropriate graduate classes at a nearby university or online. Still another district might not have districtwide professional development activities, leaving it up to schools to decide how to schedule a certain amount of time for professional learning during the year. School-based PLCs thrive when districts orient their professional development days to school needs.

Please see Resource 2.10 for more information about professional learning activities and agendas for PLCs. You'll also encounter some of these activities up close and personal in later chapters.

A New Way of Looking at Credit for Professional Learning. Professional development credits are conventionally awarded according to time (just as student credits are still awarded according to seat time in most schools!). "Credits" for professional development accrue according to duration; enough time in a district-workshop or a university class leads to license renewal and/or a jump on the salary scale. The system is straightforward, and districts (and states) know exactly how to count conventional professional development experiences.

But professional learning does not always happen in neat increments of half-a-day or more or as predictably as a class. School staff may spend one day listening to a guest speaker, getting new ideas about school improvement, but after that, time varies immensely. As an example, let's look at a simplified version of what an action research team might do related to ideas gleaned from a guest speaker:

1. The team meets for 2 hours after school to plan an action research project related to implementing the speaker's ideas.

2. The five members of the team collect initial data in classrooms, spending about a half hour in each classroom during school hours. A substitute rotates among their classrooms.

3. The team decides to research the innovation. Two members spend a half-day in the university library, and then all five gather to discuss what they found.

4. The team begins to plan the innovation. They share lesson plans in a tuning protocol after school. They agree to coach each other during the implementation.

5. As they implement their lessons over the next 3 months, they are observed by at least one other member of the team, requiring a substitute.

6. The team meets on an early-release day to share their observations and problem-solve (and give each other courage to continue!).

7. The team meets for a couple of hours to finalize plans for an assessment that relates to the initial data team members collected.

8. The team collects data through the assessment and through classroom observations such as the ones they did to start the action research project.

9. The team reports its outcomes at a faculty meeting and then to the Board of Education at one of the Board's meetings. Later, the team makes presentations to other schools during their faculty meetings.

How is the district to recognize these many, productive hours of professional learning? How will they be counted toward contract renewal? Also, how is the district going to budget for substitutes and for time outside the contract? It's important for schools to have one or more advocates at the district level to address these professional learning needs so that professional learning happens and counts as much as (or more than) the formalized professional development that used to be the basis of advancement on the salary scale and renewal of contract.

Size of School, Staff, Groups. Size is another aspect of structure, one that a school cannot usually control but one that affects professional learning. The number of teachers and staff assigned to a school corresponds to the number of students attending that school; obviously, the greater the number of students, the greater the number of staff. Small schools, with fewer students and staff, can organize themselves into a variety of structures for professional learning, including whole-school PLCs. Larger schools, with more students and staff, have to figure out how to organize themselves into smaller groups for learning—and this applies not only to student groups but also to adult groups.

Generally speaking, an effective PLC has between three and 12 members. But remember Resource 1.5? PLCs can take a number of different forms. In a relatively large school, like GHMS, there might be a Design Team. There might also be a number of subgroups of the whole-faculty PLC—as you will discover in later chapters. Or PLCs can form around grade levels, subject areas, or shared students, in which case the PLC might be interdisciplinary. Interdisciplinary PLCs seem counterintuitive, but they can be incredibly dynamic. There's nothing like an English teacher leveling a mathematics teacher with a question such as, "But, why do you do that?" and vice versa. Teachers from different content areas may speak for students when they make comments or ask questions about teaching and learning.

Space. The third aspect of structure affecting professional learning is space. Simply put, there needs to be space in the school for a whole professional learning community to meet. If the PLC is the whole school, then room must be found for the faculty and staff in the whole school to meet. If the school is large, that space might not be particularly conducive to learning—an auditorium with fixed seats in rows, a gymnasium with bleachers, a lunchroom with tiny seats attached to folding tables (not comfortable for long!) or an acoustically challenging multipurpose room in which tables and chairs can be arranged. Sometimes unused classrooms become adult learning centers—best without primary (or even secondary) desks, however.

The best space for professional learning seems to be around a single table that allows everyone to see everyone else and be seen by everyone else. Gathering the entire faculty and staff of a large school around a single table may be daunting unless the school features a truly Arthurian Round Table. So, a large school may need to consider organizing in smaller groups that can meet in smaller spaces.

One or more permanent adult learning spaces—ones not used by students during the school day—work best. Besides being used for professional learning purposes (PLC gatherings, coaching meetings, tuning protocols, etc.), these spaces may be meeting places for lunch or planning periods. Furnish these rooms with a variety of educational materials, some up-to-date hardware and software, comfortable chairs, and movable tables and chairs. Add a refrigerator, microwave, sink, and restroom, and you have an ideal space for adult learning.

Governance in Learning Communities

Governance is an aspect of schools that either promotes or curbs professional learning. Governance is the distribution of power and authority. In the 1990s, principals were reinvented as instructional leaders rather than managers of schools. In the first decade of the 21st century, the concept of one instructional leader per school morphed into shared leadership, and teachers were invited to participate in the planning and implementation of school improvement initiatives. Shared leadership—or distributed leadership—is important for professional learning. (In Chapter 1, you read about the various leadership assets a school needs—the list was meant to suggest that no one person can provide all those talents but, together, a team can.) You also read about the many tasks a leader has to accomplish to set up and facilitate a meeting. You can probably imagine that no one person can sufficiently attend to implementation of efforts related to important change; a whole staff needs to do so.

A hierarchy interferes with shared leadership. Each member of a school faculty or staff needs to be equal—at least in terms of learning. Some may know less, some more, about what it takes for students to succeed. Some may specialize in a particular area and know more in that area (such as district policy), but no one knows more in all areas affecting student learning. Still, decisions need to be made, and PLCs thrive when members know which decisions need to be made by which person, and how those decisions are made. PLCs that tip-toe around making decisions, worrying that some things might be out of their control or wondering what the principal's viewpoint is on those things, can stumble and fall. PLC Paralysis occurs when a PLC decides to wait for the principal's cues about how to proceed. Sometimes, PLC Paralysis seems intentional, a way of postponing the scary process of making significant change.

Resource 2.11, which gives a decision-making matrix, can help a PLC gain clarity about who makes decisions and how they are made.

Principals. A functioning PLC calls for skills that, according to Charlotte Roberts (2000), go beyond what she calls "The Principal Do-Right" model. The do-right principal must remain in control no matter what; must win (or appear to win); must not show negative feelings (things might seem out of control); and must remain rational—no emotions! (pp. 412–413).

What are some aspects of leadership for today's schools? Roberts suggests the following four characteristics of leaders: Engagement, Systems Thinking, Learning, and Self-Awareness.

The survey included as Resource 2.12 is one way a principal can evaluate herself and have her faculty and staff do so, too. An interesting discussion ensues when the principal shares results of the survey and seeks help to improve leadership.

Engagement of Leaders. An engaged principal recognizes problems and does something about them. The engaged principal has the proverbial "eyes in the back of the head." The engaged principal does not try to solve problems alone in her office—a pretty lonely job—but brings problems to the attention of faculty and staff in terms of the question, "How can we deal with this issue? How can we address and even resolve the problem?"

The principal with blinders on may not want to see the problems because he fears problems indicate some lack of leadership: No problems = good leadership. The principal who seeks to protect her teachers from problems underrates the professionalism of staff. "I just can't ask them to do one thing more," this principal might say; "they're overwhelmed as it is." Chances are, this principal's faculty and staff not only know about the problem but are being affected by it, sometimes in ways that erode the learning environment in their classrooms. Principals who hope problems will resolve themselves are kidding themselves, especially in the complex world of today's schools where systems effects are far-ranging, even though they might stem from what seems an insignificant incident.

Principals can be engaged in professional learning by being in the midst of professional learning activities, not in the office returning phone calls and doing paperwork while faculty and staff engage in professional learning. Engaged principals don't just introduce the guest speaker or workshop presenter—and then disappear. Principals do more than manage the school (keep things running) and students (monitor the hall) and run meetings. Principals may even have their own PLCs, times when they can meet with other principals to address real problems.

The principal who does not want to see problems or bring them to staff and faculty to resolve may be an administrator who is not engaged . . . and a disengaged principal diminishes the effect of professional learning.

Leaders and Systems Thinking. A leader who does not see his or her school as a system itself (and as a part of a larger system) is more likely to use short-term solutions to solve problems—the Band-Aid, silver-bullet, magical, one-size-fits-all cure to problems or approach to school improvement. A nonsystemic approach, for example, may feature professional development days—3 or 4 days built into the district's schedule for workshop attendance, planning, or grading. Teachers go their own ways, some learning about differentiated instruction, some learning about formative assessment, others learning about a new computer program. After professional development days, teachers may have a path to improvement within their own classrooms—but nothing that is schoolwide—and they may wander off that path when the going gets tough for them.

Leaders—perhaps at the district level—who decided that this type of professional development is sufficient may not be aware that such a design, lacking focus, may not lead to implementation even within the individual classroom. This type of professional development fails at promoting significant change at the school level. Principals who think in terms of systems are likely to gather as many stakeholders as possible at least once a year to engage in visual dialogue (see Chapter 3) to map and analyze system needs from all points of view. Professional learning opportunities then follow from the systems analysis—individualized to the school, powerful because of its focus, and likely to result in significant change for students.

Leaders Leading Learning. The principal who leads learning is probably not relying on the authority of his or her title to run the school. This person does not need to be the expert with all the solutions. Instead, this person seeks solutions alongside staff and students. This person admits, "I don't know," and follows that confession with a vow: "But, together, we can find out." One principal I know designated himself "head-learner," but he was willing to admit that anyone—including students—could join him in that category. What a rich learning community resulted!

The context for professional learning is considerably enhanced when the leaders are willing to participate in the learning activities themselves, really participate, not just sit there to show support for their teachers.

Leaders Who Are Self-Aware. Each of the other three characteristics relies to some extent on self-awareness. Powerful principals are those who can say they don't know but will work with others to find out. These are principals who may themselves keep journals, put together portfolios, spend time reflecting on their own work, even work with a mentor. At the very least, self-aware principals are eager to engage in professional learning with staff members. Principals who are self-aware will be more likely to sponsor self-study activities for their staff.

RESOURCES IN LEARNING COMMUNITIES

Resources generally include allocations of time and money. Many powerful learning designs do not require a lot of money, but they do require time, and time may be costly if educators are paid for their after-school, weekend, holiday, or summer professional learning—as they should be. Sometimes schools can solve the time and money problem by embedding professional learning within the school day, perhaps as an early-release or late-start day for students twice a month or more. This move requires some close collaboration with parents, the school community, and the district office. It affects the entire school community, from childcare to bus routes.

Some schools can manage early-release or late-start days by having others work with students (eliminating the childcare and bus route problems). For example, a school can enlist classroom aides to work with students on special projects during that time (although that makes it less likely that the classroom aides can engage in professional learning themselves or alongside the teachers they support). A school can also ask the community for help—for example, some schools schedule service projects, mentorships, or internships on professional learning days, but these efforts need someone to coordinate them.

In some schools, the faculty and staff split their professional learning time. Some are part of an A schedule, for example, and group students to work on interdisciplinary projects, while their B schedule colleagues meet in PLCs. Next week, the A schedule faculty and staff will meet in their PLCs while the B faculty and staff work with all students on their projects.

A district may address the problem by including professional development days in the calendar—perhaps one at the beginning of the year before students come back to school, one at the beginning of January before students come back after winter vacation, and one on the day after the last day of school for students. Or, the district might schedule these days at the beginning or end of marking periods (quarters and semesters). As many of these district-scheduled days as possible should be turned over to schools to use for professional learning.

The best resource for looking at time as a resource is NSDC's book *Finding Time for Professional Learning*, edited by Valerie von Frank (2008). This book features real solutions from real schools and districts. (A few of these solutions can be found in Resource 2.13.) The key to finding a solution, however, lies within. Sometimes we have to reinvent the wheel. Sometimes school faculty and staff—having read about others' solutions—need to make their first activity a "finding time" activity during which they comb through their schedule looking for ways to schedule professional learning time. Similarly, a PLC can meet to explore sources of funding, public and private, for work outside the school contract. The bottom line—as I tell people in PLC workshops—is that nobody is going to hand you extra time (or extra money). You have to figure it out yourself and take your solution(s) to those who can help you. P.S. Don't take the problem to those who can help you—take the SOLUTIONS!

Wisely, Josie distributed her handout but did not launch discussion of it. The handout reassured the Design Team that someone had thought through the how *part of implementing PLCs. Forrest glanced at the document and said, "Thank you," but even he put it away when Roz said quietly, "I think it's time for this Design Team to get down to, well, design. We need to focus on the agenda for the first meeting of the entire faculty and staff. It's only 2 weeks away. Gulp!"*

"This is where I get cold feet," Dottie said. "I don't think I can make a presentation to the faculty."

"Actually, I don't feel comfortable making presentations to adults, either," Andy said.

"I'm thinking," Tasha said slowly, "that what we do not do is present something."

"It's more like facilitating," Aaron said. "Something like what we did today."

"Well, I'm not sure how to do that either," Dottie said, "Facilitating!"

Josie had been sitting quietly and then said, "I think we can get some help from the district in terms of facilitating. Why don't I contact someone there?"

"In the meantime," Kelly said, "we want to do about what we did today, don't we? Isn't that what we agreed, that everyone needs to go through the same process so we all start out with the same understandings?"

"Yes," Roz said, "I still think that's important. So, let's just expand today's agenda for our first whole-school PLC meeting."

"And," Dottie said, "let's divide up the facilitating so no one has to do all of it."

Tasha agreed, "I'd be glad to start us off, and then we can hand off the responsibilities to each other, kind of build a segue from one activity to another."

"I think we need to end with 'Next Steps,'" Aaron said. "And we need to get others involved."

"What may help," Tasha said, "is the action-oriented agenda we used at the conference this summer. That kind of agenda lets participants know what is expected of them in terms of each item." She showed the group an agenda from the summer, and the group began to create one themselves on a piece of chart paper.

As they worked, they reminded each other that, although they had a full day to accomplish this agenda, teachers would be a little leery at first about spending a full day doing this work when they could be in their classrooms, getting ready for students to return.

Tasha remarked wryly, "They'll have to unlearn what they know about professional development, won't they?" The group chuckled—the faculty was usually barely tolerant of the typical "first-day-back" motivational speakers provided by the district.

"They'll know something different is happening," Aaron said, "because of all the e-mail they've gotten from us this year, the survey and all."

"And," Kelly said, "this will be very different from the 'sage on the stage' stuff we usually get on the first day."

"Drive-by professional development!"

"Sit 'n' git. Spit 'n' pray."

"Seagull-style professional development!"

"What?"

"You know, flies by, drops a load and moves on!"

After the fun, they got right to work, creating this agenda:

Agenda Item/ Activity	Why Important	Details	Results Expected
Welcome and Introductions	People may not know each other. There are three new teachers.	Tasha will welcome them and share this essential question, "How can GHMS engage in professional learning in order to help all students learn?" She will have the whole group break into small groups to introduce themselves using the Pocket Partner process and discuss the essential question. She will share the agenda, including outcomes.	Participants will know each other better than they did before this meeting. They will have ideas about professional learning at GHMS (kind of a KWL chart).
Telling the Story So Far	So there's no mystery about what's happened up to this point. Share student test data from the previous year (and Josie's dream!). Take the story to the Design Team meeting, and share the characteristics of the Design Team as they currently stand (able to be changed).	Aaron will tell in story form ("Once upon a time, there were three teachers who went to a conference . . . and a principal who was having bad dreams. . . .") Handout of Design Team characteristics (Resource 2.14) Test score data for the previous year.	Understanding
Setting Norms	So people have some say in how the group works	Dottie will share the Design Team starter norms (Resource 1.15) and ask the group to discuss them in small groups and declare their opinions ("adopt as-is for a while" or "change immediately")	Decision
Why, What and How	So everyone understands that all three categories of change will be addressed.	Robbie will lead by showing the TED videotape of Simon Sinek Discussion Chart on **why**, small groups add to it, share with whole group	Deep understanding of why, readiness for what and how
Why Would We Want to Learn	So we can focus on purpose	Aaron will lead discussion on three questions	Passion around making changes at GHMS

(Continued)

(Continued)

Agenda Item/ Activity	Why Important	Details	Results Expected
Prioritizing Purposes and Needs	So we can have a manageable list of needs/purposes	Robbie will issue 10 dots to each participant for voting on purposes/needs	Eight to 10 prioritized purposes for adult learning
What Is a PLC?	So everyone will know what a PLC is and how it can help to address purposes/ needs through adult learning.	Packet (Resources 1.1, 1.2, 1.3, 1.4, 1.6 1.7, 1.8, 1.17). Activity possibilities from Chapter 2, Resource 2.1. Andy will have participants divide into groups of six to complete and then have them share out their understanding regarding PLCs.	Understanding and sharing so others understand.
Barriers and Boosters	So the entire faculty thinks of these, the way the Design Team did. No need to show the group the work the Design Team did.	Kelly will do with a Force Field Analysis Sheet (Resource 1.18).	Understanding
Ideas on Organizing: How We'll Work	This is best decided by the people who will do the work.	Report from Josie about district support. Initial ideas from the Design Team. Brainstorming who, what, when, where, and how.	A variety of possibilities
Prioritizing	So the faculty can select the mechanisms that will work for them.	Robbie will lead people in making 'marker marks'. People will indicate support for a mechanism that works for them by making a tic mark beside it.	Choosing logistical elements that will work
Processing	So people can make sense of the experience.	Tasha will lead, activity TBD	Processing
Action Planning	So the faculty can choose to be on a specialty team to accomplish the most important first activities.	Josie will lead, having faculty divide into priority interests and use the planning template (Resource 2.15) to plan first steps.	Participating and planning

Agenda Item/ Activity	Why Important	Details	Results Expected
Closure	To assess how they have done at norms and bring closure to the meeting.	Tasha will ask participants to individually rate how THEY did on the norms and then rate how they think the WHOLE GROUP did. She'll take suggestions. Then, she'll have participants share their Best Hopes and Worst Fears (see the Chadwick process in Chapter 1).	Evaluation Understanding

At the end of the Design Team meeting, the group shared high fives around the room, checked norms (they decided they hadn't violated any), and engaged in a closure activity Aaron proposed: "Let's go around the room and share any aha moments we had today."

Three days later, Tasha had all the survey results. She sent an e-mail, as follows, to her colleagues on the design team.

To: Design Team
From: Tasha
Subject: Panic!!!! ☹

Scores system survey mostly 1s and 2s, very, very low. Not sure we're really ready 2 start w/ PLCs and professional learning. Maybe rethink! Let's change the tire on 777 b4 take off!

To: Design Team
From: Aaron
Subject: Don't push the panic button!

Low scores no surprise. Remember, T, we lrnd if schools waited til truly ready they'd wait 4ever. Never get started. We just have to get started. ☺

P.S. Maybe don't change the tire, just pump more air into it.

To: Design Team
From: Dottie
Subject: Getting Started

We can do it, Tasha. I'm proud to be a part of this distinguished group. As I looked around the room at us—the first Design Team—I was reassured. We are people who get things done. It'll happen. Don't worry. T ☺☺

P.S. I don't know what to advise about the tire, but I think we have to "take-off" as scheduled. We have someplace to get to: better learning for all students! We can't wait any longer.

To: Design Team
From: Josie
Subject: Ditto

We're ready. Survey items can guide work, but not dictate it. Bet: When we look at the survey again at the end of the year, we'll discover that we've moved up by at least one number of each of the survey items. We can do it.

A Few "Aha" Moments from the Design Team:

"This is so different from anything we've ever done."

"It is really respectful."

"It isn't about doing something to someone else. It's about engaging them in what the whole school will do."

"I really didn't know much about you folks . . . until now!"

P.S. We'll be able to change a 777's tire in mid-air by January!

To: Design Team
From: Tasha
Subject: Let's Go For It!

UR right. I panicked. It'll be good. Great! But, don't think I will take you up on that bet, Josie. We're going to build our readiness to be PLCs as we work together. . .

P.S. I'm not gonna worry about that tire, not with the crew we have.

To: Design Team Members
From: Forrest
Subject: Logistics

I took Josie's handout home and prepared a possible org chart for our work. Take a look at it and let me know what you think.

PRESENTING AND FACILITATING

Josie's district contact, Stephanie Hodges, provided some materials about facilitating. Presenting and facilitating are two different approaches to working with groups. Many professional learning activities require facilitating, but some may require some kind of presentation, too. Here is a chart of key differences:

Presenting	Facilitating
Presenters have something to share with others: special knowledge, a classroom experience, student work. The job of the presenter is to share what they have so that others understand it (and, sometimes, can take action as a result of the presentation).	Everyone has something to share; the job of the facilitator is to provide a structure for sharing, listening, and understanding. The group may engage in dialogue, discussion; it may also decide to take action.
The group focus is on the presenter.	The group focus is on everyone in the group (including themselves and their own learning) but usually not on the facilitator, except for structure.
The presenter has a clear vision of the outcome of the presentations.	The facilitator may not know where the group work will lead, except generally.
The presenter responds to questions in a (sometimes separate) Q & A session.	Group interaction is usually in the form of dialogue, which includes statements, questions, responses, summaries, etc.
Presenters usually make statements.	Facilitators often ask questions; facilitated groups may engage primarily in dialogue.
Presenters take people through their topics in as much detail as necessary, step by step.	Facilitators may ask individuals and groups to be self-directed, that is, study materials on their own, sharing ideas, commenting, and taking action when ready.

Presenters have special roles in protocols, such as the tuning protocol, which are discussed in Chapter 6.

Sometimes multiple presenters organize their presentations to be sequential . . . or they speak as a panel. Having multiple *facilitators* (what the Design Team decided on for the whole-school PLC) is a bit more complicated. It requires good coordination and close listening so that facilitators can help participants transition from one activity to another. Facilitators can say something like this to establish the logic of the meeting: "Remember how you did *X*? Well, now we're going to have you build on *X* by doing *Y*."

You'll notice that the Design Team decided on facilitation rather than presentation in their agenda for the whole PLC—much to the relief of Dottie and others! One item on the agenda in particular *could* have been accomplished through simple presentation. Andy, the facilitator of the learning about PLCs, could simply have read aloud information on Resources 1.1, 1.2, 1.3, 1.4, and so forth to help people understand what PLCs are . . . much to their boredom. Instead, the Design Team decided to have participants work through the materials themselves in small groups and present what they understood through a variety of mechanisms: through a metaphor, an acrostic poem, a mind box, or a schematic. Participants helped each other understand the handouts and worked together to create a way to share what they had learned, much to the delight (and learning!) of other participants.

One reason the Design Team decided *not* to present the handouts is that some of them had already been distributed to faculty and staff—and "covering them" would have been redundant (and, possibly, insulting). Another reason for choosing a group process rather than a front-of-the-room process to gain common understanding of PLCs is that the handouts were written to be self-explanatory. A final reason is that the Design Team wanted the entire faculty and staff to experience something as different from what they were accustomed to (presentations) as possible. The Design Team wanted faculty and staff to be self-directed, perhaps for the first time, managing their own time and accomplishing a task by themselves. This experience would be the first of many self-managing experiences that are common in PLCs.

For more on facilitating, go to Resource 2.16, where you will learn

- Why essential questions are, well, essential, and how to frame them for an agenda
- Why to write outcomes and how to do so, using a template of KUD (Know, Understand, Do from Cindy Strickland 2009, p. 167)
- Agendas
- Agenda Logic
  - Simple or Elaborated Agendas
- Sharing the Essential Question and Outcomes
  - Times
  - Components of an Agenda
  - Breaks

YOUR TURN: WHAT ARE YOU LEARNING?

Dottie stated definitively, "What have I learned? Well, unlearning, that's it. I had never thought about the need to unlearn something before Tasha brought it up. I've been around a long time, and I've accumulated a whole host of automatic responses to things, and sometimes I go into overdrive and simply respond the way I'm used to. I'm learning that this kind of work requires attention. I have to be mindful about what's going on. I have to consider my responses. I may have to unlearn my typical responses."

What did you learn from this chapter?

SO WHAT?

"Unlearning is important to me, and I suspect it will be important to a lot of the Glen Haven Middle School staff. We bring a lot of experiences to our work here, some from our childhoods, growing up, attending this thing called 'school.' We have to unlearn some of those things to move forward. I need to keep 'unlearning' in mind so that I keep 'learning.'"

What does your learning mean to you? Why is your learning important to you?

NOW WHAT?

Dottie continued, "I am going to need to be very patient with myself and others. I think I will pause for 10 seconds before saying anything, just to give myself a chance to check whether my response comes from the past or present, whether it represents something I'm trying to unlearn or something I'm trying to learn. I sure hope I can do this."

What might you do next in terms of your learning?

RESOURCES FOR CHAPTER 2

2.1 Processing Experiences

2.2 Survey on Learning Communities, Leadership and Resources

2.3 Survey Based on a School Improvement Focus

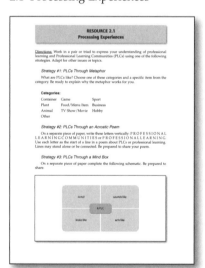

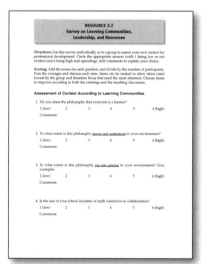

2.4 Template of a Systems Approach

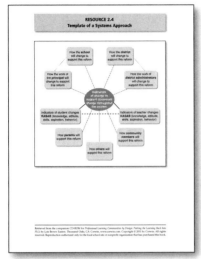

2.5 KASB

2.6 A Rubric Based on a Systems Approach

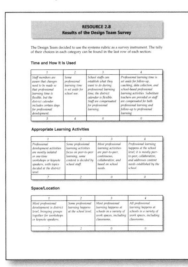

2.7 A Survey Related to What People in PLCs Do

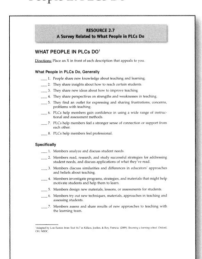

2.8 Results of the Design Team Survey

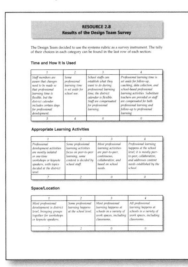

2.9 Identifying Purpose Template

2.10 PLC Agendas and Activities

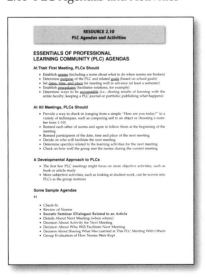

2.11 Decision-making Matrix

2.12 Principal Survey

2.13 Some Examples of Finding Time for Professional Learning

RESOURCE 2.13
Some Examples of Finding Time for Professional Learning

2.14 GHMS Design Team Characteristics

RESOURCE 2.14
GHMS Design Team Characteristics

2.15 An Initial Steps Agenda Template

RESOURCE 2.15
An Initial Steps Agenda Template

2.16 More About Facilitating

RESOURCE 2.16
More About Facilitating

2.17 An Elaborated Agenda Template

RESOURCE 2.17
An Elaborated Agenda Template

Pursuing the Need to Know; Making Sense of Data (August–October)

I n which the Design Team debriefs the previous day's all-faculty PLC meeting with joy and fear; in which a Data Specialty Team is formed and collects—what else?—data, and the faculty analyze these data, arriving at five goals for themselves.

"Ahem. . . . This meeting will now come to order," Robbie stated, then louder: "Ahem. . . . This meeting will now come to order." She paused and then turned to Andy next to her. "I've always wanted to say that." The meeting did not come to order; in fact, the chatter in the room increased in volume and enthusiasm. Andy took off his shoe and handed it to her: "Pull a Khrushchev," he said, and she pounded his shoe on the table. That got the attention of the Design Team, who, laughingly, "came to order" around the meeting table.

It was only a day after the mid-August meeting of the whole school as a PLC. Josie had arranged with the superintendent to let the Glen Haven Middle School (GHMS) faculty attend their own meeting rather than going to the customary opening-day workshop. With only 3 more days to get ready for students who would show up on August 21, Robbie wanted to get this meeting started. She reminded the group of the bargain she had struck with them at the meeting to plan the first PLC meeting and its debriefing. "I facilitate. You cooperate," she had said, and they had wholeheartedly agreed to the arrangement.

"So, take a look at this agenda," she said and unfolded a piece of chart paper on the wall in back of her.

Agenda Item	Results Expected
Check-In	Participation
Feedback From Staff: Online Survey	Understanding
Norms	Commitment to or change in norms
Results of PLC Activities	Understanding
What We Have Learned	Reflection
Next Steps	Action

Best

"No one walked out!"

"It went pretty much as planned."

"Energy was high all day—even though it was the first day back for faculty."

"Even though they were already thinking about their classes and classrooms."

"Even though they were thinking ahead to the weekend."

"They seemed surprised at how we ran the meeting."

"They kept looking at you, Josie, but you didn't step in and take over."

"Not that you wouldn't have been good!"

"I think we changed the school culture—for the better—in just one day."

"Just by doing one meeting differently."

Worst

"I think we've set ourselves up. We're going to have to produce."

"Nobody walked out! Just kidding."

"I felt some pressure to perform, not individually but as a group."

"We could have done much more faster if we'd had a dictator and were just told to do it."

"Who would like THAT?"

"I got hungry around 2:00."

"The room was too cold."

"It was too hot."

"It seemed a little messy at times, chaotic."

"That's group process for you."

"I'm scared out of my mind. What have we taken on?"

She then introduced the check-in by asking, "What was the best in terms of our first PLC meeting?" You can read some of their responses in the box.

She followed up with, "What was worst about our meeting?" See their "worst" in the box below.

"Overall," Robbie said, when everyone who wanted to had shared their 'worsts,' "what number, 1 to 10, would you give the day?" After a moment of quiet, people held up fingers to represent their scores—they ranged from a 7 to a 10. "I think I'll prepare a set of cards with the numbers 1 to 10 on each so we can do this like judges in the Olympics used to do!"

"Let's say it's about a 7.33321," Andy stated, to laughter. The group, feeling exultant, toasted each other with their water bottles.

"So let's keep in mind our own perspectives about the meeting and let's hear more from Andy, then."

"Here are the results of the feedback form we put online—over 80% of the faculty and staff responded to it!" Andy said. He distributed a single page to them (Figure 3.1).

Figure 3.1 Results of Staff Feedback Regarding the First PLC Meeting

The evaluation of the day was an outcomes-based form with a 4-point scale (1 = low; 4 = high):

PARTICIPANTS WILL <u>KNOW</u>:

How the GHMS process relates to professional learning and PLCs.

# of Respondents	Range of Responses	Mean Response
50	2–4	3.725

What PLCs are.

# of Respondents	Range of Responses	Mean Response
50	1–4	3.015

PARTICIPANTS WILL <u>UNDERSTAND</u>:

What PLCs might look like at GHMS.

# of Respondents	Range of Responses	Mean Response
49	2–4	3.800

How the Design Team works with PLCs and specialty teams.

# of Respondents	Range of Responses	Mean Response
49	2–4	3.666

Why PLCs and professional learning might be important at GHMS.

# of Respondents	Range of Responses	Mean Response
49	1–4	3.004

How barriers and boosters might affect GHMS's work in PLCs.

# of Respondents	Range of Responses	Mean Response
49	1–4	3.212

(Continued)

Figure 3.1 (Continued)

PARTICIPANTS WILL BE ABLE TO <u>DO</u>:

Use the norms to engage in the meeting.

# of Respondents	Range of Responses	Mean Response
49	1–4	3.113

Offer suggestions for professional learning activities of the PLC.

# of Respondents	Range of Responses	Mean Response
49	2–4	3.881

Prioritize the suggestions.

# of Respondents	Range of Responses	Mean Response
49	2–4	3.603

Create first-step plans for the most-important suggestions.

# of Respondents	Range of Responses	Mean Response
49	1–4	3.114

First Design Team

Josie Bermudez, Principal

Kelly Bosco, Science, Seventh and Eighth Grades

Tasha Peart, Fitness and Health, Seventh and Eighth Grades

Aaron Dobroski, Language Arts, Seventh and Eighth Grades

Dottie Gibbon, Aide

Forrest Long, Counselor

Roz Best, School Coach

Andy Mevoli, Mathematics, Sixth-Grade Core + Seventh and Eighth Grades

Robbie Beckel, Language Arts, Seventh and Eighth Grades

"It looks like we lost someone after the first couple of items, but those scores are pretty good," Roz commented.

"I can give you how many people scored at each level for each item," Andy said. *"I can also break down the scores by role. I can. . . ."*

"Bless you!" Dottie interrupted. *"I couldn't do all that! I'm so glad you are on this Design Team."*

"Well," Andy said, *"I do sort of enjoy this stuff."*

"I think we have some good products from the activities themselves. Can those be considered data?" Kelly asked.

"I think they can," Andy replied. *"They're not numbers, but the activities were data-directed. By that, I mean that they yielded information."* Kelly told the group that he had typed up what was on the chart paper from the various PLC activities. Josie suggested that she investigate getting a work-study student from the high school who might want to be their typist from then on.

Kelly smiled broadly and said, *"Great idea!"* Then he suggested, *"I think these should be the first things we put into a PLC portfolio for Glen Haven. We need to archive what happens along the way. We need to be able to show what we're doing and learning. I guess . . . I guess I volunteer to take care of that."*

"Be the librarian?" Tasha asked.

"Or the curator," Kelly responded. "Let's call me the keeper."

"So," he said, "here's a list of what's already in the portfolio." He rattled off the list and then mentioned that he'd attached a note to each item about when and how it was used and something about its effect. He asked the Design Team for a time in October to display the portfolio and record members' reflections on its contents. He bowed slightly to a light round of applause.

"Thanks, Kelly! So, moving on, how about our norms?" Robbie asked. And the group dug out the norms they had settled on when they first met as a Design Team. Robbie asked for a "Fist-to-Five," about committing to them and got fours and fives around the table.

Let's examine a few ideas that emerged from this part of the Design Team meeting.

DATA?

Strictly speaking, data are numbers (statistics, facts, records). Broadly speaking, *data* and *factual information* are synonyms. Information—of all kinds—helps a system learn. The Design Team is smart to collect both numbers and results of work—both provide important information.

To the extent possible, data should be unfiltered—it should come to people who need it without some else's summary or conclusion. Figure 3.1 is a good example of the right amount of detail, presented in the right way. It contains both a range of marks and an average. Andy could have shared the distribution among the marks—how many marked each number—but his average accounts for that. Because Andy did not summarize the data for the Design Team, they were able to study it and remark themselves that the scores were pretty good. Later, if they want to, they can discuss the differences in the averages for each item, so it's good that Andy carried them out to the third place.

Andy described useful PLC activities as "data-directed"; that is, they yield information. As you design PLC activities, ask yourself how the activities can produce information that the group itself can use.

PLC PORTFOLIOS

Kelly proposed what all PLCs should do—sooner rather than later: Construct a portfolio system. Sometimes PLCs (or task forces, committees, or teams) wait until they near the end of their work to realize that they should have archived pieces of it—and then they have to dig around in computer files, paper files, and round files, hoping they have what they need to trace their progress.

Portfolio systems accomplish some important goals for a PLC:

- They help the PLC keep track of progress—members can look back, realize the distance they have come in terms of their work—and celebrate.
- They help the PLC keep track of how they were doing as a PLC, especially since in most portfolio systems, members write a reflection on what they are archiving.

- They are useful for communicating what the PLC has done.
- They are a good form of accountability for the PLC.

The storage system can take a variety of forms. However, it should be a system for the PLC only, nothing else. It can be a box or other container; it can be a scrapbook. It can be organized according to meetings (by date of meeting) or by projects, tasks, and/or activities.

Although one member of the PLC (who may call himself or herself a librarian, archivist, keeper, or curator) takes charge of the portfolio, everyone in the PLC contributes to it in terms of

- determining what should go into the portfolio and
- reflecting on the meaning of the items that go into the portfolio. Reflections can be stated in terms of what members of the PLC learned related to the items or why the item was important to the PLC.

The librarian/curator/archivist may want to keep a log of entries by date and file name. An online portfolio is possible, as long as materials can be scanned in and the portfolio is accessible to everyone.

Occasionally, the PLC (or, in the case of GHMS, the Design Team) may want to do Portfolio Presentations to gauge progress.

The process of creating a portfolio system is straightforward:

- Collect what you already have from meetings, activities, projects, and tasks and file this information.
- At a PLC meeting, take out these artifacts and examine briefly. As a group (or individually, as preferred), write a reflection on that meeting, activity, project, or task. Write about what you learned as a result of that activity.
- At a PLC meeting, consider what you learned through that meeting, activity, project, or task.
- File both artifacts and reflections together.
- Celebrate your progress.
- Continue the process of filing artifacts of meetings, activities, projects, and tasks . . . reflecting on what you file as individuals or as a group . . . and summarizing what you learned as a result of them.

Kelly started the GHMS portfolio in a file box, with files labeled by date. You'll find a list of initial contents of the portfolio in the box.

GHMS PLC's Portfolio: Table of Contents

June & July, Year One

- Definition and Description of Professional Learning & PLCs
- Memo to Faculty
- Online Survey and Results
- Characteristics of Powerful Professional Learning
- Starting PLCs

FIST-TO-FIVE AND OTHER WAYS TO GAUGE DEGREE OF AGREEMENT

Fist-to-Five is one of many processing activities designed to gauge a group's level of agreement with an idea, proposal, or action. Once the item has been stated clearly and succinctly (perhaps even written on a piece of chart paper), members of a group indicate their willingness to commit to it by holding up one hand with zero to five fingers extended. Here is what they mean:

0 fingers (a fist) = I do not at all support this. In fact, I will work against it.

1 finger = I don't support this, but I won't work against it.

2 fingers = I don't really support this, but I'm OK with it; I won't work against it.

3 fingers = I'm OK with this; I will neither defend it nor work against it.

4 fingers = I like this; I'll support it.

5 fingers = I really like this; I'll work to support it; I'm committed and will take action.

A fist or one or two fingers should bring a halt to the process so that the whole group can explore not only what caused problems for those who were not supportive but also amend the idea, proposal, or action. Sometimes a group extends the revision process to include those who held up three fingers. Any revision requires another Fist-to-Five action and subsequent revision (or abandonment) of the idea, proposal, or action.

Three or four fingers means that the group is largely supportive of an idea, proposal, or action and committed to it.

Some groups engage in Fist-to-Five several times before reaching consensus, checking in with each other about their ideas early in the process, rather than waiting until the group must decide. You will find other ways to gauge agreement in Resource 3.1.

- Organizing a PLC
- Characteristics of the Design Team
- Leadership Assets & Roles
- A List of Members on the Investigative Team
- Memo Inviting Faculty & Staff to be Members of the Design Team
- Agenda for First Design Team Meeting
- A List of Members of the Design Team
- Norms Developed by the Investigative Team
- Investigative Team Best Hopes and Worst Fears
- Article: *Leader and Learner*
- Descriptions of Processes Used (Delphi, Pocket Partners, etc.)

August Year One

- NSDC Standards
- Surveys & Rubric About Context
- Results of the Survey GHMS Used
- Agenda for the First PLC Meeting
- Essential Question and Outcomes for the First PLC Meeting
- Processing Activities
- Materials Generated in the First PLC Meeting

Robbie looked around the room. "Do you remember how people responded to the questions we asked after the videotape of Simon Sinek?"

"A great videotape, by the way," someone said.

Kelly distributed a handout from his notes . "Here are the questions," he said, "and here are the responses. Remember, there were 50 of us there, not everyone. Also remember that we didn't ask the third question: "Why do we believe these changes will result in an affirmative answer to the question, 'Are we doing the best we can in terms of educating young people?'"

1. "Are we doing the best we can in terms of educating young people?"

| No = 47 | Yes = 2 | Somewhat = 1 |

2. If not, "What do we need to change or improve?" See the following list:

Parent communications	Assessment—school
Boring curriculum	Assessment—class
Teacher-centered curriculum	Grades
Active engagement	Gangs/cliques
Student involvement	Ninth-grade transition
Student focus	Fifth-grade transition
After-school activities	Don't know enough
Sports	Business models
Intramurals	Professional development
Clubs	Time, time, time
Awards and recognition	Celebrating kids
Interruptions to the day	Knowing each other as faculty
Schedules	Trust
Lunch periods	Relationships with students
Longer classes	Relationships with faculty
Like sixth grade	What aides do
More data	Have demographics changed?
Student data	What do people think about us?
Community changes	What do we do that works?
Faculty interests	Can we get better?
Parent involvement	Literacy
District regulations	What does success look like?
Math skills	What district changes are coming?
State rules/laws	Sixth-grade team—all grades?
Test scores	RtI (Response to Intervention)
Assessment—district	Administrators' needs

After the Design Team scanned the list, Robbie commented, "They were all over the place weren't they? Some are solutions, not problems."

"Well, I see some connections," Roz said. "There are some things here about needing more information. There are some about school culture. There are some about school programs—not just curriculum, instruction, and assessment, but also what kids DO here."

"I wrote down what some of them said," Dottie commented. Andy smiled at Dottie and said quietly, "Bless you, Dottie. I couldn't do all that! I'm so glad you are on this Design Team!" Robbie asked her to read what she had heard.

"Remember that we did a 'go-round' after the story telling, including the test-score handout, where they could make a comment, say 'ditto' or 'pass' if they had no comment, but they could not discuss things. They really focused on test scores, maybe because that's what they know best. Here's what they said:"

"I was shocked at how low our math scores are."

"The language arts scores aren't anything to celebrate!"

"We're pretty stagnant or going down."

"I had no idea that there was such a difference between some groups of students and others."

"And the gap is getting wider."

"So many students seem to be struggling."

"Or just don't care. They've dropped out even though they're still in school."

"Ditto."

"Pass."

"We can't just ignore what's been happening slowly and insidiously over time."

"It's not OK."

"We can't let so many students fail."

"Or fail to do well on the tests that measure how they're doing."

"Or we're doing."

"We need more information."

"I think we're doing a pretty good job, actually. The students have changed. They're not coming from the same types of homes they used to."

Dottie concluded, "The go-round continued until most people were passing or saying 'ditto,' and then, remember, Alice said, 'The most important thing for me is that we need more information. Scores—even comparisons over time—don't tell us enough.'"

"Thanks, Dottie. That gives us some insight on the brainstormed list," Robbie said. "We asked how many thought they needed more information . . . or needed to learn. I think everybody raised a hand. Then, we gave them the dots to vote on highest needs/purposes. Here is the list of what got the most dots:"

Teacher-centered curriculum	*Professional development*
Student focus	*Time, time, time*
Active engagement	*Celebrating kids*
Schedules	*Relationships with students*
More data	*Relationships with faculty*
Literacy	*What do people think about us?*
District expectations	*What do we do that works?*
Assessment—state	*Math skills*
Don't know enough	*How can we get better*

Robbie added, "These got 10 or more dots each, but I didn't put them into priority order. I think it's interesting to note how many people want more information. I think I do, too."

"There's a lot of focus on students," Forrest noted. "Relationships, celebrating kids."

Robbie glanced at her watch, "Speaking of 'time, time, time,' we need to debrief the rest of the meeting and then come back to these priority needs." She asked, "Do you think almost everyone understands what a PLC is?"

Andy responded, "I think they know what a PLC is, but I'm not sure they understand. Know what I mean?"

Dottie added, "Well, I'm not sure we really understand either, but let's keep going. We'll learn as we go."

"TMI," Tasha said. "Our materials were pretty overwhelming to them, but we got some good metaphors and acrostic poems. I kept what they created in case we want to refer later to their initial thoughts about PLCs."

"What did you think of their barriers and boosters?" Robbie pushed on.

"About like ours," Forrest said. "But, as I said earlier, we really need to resolve the barriers and boost the . . . um . . . boosters."

"Forrest, you saved the day in terms of how we might organize ourselves," Robbie said. She held up the schematic, Figure 3.2, to remind people. "If we hadn't had that, our brainstorming 'how' wouldn't have been much use. It would have been all over the place. It was a good 'strawman,' er, make that 'strawdog' so as not to be sexist!"

Josie said, "It was interesting to see how the whole faculty appreciated your embedded structures . . . they commented mostly on the particulars but liked the general design."

Figure 3.2 Forrest's Organizational Chart

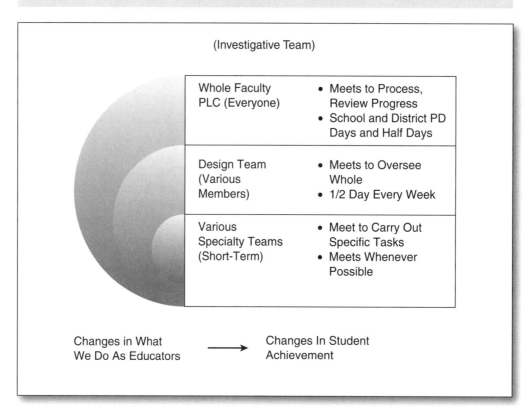

"We never did get to prioritizing their suggestions related to how we do our work, but I do have them written down," Forrest said. "And," he said, "I thought their taking the next step—planning the first specialty teams and first steps for those teams—rather got to prioritizing, just by how they organized themselves around some top concerns."

"So, let's go there," Robbie said. "We have action planning for which purposes?"

"Well," Andy said, "we have some planning for getting more information." He flipped through the planning templates that had been at least partially completed. (See the blank template in Resource 2.15.)

Josie said, "Let's ask the team that worked on that action plan to join us at lunch on that Friday, then. Sack lunches. I'll bring iced tea and lemonade. I think we may have our first specialty team—the Data Specialty Team!"

"The only other action plans we have are for Student-Centered Curriculum, Time, Celebrating Kids, and Relationships With Students. I know that other priorities were worked on, but I'll bet the groups didn't get very far and some may have kept their plans," Robbie said.

"I have a list of who worked on which action plans, so we'll know who to go to when we're ready," Kelly said.

Robbie nodded to the whole group, smiled, and mouthed the word "Thanks." Then she proceeded to draw the meeting to a close, checking on how they did on norms and asking the group to rate the effectiveness of the meeting on a 1 to 6 point scale with one comment on what went well and another on what could have been improved. She had them score and comment on sticky notes and collected these as the Design Team left, promising to share results at next week's meeting, which she would cofacilitate with Tasha.

Let's take a closer look at what happened during this segment of the Design Team meeting.

NATURE OF INITIAL PLANNING

You might have noticed that the template for initial planning directed people to plan only the first steps. It admonished: "Don't plan too much until the whole group is together!" Remember "Thems as does the doin', does the decidin'." Keep in mind that, although we need to be sure of our purposes and orient our actions toward them, we would be foolish to plan all the steps at once. It's better to plan a cluster of steps, gather data as you go, revisit purpose, and then plan the next cluster.

A "STRAWDOG"

Sometimes it's useful to have something, anything, written down for people to consider when they are brainstorming. Starting "from scratch" with a general question such as, "How shall we organize ourselves?" sometimes paralyzes people. The subject is too big; they don't know where to start. Drafting a "strawdog" and sharing it as such gives people a starting place. Invite them to comment on the "strawdog" first: "How should this be modified? Does this represent what we want? What does this mean for us?" Do not be too attached to your "strawdog." People may go along with and discuss details related to it . . . or they may entirely revise it.

IMPORTANCE OF DATA COLLECTION

What's the first thing that comes to mind when you hear the word *data*? For many, the response is an epithet followed by a groan. Data don't have to be dry and boring. They can be vibrant, exciting, and alive. Data aren't just numbers and formulae.

Josie consulted the district data person before the Data Specialty Team convened, and he recommended that the Glen Haven Design Team look into the work of Victoria Bernhardt (2004, 2008).

Bernhardt (2008) maintains,

> Data are critical in understanding how an organization is doing in terms of its processes, procedures, and student learning results. Understanding data leads to knowing what to do to improve those results. To effectively turn data analysis into meaningful action, all staff must understand the data and know what they personally must do for the system to improve. (p. 126)

She continues, "The power of data analysis as a professional development activity comes from many facets:

- Data are real—therefore the work is real.
- Most teachers do not typically see their whole school's data, so they might not know the health of the organization and what they and their colleagues can do to improve it.
- The focus is on improving learning for all learners.
- The focus is on improving the quality of the work done in the organization—at all levels.
- The professional development is collaborative.
- The work that is done is in the context of a professional learning community.
- Analyzing data honors the staff's expertise, experience, and professional knowledge.
- Data analysis requires reflection and inquiry.
- The work helps uncover findings that lead to change.
- Data analysis conversations can be built into the work week.
- Data analysis includes all staff in the work and every stakeholder's voice is heard through the data (p. 126).

Data Specialty Team

Josie Bermudez, Principal

Tasha Peart, Fitness and Health, Seventh and Eighth Grades

Andy Mevoli, Mathematics, Sixth-Grade Core + Seventh and Eighth Grades

Alice Rodas, Head of Library/Media

Judith Maestas (Judy), Aide for Social Studies & Focus for Sixth-Grade Core

Bobbie DeSantis, Social Studies, Sixth-Grade Core

Dinh Tuan, Band/Orchestra 1, Sixth-Grade Explore

K. D. Weg, Seventh- and Eighth-Grade Language Arts

She cautions, however, that data collection amounting to test scores and little else is not particularly helpful.

Reprinted with permission of the National Staff Development Council, www.nsdc.org. All rights reserved.

KEY ELEMENTS OF DATA COLLECTION

Bernhardt has two key recommendations, which Josie shared with the Data Specialty Team at their first meeting on Thursday:

1. Collect and analyze four kinds of data:
   a. Student achievement data (not just test scores)
   b. Demographics (student, staff, community)

    c. Perception data (impressions of the school from students, staff, parents, community members, other)

    d. Process data (what it is the school currently does to help students learn).

2. Practice with another school's data before working with your own data.

You can read a more complete description of these four categories of data in Resource 3.2, expressed in a slightly different way in Resource 3.3.

The hardest of the four categories to understand may be *processes*. Here are categories that the GHMS Data Specialty Team used to collect information about processes:

Common Instructional Strategies (literature circles, for example)

Structures For Academic Help

Clubs and Activities, General

Academically Related Clubs and Activities

Interscholastic Sports

Intramural Sports

Special Opportunities (Community Day, International Week, for example)

Parent/Community Organizations

USING BERNHARDT'S FOUR CATEGORIES OF DATA

Bernhardt provides data in all four categories from a school called Magnolia Middle School (2008). Educators can use her data sample or use the data sample related to Glen Haven Middle School, which is included on the CD that accompanies this book as Resource 3.4. Either data set will help your own group practice processes of analysis with another school's data before they attend to their own data.

One way to analyze data collected according to Bernhardt's four categories is to cross-reference it. Another way is to make predictions on the basis of it. Visual dialogue and gallery tours help people move to action.

At their lunch meeting, the Data Specialty Team decided that the first thing to do was to engage the entire GHMS faculty in analyzing Magnolia's data, just as the readers of this book might decide to analyze GHMS's data (Resource 3.4) as practice for the real thing. They reasoned: Magnolia data are available. We want the GHMS faculty to see the data available from another school before deciding what to collect for GHMS. We want the GHMS PLC to experience a data analysis process before using a similar process with our own data. We want them to be confident about analysis of data.

The Data Specialty Team chose the September 18 early-release half-day so that the whole PLC could practice data analysis. On that half-day, after check-in, K.D. from the Data Specialty Team shared information about Bernhardt with the whole faculty, especially the need to begin with a sample school's data (and then go to their own data) and the four categories of data (Resources 3.2 and 3.3). Then, he and Tasha led the group through the cross-referencing process.

ONE PROCESS FOR ANALYZING DATA: CROSS-REFERENCING

The process that the GHMS used to practice analysis of data, based on the recommendations of the district's data person, is a cross-referencing process. It can also be seen as a triangulating process (involving four sets of information). For its practice session, GHMS used Magnolia Middle School data, but you might want to use GHMS's data (Resource 3.4) for your own practice session.

The cross-referencing process helps people seek meaning in data without being overwhelmed. Here is a summary of the process. You will find a complete description of the steps of this process on Resource 3.5, with worksheets on Resources 3.6 and 3.7.

1. Divide the whole group into the four data categories and have each category group look for strengths and weaknesses, and patterns and anomalies within that data category. Have them record these on Resource 3.6.

2. Have someone in any of the category groups share one strength. (Use Resource 3.7.)

3. Have those who worked in other categories contribute what they notice in their own category that corroborates or contradicts that strength.

4. Repeat with other strengths in any category.

5. Repeat the process with a challenge in any category of data.

6. Repeat with other challenges.

7. Discuss implications of your work findings— "So What?" (What do these observations mean?) and "Now What?" (What might we do next?) Note: You might simply want additional data.

Reactions to Practicing Data Analysis

"I was surprised. That wasn't what I thought data analysis was at all."

"I'm embarrassed to say that it was—actually—kind of interesting."

"I think Magnolia School missed out on collecting some important data."

"I think I know what to do now in terms of what we should collect."

"I still hate data—but I think we have to collect a variety of data, not just test scores, and see what all the data tell us."

"The analysis—strengths, challenges, and all that—helped me see how data can be used."

"I like the cross-referencing. It was interesting how data in one area matched data in another area—or not."

"Is it day-tuh or daaaaa-tuh?"

"Whatever."

At the end of their all-school PLC practice run with data, Alice, the library media specialist who served on the Data Specialty Team (but wasn't a Design Team member), said cheerfully, "That wasn't so bad, was it?" The few groans she heard were half-hearted, but several people waggled their hands (the deaf sign for applause) to show appreciation.

Then, Alice had them process the experience by asking them to write about it: What had they learned about data collection and analysis? What had they learned about Magnolia School? What could they apply to their own process of data collection and analysis? The half-day ended with a few declarations (see box).

The Data Specialty Team met on Friday after the school's practice run with Magnolia. First, they decided to collect information about the faculty's interest in collecting and analyzing data related to GHMS. They put the survey (see Figure 3.3) online and had a 98% return rate.

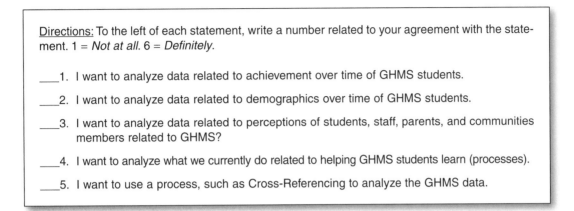

Figure 3.3 Survey on Data Collection

<u>Directions:</u> To the left of each statement, write a number related to your agreement with the statement. 1 = *Not at all.* 6 = *Definitely.*

___1. I want to analyze data related to achievement over time of GHMS students.

___2. I want to analyze data related to demographics over time of GHMS students.

___3. I want to analyze data related to perceptions of students, staff, parents, and communities members related to GHMS?

___4. I want to analyze what we currently do related to helping GHMS students learn (processes).

___5. I want to use a process, such as Cross-Referencing to analyze the GHMS data.

Having experienced the practice process with Magnolia Middle School data, respondents were nearly unanimous in their interest in collecting and analyzing GHMS data in the four categories and doing something like the cross-referencing process to analyze their own data. One respondent commented, "I don't exactly WANT these things (that word's a little strong), but I think they're things we should do."

It was patently clear that the first job of the Data Specialty Team would be to access their own, "real" data. They had achievement test scores, but where would they find demographic data? How could they get perception data? How would they collect information on the processes that educators and community members at Glen Haven use to help students succeed in school?

They decided that they needed to form specialty teams within their specialty team. They decided to divide the work and themselves according to the four categories: Achievement, Demographics, Perceptions, and Processes. Each task team had two members of the original Data Specialty Team on it and recruited two or three other faculty members to join the effort. The Data Specialty Team became an oversight team, much like the Design Team, but focused on coherence in terms of data collection and analysis.

Josie announced that she was repurposing her October 1 faculty meeting so the Data Specialty Team could meet. Josie also provided the Data Specialty Team afternoon subs one day and persuaded the district to let GHMS forgo the district professional development day so that faculty and staff could conduct data analysis on the school's own data.

In place of the faculty meeting, Josie sent out an e-mail to all faculty and staff containing announcements and items of interest she would have shared at the faculty meeting. In addition to Josie's faculty meeting announcements and items, faculty and staff members also received a report from the Data Specialty Team about what they had heard from the survey and how they had revised plans:

1. *We think it's important to gather our own data and analyze it.*

2. *To that end, the Data Analysis Specialty Team will work in four task teams, one for each of Bernhardt's categories.*

3. *We will get achievement data from the district's assessment staff, going back 3 years and disaggregated according to certain demographics. We will also collect student work to be analyzed.*

4. *We will get demographic data for the last 3 years from the district office, broken down as specifically as possible.*

5. *We will have a survey day during which students, staff, and parents will complete surveys. We will work with the parent-teacher organization to invite parents to a Data Dessert after school in order to complete the surveys, which will be online as well as on paper. A high school student doing an internship at GHMS will enter the responses that are not online.*

6. *We will spend the October early-release half-day doing an artifact hunt to discover all the processes that the school currently offers to help students learn.*

7. *We will engage in a data analysis process similar to what we did with Magnolia Middle School, but with our own data to cross-reference, and then we'll do visual dialogue and a gallery tour to plan what to do next.*

8. **Wouldn't YOU like to participate in Task Three, Four, Five or Six?** *Let us know!*

The Data Specialty Team prepared chart paper with Tasks 3 through 6 above and divided themselves up, two per task. They posted this chart paper in the hallway leading to the teachers' lounge so that all could see it. The invitation to their colleagues worked (amazingly!), and there were as many as five people per task ready to take on the work. These task teams met for about 15 minutes during the repurposed faculty meeting to plan their first steps.

The task teams worked hard. You can read some of the issues they considered as they planned GHMS's data collection: Achievement (Resource 3.8), Demographics (Resource 3.9 with a menu of demographic categories on Resource 3.10), Perceptions (Resource 3.11 with the survey GHMS used in Resource 3.12). Here are a few details related to their work:

PAINTING A PICTURE WITH DATA

Libby, a math teacher who was a member of the task team collecting achievement data, decided to create graphs to represent some of the data. What a good idea! As Bernhardt declares, "Gathering data is important. Graphing the data is equally important. Graphing the data turns the information into a picture that everyone can see at the same time. Graphs are easier for most people to comprehend." A graph tells a story over time and in terms of related elements. One source Bernhardt recommends for making a graph is available at http://eff.csuchico.edu/downloads/Demo_Templates/Demo_Templates.zip. It features templates that allow users to "find the appropriate graph, enter the numbers, and watch the graphs build. If you are creating the graphs from scratch, Microsoft Excel® is the best tool" (Bernhardt, 2008, pp. 128–129).

PERCEPTION DATA: SURVEYS

Surveys are one way schools can obtain perception data from the various stakeholders in the system: students, faculty and staff, parents, community members, and others. Other perception data can be gained through focus groups and interviews. Surveys are, often, the best way to begin collecting perception data—they are less time-consuming for the data collectors, are likely to involve more people than interviews and focus groups, and are usually easier to analyze than open-ended responses to interviews and focus questions. In fact, interviews and focus questions are valuable follow-up tools to surveys, as you will read in the next chapter.

Bernhardt recommends that schools

> using surveys might consider administering questionnaires online. Online administration results in quick returns. Staff members get a real boost when they see the data flowing in quickly. Start with the staff questionnaire so staff can know what they need to do to help administer questionnaires to students and parents. Consider giving the student questionnaire during school, and the parent questionnaire at parent-teacher conferences. (Bernhardt, 2008, p. 128)

Often districts have already engaged in survey research. A school like GHMS might be able to obtain from district staff surveys for parents, nonparent community members, teachers, other school staff, and students. With modification, they might be able to use these surveys and, on specific items, compare the district results with their own results.

THE ARTIFACT HUNT FOR SCHOOL PROCESSES

Many times, process data is buried within other data. For example, as Bernhardt points out,

> School process data sometimes are hard to analyze by themselves. They show up in the other categories of data, however, and they need the other categories to make the most sense. The Magnolia teachers, looking at data from the example school, saw a lot of process data in the demographic and question-naire data. For example, the number of students identified as learning disa-bled or gifted and the number of students getting high school credit for middle school work implied processes, and staff wanted to know more about how students were identified for these programs. (Bernhardt, 2008, p. 127)

An Artifact Hunt (which originated with Suzanne Bailey [personal communica-tion]) helps make process data more tangible (and is fun, besides!). The key is relat-ing the collected artifacts to their significance in terms of teaching and learning.

Carolyn J. Downey and her coauthors recommend "reading the walls" as part of classroom walk-throughs. "Reading the walls" is akin to an artifact hunt; the only difference is that walls are not the only parts of a building "read" by a touring group (indeed, Downey and her coauthors probably had more in mind than walls, too) (Downey, Steffy, English, Frase, & Poston, 2004). The following description is adapted from *Engaging the Disengaged* (Easton, 2008b, pp. xliv–xlv).

An artifact hunt engages people in noticing any part of an organization's struc-ture that is used for displaying what that organization does—on floors, ceilings, windows; in display cases and on bulletin boards and doors; in closets, whole class-rooms, hallways, offices, restrooms, common areas; on desks and tables; what's featured in the library; what kind of media are available; in backstage areas, locker rooms; what's on signs; in outdoor school spaces. Investigators might note the con-dition of the school's spaces. Others might scrutinize public documents that describe the school: parent, student, and staff handbooks; rules; report cards; yearbooks; cur-riculum guides; accreditation documents; reports; police records; policies, proce-dures, steps; letters to and from people interested in the school; letters to the editor of the local paper; news stories; the school's website. Some may want to explore the school as a visitor might. This activity is a way of deducing what a school values, what its culture is, and what it does to help students learn.

An artifact team should begin by listing all aspects of the school (similar to the list above) that might yield information about the school. Then, they should divide up the research tasks, collecting what they can in a short period a time. In fact, the group decides to declare a time limit, as artifact hunts can continue, well, forever, as people discover more evidence of a school's culture and processes. "We have one hour," someone might say. "Go!" After only an hour, a team probably has as much as it needs to perform a decent analysis. Suggest that members work individually or in pairs on their piece of the search.

Members of an artifact team do not actually have to bring artifacts with them to the group's meeting space. (Think of hauling the trophy case from the front entry-way to the library, where the artifact team is meeting!) Instead, members need to note on a chart like the following chart what they noticed as they hunted through the building or documents that were available, leaving the third column blank.

Artifact Description	Where Found	Meaning

Following their artifact search, participants work together, perhaps in small groups at first and then as a whole group, to identify what their artifacts say about the culture and processes of the school. You will find a sample dialogue in the box on this page.

At some point, the charts need to be combined and commonalities identified. Then, as the whole school goes through the cross-referencing (or another) process, a team for processes should use the combined lists to supply information that supports or contradicts data from some other category (such as achievement, demographics, or perception data). Eventually, of course, the whole faculty should look at the artifacts list in order to ask key questions such as these: "Is this the culture we want? If not, what do we want? And what would we do to create that kind of culture?" The last step leads, of course, to new artifacts.

Involving more than those who work in a building in an artifact search can be valuable. For example, students and parents might be invited to participate in a school artifact search. An organization such as a teacher center might invite some of its clients. A district might involve board members as well as teachers and administrators from schools. Any organization might involve someone from outside that organization to help conduct an artifact search—someone who sees with "fresh eyes."

A Sample Artifact Dialogue

Person 1: I saw how many trophies are in the display case. They go back quite a way, but we don't have any current ones.

At a meeting with the Data Specialty Team, Bobbie De Santis suggested that the team might invite the whole faculty to engage in a preliminary data analysis process related to their own data, this process based on making predictions and then checking data to confirm or deny the predictions (in part or wholly). She hoped that predictions about the real data would *whet people's appetites for the data analysis day at the end of the month.*

With their approval, she wrote an e-mail to the faculty and attached a packet related to data prediction (Resources 3.13 and 3.14). Here's her e-mail: "This is an invitation! You might want to prepare for looking at our own data at the end of the month by making a few predictions about the data. You can make predictions in terms of achievement, demographics, perceptions, or processes. You can e-mail me your predictions or write them out and put them into my mailbox."

Alice Rodas, also a member of the Data Specialty Team, asked a key question: "So, what do we do after we analyze the data . . . according to predictions as well as according to cross-referencing? What do we do next?"

Josie offered this: "I learned a strategy at a conference that we can use. It's called visual dialogue, and it can help us reach consensus about what to do next. I'll find out more about it and let you know."

At the end of this meeting, Dinh Tuan asked another key question: "Can we collect the data in time?"

"We will," Tasha said, "we just will!"

Let's examine some aspects of this discussion.

> The trophies and the case have not been dusted.
>
> Person 2: That may mean that we used to believe that athletics was important but we don't anymore? Is our culture supportive of athletic ability? How many interscholastic teams do we have?
>
> Do we have any intramural teams?
>
> Person 1: I looked in the principal's office. All of his pictures are of scholastic events, such as the time the debate club won the regional tournament. He didn't have any pictures of athletics.
>
> Person 2: Well, I looked at the schedule for last year, and it's clear that practices for sports are scheduled, but so are many other student activities.
>
> Person 1: I suppose we could say that the culture of this school supports sports activities as well as other extracurricular activities. Perhaps we believe in the well-rounded individual. Let's see what others found.

WHAT, SO WHAT, AND NOW WHAT

Neither data analysis process is powerful enough for focused action, however. Another step is needed, one that leads to action. You are already familiar with the *What*, *So What*, and *Now What* prompts that end each chapter in this book. They come from the work of Laura Lipton and Bruce Wellman (2004). These end-of-chapter prompts invite you to think about your learning: What are you learning? What does your learning mean/why is it important to you? What will you do in terms of your learning?

These three prompts can also be used to gain consensus about next steps related to data analysis. The *What* question can be answered in terms of what you have learned from data analysis. The *So What* question can be answered in terms of what your conclusions mean, and the *Now What* question in terms of what you will do next. Sometimes, data analysis stops short of the *Now What* part, and people come away from the process thinking, "Oh, that was nice" but not having a clear vision of what to do in terms of the analysis (literally, "Now what?").

Here is one way to solidify *So What* and *Now What*.

A WAY TO GET TO *NOW WHAT:* VISUAL DIALOGUE AND GALLERY TOURS

Visual dialogue, described below and, more fully, in Resource 3.15, is a powerful tool for activating the *So What* and *Now What* processes of analysis. It helps individuals "get their voices in the room" in terms of what happens next; and it helps a group build consensus. The gallery tour process, often used in conjunction with visual dialogue, helps a group decide together what needs to be done next. Resource 3.16 provides directions for visual dialogue. Resource 3.17 provides directions for gallery tours. Resource 3.18 provides a template for visual dialogue on *What*, *So What*, and *Now What*.

Visual Dialogue and Gallery Tours: A Brief Description

Although you can read more about visual dialogue and gallery tours on Resource 3.15, this brief description will help you visualize what the whole GHMS PLC did to corral consensus (adapted from Suzanne Bailey and Lois Easton, 2008, "Visual Dialogue," *Powerful Designs for Professional Learning*).

Visual dialogue (and the gallery tour that follows most visual dialogue) is a powerful tool to use in meetings to get all voices in the room, ideas in front of a group, and the real possibility of consensus. In a visual dialogue, groups of six to 10 people work simultaneously on the same large templates posted on the wall. The template is a diagram that guides thought processes. Participants sit in a horseshoe-shaped configuration in front of the template and decide together what to write or draw on the template. After the groups have completed the template, the groups reassemble in mixed groups (one from each original group) to do a "gallery tour." The gallery tour groups move from template to template, studying each one, noticing commonalities and differences. The person in each group who worked on the template serves as a "docent" when his or her gallery tour groups stops by that template. Through this process, group members achieve some degree of consensus when the whole group convenes.

Let's take a look at what happened on the whole-school data analysis day, including visual dialogue and a gallery tour to achieve consensus.

The late October professional development day (which the district had allowed GHMS to control rather than participate in district workshops) came much too soon, but the Data Specialty Team felt prepared. After check-in ("In keeping with the four letters in data, what four-letter word would you use to describe yourself today?" Participants kept their responses "relatively" clean.), Andy and Judy, who agreed to cofacilitate the day, had previously asked Bobbie to prepare a piece of chart paper for each of the predictions, according to the template for dialogue (Resource 3.14). They began the meeting by having the PLC investigate the predictions, four examples of which follow:

- *"Student demographics have changed immensely in the last 5 years, especially in terms of intact families. More of our students come from split homes than ever before"*
- *"Achievement has gone up in reading over the past 5 years but down in mathematics"*
- *"We have great after-school programs that help students learn"*
- *"Students don't like school very much."*

Faculty members left their seats to read the posted predictions the walls and a few added predictions of their own until there were 25 predictions. Then, the whole PLC settled into scouring the data. Individuals chose the data category they wanted to work on—some concentrating on achievement data, others on demographics, still others on perceptions, and others on processes. They met with similarly interested colleagues in corners of the room and settled down to study their packets.

Though they would each get a full packet of data (data in all four of the categories), each category group started out with data in their own category only—so they would not be overwhelmed by the sheer volume of data.

An hour and a couple of pots of coffee later, the whole faculty gathered to go through the data analysis process they had experimented with using Magnolia School data. Although they stayed in their category groups, they arranged themselves in a huge circle so they could see (almost) everyone else. They checked out strengths from all four data categories to see if other data supported those strengths; then they did the same with challenges. They shared a few trends and anomalies.

After a well-deserved lunch break, those who had made predictions stood next to the chart paper on which they had recorded their predictions. The rest of the faculty roamed from chart to chart to help the predictors complete these categories on the prediction worksheet (Resource 3.14):

1. *Prediction/Assumption*

2. *Exploration/Observation: Data Facts (X, which confirms/ denies—or partially so—the prediction/assumption)*

3. *Explanation/Correlation (If X is true, why might that be so?)*

4. *Taking Action (If we changed X in some way, what might happen?)*

Several times, a semiembarrassed laugh rang out when a predictor observed how wrong he or she had been, how contradictory the data were! More interesting were predictions that were somewhat wrong . . . and somewhat right.

Finally, the whole faculty broke into prearranged, mixed groups to do visual dialogue on next steps, using as their template the design on Resource 3.18. Afterwards, they did a quick gallery tour to seek commonalities among the visual dialogue charts. These five needs emerged as common elements on almost all the visual dialogue charts and became the GHMS PLC goals or purposes for the next few months (and the next couple of chapters):

1. *Get more information about students, from students.*

2. *Work on ways to engage students in their own learning; help them become more self-directed learners.*

3. *Make literacy a priority across the curriculum (including listening and speaking).*

4. *Hold regular special meetings, like the Data Dessert, to bring parents into the school (not just PTO meetings or parent conferences).*

5. *Ask the district for help (expertise, time, funding, resources).*

Closing Activity

- I used to think data analysis was something I couldn't do, but now I know I can do it (but I still don't particularly like it!).

- I used to think I knew a lot about Glen Haven, but I didn't know much, really.

- I used to think that only math types liked data, but, even though I'm an art teacher, I really like what we did.

- I used to think students were pretty happy here, but I guess they're not entirely engaged.

- I used to wish for the day to be over and now I really wish for the day to be over—I'm exhausted!

- I used to think my colleagues were smart and now I know how smart they are.

- I used to hope that professional development days would disappear, but—if this is professional development, I'm enjoying it

- I used to hate meetings, but I enjoy working with my colleagues like this.

- I used to just plan lessons and grade papers, but now I'm going to have to think more about teaching and learning.

- I used to hide away in my cubicle, but now I am going to interact more with my colleagues.

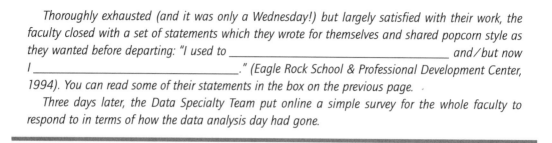

Thoroughly exhausted (and it was only a Wednesday!) but largely satisfied with their work, the faculty closed with a set of statements which they wrote for themselves and shared popcorn style as they wanted before departing: "I used to _____ and/but now I _____." (Eagle Rock School & Professional Development Center, 1994). You can read some of their statements in the box on the previous page.

Three days later, the Data Specialty Team put online a simple survey for the whole faculty to respond to in terms of how the data analysis day had gone.

Let's consider some moves the Data Specialty Team used to help the whole PLC work well.

CHECK-IN

Meetings may or may not deserve the sobriquet "Worst Professional Experience in a Lifetime." Faculty meetings, in particular, have gained notoriety for being dull, repetitive, and a waste of time, with a frequent comment being, "We could have read *this* [whatever it was] in a memo or e-mail." During their August meeting, Josie suggested to the Design Team that she could switch her faculty meetings from items on an agenda to professional learning. "Isn't it interesting," she noted, "that I see them as *my* faculty meetings?"

The Design Team wanted to use the first few minutes of each PLC meeting to check in with each other. If possible, they also wanted to use the check-in as a way to *focus* (some were old enough to remember Madeline Hunter's "anticipatory set"; others operated according to the current practice of accessing background knowledge). Especially after a full day of teaching, focusing is important. Check-in also allows each individual to get his/her voice "into the room." Finally, check-in allows the facilitator(s) to take the temperature of the group—individual and whole group "well-being"—in terms of the work that the group will be doing. Through check-in, participants can express frustration or elation . . . and every emotion in between.

You encountered some ways to begin meetings in Chapter 1 (see Resource 1.14). You can investigate some additional processes—focusing more on checking in and focusing on the topic—in Resource 3.19.

ALTERNATIVES TO TRADITIONAL FACULTY MEETINGS: HOW TO GET THE INFORMATION OUT THERE

With the help of the Design Team, Josie faced the fact that she *liked* leading faculty meetings; she liked making announcements, especially of exciting events to come. She liked making up agendas. She liked directing faculty activities, such as responding to an article. She liked sharing pithy quotes about education. She liked sharing her own experiences. She liked leading discussions. She liked being the leader during these times, all eyes on her, everyone following her agenda. Faculty meetings in the traditional sense were hard to give up.

She made the first step a year before the PLC started when she invited the faculty to submit agenda items and then choose which items they'd like to discuss during faculty meetings. She added her own items.

As you have read in this chapter, this year she began to repurpose faculty meetings. When she held faculty meetings and asked for items, she noticed that gradually the number of items submitted shrank to a pitiful few. As this year progressed, Josie realized that faculty members were communicating in different ways. They were paying attention to voicemail and e-mail. They communicated in person. They didn't feel the need to command the attention of everyone at a faculty meeting.

Naturally, in an emergency or on the way to a major decision, Josie could call a staff meeting, but she usually preceded the meeting with an e-mail or voicemail message outlining the need and purpose of the meeting. She often asked, "Do we need to meet?" or "Can you let me know how you feel by return mail?"

Sometimes she went too far. Several times during the year the Design Team as a whole or other faculty members said to her, "We need a meeting on this." No problem.

The other move Josie made a year before PLCs was to introduce her faculty to meetings as professional learning. Instead of loading an agenda with items, she would plan a short agenda and then engage the faculty in study of an article using a discussion protocol such as "Three Levels of Text," Resource 1.13.

Several teachers suggested the use of the hallway leading to the faculty lounge as a living bulletin board. They allowed only "really important stuff" to be posted there (not everyday announcements) and sometimes required faculty to sign off once they had read the information. One side of the wall became a graffiti board of sorts as faculty took on weighty issues such as "Do we test our students too much?" and posted their responses, sometimes written, sometimes drawn, always worth reading.

As the year progressed, the faculty adopted the attitude of "If you don't know, you didn't try to know" and passed along this culture to new teachers as they arrived. They were determined not to spend precious meeting time in activities that served little useful purpose and deprived them of time to concentrate on teaching and learning.

DISTRICT SUPPORT

Perhaps you were surprised that the district so readily excused GHMS from attending the districtwide professional development days. Although schools (and their classrooms) are where changes happen to improve student learning, those at the district level are quite important to those changes. You read some ideas about how districts might change in Chapter 2. See Resource 3.20 for suggestions for how district-level people can help schools make needed changes.

YOUR TURN: WHAT ARE YOU LEARING?

Sanjay Misra, a science teacher in the sixth-grade core, commented on his learning during the data analysis day: "Well, certainly I was surprised! The day was not at all what I expected. I am accustomed to 'sit and get,' and we didn't sit much. We didn't get much either. We produced a whole lot, however. I'm learning that professional development—make that professional learning—is quite different from what I'm used to."

What did you learn from this chapter?

SO WHAT?

Misra continued, "I think a lot of us engage in professional learning in the sixth-grade core, but we've been pretty isolated. We work as a team, but we don't share much with seventh- and eighth-grade teachers. That's a shame, truly."

What is important to you about your learning?

NOW WHAT?

Misra concluded, "We must be able to share across grade levels—not only what we are doing but how. I think we in the sixth-grade core have a lot to share . . . and we have a lot to learn. I'm going to talk with my colleagues in the core about how we might share. And, I will write a proposal to the Design Team."

What might you do about your learning as a first step?

RESOURCES FOR CHAPTER 3

3.1 Fist-to-Five and Other Ways to Gauge Agreement

3.2 Four Categories of Data

3.3 Template for the Types of Data Available

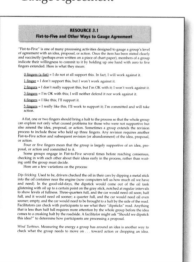

3.4 Glen Haven Middle School Data

RESOURCE 3.4
Glen Haven Middle School Data

A. School Profile

B. Demographics—Students

C. Demographics—Administrators, Faculty and Staff

D. Achievement

E. Conditions for Learning (Processes)—School

F. Conditions for Learning (Processes)—District

G. Perception Survey Results

H. Graphs to Support Some Data

3.5 Steps for Cross-Referencing Data

RESOURCE 3.5
Steps for Cross-Referencing Data

Have the whole group browse all the data first, just to see what's there. They might jot down some notes in each of the data categories (Resource 3.6):

1. Have the whole group divide into four groups to study data in a preferred category. Keep category groups to 10 or fewer if possible (so you may have more than one group in a category) so that everyone gets sufficient "air time." If more than one group works on a category, then both (or more) data category groups report what they've learned. As an alternative, simply assign the categories to parts of the room—one quarter of participants for each of the four data categories—and have participants go to the "corner" they prefer.

2. Distribute the data worksheet to participants in each data category (use Resource 3.6). Give ample time for studying and discussing the data in their own category. Breaking down a mass of data into the four categories helps to make data analysis a much less overwhelming process for faculty who flinch at the word "data." Allowing open discussion also helps to break down the fear of data, as people listen to each other and discover that what they noticed in the data is legitimate and that what other people notice is similarly illuminating.

3. Referring only to their own category, group members should decide what the data say about the school in terms of strengths, challenges, trends, and anomalies. The first two analysis points—strengths and challenges—focus on what the data show about what's working in the school, as well as what needs attention. The second two data points allow group members to decide whether or not there is a pattern to the data (a theme or trend). They can also keep in mind items that do not really fit within that pattern—anomalies—but are interesting or compelling in some way.

4. The process group may have a harder time categorizing the data about what the sample school actually does to help students learn. However, members of this group can look at what the school does and what it does not do. For example, a strength might be the number of after-school clubs offered; a challenge might be that few awards honor academic achievements. A trend might be that fewer students are seeking tutors; an anomaly might be that one grade level's parent group is particularly active, while the others are not.

5. Ask groups to identify something particularly striking as a strength in their data category and be ready to share that.

6. Have the category groups come together if they have been physically separated, sitting in a large circle if possible so they can see other groups but still remaining together as a category group.

7. Ask a spokesperson from one category group to begin with its "striking" strength, having others write down that phenomenon on Resource 3.7.

3.6 Worksheet on Data Collection

RESOURCE 3.6
Worksheet on Data Collection

I/we investigated (circle one):

Student Learning Data   **Demographic Data**

Perceptions Data   **School Process Data**

Then describe what you noticed in terms of Strengths, Challenges, Trends/Consistencies, Anomalies/Oddities.

Strengths	Challenges
Trends/Consistencies*	Anomalies/Oddities*

*If you are not using visual dialogue and gallery tours to get to SO WHAT and NOW WHAT, change these categories to the What and **Now What** to accomplish these steps.

3.7 Worksheet for Cross-Category Discussion

RESOURCE 3.7
Worksheet for Cross-Category Discussion

1. Work across the categories (the whole group). Begin with any strength, in any category of data. Work with that strength across all four categories, with those who studied the data in that category contributing what they noticed.

2. Go to challenges in any category of data. Work with that challenge across all four categories, with those who studied the data in that category contributing what they noticed.

3. Discuss implications to your work, which may include needing additional data.

4. Then do the same with Challenges.

Strength #1: _____   Data Category: _____

Student Learning Data	Demographic Data	Perceptions Data	Processes Data

Implications:

3.8 Considerations Related to Achievement Data

RESOURCE 3.8
Considerations Related to Achievement Data

Test Scores. Test scores in a school, district, and state are relatively easy to get since the No Child Left Behind (NCLB) Act of 2001 and Race to the Top (2010). Most districts and states post scores on their websites by school, shown over time and disaggregated by a number of factors, such as gender, race/ethnicity, and even mobility. Scores are often posted in newspapers and linked from local real estate agents' websites. These tests are nationally normed and usually multiple-choice, so an answer key (rather than a teacher's possible subjective ruling) dictates the "right" answer (although it can be argued that the answer key and the set of "distractors" or wrong answers represent a certain sort of bias).

Unfortunately, test scores are high-stakes. Diane Ravitch wrote about how her educational philosophy had changed in *The Death and Life of the American School System: How Testing and Choice Are Undermining Education* (2009). Once she believed that "testing would shine a spotlight on low-performing schools, and choice would create opportunities for poor kids to leave for better schools" (pp. 3–4). Later, however, she "grew increasingly disaffected from both the choice movement and the accountability movement. I was beginning to see the downside of both and to understand that they were not solutions to our educational dilemmas" (p. 12). She realized that "accountability, now a shibboleth that everyone applauds, had become mechanistic and even antithetical to good education. Testing, I realized with dismay, had become a central preoccupation in the schools and was not just a measure but an end in itself" (p. 12).

As I wrote in *Engaging the Disengaged*, "Results of testing usually provide little help to educators. Scores themselves are too general for generating important changes in curriculum and instruction. Item analysis reduces learning to bits of knowledge such as 'mass count nouns' (jury and audience, for example)" (Easton, 2008, pp. 4–7).

Another problem with looking at achievement through test scores:

Tests are a proxy for the real thing—demonstration of real knowledge and skills. Educators cannot be sure what they are witnessing in students' selected answers. Does a selected answer really represent what students know and can do or simply what they chose to mark on the answer sheet? Moreover, tests seldom point towards what students need to know or do—what errors they might be making when they select the wrong item. As Mina Shaughnessy so wisely pointed out in 1977, understanding errors in thinking—and delving into students' "world views" to understand why they made and clung to their errors—is one of the best ways educators can help students learn" (Easton, 2008, p. 7).

I would certainly not recommend more testing so that educators could glean more knowledge about students' learning needs (as if they could with the testing we have now). Testing time (and intense preparation for testing) takes away opportunity to

3.9 Considerations Related to Demographic Data

RESOURCE 3.9
Considerations Related to Demographic Data

If possible, have someone at the district level (which is required to maintain data on several demographic features of the district over a period of years) provide your school with demographics relating to three populations: students, faculty and staff, and community. The best demographic data are historic, going back at least three years, and up-to-date. As Glen Haven Middle School (GHMS) discovered from the district's data administrator, the district had aligned demographics to some of the test score disaggregations and had more demographic data than the middle school could ever use! The problem quickly became a problem of choice, and the Design Team had to tell the district test coordinator (who was delighted to be consulted) that she had sent enough to occupy them for several months, if not years.

Bernhardt lists some aspects of demographics that should be considered on Resource 3.10. Many demographic data are required by No Child Left Behind (NCLB) (as of the publication of this book), and they are marked with an asterisk on Resource 3.10. This material comes originally from Bernhardt's book (Bernhardt, V. [2004]. *Data analysis for continuous school improvement*. Larchmont, NY: Eye on Education). It was used with permission in Easton, L. B. (2008). *Powerful designs for professional development*. Oxford, OH: NSDC.

3.10 Demographics: A Menu

3.11 Considerations Related to Perception Data

3.12 The GHMS Perceptions Survey

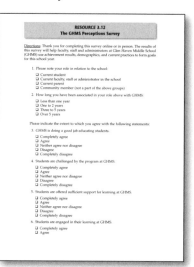

3.13 Another Process for Analyzing Data: Predictions

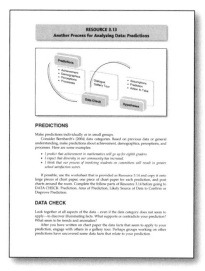

3.14 Dialogue on the Basis of Predictions: An Example and a Blank Template

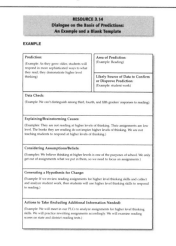

3.15 Description of Visual Dialogue and Gallery Tours

3.16 Directions for Visual Dialogue

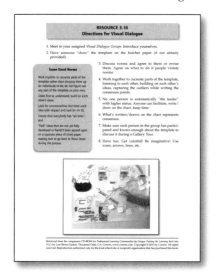

3.17 Directions for Gallery Tours

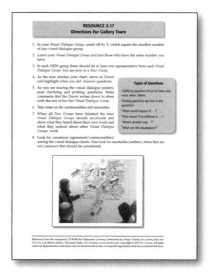

3.18 Template For Visual Dialogue on the So What and Now What of Data Analysis

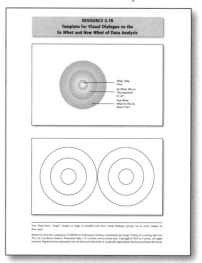

3.19 Checking In and Focusing at the Beginning of a Meeting

3.20 District Support of School-Based Change Efforts

Finding Processes for Working Together (November and December)

I n which the Design Team meets to consider what they had wrought so far. The Design Team and the Data Specialty Team get into it! Also, the Professional Learning Community (PLC) understands and appreciates individual differences and learns to work together better, and various specialty teams collect more data from and about students. In which it was a miracle *anything* got done with all the vacations and holidays!

Snow had begun to stick to streets outside Glen Haven Middle School (GHMS) by the time the Design Team and the Data Specialty Team met after school during the early-release half-day on November 13. The flakes, heavy and wet, accumulated quickly and both staff and students prayed for "Snow Day" tomorrow even though they knew they'd have to make up the day in the spring.

Forrest had agreed to facilitate this meeting, the first after the all-day data analysis day, and he pumped an old-fashioned car horn—one, loud "oo-ooga"—to get the group's attention. One more "oo-ooga," and the group had taken seats around the donut-shaped table in the library media center.

First Design Team + 1

Josie Bermudez, Principal

Kelly Bosco, Science, Seventh and Eighth Grades

Tasha Peart, Fitness and Health, Seventh and Eighth Grades

Aaron Dobroski, Language Arts, Seventh and Eighth Grades

Dottie Gibbon, Aide

Forrest Long, Counselor

Roz Best, School Coach

Andy Mevoli, Mathematics, Sixth-Grade Core + Seventh and Eighth Grades

Robbie Beckel, Language Arts, Seventh and Eighth Grades

Ariel Aboud, Social Studies, Sixth-Grade Core

"Welcome," he said as he looked around the table. "Welcome to the Data Specialty Team. Welcome to Ariel, who volunteered to be part of the Design Team for at least 3 months." He led the group in applause.

"Here's an agenda I worked out with Robbie, who facilitated the last Design Team meeting—thanks, Robbie, for helping me!" He distributed an agenda (shown below).

He asked the Design Team and the Data Specialty Team to use Fist-to-Five (see Chapter 3) to declare whether or not the agenda worked for them. Getting no fists, ones, twos or threes, he said, "Good to go, then. Let's check in. Since our more recent

Agenda Item	Results Expected
Check-in	Participation
Norms	Commitment to or change in norms
Analysis of data work	Participation
Next steps and how to approach them	Contribution of ideas; commitment
New items	Contribution
Closure	Participation

meeting was all about data, let's take the four letters in data and do check-in acrostic poems. You know, put the letters D A T A down the side of your paper and write something after each letter that expresses how you're thinking about data now. You can work in pairs if you'd like."

Working individually or in pairs, the group approached the task with zeal. Forrest asked each individual to share how he or she was doing using a number from 1 to 10 and then had them share acrostic poems, which varied widely. After announcing that she was a "7" but would be a "9" if there was a Snow Day tomorrow, Judith Maestas and Bobbie DiSantis shared their poem:

D *ang it! I still don't like data*

A *fter a whole day of looking at it*

T *he time has come to look beyond it*

A *t our students.*

K. D. Weg and Ariel Aboud shared this poem:

D *stands for more than* <u>data</u>

A *stands for more than* <u>achievement</u>

T *stands for more than the* <u>time</u> *we put into data analysis*

A *stands for the* <u>actual insights</u> *we got into Glen Haven last week.*

Each poem brought nods of understanding and applause. Some brought laughter, as well. It was a good way to start the meeting.

"How about norms?" Forrest asked, according to the agenda.

Kelly said, "One norm I would really like to be sure we follow is looking at the norms at the beginning and end of each meeting. We should do what we're doing now before each meeting—just to make sure we don't need to amend the norms before starting our work. And, we should look at the norms after each meeting to see if we've met them. We need to be sure to preserve the time, even when we're most rushed."

"Fist-to-Five on that?" Forrest asked, and the group held up fours and fives. "Agreed. Let's add that to our closure activity." Then he turned the meeting over to the data team.

Dinh spoke up, with a slight laugh. "Somehow," he said, "I was elected to speak for the Data Specialty Team. I was very careful not to be late to meetings. I never went out of the room during a meeting. I stayed late and, still . . . I was elected." The whole group, catching his drift about how leaders are sometimes "trapped" into leadership roles, laughed with him.

"Anyway," he said, "you'll remember that we put a simple survey online a couple of days after the all-day data analysis meeting. At this point, all but three staff and faculty members, two of whom are here today, have responded to the survey." He shaded his eyes with one hand and looked around the table, catching the eyes of nearly everyone. "These two shall remain nameless."

> **Data Specialty Team**
>
> Josie Bermudez, Principal
>
> Tasha Peart, Fitness and Health, Seventh and Eighth Grades
>
> Andy Mevoli, Mathematics, Sixth-Grade Core + Seventh and Eighth Grades
>
> Alice Rodas, Head of Library/Media
>
> Judith Maestas (Judy), Aide for Social Studies & Focus for Sixth Grade
>
> Bobbie DeSantis, Social Studies, Sixth-Grade Core
>
> Dinh Tuan, Band/Orchestra 1, Sixth-Grade Explore
>
> K. D. Weg, Seventh- and Eighth-Grade Language Arts

"I won't give you the statistics, but I'll summarize what we learned on our 4-point scale:

"Nearly 90% of the staff agreed or strongly agreed that the day was valuable.

"Over 80% of the staff agreed or strongly agreed that they had learned something worthwhile during the day.

"Over 95% agreed or strongly agreed that they knew more about Glen Haven than before the data analysis day.

"Over 75% agreed or strongly agreed that they enjoyed working with their colleagues.

"Only about 50% agreed or strongly agreed that the data point the way to worthwhile school improvement goals.

"I don't know what the last item really signifies," he admitted. "Is it that the data do not point to goals? Or is it that the goals are not worthwhile? I think we need to ask the question again."

"Let's take a look at those goals," Josie said. Forrest unfurled a banner on which someone had written in fine calligraphy the goals that emerged from the data analysis day. "Remember," she said, "these are the purposes for our work."

1. *Get more information about students, from students.*

2. *Work on ways to engage students in their own learning; help them become more self-directed learners.*

3. *Make literacy a priority across the curriculum (including listening and speaking).*

4. *Hold regular special meetings, like the Data Dessert, to bring parents into the school (not just PTA meetings or parent conferences).*

5. *Ask the district for help (expertise, time, funding, resources).*

As the group reread the goals, appreciating the artistry of the banner, Josie asked a more pointed question: "Could we have gotten to these goals without looking at data?" Around the table heads wagged back and forth, signaling a no answer to her question.

"I think we might have gotten to similar goals without data," Bobbie said, "but these have substance because they came as a result of analyzing data."

"They're a little confusing," Tasha said, "because they're a mix of process and content."

"Is five the right number of goals?" Alice asked. *"Also, is there some order to the goals? Do we have to do some right away and some later? Do some depend on the completion of others?"*

"These are some of the questions we have been asking ourselves," Dinh explained, *"so we did a chart to analyze the goals."*

"Sounds just like what a Data Specialty Team would do," Aaron commented, with a smile of appreciation. Dinh distributed the following chart:

Goal	Process/Content	Implementation Notes
Get more information about students, from students.	Both. Process is getting more information through interviews, focus groups, shadowing, looking at student work. Content is the information we'll get.	This comes first and is ongoing. We need new specialty teams for each process we'll use. We'll need to meet again and revisit goals once we know more.
Work on ways to engage students in their own learning; help them become more self-directed learners.	This is both. Process is the way we learn (professional learning) as adults. Content is engagement.	The ultimate goal is engagement. How will we know whether or not students become more engaged as a result of our efforts? How will we know what self-direction looks like? This comes second, after we know more about what students need.
Make literacy a priority across the curriculum (including listening and speaking).	This is both. The process is making literacy a priority. The content is literacy.	We need to learn more about literacy. Then we need to evaluate how well we support literacy. Then we need to fill the gap between what we currently do and what we want to do in terms of literacy. This comes second after we know more about what students need.
Hold regular special meetings, like the Data Dessert, to bring parents into the school (not just parent-teacher meetings or parent conferences).	This is process—bringing parents (and other community members?) together. We don't know what the content of the process would be.	We need to ask parents what they think of this process. Also other community members. We need to understand content in terms of what they want and what we want. This comes second after we know more about if parents want this and what they need.
Ask the district for help (expertise, time, funding, resources).	This is process, mostly, although content is implied in parentheses.	We've already started by asking for help in data analysis; also, getting the district to let us use the early-release and PD days for our own purposes. The content will depend on what we need. This comes first and is ongoing as we proceed.

Dinh gave the group a couple of minutes to study the chart and then he commented, "So the Data Specialty Team thinks that what we need first is . . . more data!"

Aaron spoke up: "Sheesh! That'll be a hard sell."

"We run the risk of collecting and analyzing data but not doing anything," Robbie said. "You know, the planning-doing conundrum."

"Well," Dinh said, "I'm speaking without consulting the rest of my team, but I think some of the data collection is actually doing, not just collecting and analyzing."

"Meaning?" Aaron said.

"Meaning that we'll be doing something we have never done when we collect additional data. Like looking at student work. Like shadowing students. Like interviewing them. Holding focus groups."

"And these things," Roz suggested, "might be doing things in the finest sense. I mean, these things might be culture-changing."

"But, they won't change students into being more self-directed or more literate," Aaron pointed out.

"Not immediately and not directly," Roz said, "but they'll change the culture by changing the emphasis. We'll be looking at students with some expectations—when we look at their work, see how their day goes, learn what they need to be learners."

The group was silent, contemplating all this.

"I don't think we can reject these goals," Dinh said, "because they came from the entire faculty and staff. None of them is a bad goal, really. Our job is to make them work and make sure the results improve the school."

"But, remember," Josie said, "one of the roles of the Design Team is to look at the big picture . . . to subject the pieces of the picture to the whole purpose of our PLC work."

"So, what's wrong with starting with the three goals that are less content-specific—getting more information from students, getting more information from parents, and communicating with the district—and then checking out the more content-specific goals related to self-direction and literacy?" Tasha asked.

Again, silence, as the group considered her idea.

"I am completely opposed to that idea," K. D. said. Up to this point, he had not spoken . "I vote no. I think we form specialty teams, one per goal, and go from there. I don't think we have any right—or, well, the Design Team doesn't have any right—to modify the goals. That should be up to the specialty teams. We go with what the faculty and staff decided."

"Actually, I agree with K. D.," Forrest said. "Because they came from the entire faculty, we have no right to mess with the goals . We just go with them all, as they are. I say we should vote."

Roz spoke up, "I'm not in favor of voting, Forrest. I think we need to think more about this."

"If we were to do a Fist-to-Five," Forrest said, taking back his role as facilitator, "how would people vote?" He looked around the table. Some people had their hands up with a fist or with one, two, three, four, or five fingers showing. Others—about half—had their hands down.

"What are we voting on, exactly?" Alice said.

Oh-oh. We need to look at what might be going on with the Design and Data Specialty Teams.

THE FIRST ROADBLOCK

The Design and the Data Specialty Teams had hit their first roadblock—but not the only, nor the last—in the difficult process of school change. Some members of the two teams wanted to make a decision, and some were not yet ready to do so. One reason for the snag is the variety of expectations individuals have in terms of how meetings should go and what roles they want to play related to accomplishing outcomes. Individuals have preferred ways of acting during meetings (usually related to some aspect of meetings they excel at, such as thinking logistically) and preferred ways for meetings to go (such as problem-to-solution). Individuals do not shed their distinct preferences when they work in teams.

Another reason that teams falter relates to a skill that few people have naturally—the ability to engage in dialogue and inquiry. Most people are accustomed to discussion, or even debate, in meetings. Most meetings feature discussion or debate as the main way to achieve an outcome, often a decision leading to action. Dialogue is, however, a feature of collaborative teamwork and of many protocols and professional learning designs used in PLCs. Individuals in a team need to learn and practice dialogue and identify when it is to be used, even to the extent of saying, "Let's have 15 minutes of dialogue on this issue before we go into discussion and reach a decision."

The two reasons are related, as you will see.

INDIVIDUAL DIFFERENCES WITHIN A TEAM

You may remember Dottie's comment in Chapter 3 to Andy: "Bless you! I couldn't do all that! I'm so glad you are on this Design Team." She was delighted that he could analyze responses to a survey, something she did not feel she could do (or perhaps didn't want to do). You may also remember that, later in that chapter, Andy commented to Dottie about how grateful he was that she could do something he didn't feel he could do: "Bless you, Dottie. I couldn't do all that! I'm so glad you are on this Design Team!" He wasn't being sarcastic; he realized how unlikely he would be to capture, almost verbatim, what people were saying. Remember how Kelly volunteered to be the keeper of the Design Team portfolio? These Design Team members were all expressing their preferences within the team.

Anyone who expects that individuals within a team are going to behave consistently—seeing and acting upon issues exactly alike over a period of time—is going to be disappointed. Facilitating a meeting in which individual meeting preferences have not been identified can be perilous for both the facilitator and participants. On the other hand, having a variety of people participate in meetings—bringing different skills, talents, and interests to a group—can be exhilarating.

Personality inventories help people in a group understand individual preferences in terms of working together. One of the best is the Meyers-Briggs® and any of a number of variations that have been created on the basis of this inventory. The MBTI® (or Meyers-Briggs Type Inventory®) was created by Isabel Briggs Myers and her mother, Katharine Briggs, to show that "much seemingly random variation in the behavior is actually quite orderly and consistent, being due to basic differences in the ways individuals prefer to use their perception and judgment" (http://www.myersbriggs.org).

One popular version of the MBTI® is True Colors®, in which four basic types are rendered as colors (blue, green, gold, orange). Jane Kise (2006, 2008; Kise & Russell, 2010) has applied the MBTI® to differentiation in terms of teaching, coaching, and leadership.

One approach that is particularly useful in groups is called Four Corners (or, sometimes, Four Compass Points). You'll find a set of directions for using Four

Corners as Resource 4.1. Basically, people decide what they prefer to do (and are good at) in terms of working in groups:

- Taking action
- Attending to community well-being
- Figuring out structure or logistics
- Keeping in mind the vision

In Four Corners, they join others with the same preferences in one of four corners of a room—no equivocating by standing in the very middle or between any two of the corners—and, there, they talk about what they bring to a group through their preferences, as well as what they do that may drive others crazy. For example, the "vision" group often says, "We keep the eye on the big picture, but we sometimes dismay the action people who don't want to fuss around with all the fuzzy stuff, just get right to first steps." Each preference group shares (often on a piece of chart paper) what it contributes to group work as well as how the preference frustrates others. Each group may also share other signifying details, such as a famous person (real, fictional, alive, or dead) who represents that preference, and a motto or saying that might be used to describe them.

The whole group, then, has more understanding of the contributions individuals make (which may have seemed distractions or obstructions before this activity). When a group forms, its members may benefit from sharing their preferences before starting work.

As with MBTI® and True Colors,® we do not usually participate in a group according to only one preference; in fact, most people have the capacity for all four (or more, depending on the instrument) meeting skills. But "structure" people might be more likely to chafe at an extended check-in process ("How is everyone today?") than "community" people, and "community" people are more likely than "structure" people to sense that some members of the group are not getting their voices into the room.

Individuals can also develop and use nondominant behaviors when needed. They can learn to understand the demands of a task and "rise to the occasion" with behaviors that are neither customary nor particularly satisfying to them.

A group composed of mixed preferences is likely to get good work done as long as its members are aware and considerate of others' preferences. This does not mean that people wear sticky notes on their foreheads identifying their preferences! It does mean that a group might start its work by sharing preferences and agreeing to an outcome and agenda that rely on having all preferences. (An example is, "What do we need to do to engage parents in the life of this school?" A nonexample is, "How will we structure our first parent meeting?" The former engages all preferences; the latter engages the action and structure people more than the vision and community people.)

At Glen Haven, those who volunteered for the Design Team and the Data Specialty Team probably did so according to preferences. Prediction: The Design Team has more members who like to see the big picture and keep in mind the vision than those who use other preferences. Prediction: The Data Specialty Team has more members interested in the structure (who, what, when, where, why, and how—to use the journalistic heuristic) than those evidencing other preferences. We'll see later whether these predictions are accurate.

Knowing preferences can help members of a PLC shape agendas and activities. Design Team and PLC members can ask four questions about an agenda or activity:

- What is our vision (or purpose)? How will we keep our vision (or purpose) in front of us as we work?
- How will we get to action?
- How will we structure our work? What's the structure of the final outcome?
- How will we attend to the various needs of the people involved in this meeting or this work?

At Glen Haven, a subcommittee of the Data Specialty Team plus others on the faculty joined forces to plan Dessert Night; several did so because they were interested in community; others did so because they were interested in structure (shaping the details). At the same time, this subcommittee also had to keep in mind the vision (why they were designing the Dessert Night) and what they had to do to make Dessert Night work (action).

DIALOGUE AND DISCUSSION

Understanding individual differences within a team is an important first step. The next step is learning a basic skill related to teamwork: dialogue. It is clear that K. D. and Forrest are experiencing some frustrations related to the group's work and may, therefore, have different group preferences. They might have been expressing anxiety about getting to some action or structuring work. They might not have been aware that some members of the group had not participated (perhaps were not ready to speak) or did not have a clear picture of the big idea being discussed, which can be summarized as, "Basically, who's in charge or who decides—the whole faculty or the Design Team?" It is also clear that they want to move into decision making. They might not have recognized others' need for continued and deepening dialogue before making a decision. They might not have known what dialogue is and when and why it's used.

All teams need to understand *as a team and as individual members of a team* what dialogue is and when to use it. This means that team members can distinguish dialogue from discussion (or, in its extreme, debate) as well as recognize when to use each. This two-level skill is not a skill to be left up to chance; teams need to openly, directly, and intentionally talk about dialogue and discussion, and they need to have an ongoing process for determining when to use which process.

I have revised a diagram that Robert Garmston and Bruce Wellman (1999, p. 52) provide to distinguish dialogue and discussion (see Resource 4.2). A group that knows the differences and has practiced dialogue decides whether or not to engage in dialogue by looking at the purpose of their work. Sometimes the purpose of a meeting is to generate lots of possibilities, in which case dialogue may be the only process a group uses. Sometimes the goal of a meeting is to make a decision based on lots of good ideas, in which case dialogue is followed by discussion. Sometimes, when the content is given, no dialogue is needed, just discussion leading to a decision on one of the given ideas. Garmston and Wellman call the decision about whether to use dialogue or discussion a *deliberation point*. In a meeting, the deliberation point needs to be obvious and overt, not secret and certainly not assumptive. Rather than hoping that "everyone knows" that we're going to engage in dialogue, a good facilitator says, "Let's have a dialogue on this issue for a few minutes and then determine if we're ready to discuss it and make a decision."

In dialogue, a group agrees to take an inquiry rather than an advocacy stance. Garmston and Wellman call this the "balcony view," a standing-above-the-fray position, a position that focuses on seeing many points of view rather than just one. Participants agree not to form any lock-jaw opinions or take any sides during dialogue (a phenomenon Garmston and Wellman call "suspension"). Participants are open to any idea, constantly reconsidering their own and others' ideas as they listen to new contributions. They are serious (more than convivial, doing more than just going along with the crowd), but they don't judge ideas. They are likely to state ideas as hypotheses: "I wonder what would happen if. . . ." or "What do you think of. . . ?" They muse aloud about possibilities. They build on each others' ideas. They question in order to be certain they have gotten "it." At the end, in addition to a bevy of beautiful ideas, they have deeper understanding than they did before the dialogue. As Stephen R. Covey says, "Seek first to understand, then to be understood" (1991, p. 45), and that's what people do in dialogue.

Discussion has an entirely different feel to it. People begin to be wed to an idea and are likely to state their "side" clearly, although they may be willing to modify it as they hear from others and absorb different points of view. They are "in the pit," according to Garmston and Wellman (1999). They may also be said to be "in the fray" or "in the middle of it," although discussion is often quite civil (unlike debate, which can sometimes be an extreme form of discussion during which participants line up to present their own ideas—and nothing but those ideas—in a most theatrical way, refuting their opponents' ideas point by point). The endpoint of discussion is a decision, which may entail a vote or simply consensus. The endpoint of debate is a winner (and, sometimes, that seems the endpoint of discussion, too).

When a decision is needed, dialogue can become discussion after a variety of ideas has been presented. However, it should be clear to all participants that the process will start with dialogue and proceed with dialogue until a call is made to switch to discussion (a call that may be made by a facilitator, a Fist-to-Five, or other means). Someone needs to announce, "We're moving now from dialogue to discussion. At the end of our discussion, we need to have a decision." A decision leads to action, which leads to results.

Is it enough for meeting participants to engage in dialogue? The answer depends, of course, on the purpose of the meeting. The answer is yes when people need to engage intellectually, emotionally, and socially in an issue or topic. The answer is yes when people need deep understanding. The answer is yes when having a lot of different points of view and alternative ideas is important. Dialogue is enough (at least for the moment).

This is especially true for educators, who are used to evaluating and assessing. Throughout history, teachers have been required to judge good, bad, not-so-good. Nightly, they mark papers in piles that seem to grow higher by the hour. They may read an essay, for example, and know instantly how many points or what grade it gets: "Terrible essay! A D for sure!" They may argue internally about a grade or points ("Well, maybe a C–!"), having what might be called a single-sided discussion or debate. They are alone in their classrooms (or at the kitchen table, late at night) perhaps wondering whether or not they are "giving" the right grade to whatever is in the pile. Seldom do they have a chance to have a discussion or debate with other educators about student work or educational issues—much less a dialogue!

Seldom do they have the luxury of simply describing what they see (and don't see) in student work before judging it. One of the protocols you can use to help a group focus on description before generalizing and evaluating and recommending is called "Rounds." You'll find this protocol as Resource 4.3. Most educators actually have to learn how to describe something, and they need to practice this strategy with everyday objects, such as a table before leaping to judgment. Description is a very hard skill to learn, as is dialogue.

People need to experience dialogue emotionally, forcing themselves to back away from advocacy, forcing themselves not to care (too much!) about the outcome. People need to experience dialogue socially, giving themselves a way to interact with others respectfully and thoughtfully, without an agenda.

Oscar Graybill, who wrote the chapter "Dialogue" for *Powerful Designs For Professional Learning,* 2008, provides helpful materials (Resources 4.4–4.7) related to dialogue. Resource 4.4 distinguishes succinctly between dialogue and debate (the extreme form of discussion); readers might find it useful to select one pair of descriptions that most helps them distinguish the two. Resource 4.5 lists a sample set of agreements for dialogue (a set of valuable norms, actually). Resource 4.6 provides directions for a text-based protocol, and Resource 4.7 provides a useful text that a group can use for practicing dialogue.

Here's a comparison of dialogue and discussion on the same topic, longer passing times between classes:

Dialogue	*Discussion*
Speaker 1: What I'm wondering is why we need longer passing times between classes.	Speaker 1: I'm really in favor of longer passing times between classes, and not just for students—teachers need more time as well.
Speaker 2: Well, we might look at this from both the students' and the teachers' points of view.	Speaker 2: But, if we have more passing time between classes, we'll have to lengthen the school day.
Speaker 3: Perhaps students are feeling as if they have to go to their lockers between classes; they aren't carrying with them everything they need.	Speaker 3: And, we can't do that this year without going before the school board. So, I'm in favor of tabling this issue.
Speaker 4: It might be that students try to get in text messages and return calls during their passing periods.	Speaker 4: I think we should try it for one week just to see how it goes.
Speaker 5: Not to mention, using the restroom and just walking to another hallway.	Speaker 5: I'm in favor of that.
Speaker 1: Well, do we know enough about how students are using their passing periods?	Speaker 3: Why bother? If we have to get board approval, let's just wait until next year.
Speaker 3: We might want to do a little data gathering before we proceed with this issue.	Speaker 1: I say we take a vote on this. How many in favor of lengthening the passing period?
Speaker 5: I'm wondering if teachers need a longer passing period just so they can "clean up" after one class and prepare for another.	

Speaker 3: Not to mention getting to the faculty restrooms which, for some, are pretty far away.	Speaker 4 (continuing, after a show of hands): How many are against this?
Speaker 4: Again, perhaps we ought to gather some more information before we try to make a decision.	Speaker 4 (continuing after a show of hands): Why did so many of you NOT vote?
Speaker 1: We need to look at what the state says about the requirements regarding the length of a school day, in terms of actually being in classes.	Speaker 5: I think we should just table this idea until next year.
Speaker 4: I'm wondering what other high schools are doing, both in our district and other districts.	
Speaker 5: What if we table this until we can get some more information? We're not ready to make a decision yet.	

Both groups ended up at the same point, but the dialogue group was more productive, by far, than the discussion group. A useful set of "talking points" about lengthening the passing period came up in the dialogue, while the discussion started and ended with unelaborated positions or stands on the issue. The dialogue group knows what to do next; the discussion group might be feeling frustrated ("Wasted our time.") because members don't understand the issues, and the group may not follow up on the topic in any more productive way—if, indeed, they follow up at all. If the dialogue group had had data, it could have gone on to discussion and, eventually, decision making; nevertheless, members of the dialogue group probably felt satisfied because they understood the issues and had a realistic plan for going forward.

One of the best forms of dialogue is the Socratic Seminar, which Graybill defines as "a highly motivating form of intellectual and scholarly discourse facilitated with students or adults" (Graybill, 2008, p. 136). Usually 1 or 2 hours long, Socratic Seminars are obviously connected to Socrates and the ancient Greek philosopher's practice of teaching others through asking questions. More recently, Socratic Seminars are known for their use in the Paideia program (Mortimer Adler), the Coalition of Essential Schools, and other innovative schools predicated on an inquiry-based approach to teaching and learning.

Graybill describes the goals of a Socratic Seminar as "collective inquiry and shared understanding through dialogue" (2008, p. 236). The process gives groups a chance to practice dialogue using a text (an article, a quotation, a story, etc.). Resource 4.7 provides an article that a group can use to practice dialogue in the Socratic Seminar format, along with directions. The practice dialogue relies on written text, but

> **Socratic Seminars**
>
> You can read more about the Socratic Seminars and the Paideia program in Terry Roberts's book *The Power of Paideia Schools: Defining Lives Through Learning* (1998) and about the Coalition of Essential Schools in the trio of Horace books written by Theodore Sizer. His first is *Horace's Compromise; The Dilemma of the American High School* (1984). Also check out the website www.nsrfharmony.org for materials for Socratic seminars.

groups can also practice dialogue by identifying a theme or idea members want to pursue, such as how to involve parents more in school life. In the reality of teamwork, participants may work more with a concept or idea, rather than a text.

Alice's question: "What are we voting on, exactly?" made the room go silent. Members of the Design Team and the Data Specialty Team looked at each other. Finally, Forrest spoke up, as facilitator, "I think we've gone on to the next agenda item: 'Next Steps and How to Approach Them.' But, maybe we're not ready for that yet?"

Aaron agreed, "I think we need more discussion . . . actually more dialogue . . . about the goals and the ramifications of them for our work."

"What do you mean by dialogue?" K. D. asked.

"Something we learned this summer at our conference on professional learning," Aaron responded. "Dialogue is more open than discussion, more about thinking aloud and exploring ideas."

"It's about fully understanding an issue," Tasha added. "I get the feeling that we're not completely understanding the goals and our role as the Design and Data Specialty Teams in terms of doing something about them. So, we can't make a decision or vote. We're not ready."

"Well," K. D. said, "I'm ready. I don't see the point of all this random thinking. We could go on and on and never get finished with it. We need a plan."

Forrest said, "I'm also thinking that some people in this room know things that the rest of us don't know. I wasn't aware that I was breaking a rule, really. But, apparently I was. I'm wondering if we should stop and learn a little about dialogue."

"And, I'm feeling frustrated," K. D. added. "We just need to move on."

"So, K. D.," Tasha said, "I'm understanding your frustration. That's how I feel a lot of the time in meetings, but I've learned that the way I feel is not the way everybody feels. I'm wondering if we should look at our preferences in terms of meeting with each other."

Dinh spoke up, "It feels as if we're backtracking here rather than moving along according to our agenda. At this rate, we'll never get anything done!"

Josie spoke up, "I'm learning that the hard work of change—which is what we're involved in— often feels like this. A group gets to a certain point and then discovers that it needs something else. It can go on, regardless, or it can stop and address what is needed. A group that goes on, despite the pressure of a problem, often gets blocked later. One way or another, needs, well, need to be addressed."

"So," Forrest said, attending to his facilitator duties, "shall we just end this meeting, like this?"

"That doesn't feel good," Dottie commented. She hadn't said much during the meeting, but suddenly she leaned forward and addressed the group: "This is not failure. This is learning. We haven't been on teams before, like this. The teams we've had before have had little things to deal with—simple, quick, like that." She snapped her fingers. "We need to learn how to be on teams. So, let's stop where we are, be glad we have goals and some ideas for implementing them, and let's plan our next meeting to focus on us as a team—or a couple of teams working together." She sat back.

Silence, then a murmured "Huzzah!" and a smattering of applause.

Josie said, "I know someone who can teach us dialogue."

Roz added, "And, I can help with group meeting preferences. We can do this fun activity called Four Corners. We need to schedule two more meetings: one to address our needs as a team and one to continue this agenda."

Josie spoke up, "Why don't we use the faculty meeting on the 26th of November to look at group meeting preferences—I can get out voicemails and e-mails rather than hold the faculty meeting. And, perhaps, we can practice dialogue with the heart of the issue we've run into—kind of two birds with one stone?"

"And," Dinh added, "we need to let the whole school know what we're doing. How shall we do that?"
"I think I can draw a comic strip of us, working, on the graffiti board," Ariel volunteered, "You know,

three panels, the beginning of our meeting, the middle, and where we are now."

"I suspect that the rest of the faculty will want to look at group meeting preferences and dialogue, too," Dinh said. "When can we do that?"

It happened as Dinh predicted. First, during the time set aside for the November 26 faculty meeting that Josie gave up, the Design Team and the Data Specialty Team met to learn about their meeting preferences and also to learn and practice dialogue. The district director of professional development, Stephanie Hodges, did not let them practice dialogue with the issue that had stalled their work; instead, she asked them to practice on a rather benign text. So, Josie once again surrendered a faculty meeting so that the two teams could get back to how to implement the five goals. When Tasha questioned her about giving up so many faculty meetings, Josie said, "What the Design and the Data Specialty Teams are doing is the heart of this school. The details can be dealt with in other ways."

Naturally, the faculty had sniffed out the problem—the roadblock that stopped the work of the Design Team and the Data Specialty Team—almost before that meeting had ended. They read and discussed Ariel's cartoon. They talked to members of both teams. And they were curious about preferences and dialogue. Even before the Design Team and the Data Specialty Team met to learn about preferences and learn and practice dialogue, some faculty members said, "We'd like to do this, too," so Josie decided to use December's early-release half-day to engage the whole faculty in discovering and understanding preferences and learning and practicing dialogue, with Roz and Stephanie facilitating.

Let's take a closer look at what the Design and Data Specialty Teams need—as well as what the whole PLC may need—another example of the necessity of redundancy or mirroring of processes (see Chapter 2).

TRUST

Building trust is so fundamental to the success of groups that it is often the foundation of group processes. The founder and president of the Table Group, a management consulting firm that specializes in executive team development and organizational health, Patrick Lencioni, puts absence of trust at the bottom of a pyramid of group dysfunctions in *The Five Dysfunctions of a Team: A Field Guide for*

Leaders, Managers, and Facilitators (2002, p. 6). It is the #1 dysfunction. Only when absence of trust is addressed and trust built, can teams address the other dysfunctions: #2, fear of conflict; #3, lack of commitment; #4, avoidance of accountability; and #5, inattention to results.

A group can go through all sorts of trust-building activities, from deciding together who will survive a blizzard to falling backwards off a platform into the strong arms of their colleagues, but real trust is built when people practice using particular skills to tackle a wicked problem (see Chapter 1). Trust-building activities are fun—and I've survived even the harshest of them—but trust is, itself, a warm, genuine feeling of empathy and pride when a group accomplishes a real task together, overcoming personal, social, and societal barriers to the work. Trust is a soft, satisfied smile, not a rush of relief when you make it to the end of the zip line.

Consider these premises about trust:

1. We need trust in order to share leadership, rather than having one "appointed" leader or taking on the leadership role ourselves.

2. Trust is built on understanding.

3. One reason we lack trust is our lack of understanding of other's mental models . . . and our lack of communication about our own mental models.

4. The problems we encounter in education are usually "wicked" problems, not simple, linear problems. They are "tenacious and nonlinear. They contain unpredictable barriers and recur, folding back on themselves. . . . Existing ways of thinking cannot handle wicked problems. Individuals and groups require new mental models for problem finding and problem approaches" (Garmston & Wellman, 1999, p. 223).

Although the others have already been discussed in this book, the premise in #3 deserves some attention. Peter Senge and his colleagues suggest that one barrier to understanding, and therefore trust, lies in our own and others' mental models: "The semipermanent unspoken 'maps' of the world which people hold in their long-term memory, and the short-term perceptions which people build up as part of their everyday reasoning processes. Short-term can become long-term. Both long-term and short-term can be modified" (2000, p. 237).

We form our mental maps beginning with observation of some phenomenon. From among the many impressions we get about that phenomenon, we choose one or more and add meaning, imbuing each impression with not only a definition but also a connotation or feeling. We make assumptions, draw conclusions, and develop beliefs about the world based on our laden observations and impressions. We act according to our assumptions, conclusions, and beliefs. We may not be aware of nor share with anyone else what has caused us to take action. Others may see only the action and may derive their own explanations for what we did, based on their own mental models! They may react accordingly. What an unproductive loop that becomes!

For example, we may have heard a colleague make a joke at the expense of another. We registered the tone and volume of the acerbic comment, the comment itself, and the listener's astonished and then hurt reaction to the comment. We assume that the person making the comment is capable of making such comments to others. We become wary about working with this colleague and, when we find ourselves on a team together, watch what we say, unwilling to put ourselves on the receiving end of a bruising but humorously meant story. People—including the one who made the joke in the first place—wonder why we seem estranged.

This quick and natural mental process from observation to action is often referred to as a ladder of inference since each step builds upon a supposition related to the previous steps.

Only when we access our own mental models can we get beyond their restrictions. Only when we share our mental models can people understand why we do what we do. Only when we try—politely!—to access others' mental models can we get beyond actions that puzzle us or prevent trust. Here are the steps that must be taken:

1. Become more aware of your own thinking and reasoning (reflection).

2. Make your thinking and reasoning more visible to others (advocacy).

3. Inquire into others' thinking and reasoning (inquiry).

You can find processes for accessing and sharing mental models on Resource 4.8. The schematic below, Figure 4.1, provides another way of examining trust in a group:

Figure 4.1   A Way to Examine Trust

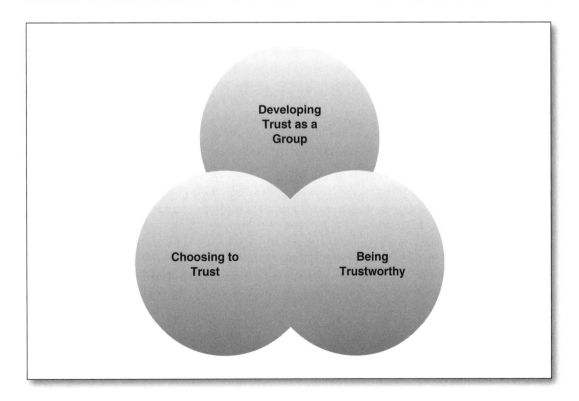

To develop trust as a group, we must first choose to trust and be trustworthy ourselves. Here are two case studies of participants in a PLC who may hold trust hostage by either not trusting or not being trustworthy:

Case #1: "I choose to withhold my ideas or I may look to someone else as the expert to further the thinking in the group. When a problem is surfaced in the PLC, I immediately start looking for a silver bullet or quick fix. I spend my time thinking how this PLC is being mandated from the administration and I have other kinds of work I want to be doing right now" (Hord, Roussin, & Sommers, 2010, p. 120).

Case #2: "I participate in parking lot conversations on topics related to our PLC. I show up having the 'right' answer and speak with authority about what I know is the right thing to do. When an innovative or compelling idea is presented, I immediately move the group back to the practical tasks at hand" (Hord et al., 2010, p. 120).

Here is a best-case scenario (also from Hord et al., 2010, p. 120):

Case #3: "I embrace all ideas presented in the PLC with curiosity and wonderment. I find myself interested in how others think and see the world around them. I find a balance between advocacy and inquiry when expressing myself in a PLC. I notice when I get hooked to an idea or belief and pause long enough to determine if that block is helpful to others and me. I actively interrogate reality. I use learning in the group to see others and myself in order to be more effective in my work."

Hord et al. (2010) describe as "facets" several important elements of trust: Honesty, Competence, Reliability, Openness, and Benevolence (pp. 126–127). Evidence of these facets in everyone involved in a PLC goes a long way toward "building, nurturing and sustaining PLC relationships" (p. 126).

You can read two articles about trust in Resource 4.9.

BLINDERS

By now, you might have wondered, "Is this group blind to the real problems in the school? Do they have blinders on?" You examined the achievement data in Chapter 3. You noticed the mathematics scores. Why didn't the Design Team or the whole PLC initiate a focus on mathematics? Why did literacy, a subject in which the scores are much better, make it onto the list of five goals?

There's no real answer to that question, of course. Surely the mathematics teachers and others noticed those scores. Perhaps they did not feel that improving learning (not just test scores) in mathematics was worthy of all-school investigation, thinking that it's the purview of the Mathematics Department. Perhaps, those whose attention was caught by the mathematics scores saw them as so appallingly bad that they felt hopeless. There might have been some resignation—"We're never going to do better in math, given *X*, *Y*, and *Z*." You can guess what *X*, *Y*, and *Z* are. Perhaps those who noticed the mathematics scores despaired of teaching mathematics any differently, not knowing about strides in mathematics education, especially those related to a professional learning strategy called lesson study, that you will learn about in a Chapter 8.

Perhaps the whole faculty will, later, fixate on mathematics but, at the beginning, they were unwilling to go there. Should Josie have intervened? She could have suggested a mathematics goal, but perhaps she recognized that the literacy goal, itself, would address reading mathematics content, one of the problems that students have in understanding math. She could have mandated that one of the goals be related to mathematics, but that would have been out of character for her in her new role as leading learner. Like many things, perhaps Josie had to just bite her tongue to keep from blurting out, "But, what about mathematics?" trusting the group to get to math when ready.

PREDICTIONS AND RESULTS OF FOUR CORNERS

You may be curious about how Four Corners went for the Design and Data Specialty Teams and the whole faculty. You might enjoy reading about how they experienced the process on Resource 4.10, but here are the data. As you examine the preferences selected by the team members, imagine what team members will need to do in meetings so that everyone has a voice and all four preferences are represented in the process. Imagine how they might need to adjust their group work to compensate for having too many or too few people with preferences in any of the four corners.

Preference	Design Team Percentage (n = 9)	Data Specialty Team Percentage (n = 8)	Whole Faculty Percentage (n = 51)
Vision	55	25	27
Action	11	12	23
Community	11	12	18
Structure	22	50	32

December was a crazy month and not just for the usual reasons. Just to recap, on Tuesday, November 26, the Design Team and the Data Specialty Team met during the faculty meeting time that Josie had repurposed so that they could explore preferences and learn and practice dialogue. On the 17th, both teams met again to have a dialogue about the five goals and reach some consensus, which they could present to the whole faculty the next day. On the 18th, an early-release half-day, the whole faculty met to explore preferences, learn and practice dialogue . . . and consider action plans for the goals. On the 19th, the Design Team met one last time before the end of the calendar year.

The most critical meeting was held on the 17th. It was at this meeting that the Design Team and the Data Specialty Team had to apply what they knew about preferences and dialogue to their roadblock. It was not easy. Forrest—bless his heart—agreed to facilitate again and started the meeting with, "So, where were we?" A little laughter set the tone for a positive meeting. So did this revised agenda:

Agenda Item	Results Expected
Check-in: How are we similar to and different from our preferences?	Participation
Norms	Commitment to or change in norms
Outcome for the day	Commitment to an outcome
Dialogue on the role of the Design Team and other teams (with a focus on how to implement the five goals)	Contribution of ideas; understanding
Dialogue on implementation of the five goals; discussion; decision	Contribution; decision about what to present to faculty the next day
Closure	Participation

Through check-in, many of the team members admitted that, yes, they definitely had a preference for a particular role and type of meeting—but each agreed to acknowledge, respect and rely on others' perspectives. Roz asked if she could summarize preferences, as she saw them. The group listened carefully as she said, "We have a lot of vision people on these two teams. That can frustrate the rest of us. We only have one community well-being person, Dottie. We'll need to help her spot difficulties and make sure that all of us are getting our voices in the room. We have two structure people and two action people. At some point, we're really going to need them to help us move on."

The two teams agreed to norms, with a special emphasis on the first one and the Seven Norms of Collaboration from Robert Garmston and Bruce Wellman (see Resource 1.14):

1. We will first inquire about another person's thinking before offering our own ideas.

They wrestled with the next item on the agenda: "outcome for the day," not sure what it might be. After some dialogue and Kelly's charting of key words that came up for them, Aaron wrote a draft of an outcome on the white board and, after some wordsmithing, the group agreed to this:

We will have a draft of a plan for implementing the five goals that will be respectful of the whole faculty and move our work ahead in the most expeditious manner.

Dialogue Questions and Comments They Used

"Help me to understand. . . ."

"Here's what I think you said. . . ."

"I'm wondering. . . ."

"What does that look in real life?"

"One example of that might be. . . ."

"As I see it. . . ."

"What's the difference between. . . ?"

"What if we. . . ?"

"I like that idea and I wonder what you would think if we tweaked it like this. . ."

"Let me see if I've got this straight. . . ."

"What do other people think?"

"What would be the chief barriers to this? How could we overcome these?"

Aaron led them in a mock ceremony: "Raise your right hand and repeat after me. I do solemnly swear . . . to do my best . . . to uphold the processes of this meeting . . . in order to achieve the outcome . . . we have agreed upon. . . ."

"Sheesh," Tasha said in a whisper loud enough for everyone to hear. "If it takes this long to settle on an outcome, how long will it take to decide what to do about the PLC goals?" She was "just kidding," but one or two other people nodded. "I know . . . I know . . . we'll get good at this . . . it'll come naturally at some point . . . it's part of the process we have to go through." She was reciting some of the things she, herself, had said to the Design Team. People chuckled . . . a bit.

Then they dug into their first dialogue, using as their "text" the statements the Investigative Team had drafted to describe the Design Team (Resource 2.14). With a brisk rubbing of his hands together, Forrest announced, "Let's go into dialogue about the role of the Design Team. Who would like to start?"

Dinh began, "I think we got stuck on what the Design Team can and should do (with or without the Data Specialty Team) in terms of what the whole faculty decides." You can read in the box some of the "dialogue-type" questions or statements you would have heard if you had been there.

After about 12 minutes, Dinh said, "Here's what I understand: The Design Team will always start and end with what the whole faculty wants. That means that we begin our deliberations with what we've heard from them, and we end them by taking subsequent drafts back to them to be reviewed and revised if necessary. It will be a transparent process."

Nods around the table indicated consent, so Forrest asked, "Do we need to do more dialogue on this topic?" The nods changed direction and so he said, "Let's continue dialogue regarding the five goals. What are we thinking?"

At the end of another 10 minutes of dialogue, Forrest asked if the team felt ready to go into discussion. A Fist-to-Five with fours and fives. Robbie recorded on chart paper the key ideas as the group engaged in discussion. By the end of a short discussion, the group had agreed on five essentials of implementation:

1. *There will be two tiers for these goals: Tier 1 and Tier 2. Glen Haven will work on Tier 1 goals before going on to Tier 2.*

2. *Other tiers may be named as new tasks come up.*

3. *Tier 1 will focus on the process goals, particularly the gathering of student data, which might affect the two content goals (literacy and self-directed students).*

4. *Tier 2 will be modified, as necessary, according to what is discovered in the implementation of the Tier 1 goals.*

5. *We'll take this idea to the whole PLC to see if it meets with approval or can be improved.*

Nearly an hour had passed, and team members looked spent. They made a plan to present these essentials of implementation to the whole faculty after the PLC had done Four Corners and learned and practiced dialogue.

Nods of assent around the room. "Let's have some closure. How did we do on the norms? Kelly, why don't you read each norm to us and let us come up with a number from 1 to 10, with 10 being high. I'll record the numbers."

This process made the norms (Resource 1.15) they had been using come alive for the group. Andy commented that they would not have been able to rate their adherence to some of these norms high in their first meeting: "A lot of these norms point to dialogue." Tasha pointed out that they were not meeting the norm for using student data . . . yet. "We don't have one norm we need," Kelly said, "the one about what we do if we violate the norms." Overall, however, team members seemed proud of the work they had accomplished at this meeting. . . as well as HOW they had accomplished it.

On the 18th, the whole faculty enjoyed Four Corners, learned and practiced dialogue, and approved the five essentials of implementation the Design and the Data specialty team had worked on. Then, they divided into small groups according to the Tier 1 and Tier 2 goals, and brainstormed some implementation possibilities and the results they wanted for each goal. Design Team members facilitated the small groups, recorded their ideas on a template, and posted them for a Gallery Tour (see Resource 3.17).

PROPOSED ACTION PLAN

Tier 1 Goals	Implementation	Results
Get more information about students, from students.	Form four specialty teams to (1) interview students, (2) hold focus groups, (3) shadow students at other middle schools and Glen Haven, and (4) collect student work. Collect data. Analyze data. Present data to staff.	A plan for interviews, focus groups, shadowing, and collecting student work. Implementation of the plan. A summary of the results from each of the four strategies. Staff discussion of the results and application of ideas from the data to future work.

(Continued)

(Continued)

Tier 1 Goals	Implementation	Results
Hold regular special meetings, like the Data Dessert, to bring parents into the school (not just PTO meetings or parent conferences).	Form one or more specialty teams to (1) interview parents to find out what they want and need and (2) survey other schools within and outside district to discover how they work with parents. Propose to the whole faculty a set of activities to involve parents.	Information about ways to work with parents effectively. A draft set of activities for working with parents. A schedule of activities to use during the remainder of the year.
Ask the district for help (expertise, time, funding, resources).	Form a specialty team to do the following: Survey the faculty about possible district resources: what's available and what might be needed. Make a presentation to district administrators (and the board?) about what's happening at Glen Haven and what Glen Haven needs from the district. Follow-up.	A list of what the district might be able to offer. A list of what the school needs. A presentation to district administrators about what the school is doing and what it needs. A plan for following up on the presentation.
Tier 2 Goals	Implementation	Results
Work on ways to engage students in their own learning; help them become more self-directed learners.	Incorporate questions related to self-direction and engagement in learning into interviews and focus groups; look for evidence of self-direction and engagement during shadowing. Analyze results of interviews, focus groups and shadowing in part on the basis of self-direction and engagement.	Questions related to self-direction and engagement. Descriptors of self-direction and engagement. Data from interviews, focus groups, and shadowing, analyzed according to descriptors of self-direction and engagement. Report to whole faculty. Discussion about what to do next.
Make literacy a priority across the curriculum (including listening and speaking).	Form a specialty team to focus on literacy; this team will reanalyze data related to literacy and report to whole faculty. Incorporate questions related to literacy and learning into interviews and focus groups; look for evidence of literacy skills during shadowing. Analyze results of interviews, focus groups, and shadowing in part on the basis of literacy.	Analysis of data related to literacy (all four data categories). Analysis of data from the four specialty teams (who interviewed, held focus groups, shadowed, or collected student work) in terms of literacy. Presentation to whole faculty. Discussion of data results. Application to future work.

At the end of the Gallery Tour, the whole PLC met again to share reactions to the small-group work:

- *We're not ready to analyze student work. Let's delay that part of student data collection.*
- *We need to get information about the district from the district, not just what we know about the district. We also need to know what's going on in other schools. They may have expertise to offer. In other words, we need to research resources in the district, school-by-school.*
- *We should not be planning activities for parents until we have an overall plan for parent involvement: purpose/goals, rationale, outcomes, possible processes, etc.*

The overwhelming sentiment at the end of the whole faculty early-release half-day was a sigh of completion (or was it exhaustion?). "Look at all we've done since September," one faculty member said.

The Design Team met the next day, just 2 days before school let out for the winter holiday. Josie gave each a small candle and provided a chocolate frosted sheet cake scripted with the word "Congratulations!" She asked members of the Design Team to light a candle, share some aspect of their work that they were proud of, and put the candle on the cake. She ran out of candles, but the Design Team did not run out of "prouds."

Before the cake went up in smoke and smoke detectors summoned firefighters, Josie blew out the candles and cut the cake into squares. As they munched around hardening globs of candle wax on their pieces of the cake, they kept talking. Robbie voiced a fear that momentum would dissipate over the holidays, especially as teachers and students began to prepare for spring state tests. Roz responded, "Oh, but we have such great things to do in January—the student interviews and focus groups, going to other schools."

"Right now," Dottie confessed, "I'm so crazed about getting ready for the holidays that I can't much think about after the holidays."

GO SLOW TO GO FAST

Group work never goes exactly as planned. What happened to the Design Team and the Data Specialty Team is a case in point. Things were going along wonderfully until K. D. and Forrest questioned the process. Bang! The meeting was derailed. It took another whole meeting for the process to get back on track, and then the whole faculty had to detour to catch up with the learning of the Design and Data Specialty Teams. But, then, look what they accomplished at the December 18 meeting!

Sometimes it may seem as if a dictatorship is the only way to go in terms of school change. And, yes, dictatorship might be easier . . . but less rich and fulfilling and less likely to get substantive and lasting results. Educational historian Diane Ravitch makes this point in Chapter 4 of her book *The Death and Life of the American School System* (2009). She describes reform in San Diego from 1998 to 2005, which came from the top and was heavily resisted by those who were forced to implement it.

The idea of "going slow to go fast" comes from the business world. It appeared in 1995 in an article by that name in *The McKinsey Quarterly*. The authors of that article, Nathaniel J. Mass and Brad Berkson, acknowledge that "speed is of the essence—but so are quality and cost" in terms of product development (p. 19). It's hard to look at school change as a "product," but the idea of finding out what's needed to improve student learning and then doing it can, perhaps, be likened to "product development."

One product development problem that Mass and Berkson acknowledge particularly applies to educational change. They speak of setting aggressive targets. The politician, for example, has aggressive targets. So might a superintendent and

Benchmarks

Benchmark has an interesting etymology. According to Kathleen Taylor, in "The Learned Word" (2010, p. 7), *benchmark* comes from the lexicon of surveyors: "Long-ago surveyors [placed] a *mark* into a fixed and endurable object . . . and [used] these immutable *marks* to indicate to those who came after them that someone has assessed the elevation." Once they have obtained the measure of the *mark*, surveyors place an "angle iron *bench*" on the spot. "That *bench mark* provides a reliable placement for positioning surveyors' leveling rods and serves as a solid, physical reference point against which other measurements are taken." The word, once two words, is now used in education to serve "as as a standard by which others may be measured or judged" (in Taylor, from www.merriam-webster.com/dictionary/benchmark).

elected district board members. And it's all right to have targets. It's even better to have targets that can be benchmarked (that is, have signposts of success along the way).

The best way to have targets and benchmarks is to use what Mass and Berkson call "feedback loops" so that progress toward the targets can be monitored and changed, as needed. Mass and Berkson's "feedback loops" derive from systems thinking and involve process verification, ramp-up, phase gates (downstream and upstream), hard- and soft-screening, and other aspects of product development that don't automatically translate to education.

But feedback is very important to educational change. Norms that provide for feedback help ensure that it will occur. K. D. and Forrest felt comfortable enough with the group and the norms for the group that they could object to the process. The surveys that proliferate at Glen Haven are an active way to get feedback. The surveys lead to better "product development," but Glen Haven teams haven't stopped there—they have usually found ways to take a "product" or a revision back to the whole faculty to see if they approve of it. Additional feedback leads to revision, which may lead to additional feedback. Glen Haven has an advantage that business entrepreneurs and manufacturers don't: Faculty (and students, as the PLC work progresses) can respond to ideas and processes immediately, unlike consumers who are usually somewhat removed in time and space from those whose "products" they're trying.

Aggressive schedules (as Mass and Berkson describe them) can often have "the opposite of what was intended: namely longer delays with lower quality." Translated into education, this means that the reform might take longer and not be wholly satisfactory if rushed. Hasty decisions and actions not thoroughly thought through can actually stymie change.

The sooner the necessity for change is detected, the better. That's why feedback needs to start at the beginning of a school change process, almost before people know exactly what they are to change. This is especially difficult for educators who are often told *what* to change before they have even discovered *why* there needs to be a change! They may get direct professional development on a specific strategy for teaching reading, for example, and are expected to implement it, even if they're not sure there is a problem with reading or cannot describe the problem well enough to seek a solution. What a waste of people, time, and money!

Above all, the change must be looked at systemically, whether it is occurring in a business or a school. Mass and Berkson discuss various steps ("concept generation, design, prototype testing, pilot operations, and manufacturing ramp-up") that might have some corollary in education. These cannot be short-cut. They also discuss needed resources and how prepared an organization is to supply these at each step.

What can go wrong in manufacturing can go wrong in education: "slippages," "firefighting," and "inferior quality." Perhaps the objections raised by K. D. and

Forrest can be seen as a slippage. And who knows what might happen in February if the Board of Education decrees a new policy—the Glen Haven educators may need to do some firefighting. What if something they want to do to enhance literacy turns out not to work? Should they just keep using that instructional strategy?

The instant fix—the "going fast to not go anywhere phenomenon"—is sometimes called "the silver bullet" or the "band-aid" approach. Manufacturers usually find this approach unproductive (witness Toyota's 2010 problems with the gas pedal), and educators do, too. A "lot of fuss leading to nothing," one educator quipped at a workshop.

So, be prepared to go slow. Have targets and reasonable benchmarks of success, but also have active feedback mechanisms so that the targets—and benchmarks and processes you are following to achieve these—can be modified according to real and timely data from participants (including students) in the effort to improve your school.

DEALING WITH DIFFICULT PEOPLE

Perhaps you thought that Forrest and K. D. were being obstructionists. Everything was going so smoothly at the first joint meeting between the Design Team and the Data Specialty Team. Then K. D. said, basically, "Let's get on with this process and vote," and Forrest agreed. Everything stopped. A couple of people stepped in to acknowledge their feelings about the progress of the meeting and to suggest some approaches to understanding different ways of thinking and working together. And, the groups took a detour, which seemed to work, and then returned to the work they had seemingly abandoned and seemed to succeed at it.

Were K. D. and Forrest obstructionists? Four Corners (and its basis in the MBTI®) suggests that they were not; they simply had needs and styles that were different from those being expressed. In fact, others may have been feeling exactly the way K. D. and Forrest were feeling but did not speak up.

Certainly, there are meeting behaviors that—if not obstructionist—are downright disruptive. You might enjoy reading about them in Resource 4.11: the warm body, the side conversationalist, and others.

One way to handle "difficult people" is through reference to the norms. Call for a "norm check" and let the group discuss whether or not it is working according to norms. Another way is to respond directly to the behavior. Someone can say, "Ed, we really like your stories; they are always so interesting. However, they are getting us off-track. Let's save them for a beer after this meeting." Or, "You don't really mean that, do you, [name of sarcastic person]?" Or, "Nancy, we haven't heard from you yet. We don't want to pressure you to say something, but we sure don't want to miss out on anything you have to offer either." You can probably imagine a variety of ways to directly, and kindly, respond to disruptions.

Skeptics and Cynics

Tony Wagner distinguishes between skeptics and cynics. He maintains, "They may sound alike but in fact have very different motives. The skeptics are usually experienced and committed educators whose concerns must be understood and addressed, while the cynics are the teachers who have given up" (p. 23). In fact, he suggests, the cynics are the ones who shouldn't be teaching . . . and certainly shouldn't be working on a committee to improve a school. At this point, neither K. D. nor Forrest seems to be a cynic. (Access at http://www.schoolchange.org/articles/leadership_for_learning.html)

Another way is to speak personally to the person who has been disruptive. After a meeting, you (or someone who knows the person well) might approach the person who has disrupted proceedings with a question, "How are things going in the meeting for you? I noticed that you [action] and, sometimes, that indicates that things are not going well. . . ." And it can be true that things are not going well for the person who disrupted the meeting. The reasons range from a bad situation at home to not understanding the purpose of the meeting, from feeling inadequate to worrying about a student.

Ann Delehant (2007) offers a set of suggestions for responding to specific disruptions in a meeting (Resource 4.12). General strategies include

- A suggestion box for anonymous submissions (with the understanding that they will be read and seriously considered at a meeting).
- Crayons and construction paper on meeting tables.
- A graffiti board. Glen Haven put one up in the hallway leading to the faculty lounge. These can also be used to take the edge out of edgy meetings.
- A *Parking Lot* at every meeting, along with a set of stickies with attention given to items by the end of the meeting.

People who are suffering silently usually don't suffer long that way; they speak up or act out according to what's bothering them.

STRATEGIC PLANNING

You might be wondering why **someone** has not drafted some kind of strategic plan: Josie, the Design Team, Stephanie Hodges with other district administrators. Sometimes, strategic planning is the way to go; in other situations, strategic planning can actually be a barrier to action. The difference is related to the messiness of the work to be done—what Garmston and Wellman called "wickedness" (see Chapter 1). The changes at Glen Haven are, at this point, unpredictable. Although there are some overall purposes for working together in PLCs, and PLC members have some information, they recognize the need to collect more data. They wisely are postponing planning until they know more, until the data themselves announce what must be done. Once they know what must be done, they can probably engage in some strategic planning around specific outcomes. Until then, they prudently plan the next one or two steps only, taking a "wait 'n' see" attitude about the next steps, never mind a plan, until they get results from the first steps.

Strategic planning before the moment is right is an exhausting process. Many groups sprint so fast from idea to strategic planning that they arrive out of breath. They are so exhausted by planning that they have little energy to go on to action; they may get caught in the planning-doing conundrum (see Chapter 1). Strategic plans can be very complex, sometimes requiring extended deliberation on the following:

- Vision (see Chapter 1)
- Mission and goals (see Chapter 9)
- An environmental scan (comparable to the analysis of context described in Chapter 2)
- Formulation and analysis of strategies (perhaps using a SWOT Analysis—Strengths, Weaknesses, Opportunities, and Threats—Resource 4.13; or the Force Field Analysis strategy, Barriers and Boosters, Resource 1.18)

- Implementation strategy (steps to be taken, by whom, when and where; expected results)
- Evaluation of strategic plan

Ultimately, a strategic plan needs to be submitted to some key questions:

1. Does the plan result in work that is real and really important to the goal?

2. Is the plan doable? Does our organization have the capacity to follow the plan and be successful?

3. Is anybody doing anything to carry out the plan (or are they resting after the exhausting process of creating the plan)? Will people really do what the plan calls for?

Figure 4.2 provides a good way to analyze leverage (ability to effect significant change, #1 above) and capacity (#2 above) and works for individual steps (such as those GHMS staff are taking) and strategic planning:

Figure 4.2   Effect/Leverage and Capacity

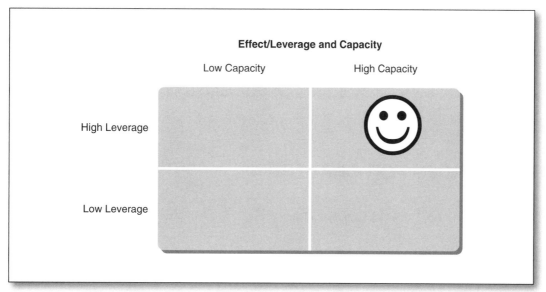

The best place for any action/plan to be, of course, is in the upper right hand corner.

Even when the time comes for a group to develop a strategic plan, it's important for the planners to understand in advance that at some point the work might sidetrack in some unpredictable way. And remember that those who create a strategic plan should be those who are going to implement that plan—"them's as does the doin' does the decidin'." You might have noticed that the Glen Haven Design Team did *not* actually plan what the specialty teams might do to interview students, hold focus groups, shadow and collect student work. Instead, they wisely left the specific planning up to the yet-to-be-formed specialty teams. Or, perhaps, the press of the holidays forced them to abrogate that responsibility. Let's imagine that they were motivated by the former.

YOUR TURN: WHAT ARE YOU LEARNING?

Forrest agreed to share his learning. "I was definitely ready to facilitate. It threw me off when the meeting [of the Design and Data Specialty teams] didn't go well. I have never been in a position like that. Things usually go smoothly for me."

What have you learned as a result of reading this chapter?

SO WHAT?

"Perhaps the problem needed to happen. I mean, perhaps it would have happened no matter who was facilitating. Maybe we just needed to deal with some ambiguity. I'm also wondering if I've ever facilitated meetings that weren't completely laid out, item-by-item, with no real thinking. I don't think I have."

What does your own learning mean to you? Why is it important?

NOW WHAT?

"I'm a little hesitant about facilitating, but I did get back on that horse, didn't I? I think I'll watch others and learn. And, I'll try facilitating again, I guess."

What will you do in terms of your own learning, based on this chapter?

RESOURCES FOR CHAPTER 4

4.1 Directions for Four Corners

4.2 Diagram: Dialogue and Discussion

4.3 Rounds Protocol

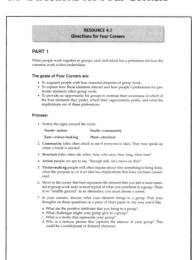

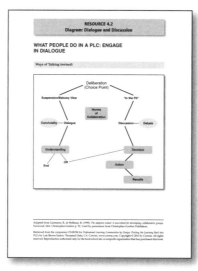

4.4 Dialogue and Debate

4.5 A Sample Set of Agreements for Dialogue

4.6 Directions for a Text-Based Dialogue

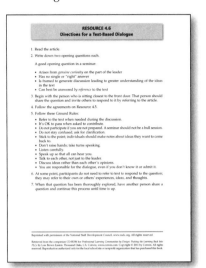

4.7 Text for a Text-Based Dialogue

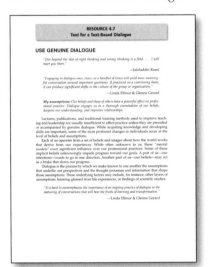

4.8 Protocols for Balancing Inquiry and Advocacy

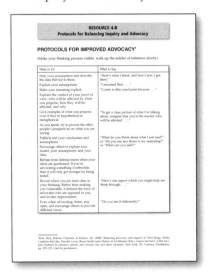

4.9 Trust Articles

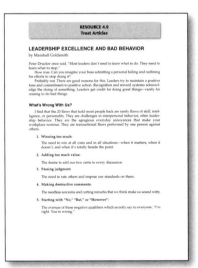

4.10 Four Corners as Experienced at GHMS

4.11 Dealing With Difficult People

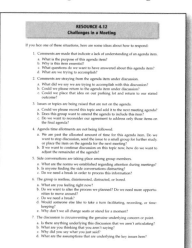

4.12 Challenges in a Meeting

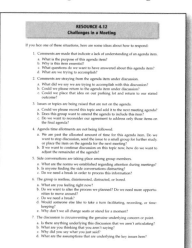

4.13 SWOT Analysis

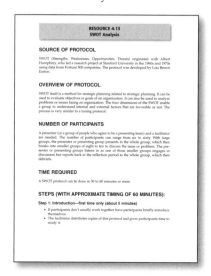

Appreciating New Data; Discovering Divergence (January–March)

In which five new specialty teams form to learn more about students, parents, community members, and the district. In which the Professional Learning Community (PLC) labors mightily to make sense of the new data and in which they focus on struggling students. In which the Design Team gets unsettling news.

Glen Haven School District historically scheduled the first day back from winter vacation as a professional development day, without students. And so it was this year. Josie wasn't able to claim the whole day for her staff, but they did get half the day to continue their PLC work. After a districtwide meeting on school safety, Glen Haven Middle School (GHMS) staff returned to the middle school for a potluck lunch and the year's first PLC.

The Design Team knew that focus was going to be a challenge. The holidays were on perpetual rewind for faculty and staff as they greeted each other and shared stories. Also, the school safety meeting had been scary because a keynote speaker led them in planning for threats, such as terrorist attacks. And everyone on the faculty was thinking about the return of students the next day.

Through e-mail, the Design Team planned a check-in to get everybody "on the same page." As people entered the library media center, they grazed not only the potluck table but also a long table on which Kelly had laid out the contents of the PLC portfolio he had been keeping. Tasha started the all-school PLC meeting with this statement: "Imagine that the book of school improvement at Glen Haven is being written, even as we speak. What would go into Chapter 1?" Based on their grazing of the portfolio table, faculty members contributed their memories "popcorn-style"—meaning that people spoke up as something occurred to them. As they did, three Design Team members charted their recollections on a piece of chart paper. A fine, full list emerged. The faculty realized that, indeed, they had accomplished a lot since August.

Ariel, the newest member of the Design Team, then led them to consider what was coming next— their own Chapter 2—by reminding them of the Proposed Action Plan they had examined before leaving for winter break. "Today," she said as members of the Design Team distributed copies of the plan to those who had forgotten it, "we have an hour or so to work with each other on specialty teams to plan actions related to our goals. Remember that we've decided to work first on Tier 1 goals, and we'll save the Tier 2 goals until we have some additional data from Tier 1 activities. Also, remember that we discovered after the Gallery Tour that we're not ready to analyze student work. Also, we need to get information from the district . . . from the district . . . and about other schools . . . from other schools. And—finally—we don't want to plan activities for parents and community until we know more about what they need and have the big picture."

Ahhhh, it was all coming back. Ariel continued, "Let's use today as a work day. In December we talked about five new specialty teams, with a member of the Design Team serving on each of them." She pointed to chart paper around the room, headed by these designations:

Interview Specialty Team

Focus Group Specialty Team

Shadowing Specialty Team

Parent and Community Members Specialty Team

District Connection Specialty Team

"Please take a moment and think about which team you'd like to work on. You don't have to work on any team—believe me, there will be more work to do later this year, and you'll get your chance. But, we'd like to have at least five members on each team. Choose your specialty team and stand by the chart. After you have worked together to create the first steps of a plan for what you're going to do on your specialty team, you can go ahead and work in your classrooms. We'll need your plans as soon as possible. We'll need your data by February 12, our early-release half-day." She paused and looked around expectantly. "I think we'll be able to find some time for you to work between now and then. Josie is dedicating the faculty meeting on January 21 to your work. So," she said, at last, "if you don't want to work on a team right now, you can go ahead and work in your classrooms. . . ."

The dates were daunting enough. Would anyone stay? The Design Team collectively held a breath, awaiting an exodus to classrooms, but many faculty and staff members walked to a piece of chart paper, enough so that each specialty team had six to eight members.

PROFESSIONALISM

What if all of the teachers had walked out and gone into their classrooms to prepare for students who were coming back the next day? You could hardly blame them! They had a lot to think about and do before 7:30 a.m. on Tuesday.

The Design Team hoped, of course, that most would stay. Design Team members were counting on the GHMS faculty to react to the invitation as professionals. Judy Wurtzel, a senior fellow at the Aspen Institute working with its Education and Society Program in Washington, D.C., describes the "old" professionalism as *autonomy*: "freedom to make decisions about what, how, and sometimes even whom to teach" which, unfortunately does not lead to instructional improvement (2007, pp. 30–31). Some who entered the profession "back in the old days" did so because they expected to shut the door and teach what and how they wanted. However, according to Wurtzel, what's needed in today's schools is "robust teacher professionalism [that] . . . places accountability for results and the use and refinement of effective practices at the core of teaching" (p. 31).

Here are six tenets of the new professionalism:

1. A professional owes her primary duty to her clients—in the case of educators, to students.

2. Professionals are accountable to the profession for results.

3. A professional has a duty to improve her own practice.

4. A professional has a duty to improve common or collective practice in the profession.

5. Professionals adhere to a body of specialized knowledge, agreed-upon standards of practice, and specific protocols for performance.

6. Professionals are expected to exercise professional judgment (Wurtzel, 2007, pp. 32–34).

It is hard to be professional when the task to be accomplished has been assigned from above, is mindless in nature, or is devoid of connection to student learning. Notice that the work to be done by the five new specialty teams is none of these; this work requires professionalism, and the GHMS faculty rose to the challenge. Professionalism, of course, is inherent in professional learning strategies such as data collection and analysis (see Resource 1.2). Although they had only a half-day to get ready for students, the task they were asked to engage in honored their professionalism.

The five specialty teams worked throughout January to prepare for the February 12 early-release day. The Design Team gave up its January meetings—letting the substitutes who were coming for them cover the classes of the specialty teams instead. Josie gave up one of her faculty meetings so the five specialty teams could work. Let's look at what the specialty teams did to prepare for the February 12 early-release half-day.

The Interview Specialty Team

The first meeting of this team turned out to be a meeting to make a plan for making a plan. It seemed ludicrous at the time, but the team agreed on a need to clarify their work before planning action. Members joked that they really needed to make a plan for making a plan to make a plan. The first issue for them was purpose: "Why have we been formed? Why do we need interviews?"

The team deliberated over these reasons for their existence:

- *The GHMS faculty and staff do not have enough data about students to plan work that will help all students learn better.*
- *The results of the survey are ambiguous.*
- *One way to clarify what students need is to interview them.*
- *We especially need evidence related to literacy and engagement since those showed up on the five goals from the faculty and are Tier 2 goals.*

It didn't take long for members of the Interview Specialty Team to realize that they should be working with the Focus Group Specialty Team, which was going to meet the next day. "Our only difference," Julianne Blake said, "is the method we'll use. Don't we want the same information? Have the same goals?" The rest of the specialty team agreed with her, and Aaron, the representative from the Design Team, texted Lorena Soltar, "Cn we invite ourselves to yr mtg tomorrow PM?" Lorena responded quickly, "R U kidding? Why wld we wnt U guys? Yes. P.S. Bring cookies." Aaron shared her message, and the group hit the grocery stores for cookies on the way to work the next morning.

The Focus Group Specialty Team

A variety of cookies and members of the Interview Design Team were enthusiastically welcomed the next day. Juli (Julianne) explained the thinking behind their request for a joint endeavor and shared their ideas about purposes. Benjamin LaSala (Ben) from the Focus Group Specialty Team spoke up, "Should we also meet with the Shadowing Specialty Team?" Juli responded for her team and then looked around to see if what she said met with their approval: "I think they're doing something a little different. They're going to be following students around to discover what students experience, here and in other schools. They will probably be working inductively. We're working deductively. We know what we need to find out because we're designing questions. They will find out . . . what they find out. They might want to do focus groups or interviews after their shadowing."

"But," said Aaron, "we should probably let them know what we're investigating?"

Nods of approval. "Remember the axiom, 'Who needs to know? Who else needs to know?'" someone said.

"I think we should go back to the survey data," Ben suggested. "We didn't do a whole lot with the results of the data when we did our analysis. I think we've got a lot of information in those results."

Five minutes of discussion—rather, dialogue—followed, and Aaron called for a decision. It was pretty unanimous: Get a clearer idea of what the survey data tell us. "We need pictures of the data first," Aaron said, "and then we need to look at the numbers and the pictures and decide what to do next in terms of interviews and focus groups." Aaron was absolutely right about the need for pictures (see Chapter 3). A team of three volunteered to create some graphs of the survey data for the next meeting. Grace Nugent volunteered to do some research about interviewing and holding focus groups with students so they would have some guidelines for their tasks at the next meeting.

At their next, combined meeting, they examined and commented on the pictures of the data (see Resource 3.4 for the numbers as well as graphs of the survey data). Using both numbers and pictures, they studied the survey data and came up with some findings (see Figure 5.1).

Figure 5.1 Findings From the Survey Data

Survey Question #1 asked respondents to identify their roles. Because responses to other questions are disaggregated by roles, the Interview and focus Specialty Teams did not analyze this question.

Survey Question #2: Length of time in school (associated with school)

Even though GHMS is an "old" school, very few people have any history of it, teachers excepted.

The community has quite a few who have "known" GHMS for 3 to 5 years, however (a series of children from the neighborhood going through it?).

Parents have had between 1 and 2 years' experience with the school (not many older siblings attending?).

Faculty has the most people who've known the school for more than 5 years, but students have known the school less than a year or only 1 to 2 years.

So, who has the history? Who is able to understand GHMS over time? Who can understand the past as it applies to the future?

Survey Question #3: GHMS is doing a good job educating students

Bias toward the middle, especially for students.

Parents and the community are pretty well balanced in terms of viewing the efficacy of the school (i.e., fairly even proportions of those in each rating).

Students are heavy on *neither agree nor disagree* or *disagree*. Perhaps combine the categories *completely disagree* and *disagree* and contrast to a combination of *agree* and *completely agree*. Omit *neither agree nor disagree* (tendency toward the middle?) (A negative attitude about the school?).

Faculty rated the item with slightly more *agree* or *completely agree* (A positive attitude about the school?).

Survey Question #4: Students are challenged by the program at GHMS

Students, again, are rather negative about this . . . or neutral.

The community is relatively balanced.

Parents are relatively favorable.

Teachers are also relatively favorable.

Survey Question #5: Students are offered sufficient support for learning at GHMS

Students *disagree* or tend toward *neither agree nor disagree* with this item.

Parents and community are rather balanced, with a few more members of the community completely agreeing.

Faculty tend to be neutral or *agree* or *completely agree* by a slight difference.

Do we need more information here? If so, what kind of information?

Survey Question #6: Students are engaged in their learning at GHMS

The picture of these data is different in terms of *X* and *Y* labels. Confusing.

Community members largely *agree* or *completely agree*.

Parents are highest in neither *agree* nor *disagree*.

Students are really high in *neither agree nor disagree,* with *disagree* coming in next.

Faculty are either *disagree* or *neither agree nor disagree* (about 20% each) or *agree* and *completely agree*.

Figure 5.1 (Continued)

Survey Question #7: Students are encouraged to grow personally at GHMS

Students are high in *neither agree nor disagree* and *disagree.*

Parents are high in *neither agree nor disagree* and *agree.* Community is high in *neither agree nor disagree, agree,* and *completely agree.*

Faculty are highest in *agree* and *completely agree.*

**Survey Question #8: Students are
provided appropriate avenues for social growth at GHMS**

Again, students are high in *neither agree nor disagree* and *disagree.*

Community is highest in *neither agree nor disagree, agree,* and *completely agree* (with *completely agree* getting more tallies).

Between 20% and 25% responded by saying they *neither agree nor disagree, agree,* or *completely agree.*

Faculty have almost even scores in *agree* and *completely agree* (their two highest choices).

Survey Question #9: Students are safe at GHMS

Again, students are highest in *neither agree nor disagree,* with their second highest tally for *disagree.*

Community members mostly *agree* or *completely agree,* with *completely agree* the highest tally.

Parents are about even in terms of *neither agree nor disagree* and *agree,* with *completely agree* next.

Faculty about evenly *agree* or *completely agree* with this statement.

**Survey Question #10: Students are
being well prepared for high school work at GHMS**

Students, again, either *neither agree nor disagree* or *disagree.*

Community members mostly complete *agree*

Parents are divided by slight differences in three categories: *neither agree nor disagree, agree,* and *completely agree.*

Faculty are almost evenly *completely agree* and *agree,* with *neither agree nor disagree* and *disagree* almost evenly tied.

"Yikes," Benjamin said. "It looks to me as if the community and parents are pretty satisfied with Glen Haven . . . or neutral. But, look at the differences between student ratings and our ratings!"

Julianne said, "In my mind, I added a question at the end of each item: Do we need more information here? If so, what kind of information?" Then she said, "One of the things we could do is fix up the survey and administer it again, especially to students."

"Help me understand what you mean by 'fix up,'" Josie ventured.

"Well, the survey seems to have been set up so that students responded generally about all students at Glen Haven: Students are being well-prepared for high school work at GHMS. They weren't asked whether the statement applied to them, so they didn't respond according to their own experiences.

Or their own opinions. We could personalize the survey, ask them if—according to their own experiences—the school is safe . . . and all of the other things we asked about ."

"What if we did that through the interviews?" Ben asked. "We could ask the general question about all students and then follow up with a personalized question, something like, "To what extent is that your experience at Glen Haven?"

"I'm thinking we have to be careful about making these interviews too long and complicated," another team member said.

"Same thing with the focus groups," someone said.

The most important decision the combined group made was to base questions for the interviews and the focus groups on the survey. Then, according to what Grace shared with them about conducting interviews (Resource 5.1) and focus groups (Resources 5.2 and 5.3), they separated and went to work on their own questions and processes.

THE INTERVIEWS

You can find questions the Interview Specialty Group prepared—and the interview script they prepared for them—on Resource 5.4. When you read the questions, please notice that the teams changed the word "completely" to "strongly." Someone pointed out to Josie that "completely" in front of either "agree" and "disagree" was superfluous, perhaps even redundant (agreement or disagreement being complete themselves, so the adverb is not needed). The team decided that the word "stronger" works because it denotes the strength of agreement or disagreement, not the completeness of it. You may agree . . . or disagree. Also notice that they did not provide a "neither disagree nor agree" choice.

One of the members of the combined specialty team found some helpful descriptions of self-directed learners in an article by Maurice Gibbons, "Pardon Me, Didn't I Just Hear a Paradigm Shift?" (2004, pp. 461–467).

- Individual approaches to learning
- Finding personal meaning in learning
- Self-motivation and ability to take the initiative
- Interest in seeking patterns
- Pursuing challenges
- Reflecting for self-understanding
- Self-guidance: knowing capacity and context
- Self-management: setting goals, making plans, taking action, timing, assessing results
- Metacognition
- Interdependence

They kept the literacy questions simple, related to how students think of themselves as readers, writers, listeners, and speakers, and how much GHMS has helped them become better in these literacy skills.

The Interview Specialty Team decided to completely randomize their selection of students, 10 from each of the three grade levels. They used a computer program to "pull names out of the hat" (see http://stattrek.com/Tables/Random.aspx or http://www.evaluationwiki.org/index.php/How_to_Use_a_Random_Number_Table), 10 per grade level (five per gender) within the grade level, and then sent notes to the parents or sponsors of the 30 students. Of the 30, all but two parents/sponsors gave permission for the interview, so they added the next two names on the list of students selected by the computer program.

They divided the interviews so that each of the five members of the team had six interviews to conduct, and would do two in each grade level. Except for one interviewee, they interviewed students who were not in their own classes. With approval of the faculty, they conducted their six interviews in a single week, using lunch and their own prep periods, pulling students out of classes for the 15-minute interview.

They followed a script (Resource 5.4) to standardize what they said and agreed that they could augment the script only if they were not getting specific answers (which left the decision to augment quite loose). They decided to begin generally ("What do you like about GHMS? What would you like to change?") and then narrow their questions to match the survey, with the addition of specific questions about engagement and literacy. They decided to eliminate the length of time the interviewee had "known" or "known about" Glen Haven, determining that the question was vague and the answers would not really help them understand what students need.

They devised a way to analyze the responses, tallying responses according to categories. They traded interview notes and analyzed each other's results. When they finished the analysis, they prepared to present interview data to the whole faculty. Their analysis can be found on Resource 5.5.

THE FOCUS GROUPS

The main difference between what the Interview Specialty Team and the Focus Group Specialty Team did is the process used by each teams. The Focus Group Specialty Team followed the procedures outlined by Harvetta Robertson and Shirley Hord (2008, pp. 53–62) in Resource 5.3. They decided to have separate grade level focus groups and randomly chose 10 students (five from each gender) from each of the grade levels (eliminating from the pool of possibilities students who were engaging in the interviews). They identified a student in each of the focus groups who could cofacilitate the focus group with one of them, and they met with each of the cofacilitators the day before the focus group days to help them understand what to do.

Another difference is the quantity of questions they wanted the student co-facilitators to ask; they reduced the number used by the interviewers considerably, coming up with these basic questions:

1. Do you think Glen Haven is doing a good job educating students? What examples/experiences do you have to illustrate your opinion?

2. Do you think Glen Haven is both challenging you and supporting you in your learning? What examples/experiences do you have to illustrate your opinion?

3. Do you think Glen Haven students are engaged in their learning? Do you think they take charge of their own learning? What examples/experiences do you have to illustrate your opinion?

4. Do you think Glen Haven helps students grow personally and socially? What examples/experiences do you have to illustrate your opinion?

5. Does Glen Haven provide a safe environment for learning? What examples/experiences do you have to illustrate your opinion?

6. Does Glen Haven help you be a better reader, writer, listener, and speaker? What examples/experiences do you have to illustrate your opinion?

7. What works at Glen Haven Middle School? What should be kept or improved?

8. What does not work at Glen Haven Middle School? What would you eliminate? What would you add?

Josie was able to figure out how to release the five teachers on the Focus Group Specialty Team for a single day by taking some classes herself, hiring two substitutes, and asking for volunteers to cover classes on their prep periods. The focus groups met in a conference room near the administrative offices (a big deal for students, since it was usually used by adults only and featured "executive" chairs) and snacked on cookies and lemonade provided by the kitchen for the focus group sessions.

For each of the focus groups (sixth, seventh, and eighth grades) there were two circles of chairs in the room, an inner circle for students, who sat around the conference table, and an outer circle of teachers. Members of the Focus Group Specialty Team took turns serving as the adult facilitator, with Ben LaSala playing that role in the seventh-grade focus group. He sat in the outer circle but close to the student facilitator, DeeAnn, who sat with her peers in the inner circle. Ben welcomed both groups and had students and teachers introduce themselves. Then, he explained the purpose and structure of the process: "Remember when we did the survey in the fall? We surveyed you and other students, your parents and other parents, community members, and ourselves as faculty and staff. This is a follow-up on that survey. We need additional information from students; we may also need additional information from parents, community members, and us, but we're going to start with you.

"DeeAnn will be cofacilitating this group with me. Mostly, DeeAnn will ask the questions and decide when more details and discussion are needed and when to move on. The rest of us—teachers—will be listening in (like 'flies on the wall'). One of us will record what you say on the chart paper around the room. If our recorder is getting what you said wrong on the chart paper, do not hesitate to correct what is written.

"We won't use your names in our notes or in our report to the rest of the faculty, although we may refer to this group as the seventh-grade focus group. We will not stop you or interrupt you. At the end we may come in with a few more questions to clarify anything we're confused about, but we'll be completely silent while you talk among yourselves.

"So, please talk freely. Even if you're afraid you may hurt our feelings, please say what needs to be said, what we need to hear. Tell us good things, too! What you say will be combined with what the other two focus groups say . . . and we pledge not to use your names anywhere in our report or when we talk about the report. This process is entirely confidential. Any questions?"

Then DeeAnn asked the first question and led students in a "round robin" response process. After that, she opened up the discussion to anyone and asked for examples before going on to the next question. Occasionally the two cofacilitators whispered about the process, which led DeeAnn to say to the other students something like, "Could we have a few more examples of how you are challenged at Glen Haven?"

In the next step, students turned their chairs to face the adults and engaged in follow-up questions framed by the teachers. In two of the focus groups there were two students per teacher, which worked well because students sometimes find a one-on-one conversation a little intimidating. In the third, one teacher chatted with three students.

The after-conversation can be the most interesting part of a focus group. Some students wanted to clarify what they had said. Some adults wanted additional details or points of view. Some—both teachers and students—just wanted to share amusing stories or anecdotes related to the focus group discussion. Laughter was common during this time, and students appeared comfortable.

Then, Ben asked the students to debrief the process: "What worked? What was hard for you?" When the students had finished their debriefing, he asked the same question of the adults, and then thanked the students and dismissed them to their classes.

After the students left, Ben asked his colleagues to reflect what they had learned. The recorder captured these immediate reflections on the chart paper, and two of the members of the Focus Group Facility took the chart paper with them to analyze in more depth and put into a bulleted report, Resource 5.6.

Members of the shadowing specialty team were unsure about how to proceed. Just what, exactly, is shadowing? Where could they go to shadow? What should they expect? What could they request? Josie suggested that one of the team contact Stephanie Hodges at the district office to get some information about shadowing. Thank goodness Stephanie knew something about shadowing, but she admitted that no schools in the district had hosted shadows or had staff who had shadowed. "You're the scouts," she said. "Come back and tell us farmers where the alligators are."

SHADOWING

The team used the information in Resource 5.7 to design their shadowing experience. They decided on two places to visit—the other middle school in the district and a neighboring middle school. Then, they wanted to shadow in Glen Haven Middle School. Josie was able to secure substitutes for three days for all five of them, running the substitute budget quite low!

They were clear about their purposes for shadowing:

- We want to know how students experience three middle schools, including our own.
- We want to focus on getting more data related to the survey students took at GHMS.
- We especially want to collect data about student engagement and literacy from what we observe.

They had also thought through how they wanted to shadow and communicated these expectations to the two outside host schools:

- We each want to follow a student to classes and all activities (excepting lunch and bathroom breaks).

- When we are in a class with the person we're shadowing, we want to do whatever the students are doing.
- We are not shadowing a student in order to evaluate a teacher or the principal. We may make reference in our notes to what a teacher or principal is doing, but we will not identify the teacher by name or any definitive characteristic.
- We will not refer to schools, teachers, or students by name. If we need to reference what we've learned, we will use an uppercase letter for the school (A, B, C), a lowercase letter (a, b, c) to refer to a teacher, and a number for the student (1, 2, 3, etc.).
- We want to be able to talk to the student before the day begins to explain what we're doing and why, and we want to talk to the student at the end of the day to debrief the experience.
- We would like to debrief with a few faculty members of the host school at the end of the school day so that we can ask questions and—if the host school wants—share our observations.
- In our report we will blend what we learned at all three schools according to themes that emerged, so our report will not be about any particular school.

Stephanie made the arrangements for both the in-district and out-of-district shadowing experiences. She offered reciprocity to both schools—"Come shadow us and give us some feedback about what happens to students at our school."

THE DISTRICT CONNECTIONS SPECIALTY TEAM

Stephanie was able to help this team as well. She sat with them over coffee one afternoon after school and went through the directory of district staff, name by name, describing the myriad responsibilities of each person. Team members organized their information by task and then name, rather than name and task. As Stephanie related what each person did, she realized that others might want a sort of "Who ya gonna call?" guide to district support, in addition to the conventional district directory by department and name. So, the process benefited the district as well as the Glen Haven Specialty Team.

She gave them the name and phone number of the person to talk to in each of Glen Haven's schools—the principal or AP, a teacher, and (because they may know more than anyone else in the school), the school administrative assistant or secretary. The team divided up the schools and agreed to ask contact persons the same starter question: "What are some of the special things people in your school do to help students learn?" Depending on the answers, they asked a variety of other questions, such as, "What is the most innovative aspect of your school?"

When the team finished, they melded their notes into an alphabetically ordered booklet called Who Who Does What in GHSD *and gave a copy to Stephanie who shared it with the superintendent, who presented it to the Board of Education. GHMS was a feather in the district's cap!*

This specialty team went one step further. At their request and with wholehearted support from the Design Team, Josie made an appointment for the Design Team to sit with the superintendent and the president of the Board of Education. It was time to let those who could be supportive know what was going on . . . and ask them for support. Aaron prepared a short PowerPoint on what GHMS had been doing—lots of bullets for executive eyes. With the basics taken care of quickly, the Design Team found that discussion came easily.

As the clock hands closed in on a quarter to the hour, the Design Team and the superintendent and board president had nearly finished their discussion. Largely, the officials were supportive. The superintendent pledged to turn over a few rocks to find miscellaneous sources of funding so that the

Glen Haven PLC could do what it needed to do. The board president wondered if any rules and regulations would get in their way and urged the Design Team to contact her if they felt blocked in any way. In return, they wanted the Design Team to do the following:

1. *Make regular reports to the superintendent, who will share them with the Board; be prepared to present to the Board.*

2. *Show the PowerPoint and make a presentation at a superintendent's Cabinet meeting; send updates to a designated member of the Cabinet (probably Stephanie, who had already been so helpful).*

3. *Allow the superintendent to share the GHMS initiative with the regional area coordinator from the State Department of Education and be prepared to make a presentation to the Department or the State Board of Education.*

4. *Submit an article for the district newsletter to the community.*

5. *Allow the superintendent to include news of GHMS's effort in his column in the local newspaper.*

6. *Begin to identify desired results and determine evidence that shows that outcomes have been attained.*

The superintendent confessed that the state was just about ready to mandate PLCs in some form and that his Cabinet had been contemplating jumping the gun by requiring that schools initiate PLCs next fall. In fact, GHMS was doing the district a favor by giving PLCs a go before a mandate could come down to schools from the district or state.

Josie ventured a thought: "I'm not sure PLCs should be mandated. Based on our experience so far, I'd rather encourage them. Or, mandate them but offer schools a lot of choices in terms of how they create PLCs. And some money to buy time for teachers to meet."

The superintendent nodded sagely, as did the president of the Board. "Your suggestion taken," the superintendent said, "and we'll pass it along and consider it ourselves. Perhaps we could have a 'lessons learned' report in the spring."

"Done," Josie said. The Design Team huddled on the stoop outside the administration building and congratulated themselves. "I think the district is actually rather proud of us and our initiative," Tasha said. "We did the right thing by having that meeting."

THE TICKET AND THE PRICE OF THE TICKET

Systems thinker Suzanne Bailey (personal letter) noticed that people value something more if they have paid for it in one way or another—cash or in-kind. If something is free, it may not be worth much—or so the thinking goes. The superintendent offered support but asked the GHMS PLC to pay for it by letting him brag about what they were doing . . . and requiring regular updates. Eventually, the superintendent wanted evidence of results. GHMS got a "ticket" in terms of financial and policy support, and they paid in terms of accountability. A good deal all around!

CHAMPIONS

Initiatives need one or more sponsors, people in a high enough place to provide detours around barriers—or remove them entirely—and provide financial and policy support. As it turned out, Stephanie Hodges, the district's director of professional development, who was contacted by Josie before the process toward becoming a PLC had even been started, was the first champion. She had been wondering how to start PLCs in the district and found one way to do so when Glen Haven approached her. She put GHMS on her radar and mentioned what they were doing frequently during formal meetings, such as Cabinet meetings, and informally as she talked with her colleagues. She looked for ways to support the GHMS PLC work . . . and was ready to do battle on policy and other barriers that threatened. Most of all, she quietly established the credibility of Glen Haven's effort so that people at the district level—especially the superintendent and board president—were not surprised. They had heard good news from a respected colleague about what Glen Haven was doing. The context had been created; they were ready to learn more good news about Glen Haven.

The last thing district-level administrators and school board members need is a surprise. Stephanie prepared these people so they could support PLCs at Glen Haven. The district, in turn, would prepare the powers at the state level. Stealth is usually not the optimum strategy for engaging in innovation.

Sponsors or champions (one or more) are essential when a school or district engages in reform.

Of all the specialty teams, the Parent and Community Members Specialty Team didn't quite get it together in time for the half-day early-release day. The problem arose in part because of family problems the unofficial leader encountered, in part because no one stepped in to take over what she might have done as leader, and in part because the group wasn't sure what its purpose was or how to fulfill that purpose. As the day for reporting out arrived, two members of the team conducted two phone interviews each with parents. They asked all of the survey questions again and asked for examples to support the interviewees' answers.

A "FAILING" TEAM

Can teams fail? Members of the Parent and Community Members Specialty Team certainly felt they had failed. There appeared to be no sense of shared leadership; the group made an assumption about who would lead the work, and this person became distracted by family problems. Also, group members were not sure exactly why they were designated a team and what they were supposed to do. Failure is rather an absolute—either you have success or not; either you fail or not. I would rather think that this team is on its way to doing something great.

One of the best ways of thinking about success and failure is only three letters long: **y e t**. The Parent and Community Members Specialty Team was not *yet* accomplishing the task the faculty set before them.

This may be Pollyanna speaking again, but snags are natural in the complexity of school change work. It's not as if those in a school can stop long enough to think through and make significant changes before starting up again. Instead, school personnel have to proceed as well as possible while life is going on all around them. It's the old changing-the-tire-on-the-jet-as-it-noses-into-the-air conundrum! What to do?

Much has been written about teams, especially about leadership teams in education (Garmston & Wellman, 1999; Gregory and Kuzmich, 2007; McKeever and the

California School Leadership Academy, (2003). Among many other characteristics, successful teams seem to have the following:

- a compelling and clear reason for existing,
- a shared sense of commitment to the task, and
- a relationship between members that allows for distributed leadership.

The Parent and Community Members Specialty Team did not feel the compulsion that the other teams felt; in fact—as is unfortunately so often the case in terms of parent involvement—this item had felt like an add-on when the whole school was creating goals in September: "Oh, yeah. We need to focus on parent engagement." The team did not really know—yet—what its compelling task was to be. What was the problem? Why had faculty decided on a goal regarding parents and community members? It was the PC (politically correct) thing to do . . . but who was "in pain" in terms of parents and community communication? What was the pain?

This team fell into one of the traps that teams fall easily into—they assumed that someone would be the leader. In fact, their designated leader may not have known of her honor, assuming, instead, that leadership would be shared. When she was not able to do the things a leader would have done, no one else stepped up. This is a clear case of operating—or, rather, not operating—on assumptions that were not shared. In fact, assumptions about leadership can be more debilitating to a team than someone who steps up, says, "I will be the leader," and takes control.

Some teams find themselves wandering around the issue of leadership—it's something they have never discussed, and so it may be assumed that any one of a team—or none of them—will take on leadership tasks. Assumptions about leadership—especially if unspoken—can be the kiss of death to a team.

What needs to happen in most teams is an early discussion of leadership and agreements to share leadership roles—to take advantage of the assets each team member brings to a team and the variety of roles each can play (Resources 1.11 and 1.12)—and to ensure that no one person is expected to "do it all" while life goes on. The Parent and Community Members Specialty Team didn't have that conversation, and team members kept waiting for the assumed leader to step up and pitch the first ball.

Another trap the team fell into is assuming that team members had to figure everything out themselves, including a purpose for the team's existence. A team has a responsibility to return to the source of their designation as a team—in this case, to the whole faculty who decided to make parent and community involvement one of five goals. And the whole faculty may need to reconsider the task: Why did we decide to make parent/community involvement one of five goals?

Finally, although the Parent and Community Members Specialty team did not realize this, perhaps there simply wasn't enough data **y e t** from students or parents to help team members understand what to approach parents about.

To get ready for the February 12 meeting, three of the Specialty Teams—the Interview, Focus Group, and Shadowing Teams—had to analyze their data so that the entire faculty could come to some conclusions about the student experience of Glen Haven and what to do about it. Thank goodness all three teams had organized their work around the survey questions. They had the basis for organizing the data they had collected. You can find their analyses in Resources 5.5, 5.6, and 5.9.

The District Connections Specialty Team also met prior to February 12—not to organize their information around the survey questions, since they had not based what they did on those questions—but to publish the resource book they had produced about support available from the district offices and other schools in the district.

The Parent and Community Members Specialty Team sent e-mails to each other to see if they could set up an emergency meeting so they'd have something to present. They couldn't find a time when all could meet, so they decided individually that all they could do at the February 12 meeting is to report their failure, convey apologies and promise to do better after February 12.

The February 12 task would be huge. The Design Team spent a terrifying 30 minutes at the Design Team meeting preceding that date wondering how in the world they would facilitate the work of the five specialty teams. It was relatively easy to consider the separate work of the District Connections and Parent and Community Member Specialty teams, but how would they honor the work of the three teams working to gain insight on how students experience school? Roz texted Stephanie about the Design Team's formidable task and heard back quickly that one thing the Design Team should do is consider having an outside facilitator—which she agreed to be. She asked Roz to call her immediately—thank goodness she was available. Through a speakerphone, she suggested a strategy for the group: sentence strips.

Stephanie said, "After you have a report from the two 'outside' groups—those working on separate topics—have the three teams that worked to gain insight into student perceptions of school list their main findings, one at a time, on a sentence strip (a strip of chart paper that will hold a single sentence). Have them use different colored markers—or different colors of paper to do so. That way, when we start moving them, we'll be able to link the color to the source of the finding."

Roz asked, "Could the specialty teams decide beforehand what their top findings are?"

"Sure," Stephanie replied. "Good idea."

"So, then what happens?" Dottie asked.

"People 'read' the walls without moving anything for a few minutes. Then, you charge people with moving similar things together. As they do so, they need to announce the commonality that has made them join ideas from different specialty teams. In fact, you might have a spare set of sentence strips in a different color to use to name the categories."

"What if they can't do this?" Kelly asked. "What if they just stand there?"

"Well," Stephanie ventured, "I don't think that will happen. Since all three were focusing in different ways on students' experiences of school, I'll bet there will be lots of duplications. One thing will happen, however, and you need to be ready for it. People will get quiet and it'll look as if nothing much is happening. Let that happen for awhile. They may need to just look at the sentence strips and the way they've been categorized. If they don't move for 5 minutes or more, then it's time to check with the group. I'll ask them whether they'd like more time to contemplate the categorization—and let them have more time if necessary."

"Is that it?" Forrest asked.

"Not really," Stephanie responded. "I hope you'll have enough time to go to the next step, which involves thinking about the repercussions of the categories, what the sentence strips suggest to you about your work, why they're important. For example, you think you're going to want to work on literacy—well, there will probably be a few sentence strips about literacy. . ."

"I would hope so!" Robbie said.

". . . and someone needs to summarize those sentence strips and ask the questions 'So What' and 'Now What.'"

"Should that be done by the whole group?" Josie asked.

"Actually, I think I'd ask the whole group to form small groups to do the 'So What' and 'Now What' work."

"So, the language arts department should work on the literacy sentence strips?" Robbie said.

"Actually, I'd make the new groups cross-disciplinary and cross-grade level. There will be some categories that do not relate to specific subjects or grades. And, I think you might want to think outside the boxes of 'my subject' or 'my grade level.'"

"So, maybe, we can begin work on the 'So What' and 'Now What' at the meeting itself, and then we can form new specialty teams to address what comes up for us?" Forrest asked.

"Sure, let's just see how far we get at the February 12 meeting," Stephanie replied.

"Wow!" Roz said. "We're lucky to have you!"

"Actually, the pleasure is mine. I'm really looking forward to learning from you. You'll help me work with other schools. Remember, you're the scouts!"

ORGANIZING A COMPLEX MEETING

Some meetings are direct and straightforward—plan the first Back-to-School night. Some meetings *at first* seem to be direct and straightforward—plan the first Back-to-School night! Once people get into the task, they discover it to be more complex than it seemed at first. Some meetings are downright complicated, from the beginning. They may involve a large number of people. They may involve many issues. There may not be any clear pathways to solutions or resolutions. There may be many resolutions or solutions. The group may not achieve consensus on any of the resolutions or solutions. Think of Garmston's and Wellman's description of "wicked" problems (Chapter 1). The February 12 meeting was going to be one wicked meeting!

As you will see, the success of complex meetings depends on a number of factors:

- Shared information
- A way for everyone in the meeting to have a "voice" (no matter how many there are)
- Norms for behavior
- A compelling purpose
- A clear-cut process
- Flexibility in the process
- Expectation of results/outcomes
- Celebration

First, the Design Team asked the Specialty Teams to post their findings (Resources 5.5, 5.6, and 5.9) on the part of the school website that the whole staff could access. They asked the District Connections Specialty Team to post their directory. The Design Team then sent a series of e-mails to the whole faculty urging them to review the posted findings. The message strengthened with each iteration until the final one said, "Beware: You will not know as much as your colleagues if you come to the February 12 meeting without having read the findings on the website!"

Knowing the situation with the Parent and Community Members Specialty Team, the Design Team didn't ask team members to post anything, but the team as a whole decided to send an e-mail to everyone that explained the situation. The team received replies that assured them that it was OK not to have something to share on February 12; in fact, one reply stated, "Hey, don't beat yourself up over this. I'm thinking you'll find out on February 12 some things you can use to frame your work. No worries, mates!"

Then the Design Team asked the Interview, Focus Group, and Shadowing Specialty Teams to reduce their analysis to 10 to 20 sentence strips, using slices of chart paper and a colored marker. A member of the Shadowing Team replied to the Design Team's e-mailed directions, "How in the world can we do that? We need at least 50 sentence strips." "Try," Tasha sent back. Resource 5.10 contains the sentence strips from each group. You'll notice that the Shadowing Specialty Team got by with 25, the other two teams with 18 each.

Working with Stephanie, the Design Team decided to frame the February 12 meeting as a "What?" "So What?" and "Now What?" meeting, adapted from the work of Lipton and Wellman (2004). You've encountered this trio of questions at the end of every chapter in this book. The "What" part of the agenda would be the findings of the various specialty teams, especially the Interview, Focus Group, and Shadowing Specialty Teams. The faculty would read the sentence strips and organize them for the "What" part. In the "So What" part, they would divide into small groups to consider each set of related sentence strips, asking themselves what the data mean to Glen Haven—what they should do about the data. In the "Now What" part, they would organize next steps. Here is the agenda the Design Team and Stephanie came up with:

Activity[1]	Purpose	Materials and Procedure	Results
Welcome & Introductions	It has been a long time since the whole PLC met. Participants will be curious about how the meeting will go. Stephanie is not known by many of the faculty.	Josie does. Introduce Stephanie and explain her role in the work of GHMS. Have the Design Team stand up to be recognized. Have members of the Specialty Teams stand to be recognized. Have anyone who worked on an earlier Specialty Team stand to be recognized.	Appreciation for all of the people who have worked in one way or another on teams. PLC meets Stephanie.
Appreciation for the work of the District Support and the Parent/Community Teams	They may feel a bit "out of it" because the rest of the day is about the other three teams. The Parent/Community Team may be feeling especially vulnerable.	Josie does—holds up a copy of the report on district support and what the other schools are doing. Reassures the Parent/Community team that their time is yet to come—that they have not "failed." Use "yet."	Appreciation for the efforts. Knowledge of resources available through the district and through other schools. Understanding the dilemma of the Parent/Community Member Specialty Team.
Check-In	Focus on reactions to the analysis of the data from the interviews, focus groups, and shadowing. People may have strong feelings about the results or analysis.	Begin with a relatively innocuous and objective question, such as "What struck you about the analysis data? What did you notice? What caught your attention as you were reviewing the data?"	Shared perceptions. Focus on the day's business.
Overview of Agenda	The meeting is complicated, and people might be worried about how it will go.	E-mail agendas in advance but provide copies and have a simplified agenda on chart paper so that people can check where they are together.	Knowledge of the process—what comes first, second, next. . . . Confidence in the meeting.

(Continued)

[1]You may have noticed that the agendas crafted by the Design Team and others have varied slightly. GHMS has not yet formalized an agenda style—and that's OK because they have kept the agenda focused on purposes and/or results.

(Continued)

Activity	Purpose	Materials and Procedure	Results
Review of Norms	This will be a difficult meeting. People will have emotional connections to the data. Stephanie suggested some additional norms—draw attention to those.	E-mail the norms in advance. Have additional print copies available. Post a copy of the norms. Someone from the Design Team should go over them, ask for changes and then commitment.	Changes to the norms, if needed. Commitment to the norms.
Gallery Tour #1	Although they read the analyses/results of the Specialty Teams, participants need to see these expressed on sentence strips.	Have sentence strips on the wall, organized by color according to Specialty Group: Interview Results, Focus Group Results, Shadowing Results. Have people count off so that they are in three mixed groups to "read the walls" and discuss what they see. Allow 10 minutes for each group to read and discuss what they see before moving on.	Understanding of the sentence-strip version of the analyses.
Reflection	Participants need time to reflect on what they read.	Use a template and have people share with those at the same table.	Deeper understanding, emotional reaction.
Categorizing the Sentence Strips	The sentence strips will be redundant. This process can get chaotic. Use a "relay race" process.	Ask for five volunteers to start the categorization. After 10 minutes, ask for replacements for these categorizers. Continue until the categories seem settled and all sentence strips have a place.	Agreed-upon categories for further work.
Gallery Tour #2	Double-check the categories. This is the first step in consensus.	Have people reconvene in their groups for the first Gallery Tour. The key question is, "Does this organization work?"	Confidence in categories.
Introduce the What, So What, and Now What Process	People need to be able to trust the process they are using. Explain the rationale.	Stephanie can take the lead on this.	In-depth thinking about each category, with attention to all the sentence strips that fit that category.

Activity	Purpose	Materials and Procedure	Results
So What	This is an important part of the task. People need to decide why something matters to them, what difference it makes, what a change in it might mean for the school. People need to be sure something is critical to them before proceeding to action, especially if what they are considering is difficult or challenging to the current system.	Have groups form around the categories (actually go to the part of the room where there are sentence strips for that category). If there are more than 10 people clustered in front of a category, invite them to form two or more groups. Provide time for them to consolidate their ideas before going to the next step. Have them write their consolidated "So What" statements on a piece of chart paper.	Understanding why action is important related to the categories and the sentence strips under them.
Reports	People need to hear the rationale for taking action according to the categories.	Have a spokesperson from each category present the "So What" statements for that category.	Understanding of the importance of the category and possible actions. Connections across categories.
Reflection and Discussion	People will need time to digest these ideas.	Have people write according to a prompt and then do "Take Ten" (or whatever number you want)—10 questions or comments before going on.	Feeling their voices are being heard. Possible addition/elimination of categories?
Now What	People need to think of first or big steps, not the whole process that needs to engage them.	Invite people to stay in their So What groups in order to plan first steps related to the category.	A few next steps—not an entire strategic plan—for each of the important categories.
Sharing Now What	People need to hear what kinds of things might be done.	Have Now What groups share the first one or two steps without elaboration.	Confidence that steps will be taken, but not too quickly.
Invitation to Work on New Specialty Teams	People need to attach themselves to work at this meeting so that they can begin deeper planning and action.	Have people move around again in order to stand by the What, So What, and Now What categories they'd like to work on. Many may stay where they are. Others may not go to a group.	Belonging to a new specialty team.
Evaluation of Meeting According to Norms	The norms can serve as a good way to evaluate how successful a meeting is.	Distribute a copy of the norms with a numeric scale. Leave room for comments. Collect. Note: May need an oral way to close meeting, too.	Chance to get and give feedback.

Comments From Check-In

- I am so depressed.
- Are we doing this bad?
- I'm glad students felt they could really, honestly, speak up.
- Is it worse here than in other middle schools?
- Do we need to pay so much attention to what students think?
- I'm glad they're paying attention to school, not just their social lives.
- I think they're right in terms of classes.
- We should pay attention to what students think.
- Our job is to think about what we're supposed to teach.
- I wasn't trained for this personal growth stuff.
- They don't need help from us in terms of social growth.
- Students are struggling here.
- We need to listen to them more often.
- We need to ask them about their learning more often.
- I'm really upset by their reactions.
- We're doing our best.
- We run the risk of losing them, starting at our school.
- They're just going through school; they're not really learning.
- What we're doing here used to work, maybe, but it doesn't work for kids today.
- I care more about my students than my subject.
- My job is to teach history, not personal growth.
- We've got to do something.
- I wonder what parents would think of these reactions to school.
- I wonder what the district would think if we made a lot of changes here.
- I'm worried that we're losing too many students in terms of their learning.

February 12: And so it happened. Not easily, of course. The planned check-in was exactly the right thing to do. People shared their reactions to what students had said in the interviews and focus groups as well as to what the shadows had learned. You can read a few of their reactions in the box.

Dottie recorded these and other comments so the Design Team could consider them later.

The faculty was still using the set of starter norms (Resource 1.15) that the Design Team used. The Design Team had already added a norm about checking on the norms before and after meetings. They had also added a norm about how to deal with people who broke norms:

We will call for a "norm check" when we think someone might be violating important norms.

Stephanie suggested a further addition, saying, "Our process today is very different from typical linear planning. It will be messy. You may be frustrated." Here is the norm she suggested.

We will call for a "process check" when we're not sure the process we're following is leading to results.

She added, "It might be that we'll alter the process in some way, but at the very least we'll clarify the process."

The categorizing of the sentence strips was less chaotic than the Design Team expected, partially because it took place in rounds. Another way to think of the process is to think of a relay race. One group got as far as it could with the sentence strips and then handed off the task to the next group. People who were not in the first round paid close attention because they knew they might be in the second or third round . . . even the fourth or fifth group if the process required that many reconsiderations. In fact, that day, there were only three rounds, those in the second round collapsing the first group's six categories into three, and the third group making a case for breaking one category into two and reinstalling one category, for a total of four categories.

Some people loathe this part of process—the organizational part—and they are glad to let others engage in it. Others see things clearly and in their own ways and want to have an impact on organization of ideas. Having volunteers for each successive group ensures that those who care are involved and those who do not care can avoid the process, but step in if needed. Usually, everyone is happy!

WAYS TO CATEGORIZE AND MOVE TOWARDS CONSENSUS

Sentence strips help groups, especially large ones, categorize items. They help groups decide, together, what they have or what they know. They move a group toward consensus. Members can see what's written on sentence strips. They are movable and adjustable. One caution: Don't throw away any sentence strips—the original strips may need to be referenced later. Or, make a record of the sentence strips before they are categorized and then record them again under their categories. A camera works well for this process, or the groups originating the sentence strips can keep a record (as happened at GHMS), or someone can enter them into a computer and put them on a website or send them out to an online group.

Another caution: Make sure that each subsequent group is accountable for what the previous group has done. They can't just ignore a category created by a previous group or a sentence strip that is an outlier. If possible, have those in each round discuss aloud with each other what they are doing and why . . . and encourage them to speak loudly enough that their reasoning can be heard by the entire group.

You can view the sentence strips created by the Interview, Focus Group, and Shadowing Specialty Teams in Resource 5.10.

Sticky notes can work well when the group is small. People can move them around a table at which all are sitting. Again, don't throw away the stickies or capture them in some way before they are categorized. And, of course, capture them under their categories.

Other ways of categorizing or prioritizing include these (information about these processes is included on Resource 5.13 and other resources in this book, noted in parentheses):

1. Delphi (see Resource 1.16)

2. Visual dialogue and gallery tours (see Resources 3.15, 3.16, and 3.17)

3. Carousel/round robin/round table with chart paper (see Resource 5.13)

4. Lenses/criteria (see Resource 5.13)

5. Fishbone analysis (see Resource 5.13)

6. Round-the-room (see Resource 5.13)

7. Stoplight (see Resource 5.13)

Voting is not a good way to get consensus, unless a group has defined consensus as some percentage of the whole: 100%? 75%? 60%? One hundred percent agreement is rare—even if people basically agree with an idea or action, they sometimes want to register some trepidation, just in case things don't turn out at the end. So a straight thumbs-up/down vote can kill an idea or action, even one that is basically good.

Try Fist-to-Five (Chapter 3) before you vote. Use this simple strategy to test the waters and then revise the idea or action, if you are able, so that everyone is relatively happy with the decision. A group can then measure consensus with the same strategy, first deciding how many fingers must be held up by everybody. Four is certainly sufficient, indicating that participants basically support the idea or action and may do something to implement the idea or action but definitely will not sabotage it.

If voting is important to the process, consider list reduction and weighted voting (Delehant, 2007, pp. 136–137). After participants brainstorm a list of ideas or action (much as the teams did when they produced the sentence strips based on analysis of their data), they should review it for clarity and revise sentences if necessary.

Then, participants should cluster the ideas under headings without eliminating any of them—this is equivalent to what Stephanie had the GHMS faculty do in the categorizing rounds.

The next step is different, however. Participants generate a set of filters or lenses for evaluating the ideas or actions. The filters could be as simple as prioritizing through the words *Essential, Important, Nice to do.* They can address the impact of the change: *All students. Most students. Some students.* Or the reach of the change: *Whole school. Grades. Classrooms. Students.* Filters can address capacity ("Can we do this?") and effect ("Will this make a difference?"). Filters can hone in on possible limitations: *Expensive. Moderately costly. Inexpensive. Immediately. In the next year. Two to 5 years.* The GHMS faculty might have wanted to survey the sentence strips according to these questions:

1. What can we affect/do something about? What is our capacity?

2. If improved, what might make the most difference for student learning? What would have the greatest effect?

Based on these lenses—perhaps using them one at a time—the group votes on each item. Majority votes indicate where on the following grid (which you encountered in Chapter 4) the item should be placed. For example, a majority vote "yes" on Question #1 (capacity) and the same for Question #2 (effect), would put the item in the upper right hand corner of the grid (high capacity and high effect). A minority vote (over 50% "no") for Question #1 and the same for Question #2 would put the item in the lower left hand corner of the grid (low capacity and low effect). A mixed vote (majority for one of the lenses, a minority in the other) would put the item in one of the other two squares. In no case should an item be discarded; also, proponents of an item can certainly restate its case in favor of the quality(ies) that got a minority vote.

	Low Capacity	*High Capacity*
High Effect		
Low Effect		

If you have an item that you want implemented, it should end up in the upper right square, of course: High capacity and high effect. You *don't* want it to be shelved in the lower left box. P.S. Sometimes categorization like this is called cost-benefit analysis.

To make final decisions, a group may want to winnow the upper right hand category a bit. This can be done through other lenses, such as Important to Parents and Not Important to Parents.

Weighted voting can also help the group reduce the final list of actions or ideas (such as those from the upper right hand box). On a large piece of chart paper or a white board, the facilitator numbers the actions or ideas to be considered and puts them on the left hand side of a grid:

	Respondent #1	*Respondent #2*	*Respondent #3*	*Respondent #4 (etc.)*
Idea/Action #1				
Idea/Action #2				
Idea/Action #3 (etc.)				

Individuals write a number (1 through 5, perhaps, with 1 being low) to indicate the importance they would give to each idea or action. The facilitator adds up the numbers and averages them . . . and, voilà, the group has a prioritized list. You can probably see that this activity takes a bit of preparation and may also take a bit of time (especially if the group is large). Voting can be done with sticky dots (spent in a variety of ways, including use of all of them for one item). Use of electronic "clickers" is one way to expedite the process.

Other ways of weighted voting occur when the number to be awarded equals the number of items, thus requiring the participants to rank order the items (if there are 10 items, each individual can use numbers 1 to 10 only once in the voting). Or, the facilitator can issue each group member a set of sticky colored dots, allowing participants to place them next to the idea/items in any way they want (for example, with six dots, a person can place all six on one item, or five on one and one on another, or two on one and four on another, etc.).

Even with this kind of voting, the process might not be over because participants should always be allowed to consider the ramifications of their voting. Through reflection and debriefing, a facilitator can help a group understand if they liked the way the voting turned out—"Do these results lead us to the desired outcomes?" A hearty discussion may ensue, with participants debating the results and working toward consensus in another way.

At GHMS, the process worked well without going into voting. Six categories emerged clearly, and the sentence strips were easily placed into them. Then, in two more rounds, described below, the GHMS staff reduced the number of categories to three and then came up with the final four.

A BROADER VIEW OF WHAT, SO WHAT, AND NOW WHAT

You have encountered this triad of questions at the end of every chapter to help you process your learning as it relates to reading this book. Although I have used the questions to help you focus on your learning (What have you learned? So, what does your learning mean? Now what are you going to do about your learning?), they can lead to other considerations. For example, the *What* question can lead to

What do we know?	What is real?
What is going on?	What are we discovering?
What are the facts?	What is happening?

The *So What* question (as either *So, what* or *So what*) can lead to these considerations:

Why is this important?	Why should we care?
What do we feel about this?	Who cares?
What does this mean for our present?	
What does this mean for our future?	
Why does this matter?	Will it matter in the future?
Will it ever matter?	What is important about this?

The *Now What* question can lead to

If/Since this matters, what do we do about it?

What do we do first? Next? Then?

What is our plan?

What outcomes or results do we want at the end of our actions?

Do we need to stop doing something, change what we're doing, add something?

The templates GHMS used to create the *So What* and *Now What* parts are included in this chapter as Resources 5.11 and 5.12.

Here are the first categories GHMS found for the three sets of sentence strips:

- School Culture (What Matters to Students; Safety; "Core" in seventh and eighth grades)
- Classroom Culture (Rigor, Personalization, Challenge, Engagement, Support, "Fun," Risk-Taking)
- Expectations: Curriculum, Instruction, and Assessment
- Personal and Social Growth/Relationships
- Literacy
- Parent Involvement in Terms of Personal and Social Growth; Surviving Middle School

Here is the second set of categories:

- School Culture (What Matters to Students; Safety; "Core" in seventh and eighth grades; Personal and Social Growth)
- Classroom Culture (Rigor, Personalization, Challenge, Engagement, Support, "Fun," Risk-Taking, Expectations, CIA, Literacy)
- Parent Involvement in Terms of Personal and Social Growth; Surviving Middle School

The third group settled on these categories, which the whole group approved using Fist-to-Five, with no three, two, one, or fist responses.

- School Culture (Parents and Community; Safety; "Core" in seventh and eighth grades, etc.)
- Classroom Culture: Student Viewpoint (Personalization, Engagement, "Fun," Support)
- Classroom Culture: Educator Viewpoint (All of the Above + Rigor, Challenge, Engagement, Risk-Taking, Expectations, CIA, Literacy)
- Parent Involvement in Terms of Personal and Social Growth; Surviving Middle School

---

The faculty divided into groups according to the category they most cared about. Because there were more than 10 people wanting to work on School Culture and both versions of Classroom Culture, the groups subdivided to consider the So What and Now What parts of the process. They met together to consolidate their work on So What and Now What before reporting to the whole group.

The meeting ended with a check on norms plus the standard questions: *What worked for you today? What could have been better?* Design team members collected surveys to be tallied and analyzed.

Then, Stephanie rapped her glass and asked for permission to speak to the whole group. Here is what she said:

I was reading a second- or third-rate novel I had picked up in desperation in the airport one day. Suddenly, I got to a part that made all the overdrawn characters and the overly coincidental plot worth the read. One character said about another, "Learning becomes her."

I was struck by that description. How nice that learning became her, just like a red hat or pearls or a nifty haircut or tie. She was enhanced by her learning. She was better because of her learning. In another sense, she became a learner. "Become" is one of those "to be" verbs that results in a predicate nominative (although I hated to teach grammar and resisted it in favor of writing, I have to admit that I understand grammar). "Learning is her." "She is learning." Or, "She = learner."

I thought about schools, including this one. I must tell you that—based on what happened today—you are learners. Learning becomes you. Congratulations! By the way, I dragged myself through the rest of that novel but found no more gems. The book ended predictably, and the characters have fled my mind. I left the book in a hotel room somewhere.

The room was quiet for enough time to be countable, and then the GHMS staff, weary as they were, rose to their feet and applauded Stephanie and themselves.

Jubilation! That's the word that describes the atmosphere at the next Design Team meeting, March 6. After they had congratulated themselves and celebrated the faculty's February 12 work, however, Josie asked to speak. She looked around at the faces of her friends and colleagues, knowing that what she would say would hurt them. "February 12 went well," she said, "for most of the staff. I have to tell you, however, that three staff members have seen me since then, and they are very upset at the way the school is going. They say they are speaking for many others. I thought you should know."

YOUR TURN: WHAT ARE YOU LEARNING?

"I don't know what the teachers are learning," DeeAnn said. "Something is different at Glen Haven Middle School this year." You'll remember that DeeAnn was the student facilitator for the seventh-grade focus group. "I'm learning that they care about Glen Haven. They really want to see us learn . . . and . . . and be happy!"

What have you learned in this chapter?

SO WHAT?

"The 'happy' part is important. I don't think we can learn if we're not happy," DeeAnn continued. "That doesn't mean that we're all smiley all the time. It just means that we look forward to going to school. I think if we have something to look forward to, then we'll learn."

Why is what you have learned from this chapter important to you?

NOW WHAT?

"I am already seeing a change in students. They are more eager to learn, I think. How do we continue this? I think teachers need to make it much more obvious to us why learning is exciting. They need to share what they love. They need to ask us to share what we love."

What are some first steps you might take to act upon what you learned?

RESOURCES FOR CHAPTER 5

5.1 Basics of Conducting Interviews With Students

5.2 Basics of Conducting Focus Groups With Students

5.3 Steps for Conducting a Focus Group

5.4 Interview Script

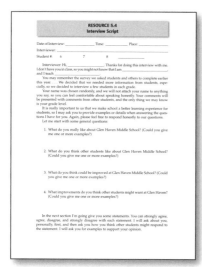

5.5 Analysis of Interview Responses

5.6 Analysis of Focus Group Comments

5.7 Shadowing Students

5.8 Classroom Observation Form for Shadowing

5.9 Analysis of Shadowing Results

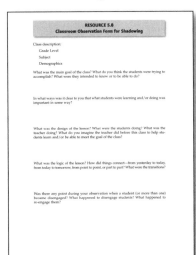

5.10 Sentence Strips

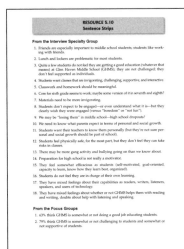

5.11 So What Template

5.12 Now What Template

5.13 Ways to Categorize and Move Towards Consensus

6

Grappling With Change; Pursuing Protocols (March and April)

In which the Design Team learns about developmental and needs-based reactions to change and in which the English Department takes off on its own: an all-staff writing assessment and an experience in using a tuning protocol with student work. Also, in which the Design Team considers a conundrum.

"That can't be," Tasha said, referring to Josie's revelation that three staff members had reported that they "and many other staff members" are very upset at the work the school is doing through the Professional Learning Community (PLC), the Design Team, and the Specialty Teams. The atmosphere in the room had changed from jubilation to gloom, thick as the gray carpet on the floor.

"We've done everything . . . everything!" Aaron claimed. "We have really worked hard to be sure everyone was on board."

"OK," Forrest said. "Who is it? I'll tell you what's going on."

Roz responded, "It really doesn't matter who it is. We need to consider what they said."

"Yeah," Forrest responded, "but who are all these other people that the complainers CLAIM they're speaking for?" The Design Team was quiet for a few moments, trying to deal with this unexpected assault on their processes.

Andy Mevoli, Mathematics, Sixth-Grade Core + Seventh and Eighth Grades

Robbie Beckel, Language Arts, Seventh and Eighth Grades

Ariel Aboud, Social Studies, Sixth-Grade Core

Forrest interrupted the silence, "Think about it. Who has not been part of any team—the Design Team, the Specialty Teams? Who doesn't really participate in PLC meetings?" He sat up straight and looked at each person around the table. Robbie thought to herself, "This is really a turnaround. I remember back in November he was not at all comfortable with the Design Team and its processes." She smiled, and Forrest thrust his chin out indignantly.

Josie said, "You know, I really don't think it makes a difference who it was. I also don't think we should assume that others are feeling the same way."

"I don't think we need their names either," said Ariel, the newest member of the Design Team. "I think we should focus on the issue, not the person."

"So, what should we do?" Andy, always the practical one.

"Let's confront the whole staff at the next early-release day!" Forrest said.

"Confront? That seems harsh, Forrest. It pits us against them. Not good," Tasha spoke up after listening quietly to her colleagues process the news. "I think we need to learn more about this . . . this dissatisfaction. What's going on? Why haven't people spoken up earlier? What are the issues? What haven't we done . . . but, more importantly, what can we do now to keep our effort from eroding?"

Aaron said with a bit of a smile, "I know you are not as old as I am. . . ."

"Har-de-har-har," Andy said. "Old?"

"Well, I remember this way of looking at people undergoing change. It was back in the 80s. Bam-Bam, I think. . . ."

Josie laughed, "I think that was the kid on the Flintstones, Aaron."

"Oh, yeah, maybe not Bam-Bam, but something like that."

"CBAM?" Josie asked.

"That's it! CBAM. Back in the 80s. It was all about how people react to change and what they need to engage in it."

"Hang on a minute," Josie said, "I'll go get a copy." Everyone else took a break but the muttering continued, especially in Forrest's corner. When Josie returned, she distributed a copy of the Concerns-Based Adoption Model developed by Gene Hall and Shirley Hord in the 1980s. "Here's what Hall and Hord mean by the word concern: 'The composite representation of the feelings, preoccupation, thought and consideration given to a particular issue or task'" (1987, p. 61).

"That's our guys," Forrest said, "concerned."

"So are we," Tasha murmured.

A THEORY OF CHANGE

My theory of change looks like the schematic on the next page (Figure 6.1).

Start in the upper left wedge of the circle with educators—including school and district administrators—engaged in professional learning, probably in PLCs. Go to the upper right wedge; there you'll see educators changing their practice. The classroom teacher effectively implements formative assessment; the school principal uses "rounds" much like those doctors do to survey the changes (City, Elmore, Fiarman, & Teitel, 2009). Go to the lower right wedge. There, students begin to change as learners. And in the lower left wedge, as a result, their achievement improves.

Around the key players, the system changes. The school itself accommodates or promotes the changes that educators are beginning to make in their classrooms and in the school as a whole. The district changes policies and practices to support

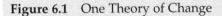

Figure 6.1 One Theory of Change

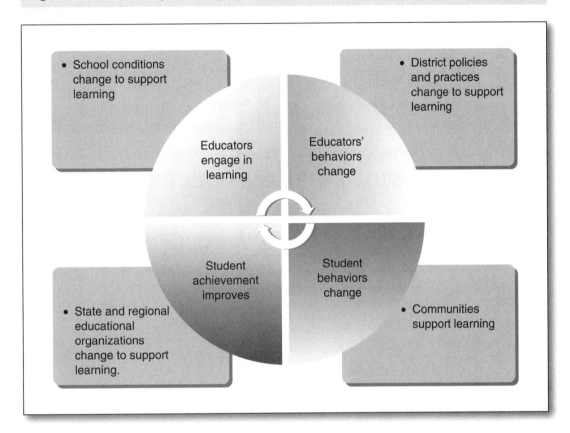

what's happening in schools and classrooms. The community, including parents, supports the changes. The state offers waivers against overly intrusive policies and drafts legislation that is supportive; regional groups, such as Boards of Cooperative Education Services (BOCES), universities, and colleges, orient themselves to support the change.

The philosophical basis for my theory is the work of Margaret Wheatley, Peter Senge, Marvin Weisbord, and other systems thinkers. The practical basis for my theory refers to what happens to people during change. I look to Shirley Hord, Gene Hall, Susan Loucks-Horsley, W. L. Rutherford, and others to understand the people side of change: how people individually and within organizations experience change and implement it. I speak in acronyms: CBAM, LofU, and IC. The best resource for "people change" is Shirley Hord and Gene Hall's 2001 book *Implementing Change: Patterns, Principles, and Potholes.* Of the 12 principles of change they describe in Chapter 1 in this book, these eight resonate the most with me:

1. Change is a process, not an event.

2. There are significant differences in what is entailed in development and implementation of an innovation.

3. An organization does not change until the individuals within it change.

4. Innovations come in different sizes.

5. Although both top-down and bottom-up change can work, a horizontal perspective is best.

6. The school is the primary unit for change.

7. Facilitating change is a team effort.

8. The context of the school influences the process of change.

Keep my theory of change in mind, as well as the Hord-Hall principles, and take a look at three models that Hord, Hall, and others developed to describe what happens to people during change.

ONE MODEL OF A THEORY OF CHANGE: THE CONCERNS-BASED ADOPTION MODEL (CBAM)

Hall and Hord (1987, 2001) are among several individuals and groups identifying three related models of change that describe what people do when approaching and going through change: Stages of Concern, Levels of Use, and Innovation Configurations.

In addition to Hall and Hord's book, I have also referenced others involved in development of the model referred to as Concerns-Based Adoption Model (fondly known as CBAM):

- Hall, G. E., & Loucks, S. F. (1978). Teacher concerns as a basis for facilitating and personalizing staff development. *Teachers College Record, 80,* 36–53.
- Hall, G. E., & Loucks, S. F. (1979). *Implementing innovations in schools: A concerns-based approach.* Austin, TX: Research and Development Center for Teacher Education, University of Texas.
- Hord, S. M., Rutherford, W. L., Huling-Austin, L., & Hall, G. E. (1987). *Taking charge of change.* Alexandria, VA: ASCD.

Here are the Stages of Concern as well as what those in a particular stage might say to indicate their concern:

Descriptor of Stage	Stages of Concern	Typical Expressions of Concern
Impact	Stage 6: Refocusing	"I have some ideas about something that would work even better."
Impact	Stage 5: Collaboration	"I am concerned about relating what I am doing with what my coworkers are doing."
Impact	Stage 4: Consequence	"How is my use affecting clients?"
Task	Stage 3: Management	"I seem to be spending all of my time getting materials ready."
Self	Stage 2: Personal	"How will using it affect me?"
Self	Stage 1: Informational	"I would like to know more about it."
	Stage 0: Awareness	"I am not concerned about it."

Perhaps you can imagine a member of the Glen Haven Middle School (GHMS) PLC working at the personal stage and thinking about herself, "We seem to be getting into some pretty major changes. I've finally figured out how to teach mathematics to my seventh graders, but I sense things are going to change. How will our work affect what I do now?"

You might be thinking that at least one of the three complainers at GHMS is at the information stage: "Just tell me what to do, and I'll do it." He or she might be frustrated because PLC members do not know exactly where they're going, or perhaps they are overwhelmed because there's such a vast universe of possibilities out there.

One way the Design Team can help individuals with their concerns is to legitimize them by sharing the CBAM model and inviting people to identify where they might be on the model. This strategy is affirming: "I'm OK. I'm not the only one who has concerns." The best way to address concerns is by acknowledging them, sharing information related to the concern (if available), and pledging to keep the concern "on the front burner." Consider a response of "I don't think we know that yet. But, I imagine by April we'll have figured that out, and it would be great to have you on the team that figures that out."

Note that one person can be at more than one stage at the same time in terms of different aspects of an innovation. Also, note that someone who seems to be at one stage on Thursday may not still be there on Friday; it may appear that this person's level of concern has regressed. In reality, the person who seems to regress may have just discovered something new about the change and has to process the discovery at an earlier stage. So, CBAM can seem recursive at times. It can even be discouraging to a change agent, monitoring stages of concern, as one person jumps ahead two and then back three stages, another stays put at one stage overlong, and a third person seems to skip a stage!

THE SECOND MODEL OF A THEORY OF CHANGE: LEVELS OF USE

Related to Stages of Concern is the second model of change: Levels of Use (LoU). Once the PLC has determined a direction and identified changes to be implemented, the Design Team can use this model to describe what people do (or don't do). Robert Marzano makes a case for examining levels of use (and doing something about them) in *What Works in Schools: Translating Research Into Action* (2003, p. 165):

> Once a specific intervention is identified it must be thoroughly implemented if a school is to expect it to impact student achievement. This might sound obvious, but the work of Eugene Hall, Shirley Hord, Susan Loucks, and their colleagues (Hall & Hord, 1987; Hall & Loucks, 1978; Hall, Loucks, Rutherford, & Newlove, 1975; Hord, Rutherford, Huling-Austin, & Hall, 1987) has shown that there are many stages of implementation. *Just because a school has provided training in a new intervention does not mean that staff members are actually using it* [italics added]. Sadly, many, if not most, interventions are not fully implemented. In fact, it is not uncommon for an intervention to be considered ineffective or marginally effective when, in fact, the intervention was improperly or only partially implemented.

One way to consider LoU is to describe what people are doing when they are at a particular level:

Category	Levels of Use	Behaviors Associated With LoU
Nonusers	0 = Nonuse	State in which the user has little or no knowledge of the innovation, no involvement with the innovation, and is doing nothing toward becoming involved.
Nonusers	I = Orientation	State in which the user has recently acquired or is acquiring information about the innovation and/or has recently explored or is exploring its value orientation and its demands upon user and user system.
Nonusers	II = Preparation	State in which the user is preparing for the first use of the innovation.
Users	III = Mechanical Use	State in which the user focuses most effort on the short-term, day-to-day use of the innovation with little time for reflection. Changes in use are made more to meet user needs than client needs. The user is primarily engaged in a stepwise attempt to master the tasks required to use the innovation, often resulting in disjointed and superficial use.
Users	IVA = Routine	Use of the innovation is stabilized. Few if any changes are being made in ongoing use. Little preparation or thought is being given to improving innovation use or its consequence.
Users	IVB = Refinement	State in which the user varies the use of the innovation to increase the impact on clients within an immediate sphere of influence. Variations are based on knowledge of both short- and long-term consequences for client.
Users	V = Integration	State in which the user is combining own efforts to use the innovation with related activities of colleagues to achieve a collective impact on clients within their common sphere of influence.
Users	VI = Renewal	State in which the user reevaluates the quality of use of the innovation, seeks major modifications of or alternatives to present innovation to achieve increased impact on clients, examines new developments in the field, and explores new goals for self and the system.

Another way to think about LoU is to examine what someone at one level needs to do to move to the next level:

Category	Behavior Needed to Move to This Level
Knowledge (0)	That which the user knows about characteristics of the innovation, how to use it, and consequences of its use. This is cognitive knowledge related to using the innovation, not feelings or attitudes.
Acquiring information (1)	Solicits information about the innovation in a variety of ways, including questioning resource person, correspondence with resource agencies, reviewing printed materials, and making visits.
Sharing (2)	Discusses the innovation with others. Shares plans, ideas, resources, outcomes, and problems related to its use.
Assessing (3)	Examines the potential or actual use of the innovation or some aspects of it. This can be a mental assessment or can involve actual collection and analysis of data.
Planning (4)	Designs and outlines short- and/or long-range steps to be taken during the process of innovation adoption, i.e., aligns resources, schedules activities, meets with others to organize and/or coordinate use of the innovation.
Status reporting (5)	Describes personal stand at the present time in relation to use of the innovation.
Performing (6)	Carries out the actions and activities entailed in operationalizing the innovation.

So, the person who was at the personal stage in terms of concern (worried about how changes might affect how she teaches seventh-grade mathematics) may, at first, be at "0" in terms of levels of use, avoiding the change. For her to move to "1," she needs to be sure she thoroughly understands the innovation, including how to use it and how it affects student learning. If possible, she gains this information from a number of sources, including observing a teacher who is already succeeding with the innovation. She gets ready for the third LoU, collaboration.

THE THIRD MODEL OF A THEORY OF CHANGE: INNOVATION CONFIGURATIONS

The third model of a theory of change related to CBAM and LoU is Innovation Configurations (ICs). This model is designed to clarify the change itself: What is it? What is it not? Early in their studies of change, Hord and Hall (2001) discovered that "users of innovations tend to adapt and, in many cases, mutate innovations! In other words, the innovation in action can take many different operational forms or configurations" (p. 38). Users of some forms experienced higher success rates than users of other forms of the innovation. In fact, usually the "developer's intended model," when implemented with fidelity resulted in the best effects" (p. 39).

Hord and Hall decided that innovations could be mapped according to the degrees of fidelity to the implementation itself. In actuality, IC maps resemble a rubric. Here is an excerpt from an IC map that was done in Douglas County School District in Colorado on student ownership and understanding of learning (understanding of standards or checkpoints, understanding of progress in relation to standards or checkpoints, understanding of what is needed to improve performance in order to achieve standards or checkpoints).

I.	II.	III.	IV.	V.
Students' focus is on the current activity.	Students' focus is on the requirements of the class and grade they receive.	Students can use the language of standards. They can state the standards and checkpoints that they are expected to learn but are unclear about where they are in meeting the standards or checkpoints of what they need to do to achieve them.	Students understand what they are expected to know and be able to do and can articulate in specific terms what it means to reach the standards or checkpoints. They can describe where they are in regard to the standards or checkpoints but are unclear what they need to do to achieve them.	Students understand what they are expected to know and be able to do and can articulate in specific terms what it means to reach the standards or checkpoints. They can describe where they are in regard to the standard and know what they need to improve to achieve it.

Source: Hall and Hord (2001, p. 46).

An IC map can be developed for any innovation. In 2003, Patricia Roy and Shirley Hord developed IC maps for implementing the standards of the National Staff Development Council (NSDC)—an innovation. The maps they developed "identify and describe in operation, the major components of new practice," in this case implementation of NSDC's standards for staff development (2003a, p. 6).

Volume I (Roy & Hord, 2003a) of the maps focuses on how teachers, the principal, central office staff members, the superintendent, and the school board can implement the standards. *Volume II* (Roy & Hord, 2005a) explores how directors of staff development, external assistance providers, institutions of higher education, state education agencies, and professional associations can implement the standards. *Volume III* examines how school-based staff developers can put the standards into practice (Killion & Harrison, 2007).

Two "field guides" help educators with implementation: *Moving NSDC's Staff Development Standards Into Practice: Innovation Configurations, Volumes I* (Roy

& Hord, 2003b) and *II* (Roy & Hord, 2005b). *A User's Guide* by Patricia Roy helps educators introduce ICs to other educators (2007).

Organized according to roles, each map describes what people in those roles would do to achieve the NSDC outcomes—the innovation—related to the NSDC standards of context, process, and content. The maps, which have six levels of proficiency, also feature a "Cross-Walk Table" of "all desired outcomes for all role groups" (p. 9). Resource 6.1 describes an IC map for teachers related to PLCs.

"I remember this," Aaron said, as the Design Team read through Josie's handout.

"Why don't you take us through it?" Josie suggested.

"Well, we were looking at cooperative learning back then," Aaron said, "and it was a real challenge for a lot of us who were used to the lecture method. Standing up front, delivering—'Stand and Deliver!'—so there was lots of concern. Some people were pretty aggressive, but others just opted out."

"What did you do?" Tasha asked.

"We did these interviews first," Aaron said. "I mean, I didn't, but someone on the staff did. They were pretty informal. Kind of fun. We stood on one leg. . . ."

ONE-LEGGED INTERVIEWS

The premise of a one-legged interview is that it should last only as long as any participant can stand on one leg. It is informal and casual, more like a conversation that occurs in passing. Gene Hall and Shirley Hord (2001) describe one-legged interviews as a useful tool for determining where people are in terms of concerns related to innovation. These interviews are not intimidating and can occur anyplace anytime (phone, e-mail, face-to-face). They are usually framed in a neutral way ("How's it going?") rather than a way that presumes an answer (such as "What's wrong with this work?"). There's no preset interview question, and there's no recording of the response, except in terms of notes made by the interviewer, who is usually a colleague (not an outsider). There's some sacrifice of accuracy and reliability (each person asking the same question and able to get the same answers), but that loss is offset by the personal interest the interviewer shows the interviewee and the good will that results when people feel honored by the question.

"We can do that!" Tasha exclaimed.

Aaron asked, "Would we ask everybody or just those who seem to be expressing a concern . . . providing Josie tells us their names."

Ariel responded, "I think we start with us! Where are we with this work? How are we doing?"

"That's a really good idea," Dottie said. "We should interview each other and then interview the rest of the staff."

"When are we going to have time to do this?" Andy asked.

"Well," Josie said, "I'm thinking this is not an activity—we won't just do it in a meeting. We'll do it over time, a couple of weeks or so. How about if we get the interviews of ourselves done by our next Design Team meeting, March 20? We have an early-release half-day on March 19, but the English Department has proposed that they use it for . . . why don't you talk about that, Robbie?"

Robbie acknowledged with a smile to Josie that she had something to say about the English Department's proposal, but first she said, "How shall we divvy up the interviews?"

Roz suggested that she'd put the names of the Design Team members in the proverbial "hat" and draw the names of both interviewees and interviewers.

"What's our question?" Forrest asked.

"Something like this," Andy suggested: "'How's it going in terms of the PLC work this year?' Is that an OK question?"

"Fits the CBAM model," Aaron said. "We had a question like that for our work on cooperative learning . . . as I remember."

Josie interjected, "We might even follow up the answer with a request for an example or elaboration, such as 'Tell me a little more' or 'Can you give me an example.'"[1]

Andy captured what the Design Team, generally, was thinking: "Sounds good. Let's try it."

"And, now—ta da!—the English Department would like to request your help on the March 19 early-release half-day," Robbie announced. "We'd like to look at student writing that day."

"All of us?" Roz asked.

"All of us," Robbie said.

"But I don't teach writing," Andy said. "Well, I mean, I do, sort of, when I make the kids write in sentences."

"That may be what we discover," Robbie said, "that we should all teach writing more, not just the English teachers."

"And I don't have the faintest idea of how to evaluate writing," Andy added.

Robbie smiled as she said, "I know it's just like saying 'the check's in the mail' but 'trust us.' We have it figured out." She spoke with some passion, "We need to do this. We have scores for the state test and we have data from the interviews and focus groups. Things are not looking good on the writing front here at Glen Haven. We need to look at real student work if we're really going to get better at writing . . . and thinking!"

"I agree," Roz said. A few "Me too" claims added an exclamation point to her statement.

"Stephanie from the district office put us in touch with an English teacher at the high school who used to run a districtwide writing assessment every year. Her name is Victoria Brandt."

"I remember doing that," Aaron said, meaning writing assessments.

"Of course you do," Robbie said, poking him in the ribs with her elbow.

"Ha-ha. Why did we stop doing that, I wonder."

Josie spoke up, "Too expensive, getting all those teachers to look at writing, but I think we can do it during our half-day early release, if the English Department is ready."

"We are," Robbie said.

"Won't it take more than an afternoon?" Andy asked.

"We don't think so," Robbie responded, and she described the process to them.

WRITING ASSESSMENT

Writing used to be tested indirectly—perhaps still is, in some places—on multiple-choice exams that required students to locate errors in sentences or choose the best detail for a topic sentence. These exams really tested only a small part of writing (editing—and a rather invalid type of editing because students found errors in

---

[1] SEDL (the Southwest Educational Development Laboratory) offers an online survey Stages of Concern Questionnaire (SoCQ) and a scoring service. The survey was written by Archie A. George, Gene E. Hall, Suzanne M. Stiegelbauer, and Brian Litke (programmer) and published in 2008. See http://www.sedl.org/pubs/catalog/items/cbam21.html.

manufactured sentences, not their own) or reading. Direct assessment of writing, rather than "measuring" it through multiple-choice tests, was one of the first performance assessment strategies to affect K–12 education. The technologies of scoring writing assessment opened up worlds of alternative assessment for other subjects.

Cooper (1977) described the reliability of the scoring process used in writing assessment. He found reliability rates as high as 97%, meaning that two trained scorers, independently scoring student writing but referencing a rubric and anchor papers, standardize their scoring enough to award the same score to papers 97% of the time. For the other 3% of the cases, a third scorer settles the differences. The "secret" is use of specific criteria (internalized or explicit) on a rubric, use of anchors (papers that match the rubric at the various scoring points), extensive training on both with a common set of papers so that scorers "agree to agree" to use the rubric and anchors to award scores, and various methods of calibration or vigilance so that the scorers do not "drift" too far from use of the rubric and anchors. It is no accident that many proponents of performance assessment, such as Grant Wiggins, are former English teachers (Easton, 1991, pp. 102–103).

Cooper (1977) and many others persuaded states and districts to engage in scoring student writing because it was more valid than making assumptions about writing based on multiple-choice tests.

Three types of scoring writing became popular: general impression scoring, primary trait scoring, and analytic trait scoring. General impression scoring (sometimes called holistic scoring) is "deciding where the paper fits within the range of papers" (Cooper, 1977, p. 12). This is the type usually used in large-scale writing assessment. The second type, primary trait, is similar to general impression scoring but focuses on a single trait that makes the difference in terms of the type of writing being scored. For example, the primary trait for persuasive writing would probably be the quality of the details or examples to support an opinion. The third type, analytic trait, translates into today's rubrics. Analytic trait lists "the prominent features or characteristics of writing" (Cooper, 1977, p. 7).

Although direct assessment of writing (or any other product or outcome) can be found reliable and valid, it does have its weaknesses. For example, most writing and other performance assessments are "point-in-time" assessments. They provide a single snapshot of writing in terms of a student, classroom, grade, school, district, or state. They may be situational in that students may be more proficient in writing one type of writing (description, for example) but less so in another genre. Writing assessments usually do not mirror the writing process—students engaged in a writing assessment are not usually encouraged to work with others to brainstorm, revise, and edit what they are doing. Writing is a one-shot deal. The same things, however, can be argued about multiple-choice tests. Direct assessment of writing is still the better way of ascertaining writing ability.

Is scoring a piece of writing more objective than scoring a multiple-choice test with an answer key? Actually, some researchers are not so sure that multiple-choice tests are objective (Alloway & Conlan, 1984, for example). Such tests are no more objective than writing assessments as they are "not designed by disinterested persons . . . all testing is contrived and artificial . . . . one can only estimate a student's total performance" (quoted in Easton, 2001, pp. 111–112).

HOW A WRITING ASSESSMENT WORKS

Resource 6.2 gives specific directions for directly assessing writing. Briefly, the process works like this:

1. Educators determine the need for a writing assessment.

2. They decide on the students from whom they'll collect a sample of writing.

3. They decide on a prompt and a process for student writing on the prompt.

4. They administer the assessment as consistently as possible. They do not let students put their names on the papers.

5. They collect papers and code them in an agreed-upon way.

6. They mix the papers from the classes or schools participating and draw a random sample of 10 from the papers. They draw a second sample of 10 to serve as backup to the first set.

7. Using a rubric if there is one (it's OK if there is no rubric—in fact, a rubric can be generated after all the papers are scored), participants read through the first set of 10 papers looking for papers that are clearly exemplary of each scoring point (a 4-point scale is ideal).

8. The group discusses these papers until they have an exemplar (known as an anchor) for each score point, perhaps even two for each score point. If needed, they use the second, backup set of papers to find anchors.

9. Then, using the anchors and the rubric (if there is one), they score all the papers reading quickly and holistically. Participants need to beware of focusing on any characteristic of writing (such as poor spelling) alone and awarding scores accordingly. They record a score on the back of the paper (often in a corner which is turned down).

10. Each paper is then read a second time by another scorer who scores the paper on a corner in the front and then checks to see if the two scores match or are 1 point apart (in which case, the final score is an average; a 2 and a 3 become a 2½).

11. Papers for which there is more than a 1-point difference need a third reader who resolves the score.

12. The papers in each category are counted to determine reliability (exact scores, scores that are 1 point apart, papers that need a third reader).

13. The papers are also quantified in other ways, as needed: total number of papers at each score, number of papers at each score for each school and/or classroom.

14. Follow-up to the scoring process can involve looking at papers (especially the anchor papers) in more depth or using the process to evaluate curriculum and instruction and other aspects of the English language arts classroom or classrooms across the curriculum.

15. **The important thing to remember about the writing assessment process is that it can be used to assess any performance.**

The English Department at GHMS had already chosen the grade level, the prompt, the process of having students write according to the prompt, the rubric, and the logistics of scoring. See the box for details.

The actual assessment process—involving all of the GHMS teachers during a half-day early-release date—went quite smoothly, facilitated by the chair of the high school English Department, Victoria Brandt, assisted by two of the middle school English teachers. The GHMS English teachers were rather proud of the prompt, thinking that it would yield even more data about how students learn best. Both the content and the process would prove valuable, in their minds, well worth the half-day early-release time.

Participants were equally interested in the topic and, overtly or not, hoped they would see something about learning in their subject area or a course they taught.

Teachers from the GHMS English Department collected the papers for analysis on Friday—they were so eager to know the results that they combined a TGIF with analysis! Here's what they learned:

- *Their reliability rate (how many papers were scored exactly alike 1 point apart).*

  - *Of nearly 300 eighth graders, 282 had completed the writing assessment (those exempted include students with individualized education programs [IEPs] that identified other test options or absent students).*

  - *Of 287 papers, 269 were scored exactly the same or differed by only 1 point, for a reliability rate of about about 94%.*

  - *16 required a third reader to resolve differences of more than 1 point.*

  - *2 papers were unscorable, both blank.*

- *The numbers and percentages of students who received the four scores or were anomalies or unscorable:*

  - *22 papers received 4s (8%).*

  - *104 received 3s (36%.)*

  - *83 papers received 2s (29%).*

  - *76 papers received 1s (26%)*

  - *2 papers were unscorable (less than 1%)*

One of the teachers had brought her computer and quickly turned the percentages into an Excel® chart. The teachers brought their drinks around to her side of the table and looked at the chart.

The scores and the chart elicited a few comments (see the box) but no clinking of glasses.

Logistics of the Writing Assessment Process

<u>Grade Level:</u> Eighth graders ("since by the end of eighth grade we will have had a chance to affect all eighth graders").

<u>Prompt:</u> Best or worst school learning experience ("since we're interested in how students engage in their learning"): a description with focus and supporting details. Actual prompt: "Think of your best school learning experience. Describe it so well that your reader is convinced that it truly was your best learning experience. Use good details to help the reader understand how good it was. You have 40 minutes to finish your paper, which can be as long as you need it to be. You may use some of the time to brainstorm ideas and make a rough draft and revise it, but be sure to have a finished final draft by the end of the 40 minutes."

<u>Rubric:</u> Based on The 6+1 Trait® Writing Model (see Resource 6.3 for more information about this model).

<u>Process:</u> Tell students that today (no advance warning) they will have a chance to show how well they write a description. Tell them that the whole faculty will be examining their papers and using them to evaluate how well Glen Haven students have learned how to write. Tell them that they should <u>not</u> put their names on their papers. Give them the prompt and read it aloud. Make sure they have paper and pens (pencil may not copy well) and set a quiet timer. Let them know when they have 15, 10, 5, and 2 minutes left. Collect papers, mix them up, and number them according to the four-digit code sequence you have chosen.

Logistics: No names on papers. Coding according to student only (not school – not needed – and not teacher – at least not in this first writing assessment process). Teachers can devise any four digit numerical code they want and keep it to themselves. They'll code the papers accordingly and turn them into the language arts classroom assistant to be mixed together).

At what they thought would be a celebratory gathering, the teachers were a little disappointed in the scores and realized that they wanted to know more:

- *How well the rubric matched real student writing at the score levels and how the rubric might be revised; and*
- *How they might want to revise curriculum, instruction, and assessment in writing.*

On Monday the English teachers sorted out their own papers to analyze scores and use with students as they wanted. At the very least, they recorded the scores their own students got. A few planned to hold individual writing conferences with students.

Figure 6.1 Percentage of Scores at Each Score Level

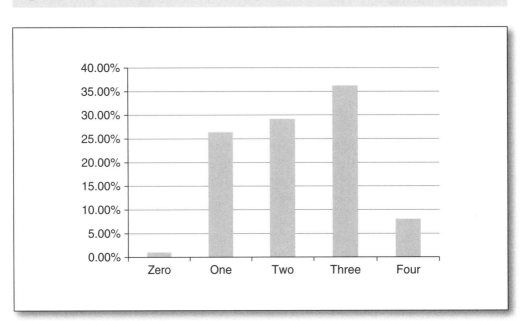

The department was also interested in burrowing deeper into the papers themselves, especially the anchor papers. They wanted to invite teachers from other departments to participate in whatever they did. Victoria suggested that they might want to do a tuning protocol or a variation on it called a descriptive review.

April was going by fast and would reach supersonic speed at the next to the last week of April when students took state tests. Only a very few weeks left for school-year learning—of both the student and teacher variety—and the passage of those weeks would soon exceed supersonic speed. The English Department asked to use part of the districtwide professional development day scheduled for early May for analysis of the papers from the writing assessment; perhaps they could engage faculty in a tuning protocol or descriptive review for the mid-May early-release half-day. Time!

In the meantime, Design Team members interviewed each other about stages of concern regarding PLC work. Here's what they found:

Figure 6.2 Stages of Concern Within the Design Team

Number and Percentage of Design Team at This Stage	Descriptor of Stage	Stages of Concern	Expressions of Concern
0 0%	Impact	Stage 6: Refocusing	"I have some ideas about something that would work even better."
1 10%	Impact	Stage 5: Collaboration	"I am concerned about relating what I am doing with what my coworkers are doing."
0 0%	Impact	Stage 4: Consequence	"How Is my use affecting clients?"
0 0%	Task	Stage 3: Management	"I seem to be spending all of my time getting materials ready."
6 50%	Self	Stage 2: Personal	"How will using it affect me?"
3 30%	Self	Stage 1: Informational	"I would like to know more about it."
0 0%	Self	Stage 0: Awareness	"I am not concerned about it."

They discussed the results—and their own responses—and talked about the effectiveness of the interview question, which was, "How's it going in terms of the PLC work this year?" with the possibility of follow-up questions to get examples.

After this prelude, "We don't need to reveal where we fit in the stages," Tasha continued, "but I will tell you that I answered in terms of collaboration. I guess I was the only one. It seems to me that we aren't implementing any one thing, but we are instigating change around here in terms of school culture, especially how we work together as adults. That's a little different from implementing a 'thing.'"

Six of the Design Team members voiced other concerns: "I'm not sure where I fit into this," Roz said. Forrest added, "I suspect our jobs are going to be different in the next couple of years." Ariel said, "I'm worried about how teachers will adapt to those new roles. What has prepared them to do their work differently? How will they reach some kind of confidence about themselves?"

Josie spoke for three of the Design Team members when she said, "I just have more questions than I had this fall. Things feel more uncertain to me. That's good, really, but kind of scary." Her colleagues waggled their hands in silent agreement.

"One thing I do know is that we need to be really careful about how we ask the questions," Kelly stated. "I discovered that my initial question "How's it going?" just to get things started was

Comments on Writing Scores

"Hmmmm. Not really much of a normal curve, is it?"

"I sure wish we had more 4s."

"If we combined the 1s and 2s, we'd have more than half of our students."

"At least there are all those 3s."

"We shouldn't 'count' zeroes."

"Why not? These were students who should have been able to write something."

"I'm a little depressed."

"What if it's our rubric? It's somehow wrong."

"Or, what if we're not teaching what we should, according to the rubric?"

"Or, we need to improve how we teach writing?"

"Or, how we assess it?"

"And, maybe we need to get the rest of the faculty more involved in writing. All the subjects use writing as thinking. We should be doing more writing in order to help students think."

"Maybe they don't feel confident about teaching writing."

"Well, maybe they wouldn't teach it, exactly."

"We could help them assign it and evaluate it according to some basic principles of quality writing."

too vague, and it took a couple of follow-up questions to narrow responses down to "going with the PLC work this year."

"I know. You were interviewing me, and I deliberately made it tough on you," Andy responded.

"It's clear that we need to ask the narrower question," Aaron commented. "It's actually very easy to listen to the answers and then follow up with more pointed questions, checking your perceptions. I found myself paraphrasing a lot, like 'So, you're feeling like this. . . .'"

He continued, "And I'm thinking that we need to be transparent about this. We need to let people know what we're doing and why."

"I don't want to tell people that some of the faculty have complained," Dottie said. "That could really bias their answers."

"How about if we just send an e-mail letting everyone know that we're wondering how people are doing with the PLC work this year and that we'll be conducting very brief and informal interviews?" Kelly suggested.

"And," Tasha said, "let's let them know that we'll take it very personally if they start dodging us in the hallways and the teachers' lounge. Just kidding."

"What if we don't happen to catch them during the week? Should we try to do the interview by e-mail?" Ariel asked.

"I'd rather not do e-mail," Tasha responded, "but we can if we simply can't reach them otherwise. Maybe it would be better if we set up a time and place to meet them through e-mail and then, if that doesn't work, ask for an e-mail response."

"I'll send the e-mail," Ariel said. "I'll send to all of you to check out before I send it to everyone."

It had been a blessedly short meeting

OTHER WAYS OF THINKING ABOUT CHANGE

CBAM essentially addresses how individuals go through change in an organization such as a school or district. There are many other ways of thinking about stages of change. William Bridges wrote several books about transitions, positing that people need help on a personal level with any kind of transition from one thing to another; even if the change is happening organizationally, individuals need to transition personally. They do so by marking an ending, going through a neutral zone (which is both scary and energizing, threatening and creative), and entering the new beginning. His books include his first *Transitions: Making Sense of Life's Changes* (2004); *Managing Transitions: Making the Most of Change* (2009); and *The Way of Transition: Embracing Life's Most Difficult Moments* (2001). Bridges: Could there be a better name for an author of books on transitions?

An often-used model of change suggests that the stages are marked by how soon people are ready to go through change. There are the "early adopters." In business, these are the ones who are ready to try something new; they are the trendsetters. According to Everett Rogers in *Diffusion of Innovations* (1962/1983) there are also people in a category called "early majority" and others in a category called "late majority." Then there are the laggards. People experiencing change distribute in a population on a normal curve unless efforts are taken to accelerate adoption. I have heard Rogers's categories likened to the settling of the West: There are the scouts, then the pioneers, then the settlers, and then the farmers.

Kurt Lewin (1947, pp. 5–41) developed an early model of the change process that depends first on unfreezing or unlearning past behavior that is no longer effective. People have to experience some cognitive dissonance (Festinger, Riecken, & Schachter, 1956) in order to be willing to unfreeze or unlearn strategies that seemed to have served them well up to the point of change. Cognitive dissonance is a sense of discomfort about what is expected and what is. It is conflict between ideas, usually one deeply held and one that is new to the individual. It is, as Suzanne Bailey, systems change expert, says, "pain in the system" (personal communication).

Recent television ads for a bank provide a good example of cognitive dissonance. A child is asked if she wants a pony and is very happy about the toy pony she is handed . . . until another child, asked the same thing, receives a real pony. Cognitive dissonance is written all over the first child's face. Data about students (and not just test scores!) often create cognitive dissonance as people who think that students are succeeding suddenly have proof that they are not. Their understanding of the world they live in is disconfirmed.

The second stage in Lewin's process is the change itself, incorporating new behaviors into personal and organizational practice, a process that usually requires some cultural changes as well as some development of new skills. In the third stage, people freeze when their behaviors are validated, rewarded, and reinforced. These behaviors become the norm of the organization and the individuals within it.

Kubler-Ross (1969/1989) first wrote about emotional stages people experience while grieving. The five stages of the Kubler-Ross Grief Model are Stage 1: Denial; Stage 2: Anger; Stage 3: Bargaining; Stage 4: Depression; and Stage 5: Acceptance. Although experiencing change in an organization does not equate to grieving over the death of a loved person, there is definitely a parallel between what people do in both situations. They may very well deny the need for change; they may get angry; they may justify not changing; they may get depressed and grieve over the way things used to be; and, finally, they may reach acceptance—or not.

Michael W. Durant (1999) altered these stages slightly to represent what happens when organizations change and individuals within them are expected to change, too:

Stage 1: Denial

Stage 2: Resistance

Stage 3: Exploration

Stage 4: Commitment

There are countless other theories of change, built upon the good ideas of people such as Peter M. Senge (1990), Stephen R. Covey (1989/2004), W. Edwards Deming (1986), and Marvin Weisbord (1987). Regardless of theory and related stages of change, organizations undergoing change (and what thriving organization does not?), including educational organizations, need to be aware of how individual people are encountering the challenges of change. And now, let's see how the faculty responded to the Design Team's informal interviews and how their responses fit the CBAM model.

Of the 58 total staff members—teaching staff, administrators, library/media personnel, and instructional assistants, the Design Team was able to interview 54 by their deadline. The e-mail to staff members actually prompted some of them to seek out Design Team members, rather than seem recalcitrant! Here's the breakdown of who was interviewed:

Category	Number Possible	Number Interviewed
Administrators	3	3
Instructional Staff	43	40
Counselors	2	2
Library/Media	3	2
Aides/Assistants	7	7
Total	58	54

Once again, the responses to the question "So, how are you doing in terms of the PLC work this year?" seemed easy to categorize:

Number and Percentage of PLC at This Stage	Descriptor of Stage	Stages of Concern	Expressions of Concern
0 0%	Impact	Stage 6: Refocusing	"I have some ideas about something that would work even better."
0 0%	Impact	Stage 5: Collaboration	"I am concerned about relating what I am doing with what my coworkers are doing."
0 0%	Impact	Stage 4: Consequence	"How is my use affecting clients?"
9 17%	Task	Stage 3: Management	"I seem to be spending all of my time getting materials ready."
18 33%	Self	Stage 2: Personal	"How will using it affect me?"
21 39%	Self	Stage 1: Informational	"I would like to know more about it."
6 11%	Self	Stage 0: Awareness	"I am not concerned about it."

Andy quickly created a graph to show them the responses. He turned his computer so that all could see this chart:

Figure 6.3 CBAM Levels for Entire Staff (*n* = 54)

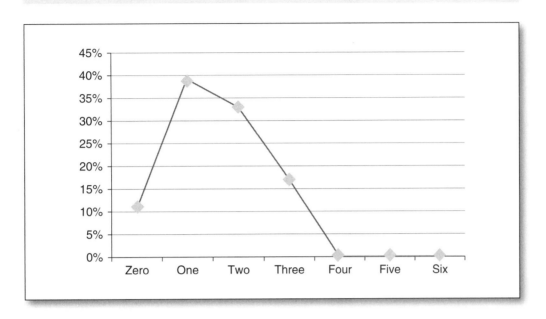

"Not surprising," Kelly said. "Like us, really."

"Most people should probably be at one or two at this point," someone said, "but I'm worried about the zero. These people don't think what we're doing will affect them?"

"I'm wondering about the threes. What are they concerned about?"

"I did a couple of interviews that I classified as threes," Dottie said, "because they were worried about keeping all the data straight, organizing for meetings, and so forth."

"Most people I talked to weren't sure what IT is. In other words, they're used to being told what to change. So far, we haven't made any changes in what we do. We aren't implementing cooperative learning, for example," Ariel said.

"I'm worried that we're too caught up in the process . . . the planning . . . that planning-doing conundrum we talked about," Andy suggested.

"Actually," Josie said, "I think there's more going on than we suspect. Sure, we haven't implemented any one thing, yet. But we have really done a whole host of things at Glen Haven that haven't been done before—the PLC meetings, the Design Team, the Specialty Teams. Faculty know there's something different. We've involved students in new ways: the surveys, the focus groups, the interviews, the writing assessment. They know something's going on. They see that the adults, as a group and individually, are concerned about making school better for them. They are witnessing adult learning. The whole culture is changing."

Spontaneous applause. Cries of "Huzzah!" and "Bravo!" That was the longest speech Josie had made, and they agreed with her. In fact, Roz added to what Josie had said, "And I suspect we're all a little different because of what we've been doing this year. Maybe not anything tangible, but we've been affected by our work with colleagues and what we're learning. We're thinking differently."

"Maybe tangible," Robbie added, "because I know I've changed some things in my classroom related to literacy and engagement, and I know others have, too. So, it hasn't been a waste of almost-a-year. Not at all. Glen Haven is a better place already for both students and us."

"So, not to disrupt the patting-on-the-back or anything," Forrest said, "but what are we going to do about the staff members who complained? Remember, that's what started this whole CBAM thing."

"Forrest," said Roz, "you'll be delighted to know that the people who did so much work on CBAM, actually thought that out." She distributed the chart below.

INTERVENTIONS

Stage 6, Refocusing	Respect and encourage teacher interests; channel their ideas and energies; act on their concerns
Stage 5, Collaboration	Provide opportunities to develop skills needed to work collaboratively; rearrange schedules so people can collaborate
Stage 4, Consequence	Provide positive feedback and needed support; provide opportunities for teachers to share knowledge and skills
Stage 3, Management	Answer specific "how to" questions; avoid considering future impact at this time
Stage 2, Personal	Address potential personal concerns directly; implement changes progressively over time
Stage 1, Informational	Provide clear and accurate information; relate changes to current practices
Stage 0, Awareness	Involve teachers in discussion and decisions; give permission not to know

Source: Hall, George, and Rutherford (1986).

"So, what should we do with this?" Forrest asked.

"Well, most important for me is no stealth," Kelly said. "I think we should be fully transparent about the results and what the possible interventions are. Actually, I don't much like that word 'interventions.' It sounds too much like getting in the way of things, rather than helping things move on."

"Agreed!" said Dottie, and others waggled their hands to signify the same.

"So, we get rid of the name, but I think we have to share what we learned from the interviews with the whole staff," Roz said, "the initial chart of the stages, the result of the surveys, the 'interventions,' which we can call 'actions' if we prefer."

"Perhaps at the next early-release half-day?" Andy suggested, consulting his calendar. "That would be April 16."

"Right after tax day!"

"Right before testing week!"

"Ugh!"

"OK," he said, "another day?"

"It's OK, Andy, to do it on April 16," Tasha said. "People were just thinking about what that day means to them. But, April 16 is soon!"

"So," Roz said, "I'm thinking that we structure the day as a 'taking stock' and 'looking into the future' day. We include the CBAM stuff as part of both 'taking stock' and 'looking into the future.'"

"I like that," Tasha said. "I'd love to plan that day with you."

"Who else?" Roz said.

"I'd like to work on that day, too," Robbie said. "And I," someone else said. "Me too." Suddenly there were four, and Josie mentioned that, perhaps, they should invite members of the whole PLC to join them. "Perhaps we can send an e-mail out thanking them for their interviews and setting up April 16 for them, including sharing the data from the interviews, and we can ask who would like to participate in planning."

"I'm getting good at e-mails," Ariel said. "I'll draft one and send it out to all of you before I send it out to all of . . . us!"

"You should have been an English teacher," Robbie commented.

GETTING BACK TO BUSINESS

Does anyone on the Design Team or the whole PLC remember what happened at the end of the February 12 early-release half-day? What's going on? Have they been so distracted by the revelation that some GHMS faculty and staff members were disaffected by what the PLC was doing that they forgot what they accomplished on February 12? Did the writing assessment that the English Department wanted the entire PLC to conduct divert their attention? Have they forgotten these goals, made on the basis of data and even more data?

- School Culture (Parents and Community; Safety; "Core" in seventh and eighth grades, etc.)
- Classroom Culture: Student Viewpoint (Personalization, Engagement, "Fun," Support)
- Classroom Culture: Educator Viewpoint (All of the Above + Rigor, Challenge, Engagement, Risk-Taking, Expectations, CIA, Literacy)
- Parent Involvement in Terms of Personal and Social Growth; Surviving Middle School

It is so easy for a school improvement process to get derailed during the school year. The announcement that three or more staff members were dissatisfied with the work of the PLC threw the entire Design Team into a tizzy, and members of the team felt they could not move on until they learned more about the discontent. Could they have moved on? Should they have simply ignored the grousers and gotten back to the goals laboriously set on February 12? And what about the birdwalk the English Department wanted to take by having the whole staff evaluate student writing? Couldn't that have been delayed?

It's easy to armchair quarterback such situations. The Design Team was particularly sensitive about people's needs, doubtless remembering their own, perhaps unpleasant, experiences of working in a group and having their needs go unmet. They had "pulled out all the stops" in terms of communicating, surveying, presenting ideas for revision . . . and, somehow, there were at least three people who were discontent.

Putting the specific situation into a larger context was exactly the right thing to do. Taking stock should be done regularly during the process of change, and so Roz's suggestion that the Design Team take stock—rather than respond to one or more complaints—led to exactly the right thing to do. The Design Team swerved from being reactive to being proactive.

Earlier in the year when Forrest and K. D. expressed discomfort at the way a meeting was going, the Design and the Data Specialty Teams attended to their needs, a process that led to learning for the entire faculty. Learning about preferences and when and how to engage in dialogue were important, positive activities for the entire school, likely to have impact well into the 2nd and 3rd years of the change effort . . . perhaps beyond. Learning about CBAM and Levels of Use and Innovation

Configurations, doing one-legged interviews, and—most importantly—validating people's concerns about the PLC process would probably have the same type of effect on the whole school.

But the Design Team is going to have to lasso the diversions and get back to the goals. That's its purpose.

Even before the whole faculty had taken stock, Victoria Brandt, the high school English teacher who had helped the Glen Haven English teachers plan and accomplish the writing assessment, invited them to participate in a process (called the tuning protocol) for looking at student work at the high school. The high school tuning protocol group was going to look at science portfolios, and Victoria felt that witnessing another process for looking at student work might help not only the GHMS English teachers but all of the faculty. Here's what happened according to Robbie, who was one of the four middle school teachers to attend this Thursday afternoon event. She took notes about the event and wrote about it for the English Department:

"Dave, a science teacher, brought several science portfolios for his interdisciplinary team to examine. Though each portfolio was more than 30 pages and bulky with drawings and charts, Dave assured them that they didn't have to read each one in depth. Nor did they have to assess them. Since members of the group knew each other well and met regularly, they introduced themselves and learned our names and indulged only in 'checking in' as a starting activity.

"Dave began with these words: 'I'm really proud of these portfolios. I think that—at last—I've found a way to link curriculum, instruction, and assessment, all in this one format, the portfolio. Things make sense to me . . . and to my students. I'd like to take you through one portfolio while you look through the others. They follow the same format.'

"Dave opened the portfolio he had kept and took us through it as we looked at the ones in front of us (he had brought enough portfolios for visitors).

"'Here's the problem. I'm not sure that portfolios stimulate students to think at the highest levels. I'm not sure what levels of thinking are represented in these portfolios, but I suspect that only the three lowest levels of Bloom are there. I definitely want science students to be analyzing, synthesizing and evaluating. So my key questions are these:

"'What can you tell me about the levels of thinking in these portfolios?

"'How can I be sure that students are working at the higher levels of Bloom?'

"Dave gave the group the remaining 8 minutes to pore through the portfolios. We did so quietly, but it was clear that the tuning protocol group had questions and they were beginning to test some hypotheses. They obviously knew about protocols and they knew that, during this part of the process, they said nothing; Dave had 'the floor' even though he had given up part of it so the group could examine the portfolios. Victoria was serving as facilitator and timekeeper and she told the group when Dave's time was up. 'Let's go on to clarifying questions,' Victoria said.

"Raul asked the first question, 'How long have you been doing portfolios in science, Dave?' He replied that he started them last year in February. 'So, it's been about a year.' Other group members asked clarifying questions until the time was up. Victoria remarked, as much for us as for the group, that they knew that they would never have all the information they needed, but they would have enough information to tune what Dave has brought them.

"After clarifying questions, they knew it was time to write. Dave repeated his key questions and all of them, including Dave, began writing with these in mind.

"Then it was time for dialogue about the questions. (They use dialogue, too!) Dave pulled back from the group slightly and turned aside so that they couldn't make eye contact with him. His slight movement helped them focus on what he had brought them to tune rather than on him. It helped them 'own' the task. They would be less likely to say, 'You' than 'It' or 'He.' Dave was a 'fly on the wall,' listening to brilliant dialogue among his trusted colleagues! He took notes so that he could respond later in the process.

"It didn't take them long to establish amongst themselves that Dave was accurate in his thinking that students were not demonstrating that they were thinking at higher levels in their portfolios. They pointed to examples in the portfolios that they had examined and in the portfolio that Dave used to illustrate the portfolio process. At last, Desmond captured the problem: 'What the students are writing about is not what they think or what they learned. It's what they did. Time after time.' The rest of the group checked out his assertion. True enough, reporting was the level of student thinking.

"Dave was rapidly taking notes, writing on one side of his paper what he heard them say and on the other his thoughts and reflections about what they said. Eventually, they switched their focus to what Dave could do to help his students think about what they were doing. They generated quite a list, ranging from the simple ('Provide a time at the end of each science activity for students to reflect on what they have done and what they learned.') to the more elaborate ('Teach students Bloom's taxonomy and have students write a thought about what they have done that matches each level of Bloom.').

"Victoria asked them midway about how they were doing with warm and cool feedback. They realized that they had become so engrossed in what Dave brought them to work on—and their own interests in using portfolios—that they might not have given Dave enough warm feedback. They quickly made up for their omission, letting Dave listen in as they talked about how impressed they were that he was using portfolios, how big a jump that was from typical ways of assessing science. They affirmed that they each wanted to do so themselves. They shared their excitement about the integrity of the portfolio process: 'It does, truly, align curriculum, instruction, and assessment.' Victoria checked on how they were doing with Dave's key questions, and they all agreed that they were addressing them almost to the exclusion of other questions that might have come up. 'That's okay,' Victoria said, 'as long as we address them.' Finally, she checked on 'airtime.' They quickly decided that no one was dominating the dialogue and everyone was getting a chance to contribute. Then, they resumed talking until time was up.

"Dave, who had been silent during the group's discussion, entered the group again, with a big grin on his face. He talked to them about what he had heard—processing it out loud in front of them, pushing their ideas deeper. He corrected some of their observations about the portfolio but concentrated on the fact—now so obvious—that the students were simply writing on or producing material that represented what they had done, not what they had learned. He exulted over the ideas for remedying the situation and added a few other ideas. The group was quiet during Dave's reflection time.

"Then, it was time for open conversation, first about the content and then about the process. Members of his group averred that they had learned immensely, even though the focus was on science and, more specifically, assessment in science. In fact, each of them declared an intent to try portfolios sometime before the end of the year. Alison asked if Dave wanted to 'tutor' the rest of them in designing portfolios for different purposes in their own content areas.

"When they began to focus on the process, the high school teachers agreed that, once again, it had worked. It protected the presenter (who, after all, had taken some risk bringing student work to be examined), and it drove the thinking deeper. Dave summarized, 'I think that, if we had just begun to talk about this, in a discussion, we wouldn't have gotten this far'" (adapted from Easton, 2009, pp. 5–7).

The GHMS English teachers were excited to share the tuning protocol process, especially as it related to science portfolios, with the Science Department.

ABOUT PROTOCOLS[2]

Dave and his group were engaging in professional learning using protocols for dialogue. The one they were using the day Dave brought portfolios is called *The Tuning Protocol*. No, a *Tuning Protocol* is not a process for tuning a radio to the clearest station, getting an instrument ready to play, or diagnosing and fixing a car. It is a process for fine-tuning what educators do using student work or professional practice. Steps for the tuning protocol are included as Resource 6.4.

Protocols, in general, are processes that help groups achieve deep understanding through dialogue, which may lead to effective decision-making, although decision-making and problem-solving are not typically the end-goals of protocols. Protocols provide structures for groups that allow them to explore ideas deeply through student work, artifacts of educator practice, texts relating to education, or problems and issues that surface during the day-to-day lives of educators.

David Allen (2004) notes that, even if protocols focus on student work, the purpose of protocols is to "move beyond grading and evaluation of the work to discussion that contributes to teachers' understandings of students' learning and their own instructional practice" (p. 9).

The National School Reform Faculty (NSRF), which developed and helped people learn many of the protocols in use today, suggests that protocols consist of guidelines for conversation." In their words, the structure of a protocol—"which everyone understands and has agreed to"—permits "a certain kind of conversation . . . which people are not in the habit of having" (www.nsrfharmony.org).

People may, at first be put off by the word "protocol". As Joe McDonald (1996) says, "Some readers . . . may think protocol a pretentious word." He declares, however, "I like the word . . . its two principal meanings reflect some deep dynamics." First, he says, "is the diplomatic meaning." A protocol "provides a way for people with different interests, even deeply antagonistic interests, to interact productively and respectfully while protecting those interests." He adds, "A protocol in the diplomatic

---

[2] Easton (2009, pp. 7–9).

sense is a kind of treaty governing a particular realm of interactions." McDonald also likes the word because of its scientific meaning: "a plan for inquiry" (p. 205).

In his book, *Assessing Student Learning: From Grading to Understanding*, David Allen more specifically describes protocols:

- They are facilitated. The facilitator may be from inside or outside the school.
- They are structured. Time is allotted for different activities and for different participants to speak—and listen.
- All those taking part share norms for participation, for example, respect for the student whose work is being discussed (1998, pp. 85–86).

In a later book, *The Facilitator's Book of Questions: Tools for Looking Together at Student and Teacher Work*, Allen and Tina Blythe elaborate: 'While different protocols vary in significant features, they all do two things: (1) provide a structure for conversation—a series of steps that a group follows in a fixed order, and (2) specify the roles different people in the group will play (typically, a facilitator, a presenter, and participants)' (2004, p. 9)

Above all, protocols provide the means for professional discussion, unlike that usually found in a faculty lounge (or even typical faculty meetings!). The student work or artifact from professional practice, the issue or text—these anchor professional conversation to the realities of educators' lives.

Finally, protocols help educators build collaborative communities, sometimes called Critical Friends Groups (CFGs) or Professional Learning Communities (PLCs). According to the NSRF,

Protocols are vehicles for building the skills—and culture—necessary for collaborative work. Thus, using protocols often allows groups to build trust by actually doing substantive work together' (www.nsrfharmony.org).

KEY CHARACTERISTICS OF PROTOCOLS[3]

As Blythe and Allen maintain in their book *The Facilitator's Book of Questions*, 'a well-designed protocol is more than the sum of its steps' (p. 20). They have a certain feel or spirit to them made up of some tensions:

- The tension between talking and listening
- The tension between discipline and play
- The tension between safety and risk
- The tension between individual learning and group learning' (2004, pp. 20–21).

They also are affected by the people who are engaged in the protocol: their experiences, backgrounds, skill, and their self-concepts as professionals. They are affected by the artifact of teaching and learning (student work or professional practice) that they are working on as well as by the facilitator of the protocol. Protocols are not as simple as they seem initially.

---

[3]Easton (2009, p. 9).

Some aspects of protocols make them difficult for some people to engage in right away. For example, according to Allen (1998, pp. 8–10), staff in traditional schools may find protocols challenging because, according to the culture in those schools, people

- Avoid controversy if at all possible.
- Seek autonomy and isolate themselves (i.e., privatize their work).
- Guard what they do and what their students do or share only in the form of *show 'n' tell*.
- Prefer to share *tips and tricks* rather than student work or deeper aspects of their professional practice (p. 11).

We can, of course, continue to engage in the same kind of professional development we've always engaged in (sage-on-the-stage) and continue to get the same results we've always gotten (see Allen's list above), or we can change culture by engaging in different ways of working with each other. As I said in both the 2004 and 2008 editions of *Powerful Designs for Professional Learning* (p. 11), "schools and districts cannot wait until the context [culture] for professional learning is perfect. Having assessed context and made as many changes in context as possible, schools and districts should engage in professional learning, such as protocols. These professional learning opportunities themselves will improve the context for powerful professional learning, and the potential for real change for all the learners in our school systems."

Protocols are an important structure for PLCs, helping people learn dialogue and collaborative skills. Through their structure, which might seem annoying at first, participants trade listening and speaking roles . . . and learn to listen better. They feel protected from interruptions (arguments and "bird walks") when they speak. They learn how to give feedback so that it can be heard (usually "warm" and "cool" feedback, with various ways of phrasing "cool" feedback). They help participants use the strategies of dialogue to go deeper into a topic. They promote inquiry.

You can discover more about protocols on Resource 6.5: roles in protocols, types of protocols, and evaluating protocols.

This e-mail went out from Tasha to other members of the Design Team on Saturday:
"Hey gang. Inside sources tell me that our Josie spent two hours with the superintendent and the Director of Personnel on Friday. Wonder what's going on???!!!"

YOUR TURN: WHAT ARE YOU LEARNING?

"I'm not sure I want my name associated with this interview. I just want to say that I'm learning that I don't belong here. It should be enough to teach my subject well in my own classroom, in my own way. I shouldn't be required to serve on teams. I don't want to do all of this 'soft' stuff, this process stuff. I don't see how a PLC will help me become a better teacher."

What about your learning related to this chapter? What can you say?

SO WHAT?

"I'm glad they are going to do the 'taking stock' exercise. That'll make them feel better, but people won't respond honestly. They'll say whatever will make the fewest waves. I will, too."

How is your learning important to you and what you do?

NOW WHAT?

"I hate to sound so negative, but I've seen these things come and go. I guess it's time for me to go."

What action(s) will you take in terms of your own learning?

RESOURCES FOR CHAPTER 6

6.1 Example of an Innovation
    Configuration Map

6.2 The Writing Assessment
    Process

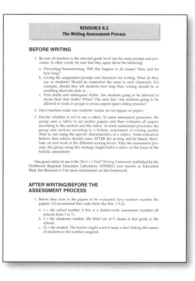

6.3 The 6+1 Trait® Writing Framework

6.4 Steps for Using the Tuning Protocol to Examine Student Work

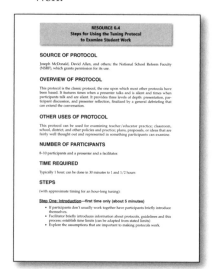

6.5 More About Protocols

6.6 A Rubric for Evaluating the Effectiveness of Protocols

7

Expanding Context; Focusing on the Future (May and June)

In which more data hits Glen Haven Middle School (and the whole district) between the eyes. In which the Design Team compares goals and plans the next PLC. In which the whole PLC takes stock and looks toward the future. In which the whole staff debates **IT** (but not Information Technology) and focuses on what to do during the summer.

Testing week ended. On the next Monday, a fine, powder-blue-sky, late April day, students were finding it hard to gear up for learning again. After all, tests usually come at the end of learning, right? "Five more weeks to learn?" they said, "Oh, m-a-A-a-A-an!" Glen Haven staff shared student sentiments but did what teachers do everywhere at this time of the year. They hitched themselves up to the wagon, shook out their weariness, and began to pull a heavy load toward the last day of school. They invented snazzy titles for everyday work ("Today we're going to play Worksheet Wonder!"), sought exciting materials, kept cheer in their voices and calm in their hearts . . . and kept track of the days, hours, and minutes left until June 6.

The morning of the districtwide professional development day early in May was relatively easy; all they and staff members across the district had to do was listen to a speaker who had a freight train of slides featuring impossible-to-read statistics. It was actually a pleasure to sit there, just listening or mentally planning the rest of the school year. The speaker was dramatic but not enough so to hold wandering minds.

The activity in the afternoon got their attention, however. The superintendent spoke about the graduate rate problem in Glen Haven, referring to what the morning speaker had said about national graduation rates. "Turn over these graduation rates, and you'll find a national dropout problem," he said, "and it's right here in Glen Haven." He showed them a slide with the following information:

Figure 7.1   Graduation Rates 1997–2007

	Class of 1997	*Class of 2007*	*Change from 1997 to 2007 (by percentage point)*
Glen Haven School District	64.8%	62.5%	−2.3
State	70.3%	66.2%	−4.1
National[1]	65.7%	68.8%	+3.1

"Remember," the superintendent said as voices rose around him. "Remember that the other side of the graduation rate is the dropout problem. If we graduate 62.5% of our students, we have 37.5% who drop out." "Wow!" "Unbelievable!" "Who would have thought that Glen Haven, a midwestern district of medium size, would have such a dropout problem?" they said to each other in a variety of ways. Then the superintendent showed them this slide:

Figure 7.2   Graduation Rates for Student Subgroups, 2007

	Glen Haven School District	State	National[2]
African American	50.9%	52.2%	53.7%
Asian American	78.4%	77.6%	80.7%
Caucasian	75.1%	74.5%	76.6%
Hispanic	50.6%	52.3%	55.5%
Native American	50.7%	51.4%	50.7%

"We're losing half of the students in some of our subgroups," some said. "Half!" "And, we're not getting better at keeping students in school; we're getting worse!"

The superintendent said, "Is our graduation rate acceptable? What should it be?" Before the buzz began, Stephanie Hodges moved the entire district staff into predetermined small groups composed of cross-sections of the district: elementary, middle, and high school teachers; teachers of different subjects; noncertificated staff; family and community members; and administrators from both the school and district level. The small groups drew their chairs together as if around campfires and tried to get past their disbelief into more useful frames of mind.

After 45 minutes of discussion, Stephanie challenged them: "What does the dropout rate in the district mean to you in your school?" She directed them to meet in rooms in different parts of the high school according to their school affiliation.

---

[1]*Education Week Diplomas Count,* 29(34: June 10, 2010), 24.

[2]*Education Week,* June 10, 2010, p. 24.

Suddenly they had cause to remember what the morning's speaker had shared with them. Quoting the esteemed yearly report called "Diplomas Count" (published by Education Week*), the speaker had said, "Every school day, more than 7,200 students fall through the cracks of America's public high schools. Three out of every 10 members of this year's graduating class, 1.3 million students in all, will fail to graduate with a diploma. The effects of this graduation crisis fall disproportionately on the nation's most vulnerable youths and communities" (Swanson, 2010, p. 22).*

Let's take a look at some issues related to this districtwide professional development day.

THE BASIS FOR THE STATISTICS

Arriving at national statistics related to graduation and/or the dropout rate used be almost impossible. There were so many ways to look at these indicators of school, district, state, and national success. Some state systems counted GEDs (General Educational Development diplomas); others counted only awarded diplomas. Some counted certificates of attendance; others counted other not-diploma categories. Some described students as "dropping out" when no one answered "here" during roll-call. Others followed up on absent students to be sure they had really dropped out, giving up only when they couldn't find particular students but trying to persuade those they did find to come back to school. Transcript transfers made the whole process messy; some schools required transcripts from previous schools for enrollment; others went ahead and enrolled students without transcripts, so the sending school received no notification of the move and counted the student as a dropout.

Finally, a method for calculating graduation rates was agreed upon and used nationwide. Called the Cumulative Promotion Index (CPI), it defines graduates as those who "graduate on time with a diploma" (*Education Week*, June 10, 2010, p. 30). The CPI "represents the high school experience as a process rather than an event, capturing the four key steps a student must take in order to graduate: three grade-to-grade promotions (9 to 10, 10 to 11, and 11 to 12) and ultimately earning a diploma (grade 12 to graduation)" (*Education Week*, June 10, 2010, p. 30). This information provides a "grade promotion ratio," which adheres to the "guidelines established under the federal No Child Left Behind Act" (*Education Week*, June 10, 2010, p. 30).

BLAME AND SHAME

If you had been able to listen into some of the school-based conversations, you might have heard comments like these:

"Well, if they'd only teach them how to read in elementary school, we wouldn't have such a problem later."

"This isn't my problem. I teach second grade, and kids are OK when they leave my classroom."

"It's really a high school problem. I wonder what they do there?"

"Do you think we have something to do with the problem, in fifth grade?"

"That's a hard grade because they go to one of the middle schools for sixth grade."

"The ninth-grade teachers need to do a better job of helping those students adjust to high school."

"I teach social studies. Kids love social studies!"

"Eighth grade is such an upheaval for students. High schools are way too depersonalized."

"My kids come back and tell me how much they loved [name the school] and me."

One of the ways of looking at how people deal with change is through the work of Kubler-Ross, whom you encountered in Chapter 6. The immediate reaction of district staff was denial: "These data can't be reflective of Glen Haven School District. We don't lose that many kids! We don't have a dropout problem! We do our best! Look at what we have to work with! Parents . . . community . . . the feeder school. . . ." The next stage, anger, may include blaming. It may also include shaming, wherein people feel they have done poorly as individuals or as a school. Blaming and shaming often occur in the Storming part of Forming-Storming-Norming-Performing (a description of group processes that you encountered in Chapter 1).

Although blaming and shaming are natural processes, they are not especially helpful. It's important for individuals and schools to move to a set of beliefs related to the following premises:

1. We need to remember that we are "in this together." All of our students are . . . *all of our students*. What we do as individuals with one set of students is insufficient, no matter how good it is, if other experiences students have are harmful (or at least, not helpful). A marvelous experience in fifth grade, the thrill of playing football in eighth grade, or the excitement of a lab experience in tenth-grade biology: These are not enough to immunize students against a toxic school culture and toxic experiences within that school, especially if students have weakened immune systems (their personal, family, and community lives).

2. We all want to get better in the work we do as educators.

3. We need each other to make sure that we all get better in the work we do.

4. We all want to be kind and courteous, *and*, to accomplish #2, we also need to be thoughtful, insightful, and provocative with each other.

WHERE ARE THE STUDENTS?

In its school-based session at the district professional development event, several GHMS staff members asked, "Where are the students? They should be here. They know exactly why they drop out. They could tell us . . . if we asked them!" Hurray!

COMMENTS ON THE PROFESSIONAL DEVELOPMENT DAY

The staff from GHMS emerged into the afternoon sunlight (still sunlight though it was 4:00!) feeling bruised and overwhelmed. They had mostly been feeling mighty proud of the work they had done during the year. The superintendent's new data felt like too much too late, even though Tasha had tried to get them to realize that these data only added fuel to the other data the group had collected and analyzed.

"It doesn't change anything," Aaron said, "it just gives us more reason to make changes according to what we know about what students need to learn."

"But," Eva asked, "what do we do about the dropout rate?" Eva Teller, a math and science teacher from the sixth-grade core, had not participated in any of the PLC work so far.

The district professional development day needed to end on a more positive note, so that participants could walk out into that wonderful sunshine with possible solutions in mind. In fact, Stephanie might have switched the morning and afternoon sessions so that the day could begin with the district-relevant data and discussion sessions. That change would have grabbed the attention of everyone. Although the guest speaker spoke mostly about the national situation, with his freight train of slides, he could have been encouraged to present some of the many success stories about states, districts, and schools improving graduation rates (see box).

GETTING PEOPLE INTO GROUPS

Sometimes it's harder to transition adults into groups than it is kindergartners into their next activity, but the transitions for the district professional development day worked well. When people arrived at the high school . . . and before they could get coffee . . . they were given nametags with numbers on them. The numbers corresponded to the hours, half hours, and quarter hours on a clock: 1:00, 1:15, 1:30, and 1:45, for example. When participants met in mixed-role groups right after the superintendent shared dropout data, they picked up their folding chairs and migrated to a sign on the wall for their hour, with the 12:00 at the front of the room and the 6:00 opposite. Once there, they found others who had their specific time and organized themselves into small groups

---

Success Stories

- Minneapolis School District's data program that allows close monitoring of "whether students pass their courses, as well as the state exams for graduation" (p. 6).
- That school district's program, "We Want You Back" (p. 8).
- The Fall River, Massachusetts, school district's attention to practicalities such as whether or not students have transportation to and from school (pp. 6–7).
- The Elgin, Illinois, school district's focus on individual school needs so as to target an intervention (p. 8).
- The Milwaukee, Wisconsin, school district, which has been working with the Wisconsin Center for Education Research on an early-warning system, what some call a "dashboard" system because dashboards "appear on principals' computer monitors the moment they log on in the morning . . . [and] summarize student and teacher attendance, as well as daily student-suspension numbers and some achievement data" (p. 4).
- Summer programs such as those provided in Cincinnati to help students transition from middle to high school.
- Stockton, California's effort to "identify students who have left high school, locate them, and lure them back, or, in some cases, to mark them off the dropout rolls after confirming that they've enrolled someplace else" (p. 9).
- Nontraditional paths to graduation, including small alternative schools, such as those in Nashville, Tennessee (p. 10).

- Graduation coaches for potential dropouts, such as those in rural South Carolina (p. 16).
- This *Education Week* special report lists 21 urban districts which "beat the odds," calling them "urban overachievers." These include Jonesboro, Arkansas; Mesa Unified in Arizona; and Long Beach Unified in California *(Education Week Diplomas Count, June 10, 2010).*

according to the quarter hour. It was noisy; it was chaotic; and it happened.

I used to try to orchestrate these transition times more than needed—and worry about them in advance—but I have learned as a facilitator to just turn my back and trust that adults will figure out how to make things work, once I've given them directions, simply and quickly. Adults are better at transitions than kindergartners, actually.

Other methods for getting people into groups include putting variously colored dots on nametags, swiping them with different colored markers or using differently colored paper for nametags. See Resource 7.1 for additional ideas on grouping.

The next day, members of the Design Team slogged into the small conference room outside Josie's office and sat quietly, trying to remember why they were there, ruminating about the previous day's shocker, and trying to forget how much they had to do. Josie brought an array of healthy snacks and a few candy bars to the meeting, and everyone went for the candy bars. It was that time of the year.

"I think we're on the right track," Roz said to summarize the Design Team's discussion regarding the previous day's news. "We know that many students start to think about dropping out in middle school."

"Or earlier," Andy said. "Did anybody catch that quote about elementary and middle schools?"

Dottie spoke up, "I got it. 'The signs that students may not last until graduation often show in the data teachers have collected in elementary and middle school.' It's from Manuel J. Rivera who used to be the superintendent in Rochester, New York. He said, 'You begin to see signs long before 9th grade— kids who don't have interest, and that begins to impact their attendance. . . . [Y]ou see kids who test quite well, but who are completely not engaged in learning.' They include some students . . . who are 'inappropriately and incorrectly' labeled as having disabilities and end up languishing in special education classes" (Aarons, 2010, p. 6).

The quotes brought a hush to the group. Finally, Josie murmured, "Just another reason we've been doing the right thing this year."

After a moment, Forrest said, "What I want to know is what those people who objected to our PLC work said in the interviews."

"Good transition, Forrest!" Tasha commented. "Let's get back to planning our last PLC meeting. We'll want to share the results of our one-legged interviews."

Robbie spoke up, "I think we need to take what those individuals said in the context of the interview results and not focus on them—whoever they are—only."

"So, taking stock is first?" Kelly asked.

"Yes," Tasha said, "let's make that first, especially the focus on CBAM and the interview results. What else?"

"Well, we need to return to our Proposed Action Plan," Josie suggested. "Is that still valid? How are we going to work toward that?"

"I think we need to have a transition between the two," Dottie ventured, "and perhaps we need to return to what we learned about our graduation rate yesterday."

"I once attended this conference in math," Ariel said, "and we did something called a future search conference, only it was modified. What we did helps people go from their current state to a preferred future. I have the name of the person who led that, and I can call her."

"I've done something like that, too," Roz said, "and it was pretty powerful. People considered what would happen if they made no changes to their current state. No one wanted to do that, so they were eager to go on to a preferred future."

"Can you get this set up in time for our half-day early release?" Tasha asked.

"Almost a week," Ariel said with a shrug and smile, "no problem."

"So maybe we do taking stock including a discussion about yesterday's shock, and then a future search to determine what we need to do. . . ."

"Don't forget all the data we've collected this year," Kelly interjected.

"Taking stock based on the data we've collected and the district graduation rate," Tasha amended.

"And, then future search to seal our commitment and a look at whether we're still 'on' with the Action Plan," Kelly added.

"There's our agenda," Tasha commented. "We're getting good at this!"

"Summer plans," Josie suggested.

"And a celebration. We deserve it," Andy said.

So, the agenda looked like this:

Activity	Purpose	Materials and Procedure
Welcome and opening activity	Get people focused	Aaron will facilitate Two truths and a lie
Agenda check	Get people focused	Agendas online (not on paper) Aaron will facilitate
Norms	Help the meeting run smoothly	Norms online; discussion; commitment Josie will facilitate
Reading the walls	People will refresh their memories	In advance, Kelly will put out materials from the PLC portfolio; Roz will give directions for taking stock/environmental scan and visual dialogue. People will start by reading the walls and will do so intermittently during visual dialogue process
Taking stock/ environmental scan; *what's* most important in terms of learning	Determine current status	Visual dialogue; brainstorming of what we know and evidence Roz will facilitate
Taking stock/ environmental scan; *so what* does our learning mean to us?	Determine what's important: so what	Gallery tours; people will form new groups to read the visual dialogue charts; they will write what's most important to them from the visual dialogue charts
Future search	Commitment to change If we do nothing. . . . If we can shape a preferred future. . . .	Discussion Ariel will facilitate

(Continued)

(Continued)

Activity	Purpose	Materials and Procedure
Goals: A review	Certify or change—these are the right goals	Aaron and Forrest will facilitate
Getting specific	Clarifying the work this summer and next fall	Tasha will facilitate
Evaluation of PLC meeting	Refocus on norms	Robbie will facilitate
Closing activity	Celebration	Robbie will facilitate Snowball activity

The whole faculty migrated from their lunches into the library media center, about as slowly as stock to slaughter. Their expressions were somber, almost as if they were longhorns heading up the ramp in Kansas City. The mood changed, however, with acknowledgement of their state and the opening activity Two Truths and a Lie. With some energy, they reviewed the agenda and pledged to abide by the norms. Then, Roz invited them to "read the walls" where Kelly had posted materials from the PLC Portfolio he had been keeping. See the box for a list of what was on the walls.

A List of What Was on the Walls		
Professional learning and professional development	The booklet on district resources	Four Corners at GHMS
Calendar of events	Results of the artifact hunt	Interview script
Starter norms	Five goals or purposes	Analysis of interview responses
Force-field analysis (barriers and boosters)	Ariel's cartoon	Analysis of focus group responses
Leadership assets	Agendas for each PLC meeting	Analysis of shadowing results
Results of the Design Team survey	Agendas for each Design Team meeting	Sentence strips
GHMS Design Team Characteristics	Names of people on the Investigative Team	Categories by round (from sentence strips)
Data in four categories: achievement, demographics, perceptions, and processes	Names of people on the Design Team	CBAM results – Design Team, whole school
Pictures of data	Names of people on each of the specialty teams	Writing assessment results

After they "read the walls," Roz had them divide into mixed groups to create a visual dialogue about what they had learned. The template was simple: a web with "What We Have Learned" in the middle:

Figure 7.3 Template for Visual Dialogue

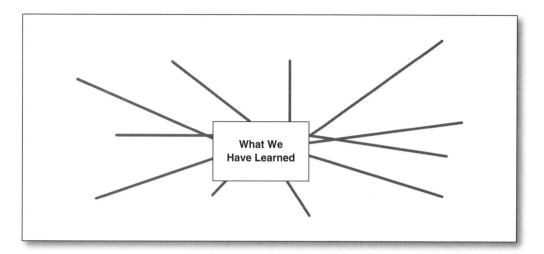

Roz charged the visual dialogue teams to complete the web with what was most important to each team in terms of learning over the past year. Some members of the visual dialogue groups went back to the "walls" as they worked.

TWO TRUTHS AND A LIE

A popular conversation starter, this activity works well in meetings, too. Aaron began this activity with reference to the time of the year: "So, it's May. How are you doing?" He let people grumble a bit before he said, "So, take a minute and scribble down three things about how you're doing now. Two should be truths; one should be a lie. Then, share these at your table. Try to guess which are truths and which is a lie." The energy soared in the room. This opening activity acknowledged where people were (exhausted) but let them have fun with their current status and with their colleagues. It took awhile for Aaron to round up the group and herd them back onto the agenda.

TAKING STOCK

You have been engaged in a version of taking stock of your learning at the end of each chapter by, first, reading the musings from someone at GHMS about What–So What–Now What and then creating your own. You read more about What–So What–Now What in Chapter 6. Taking stock focuses a bit more on the first two parts of this processing activity: What and So What.

The National School Boards Association (NSBA) describes taking stock as understanding where you are now. It "involves thorough examining of both the internal status of your district or school and the external context in which it is situated" and is accomplished through an environmental scan or collection of data to "answer questions about the present and future of the school district" (http://www.nsba.org/sbot/toolkit/ts.html).

ENVIRONMENTAL SCANS

Environmental scans are usually part of taking stock. They accomplish the following:

- develop "a common perception";
- identify "strengths, weaknesses, trends and conditions";
- draw on "internal and external information"; and
- provide a "key on-going process for internal and external honesty and openness to changing conditions" (http://www.nsba.org/sbot/toolkit/ts.html).

Tools for environmental scanning include surveys, questionnaires, interviews, and focus groups. The GHMS PLC used visual dialogue and gallery tours to "scan" their environment and take stock.

As soon as there was a significant pause among the visual dialogue groups and after looking at the quantity of writing on the webs, Roz asked the visual dialogue groups to stop their work. "What we have learned is up there," Roz said, waving her hand around the room at the visual dialogue charts on the wall. "Let's redivide ourselves so that we can do a gallery tour, so each of us can see what's on the webs. As usual, in each group we'll have a docent from each of the visual dialogue groups so that, when we come to that visual dialogue chart, we can ask questions. Here's what to do on your gallery tour: Notice commonalities among the visual dialogue charts. The commonalities will indicate what's important to us now. Notice the differences, too, but really focus on the commonalities. Why are those things so important to use? Why will they be important as we move forward?" A little confusion about dividing into Gallery Tour groups, but soon there were seven groups moving from chart to chart, their members scribbling notes at each chart while a docent explained what the visual dialogue group had done and why. (See Resources 3.15, 3.16, and 3.17 for more information on visual dialogue and gallery tours.)

After each gallery tour group had completed the circuit, Roz asked them to return to their original seats. Then she said, "What did you discover? What is common among us in terms of what's important? Why do you think these things are so important? What have we learned?" She was surprised by the first comment.

"What have we actually done," someone called out, "besides collect data?" The room got quiet. Frank Kemmerer waved his hand and then stood up, "This has been a whole lotta process, not much content."

Roz said, "Tell us more, Frank."

Somewhat reluctantly—he didn't really like speaking in front of adults—Frank stood up. "Have we done anything to help students learn this year? We've had a lot of surveys and interviews and such, but have we really done anything? I think it's been . . . a waste of a year." If silence were not already an absolute, it could be said that the room got even "silenter."

Margie Lyons raised her hand, "We didn't implement anything, like 5 years ago we implemented cooperative learning. We didn't do anything different this year."

"Ummmm," Libby Gandy said. "I did. I started listening to students more. I changed some of my strategies for teaching mathematics so they were more active. I used more groups."

Burt seconded her, "I asked my students to talk about how they learned math and what helped them and got in the way. And, I made some changes in the way I taught some of the hardest concepts."

Several people spoke at once, some raising their hands, some not. Roz stepped back into her facilitator role: "I think it's important to hear from everyone. Was this year a waste?"

Lorena Soltar, a counselor, waved her hand. "There's something different this year. I can't quantify it, but it feels as if something's stirring here. There's more energy, and it's positive energy. I get this feeling from students and staff."

"It's like we have drifted the past few years," someone else said.

"Or bogged down," another clarified.

"I hate to be corny here, but I'm feeling a little hopeful about what we can do at Glen Haven, and I haven't felt that way for some time," Anita Solazzo added.

"I, myself," Sanjay volunteered, "have made a lot of changes in science. They're only in my classroom, but students are much more engaged. They aren't as hard to control because they're interested in what we're doing."

The comments continued until Frank spoke up again, "I don't really understand what you're talking about. I don't know what it is that we're doing. All we know is that students aren't doing as well as they should. But what is IT?"

Roz wrote the word IT on a blank piece of chart paper:

"We haven't done a whole lot of the same thing," Douglas Donohue, the technology aide, pointed out. "Like cooperative learning, I mean."

"So, is IT the culture of our school?" Fatima Hoyle asked. "The way we think of students and the way they think of themselves here? The way we think of ourselves and the way students think of us here?"

"Maybe IT is not one single thing; it's lots of things, changes we make in the classroom as we become more aware of what students need," Kay Meehand pointed out.

"And," Fatima stated, "that's culture. The way we think of ourselves and our students here. The way they think of themselves and us here. The way we act toward each other."

"But," Margie said, "aren't we going to implement something as a whole faculty so that students learn better? Is it enough to make these little changes in our own classrooms?" It was "silenter" time again.

Robbie spoke up, "I think we may discover what we want to do as a whole faculty, but I can't think of any one thing we want to do now. I think just being aware of students' needs more and trying to make learning better for them in our own classrooms is a start."

"So," Roz said, "does IT look like this?" She made a new drawing:

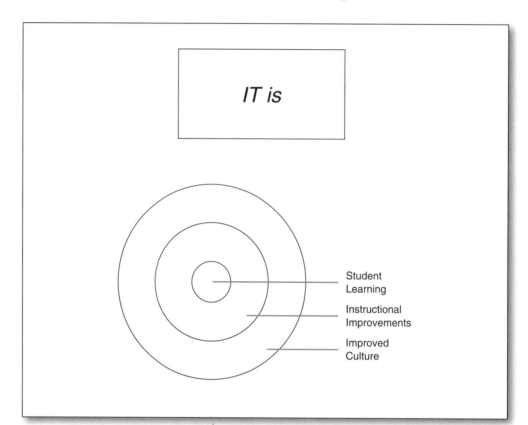

"That's a pretty simple chart," Pamela Rosario commented, "but I'm guessing that a whole lot of things fit into Instructional Improvements—like curriculum and assessment and active learning and project-based learning and standards and. . . ."

"And a whole lot fits under culture," Libby added.

IT

IT is a common problem in terms of school change, and I'm not talking about Information Technology or Interworking Techniques or Inspiration Transformations (whatever those last two are). Educators are accustomed to implementing IT—a strategy that an expert has taught them, such as cooperative learning. They implement a "thing" as a whole district (think of differentiated instruction), a school, or a grade level or department. Usually, they have not thought up IT by themselves. They have not engaged in the steps GHMS has followed to identify needs and then look for solutions.

With IT, people are pretty good about the "what" but not the "why." Sometimes, they just do the "what" because somebody told them to do so. Unfortunately, when the "what" falters, they don't have the "why" to go back to—they may not be sure what needs the "what" addresses. And sometimes, although they may understand the "what" at some level, they don't understand the deep construction of the "what," how the inventors of "what" got there. They don't know the assumptions, the model, or the logic that led to the "what" and, therefore, can't go back and rethink what they are implementing.

Training and professional development have contributed to this approach to change. Usually educators are "trained" on a strategy that they are expected to implement by a "sage on the stage," or a guru who has figured everything out for them, without really knowing their contexts. You've heard of the seagull style of professional development? A seagull flies in, drops a load, and moves on. Lately, people have been referring to this type of professional development or training as "drive-by." I've even heard it called "spit 'n' pray."

Professional learning guards against this type of professional development. There isn't an IT until there's a need for it. Once educators have understood needs through a variety of data collection and analysis strategies, they are ready to consider what to do. They're ready to look for one or more ITs. A PLC often finds that one IT doesn't fit all needs, that some people need this IT and others need that IT. At the very least, a school's ITs are going to be personalized to that school, not proclaimed from the district, state, or federal levels. (Have you had enough of IT yet? I have.)

CULTURE[3]

Fatima, Libby, and others ventured the thought that the PLC's work during the year might have had a positive effect on culture at GHMS. Just the fact that adults were meeting together to understand what's going on at GHMS had stirred the system (much like the butterfly effect). Let's look a bit more at culture. Why should schools think about culture? Here are five good reasons:

- It's there whether we think about it or not.
- Culture affects every aspect of a student's life at school.
- Culture affects the adults as much as the students.
- We can be unintentional about culture . . . or intentional.
- An unintentional culture may be a harmful culture.

School staff can fuss about program, curriculum, instruction, and assessment, but these make little difference to student learning if the culture itself is not oriented toward learning.

Culture manifests itself in a variety of ways. You can feel a school's culture when you walk through the front door. It declares itself in school design (exterior and interior), rituals, hero-making (what's in that trophy case, for example), symbolic displays, rules, and etiquette. It is a bit more hidden, but still there, in the structure of a day, governance, curriculum, instruction, assessment, events, and rewarded behaviors.

Culture is the ethos of an organization, its mores, values, customs, and traditions—and how they appear to outsiders and influence what insiders do. People say of their culture, "That's just the way we do things around here."

One of the best definitions of culture comes from Terrance Deal and Kent Peterson, as cited in Jerald (2007), who define it as an "'underground flow of feelings and folkways [wending] its way within schools' in the form of vision and values, beliefs and assumptions, rituals and ceremonies, history and stories, and physical symbols."

---

[3]This section has been adapted from Easton (2004, pp. xxix–liv).

CULTURE AS STUDENTS SEE IT

One of the best ways I know for thinking about school culture is through the eyes of students who exist within it. The best experience I've had viewing culture in this way is at Eagle Rock School and Professional Development Center (Easton, 2002, 2008) and other schools serving struggling students (and which students do *not* struggle at some point?). I have observed that students (outwardly struggling or not) are particularly sensitive to a culture that, intentionally or not, seems unfair or depersonalized. Here are five elements of culture that seem to have particularly powerful effects on students:

1. being part of a learning, not a testing, culture;

2. being part of a culture that focuses on relationships;

3. being part of a culture that focuses on community; and

4. being part of a culture that focuses on principles, not rules.

5. Being part of a democratic culture.

1. For example, struggling students seem to do better in **a learning, not a testing, culture**. Many have been tested, tested, and tested again as they struggled to find a place for themselves in schools. Tests often led to labels and special placements; in their minds, the tests had negative consequences. They made a case that these students were different (and most kids just want to fit in). Also, many struggling students do not do well on tests, even though they may know and understand tested material. Here are some comments from Eagle Rock students on <u>why</u> they didn't test well (Easton, 2008, pp. 11–13):

Lack of Confidence. David said, "I used to hate tests. Everybody thought something was wrong with me, so they kept giving me these tests. I used to freak out, and I'd get all the answers wrong. I knew something was wrong with me." Sevi confessed, "I was afraid the tests would prove that I'm not very good at things, so I messed up on purpose."

Lack of Interest. "I didn't see why we needed to take these tests. They didn't relate to what interested me," claimed Elliott. Calen said, "Mostly I was absent on test days. I hadn't been in school most of the year, so why would I go on the test days?"

Interest in Revenge on a System They Didn't Think Was Fair. Amanda confessed, "It [doing poorly on tests] was one way I could get back at school. I just made random patterns on the answer sheet and I finished first and could do anything I wanted. Well, and [get back at] the teachers and my parents and everybody that took tests so seriously."

Fear and Low Self-Esteem. "I would look around me and all the other kids were finished and I had barely started. I would get more and more nervous and then I would just give up. I knew I wouldn't do well," Manny commented.

Differences in How Students Learn and Think; Apparent Disconnect Between Learning and Test-Taking. Khalid said, "I just don't think that way. I think all the answers are right in some way." David added, "The hurry-up part of tests makes me nervous. I like to think about things."

Group Identification. "Well," said Mahkaea, "we certainly weren't the ones getting good grades and looking so preppy on test-taking days. We didn't see the point in having sharpened pencils. Nobody I knew did good on those tests." Luis added, "I definitely didn't want to be one of those kids who do good—well—on tests."

Doubt About the Relevance or Purpose of the Tests. "I never planned to go to college, so I didn't see the point of these tests," stated Adam (who, indeed, went to college and is still working toward graduation). Scott agreed, "It seemed more important to the teachers and the principal. They had a big rally, which was really stupid. And ice cream at lunch."

Once Eagle Rock students became convinced they were learners, which is what happens in a learning culture, they had a new attitude toward testing. Here's what some of them said about testing in a learning culture (Easton, 2008, pp. 12–13):

Self-Confidence as a Learner. Lauren stated, "I just feel more confident. I feel like I can do tests now." Miguel stated, "It's kind of a challenge now. I want to see if I can do them."

Seeing Testing as Part—Albeit a Small Part—of Learning. Aashli suggested, "We just learn so much at [school]. It's like college and, so, I think I can do OK on the tests. They don't bother me."

Seeing Testing as "No Big Deal." Veronica claimed: "They don't seem as hard to me now for some reason. They're kinda fun even."

Wanting to Perform Well on Tests. Tanya declared, "It's worth it to do well on tests at [my school]. I want [my school] to look good."

Seeing the Challenge in a Test. Nate said, "I just look at tests as one big problem to be solved now. And, I guess, the parts of tests are all little problems to be solved. And I know how to solve problems." Adam added, "It's really funny about what I can do now. I always thought I was too dumb to do tests but now I like to prove that I can do them."

Knowing That Tests Are Neither True Indicators nor the Only Indicators of Their Worth. Vanessa stated, "I know I'm good at some things now. I didn't need a test to tell me that."

How do students define a learning culture, one that helps them at least tolerate tests? Eagle Rock students said that learning occurs when people are

- Doing and experiencing, not just being passive and listening;
- Experiencing new input or stimulus;
- Practicing, reinforcing, and repeating or extending what they know;
- Working according to their passions and interests;
- Teaching others;
- Applying what they are learning;
- Problem-solving or struggling with ideas;
- Relating what they are learning to themselves; learning about what they value;
- Discovering and understanding their place in the world;
- Feeling empowered to act;
- Working in a safe environment;

- Motivated (feeling some compulsion about learning!);
- Reflecting;
- Feeling as if they are having fun;
- Part of a continuous connected process of learning; and
- Learning according to their own style or preferences (Easton, 2008, p. xl).

Teaching occurs when people are helping each other do what is listed above.

2. Asked by their own teachers, other educators, their own families and others, struggling students have consistently—and emphatically—named **relationships** as the key difference between schools that work for them and those that don't. Why relationships? Here's what staff and students said:

Trust and Learning. Repeatedly, the word "trust" came up for staff and students. Sevi, an Eagle Rock graduate, commented, "It is important for a relationship to exist between students and their teachers for a few reasons. Most importantly, it builds trust on both sides by allowing something deeper than a relationship limited to the classroom to grow. A sense of community is created which then creates a general feeling of support. When a teacher reaches out to a student on a more individual level, it shows the student that the teacher genuinely cares about supporting the student and is not just trying to pass them through."

Status and Hierarchy, Power and Authority. Trust is related, in what may seem a strange way, to status and hierarchy, to power and authority. Here is how students and staff frame that relationship:

Sevi elaborated, "If there is any sense of hierarchy, the student's trust, progress and willingness to listen is not based on genuine respect but on the duties of fulfilling [what] a higher power demands."

Mohammed, a former Eagle Rock instructor, commented, "Many young adults and adolescents have, for most of their lives, built [up] a distrust and suspicion toward authority. In many cases, authority is manifest in the adults in their lives: parents, teachers, police officers, babysitters, politicians, and principals. In traditional settings, the lack of respect that young people feel from those in authority leads to a repression of emotions and an overall sense of marginalization.

"Young people tend to feel that adults do not validate their emotions, thoughts, ideas and experiences. Adults regularly say, 'Don't cry!' 'Be a big boy or girl!' 'Don't yell!' 'What's wrong with you?' and 'I'll give you something to cry about!' Ultimately, this tells the young person that he or she must move away from the current experience because it is unacceptable. All subsequent events with authority only deepen this sense of marginalization."

Mohammed continued, with even more passion, "Marginalization in any context, particularly among the young, creates a suspicion of the dominant group, in this case someone in authority. In other words, young people begin to believe that all authority is equally dismissive of youth perspectives and experiences. The response, among the young, is a dismissal of authority as a whole and, more so, the values that are represented by authority. Young adults have no reason to believe that authority is really there to help them grow and learn."

Modeling Good Relationships. Students learn what they see. As Ted and Nancy Sizer maintained in their book *The Students Are Watching: Schools and the Moral*

Contract (1999) students watch what staff do—not just listen to what they say—and behave accordingly.

Modeling relationships is critical in schools—staff-to-staff, staff-to-student, and student-to-student. An Eagle Rock administrator referenced the Sizers' book as he reflected on relationships: "Human relations are at the center of any school. The way the staff treat each other provides students with a template for interacting with each other."

The Whole Person. A focus on relationships means that members of the school community are looking at not just the academic side of each other but at each other as whole persons.

Sevi commented, "If a teacher only knows a student as the student, then it is hard for the teacher to really understand the student's needs, struggles, progress, and interests. Jen, a former Eagle Rock instructor, added: "It's so crazy. Students don't come in parts. They are whole people, many faceted. So are we. But, in regular schools, we are supposed to pay attention only to how students are doing academically, only to how they learn. How can we pay attention to just their learning, when learning is a function of all of them?"

Accountability. Relationships require some form of accountability. Dan, a current Eagle Rock administrator, addressed this aspect of relationships: "Personal relationships allow for people to hold each other accountable, thus raising the proverbial 'bar.' This concept applies in both academic and personal growth arenas." Ryan, a former student, added, "If I have a relationship with someone, I'm not going to let him down. I'm going to work hard for him—and, for me, too."

Vanessa, a graduate, said wryly: "It's a lot easier not having relationships, I guess. You can just go through life not caring. But when you've built a relationship and you care about others, you really think about them and about who you are and what you do . . . in relation to them."

3. Relationships are not enough. Struggling students seem to thrive in a culture that focuses on **community**. Community gives students a chance to invest in something bigger than themselves as individuals. Addressing the greater good—and helping young people see beyond their egos—is an important aspect of community at Eagle Rock.

Even community is not enough; the word needs a powerful adjective in front of it: *Learning*. Learning communities help students and adults succeed.

Brown and Campione list among the characteristics of a learning community the "seeding, migration, and appropriation of ideas" (1998, pp. 160–161). What a fascinating concept! Members of learning communities *seed* "the environment with ideas and concepts that they value and . . . harvest those that 'take' in the community. Ideas seeded by community members *migrate* to other participants and persist over time. Participants in the classroom are free to *appropriate* vocabulary, ideas, methods, and so forth that appear initially as part of the shared discourse, and by appropriation, transform these ideas through personal interpretation" (1998, pp. 160–161).

Calling a school a learning community doesn't necessarily make it so. A real learning community is brought to life through purpose. It is nurtured. It grows and changes. It matures. Without constant care, it soon begins to wither and die.

Community is not just for students; it is for adults, as well. Adults in community, such as a PLC, discover vast benefits. (See Resource 7.2, the research of Shirley Hord on the benefits of a learning community for both adults and students.) Learning community: what a concept. Imagine everyone in a school being part of a learning community!

Jeremy, former gang member, Eagle Rock graduate, college graduate and parent, recalled the importance of community to his learning. "The benefits of the whole school learning community are intentionality (one of my favorite words) and consistency. When all actions of community are in tandem, then goals are achieved easier and with greater success."

4. A culture that is conducive to learning for struggling students has a focus on **principles, not rules**. Educators don't always look at it that way. Struggling students = discipline problems = rules.

Eagle Rock is a principle-based community. Its principles are summarized in a formula that lacks mathematical exactitude but makes up for that by being internally logical. Here's the rather imprecise (i.e., wrong mathematically) formula for Eagle Rock's principles: $8 + 5 = 10$. You can find the principles themselves on Resource 7.3. These principles guide every aspect of life at Eagle Rock, from curriculum to advisories, from service to presentations of learning, from hiring practices to restorative justice.

Here are some things to think about in terms of rules:

1. People by themselves (or guided by principles) won't do the right thing. They must be required to do the right things—through rules.

2. People deserve rules, just like they deserve punishment if they break rules.

3. The people in charge are the ones who make the rules; the people who don't have any power follow the rules so that the people in charge can live the way they want to.

4. As Stephen Covey, management guru, says, "Conflicts naturally arise out of . . . differences. Society's competitive approach to resolving the conflict and differences tends to center on 'winning as much as you can'" (1989/2004, p. 10).

5. Rules are imperfect. First, many are either too specific or too general to be applied fairly.

6. Rules are often a quick fix. "Oh-oh, we need a rule for that," someone says when a miscreant draws attention to a problem. Someone drafts a rule, and it becomes institutionalized, and then people begin to see its long-term, systemic effects . . . and may very well regret that rule.

7. Rules cannot address complexity. That's why they're broken—life is complex and rules do not always apply.

8. Rules seldom attack a root cause.

9. Rules are usually exterior. They emanate from outside us; they come from someone else—a "they," if you will, who has decided how we shall live and has the power to make that image into a law of some sort. If we disagree with the rule imposed on us from the outside, we are free to do something about it—such as go to court—where we can debate the rightness of the law.

Covey allows that in schools—at least those we currently have—which are "an artificial social system . . . , you may be able to get by if you learn how to manipulate the man-made rules, to 'play the game.' In most one-shot or short-lived human interactions, you can . . . get by and . . . make favorable impressions through charm and skill and pretending to be interested. . . . You can pick up quick, easy solutions that may work in short-term situations. But secondary traits alone have no permanent worth in long-term relationships. Eventually, if there isn't deep integrity and fundamental character strength, the challenges of life will cause true motives to surface and human relationship failure will replace short-term success" (1989/2004, p. 22).

To get more concrete, here are some principles that Covey espouses: fairness, equity, justice, integrity, honesty, trust, human dignity, service, quality or excellence, potential, growth, patience, nurturance, and encouragement. These are not practices (which are "situationally specific"); nor are they values. "Principles are the territory. Values are maps. When we value correct principles, we have truth—a knowledge of things as they are" (1989/2004, p. 35). You know you have principles when it is absurd to attempt "to live an effective life based on their opposites" (1989/2004, p. 35).

Struggling students seem to chafe against rules but love to engage in discussions of universal principles. They are more likely to accept and even defend decisions based on principles rather than rules. Principles do, however, take more time. Veteran students and staff need to acculturate new students and staff into the principles that govern the community. At Eagle Rock, this process takes the form of ERS 101, a "required" class for new students, as well as mentoring for students and staff. Important decisions require some mechanism for dialogue and discussion—a community meeting or gathering. There has to be a process for challenging decisions, and that takes time. The more that students themselves can be a part of—or even run—these events, the better the process.

Some rules still apply, the basic rules of safety. Just as traffic cannot be governed by best wishes, health and safety in a school cannot be left open to discussion. Eagle Rock has five rules (affected, in part, by the fact that the school is residential): No drugs. No smoking. No alcohol. No sex. No violence in any form.

Principles are the foundation for these rules, but the rules still apply as rules. Otherwise, Eagle Rock thrives because it is principle-centered.

Stevan, a former student, got it right when he declared, "I feel that it would be harder if there were a lot of rules. If there were, students would push them and test them to see how much stuff they can get away with. With principles, we live more responsibly because we have to think about what we do. We are in charge of ourselves a little bit more."

5. The focus on principles, not rules, leads to another aspect of culture that struggling students value: **A democratic community**. Democracy is a concept that borrows a bit from each of the other aspects of culture that help struggling students . . . and it pulls together these aspects.

Most states have a civics standard like this one: Students understand how citizens exercise the roles, rights and responsibilities of participation in civic life at all levels—local, state and national. Unfortunately, many K–12 students may only *study* democratic values; they may never *live* them in schools. In fact, while they are studying democracy, they may be experiencing contradictions to democracy in their daily school lives. Ben Barnes, former Texas House speaker and lieutenant governor, Washington lobbyist and Democratic fund-raiser, has commented that the United States needs to consider a farm club approach to democratic participation. Like baseball's farm club system, a political farm club system would "recruit and groom young people to run for office" (Weiser, 2004). Schools could be that "farm club."

But, a democratic culture is about more than living and learning democracy. It's about voice, choice, and accountability. The opportunity for students to have a say in matters that pertain to them is especially important to students who are struggling in school. To have voice, students must have information. School needs to be transparent to them. The more choices they can make, the more they have to think about what they are doing. The more choices they can make, the more accountable they will feel. See Resource 7.4 for a list of choices that schools can offer through curriculum, instruction, and assessment.

Choice and accountability are linked. Isabel spoke for a lot of struggling students when she said, "If I don't have choices and I have to do something I don't like I won't put any effort into it." Haleigh, also a student, claimed, "The more options I have, the more possibilities there are that there will be something I WANT TO DO!" As Danny, a student, said, "If people feel no control over a system, then they can easily "check-out." Jason spoke bluntly, "They [choices] are really important to me because when I was in jail I had no choices, so now I value them."

Sevi said, "Choices require responsibility and in my experience the more responsibility I have the more responsible I become. It is important for me to see the effect my choices have so I can begin to see how my choice affects my life." Ana remarked, "Choices are opportunities to direct my own life. I think . . . knowing we have the choice in our lives to succeed or fail is essential to learning responsibility."

The words *choice* and *accountability* go together. Voice, choice, and accountability are important facets of living and learning democratically.

Tasha brought the group back together with these questions:

   1. Are we doing as well as we could? Are we happy with the results we have right now?

   2. Can we get better?

There was no disagreement among the faculty: GHMS could do better.
   Frank asked one more question, "But have we made any progress this year in terms of getting better?"
   Kelly remembered what was posted on the walls and got up to point to their goals. "Here are our Tier 1 and Tier 2 Goals," he said.

TIER 1 GOALS:

1. Get more information about students, from students.

2. Hold regular special meetings, like the Data Dessert, to bring parents into the school (not just PTA meetings or parent conferences).

3. Ask the district for help (expertise, time, funding, resources).

TIER 2 GOALS:

1. Work on ways to engage students in their own learning; help them become more self-directed learners.

2. Make literacy a priority across the curriculum (including listening and speaking).

The group was amazed to look at the Tier 1 goals—they had actually accomplished two of the three goals. Kay Meehan from the English Department reminded them that they had made progress on the Tier 2 goal about literacy, and Burt reprised his comment about making changes in his mathematics classroom to help students become more self-directed.

Kelly added, "I do believe that one of the Tier 2 goals is primarily about culture, and one is primarily about improved instruction. So, our focus fits your diagram of IT, Roz, or vice-versa."

Frank had initiated a discussion about progress on goals that was a perfect segue into the next part of their agenda, the Future Search process. Before starting the group on the Future Search, Ariel stated, "Perhaps we'll want to modify those goals," Ariel said, "after we do a bit of Future Search."

FUTURE SEARCH

Marvin Weisbord and thirty-five other systems thinkers and organizational developers from around the world created future search conferences as a way of making "possible levels of action previously unobtainable . . . way beyond 'better meetings'" (Weisbord, 1992, p. xiii). Weisbord describes a "learning curve" in terms of how people solve problems. In the 1900s experts solved problems; in 1965, experts improved whole systems; in the 2000s, everybody needs to improve whole systems (1992, p. 4). He describes how "everybody" can improve whole systems in the second millennium, calling it a future search conference. As he described it, the conference, often 2 or 3 days in length, with thirty to sixty-five people, is highly focused. It consists of the following parts:

1. Review of the past (milestones)
2. Scan of the present—external (context/environment and data; forces shaping lives and institutions currently)
3. Scan of the present—internal ("prouds" and "sorries"—what to carry forward and leave behind)
4. Creation of an ideal future
5. Action planning

The future search conference has morphed over the past fifteen years. The future search conference structure that many people use now has these parts:

1. Scan of the present (context/environment and data; forces shaping lives and institutions currently)
2. Creation of an ideal future
3. Consideration of what would happen in the future if nothing changed
4. Action steps to ensure that the ideal future occurs and the status quo does not

Sometimes it's better for a group to create an ideal future first, before being influenced by current conditions. An important turning point for most groups is the dialogue about what would happen if nothing changes. Usually participants go back to the ideal future and rethink it in terms of preferred future (not necessarily ideal), incorporating some of the limitations of current conditions into the ideal. Then, they brainstorm on first steps. I usually caution a group not to go beyond first steps because one of the first steps needs to be "Think about who else needs to be involved and bring them on board."

There is no expert at a future search conference—rather, all participants are experts in that they have some experience in the system being examined. There is no external or hidden agenda. The agenda is created as participants move through the steps. There are no highly specific outcomes, just the expectation that participants will figure it out and, having done so, will take action on what needs to be done. Weisbord's formula for the successful conference is "THE RIGHT TASK + THE RIGHT PEOPLE + THE RIGHT SETTING = UNPRECEDENTED ACTIONS" (p. 8). The future search conference is the ultimate democratic process, with those who are going to be affected by the changes having a role in shaping those changes. Remember "them's as does the doin' does the decidin'"? Here's an example of that aphorism in action.

Weisbord describes core values for a future search conference (from David Angus, Gary Frank, Bob Rehm, 1989):

1. The first value is a matter of epistemology. We believe the real world is knowable to ordinary people and their knowledge can be collectively and meaningfully organized. In fact, ordinary people are an extraordinary source of information about the real world.

2. Thus, we believe people can create their own future.

3. People want opportunities to engage their heads and hearts as well as hands. They want to and are able to join the creative processes of organization rather than that being the sole domain of the organization's elite.

4. Egalitarian participation. Everyone is an equal.

5. Given the chance, people are much more likely to cooperate than fight. The [facilitator's] role is to structure opportunities to cooperate.

6. The process should empower people to feel more knowledgeable about and in control of the future.

7. Diversity should be appreciated and valued. (p. 13).

Sounds a lot like good professional learning, doesn't it?

One of the important distinctions that needs to be made is that a future search conference is not a problem-solving meeting, that is, it doesn't begin with a problem. It begins with an organization's desire for continuous improvement. It begins with acknowledgement of a past and present of good and bad and an incentive to achieve a "preferred future" (p. 49). Thus, it is more about "futuring" than "problem-solving" (p. 49).

Resource 7.5 provides worksheets I have used for a future search conference that begins with participants describing the ideal future (choosing among a variety of ways to do so) then considering current realities and what would happen if nothing changed.

Ariel's facilitation moved the PLC through the future search smoothly. Participants worked in mixed groups of 10 people to describe an ideal future. After brainstorming GHMS in the year 20__, they extracted five key words from the descriptions. Using the Delphi procedure (Resource 1.16), they merged their key words with another group's key words and continued the merge process until there were seven words that represented the future of GHMS for the whole staff. During a break, Robbie developed the key words into these sentences, one per piece of chart paper, which she posted around the room:

- *Glen Haven Middle School ensures the well-being (including physical and emotional safety) of all students and adults.*
- *Learning is engaging for students and adults; it is challenging but supported.*
- *Students see important roles for themselves in the present and future and understand how learning can help them succeed in those roles.*
- *Students are literate across the curriculum.*

After the group had read the sentences, Ariel asked them to think about and discuss this question: "What would happen if we made no changes at all in the way we 'do business' here?" Not sure they understood her, she added, "What if we just kept on doing what we're now doing?" Most of the lively discussion focused on the inability of the school to achieve the future they had designed without changes in how GHMS currently "does business." Otherwise, they commented,

"Well, we can't continue as we are now. We know too much now!"

"The data are too strong. How can we go against what we know and do the same old-same old?"

"We've already made changes. . . individually, at least. And, these seem to be working."

Ariel posed this question: "So shall we continue making changes at Glen Haven in order to improve learning for students?" The "ayes" had it, with only a single voiced "nay" from somewhere in the room.

Ignoring the single "nay," Ariel went on to current realities by saying, "Think about what we currently do here. If we were to work toward our preferred future, what would we keep? What would we drop? What would we add or change?" By the time people had completed a piece of chart paper at each table with these headings, they were feeling quite satisfied.

Key Element of the Future	Current Reality: Keep	Current Reality: Drop	Current Reality: Add or Change

Time was running out. The group had done as well as possible with a future search—but would have benefited from at least two more days and a wider variety of participants, especially people from the district and community, especially students. Ariel assured the group that the Design Team would consider next steps but not take any until the PLC could meet again. And, she asked if anyone wanted to join the Design Team. People looked around the room—you'd have to be crazy to volunteer for something new right before summer break!—but a couple of hands went up.

Josie waved her hand and, when Ariel called on her, asked for a moment to speak. Members of the Design Team, remembering Tasha's e-mail, caught each others' eyes. "Here it comes," they seemed to say. But Josie said, "We don't have much time left—and we definitely have to celebrate today's work, and the work that all of us have done all year. Before we launch our celebration, I'd like to make an announcement." She cleared her throat.

"We have some extra money—thanks to the state," she said, "but we have to spend or allocate it before July. I've already approved a great experience for two of our English teachers, K. D. and Anita. They're going to take part in the National Writing Project's summer workshop!" A round of applause.

"I have an opportunity related to one of the descriptions of our preferred future, the one about learning being engaging and challenging but supported. Has anyone heard of lesson study?" Several people raised their hands. "I'd like to have a couple of people go to a two-week workshop on lesson study. It's a great professional learning strategy, and it would be good to know more about it. It's the last week of June, and I'd like to fund another week this summer and a few days next year so that these people can continue to learn about it. Anyone interested?"

"Lesson study?" a few people whispered, but three raised their hands.

"Great!" Josie exclaimed. "And, I still have some money left over. If you have an idea that fits our preferred future, let me know. And, now, let's welcome Robbie!"

Applause, whistles, and cheers were noisy—people were getting punchy. Robbie bowed and said, with real sincerity, "I appreciate you all so much! Let's take the next few minutes to appreciate each other and what we've done together. You all have a blank piece of white paper in front of you. Write on it something you want to celebrate about our work together this year. Crumple up your paper. Make it into a snowball. It's January in May, and we're going to have a snowball fight. Ready, set, write."

People quickly wrote down a "celebration," stood up, and prepared to throw. "Ready, set, throw." The room blizzarded. "Throw again. Again. Now pick up your snowball and read it. Who would like to share what's on your snowball?" Several people did. There were appreciations for groups, such as the Design Team and the Data Specialty Team. There were lauds for Josie and other individuals. There were praises for students. There was admiration for bus drivers and lunch-room staff. Finally, Robbie said, "Sometime in the next week, post your snowballs on the graffiti wall near the faculty workroom. Sometime before you leave, read those snowballs and think about how lucky we are to be here at Glen Haven Middle School." Then, Robbie gestured to a cart that had just been rolled in to the library media center. "And, have yourself a purple, pink, or green snow cone before you leave."

And, just as the crowd started to move toward the cart, Robbie said, "Oh, hey, wait a minute. I forgot something." This almost always happens in meetings, by the way, and it's hard to bring back to order a group invited to disperse, especially when they're going for sweetened ice. When the room was moderately quiet, Robbie said, "We need to have feedback about this meeting. We'll be sending you an e-mail asking you to reflect on how well we did in terms of the norms and what worked and didn't work in terms of today's meeting. Than. . . .n. . . .k. . . .y. . . ." But by that time, people were beginning to chomp on grape, strawberry, or lime snow cones.

A SINGLE VOICE "NAY"

You may be wondering why Ariel did not stop to recognize and then address the concerns of the one person who said, "Nay," when asked, "So shall we continue making changes at Glen Haven in order to improve learning for students?" She may not have heard the "nay"; she may have been overwhelmed by the affirmative responses; she may have thought no one would respond negatively; she may have been aware of time constraints. She did the right thing.

The question was somewhat rhetorical, given the conversation that preceded it. Based on that conversation, Ariel probably should have made a statement rather than ask the question that received one "nay." If the group had not championed the continuation of changes as thoroughly as it had—absent the "nay" voice apparently— a sincere question would have been appropriate and Ariel would have appropriately attended to both yes and no responses.

Then, consider, there was only one person responding "nay," and that person may or may not have meant what he/she said. I can imagine the groans of a group that has signaled agreement when attention is given to a single person disagreeing.

How many persons saying "nay" does it take for a facilitator to pay attention? I don't know the answer to that question, but I think the appropriate way to deal with a single "nay" is after the meeting, one-on-one.

GOALS, ONCE AGAIN

How many times does a group need to focus on goals? I do know the answer to this question: many times. Over time, individuals within a group change, and the group itself changes, even if the people in the group started and stayed with it, and no others joined. A group grows its own individual and collective knowledge and understanding over time, so each time it works on goals it needs to work on goals.

Take a look at the many iterations of goals that GHMS faculty and staff formed through their PLC work. You'll find a summary of these goals on Resource 7.5. You'll find that the fabric of the goals has changed over time, with some threads repeated and some new threads introduced. Each time a group addresses goals, it recognizes patterns and is reassured; it also gets to use its own group (and individual) learning to create new patterns.

Addressing goals through a variety of formats, such as Future Search, is also a great way to triangulate work. When people assert basically the same goals through different processes they can be assured that their goals are true. They can also relish what their learning has exposed them to in terms of new goals. As with so many things, in goal-setting a real group is never "there"—finished with goals for evermore.

YOUR TURN: WHAT ARE YOU LEARNING?

Burt Reilly, the mathematics teacher who spoke up about how he has begun to translate some of his learning into his classes, commented on what he has learned. "I'm one of those people who go to a conference on just about anything, and I get something from it that I can use. I could take a conference on pottery, and I'd get something out of it. So, I may not say anything much, but I am learning all the time. It's like I'm on 'red alert' or something, always translating what people say into what I can learn."

What did you learn as you read this chapter?

SO WHAT?

"I used to think everybody was like me, so I am astonished when people say, 'This isn't about middle school or this isn't about mathematics' and then they tune out. I wish I could help them see that they can get something from everything."

Why is what you learned important to you?

NOW WHAT?

"I think I'm going to suggest to the Design Team that they end every meeting with a time for people to think about what they learned, not just what they did. Heck, I may even join the Design Team."

What will you do about your learning?

RESOURCES FOR CHAPTER 7

7.1 Other Ideas for Grouping People

7.2 Benefits of a Learning Community

7.3   8 + 5 = 10

7.4 Curriculum, Instruction, and Assessment Choices

7.5 Future Search Templates

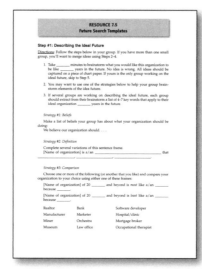

7.6 A History of GHMS's Goals

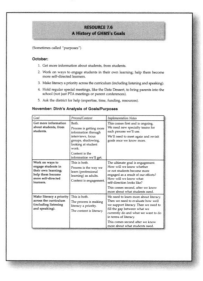

8

Exploring Leadership and Taking Action (June–August)

I n which the Design Team faces reality and in which faculty members participate in summer learning experiences. In which Josie compares Glen Haven Middle School's (GHMS's) work with the Professional Learning Community (PLC) work in another school. In which the Design Team thinks ahead to fall and the second PLC year.

"I couldn't tell the whole faculty without telling you first," Josie said to the Design Team, sitting rigidly in the chairs in the conference room next to Josie's office. "I'll be telling the whole faculty on Tuesday that I'm being transferred to E. M. Ross Middle School. Dr. Oscarsson is retiring, and the district wants me to start a PLC there."

"They have a PLC!" Aaron said.

"Well . . ." Josie started.

"Not really," Kelly said, "at least not according to what I heard."

"How can they do this?" Tasha asked. "We are doing so well . . . and you're a perfect principal for what we're doing. You understand and support us. You push us in subtle ways. You know so much, but you're willing to let us figure some things out. We've really accomplished a bond this year. . . ."

"And the district is going to tear us apart with this action," Aaron added.

"I think the district knows exactly what it's doing," Dottie said, "and it's a good decision. We'll miss you, Josie, but we can carry on." She smiled at Josie and gave her a mock salute.

"That's how I'm feeling, too. I'm very flattered by the district's request, and I know that Glen Haven's PLC is not about me. It's about you, and you can carry on." She returned the mock salute.

"How will we choose a new principal? What if that person is entirely wrong for us?"

"That's one thing I negotiated," Josie said. "You will have a big say in who takes my place. In fact, you will be the initial interview team, alone, if you want to do that. You can invite students to participate, if you'd like. Then, the Human Resources Department will get involved. Several people have already applied, and you can start by looking at their applications. Then you can interview the best candidates . . . and then you and district folks will make the final decision. If you don't want to do that, I know that the superintendent will be open to other procedures."

"Josie," Ariel started to say, "no one can. . . ."

And the rest of the Design Team chimed in, ". . .replace you!"

"I won't be far away," Josie said. "And, I'll be calling on you for your expertise. One other thing to tell you: Two of the staff members have requested a transfer, and we have one early retirement. I'll be announcing those at our last faculty meeting, along with my transfer. I want to be sure that faculty and staff—and students—have a big say in who replaces these three people, as well."

"Who are they?" Aaron asked. "Can you tell us?"

"Are they some of the complainers?" Forrest wanted to know.

"I think it would be best for me to announce those names at the last faculty meeting," Josie said. "And, prepare yourself for a bit of a farewell party then."

WHEN PRINCIPALS LEAVE

It's hard being a principal. It's hard when a school loses a principal who has done great things. It's hard for a new principal to take the place of an esteemed principal; it's even hard when a new principal replaces a less-than-esteemed principal.

Josie had principaled GHMS for 4 years, her first position as a principal after teaching for 7 years in a neighboring district and being an assistant principal at that district's high school for 4 years. Although Glen Haven School District didn't have any formal way to induct new principals, Josie found her own mentors and formed a support group with principals and assistant principals from her own and her former districts.

She transitioned slowly. Fortunately, when she took the helm at GHMS, there were no major crises onstage or in the wings. Glen Haven was in all ways a "ho-hum" school. So, the first year, in addition to everything a principal is required to do to manage schools, Josie concentrated on listening and learning. She asked questions; she tested assumptions; she vetted her observations. In her second year—in addition to spending much more time in classrooms, and doing everything else principals do —she focused on building relationships. In the third year, she began to invite teachers to join her in informal discussion groups around issues related to learning—while still continuing the conventional work of principals. She also started to ask teachers to pursue professional learning. That's how she got Kelly, Tasha, and Aaron to go to the summer workshop on PLCs. You read about the results of that conference in Chapter 1.

It's not that Josie couldn't have started a PLC herself. She knew plenty about them, and she knew that PLCs can make a difference in schools for student learning. She also knew that PLCs are less likely to be effective when mandated. She hoped that Kelly, Tasha, and Aaron would come back to GHMS enthused about PLCs—and she wasn't disappointed.

You may have wondered why Josie didn't say much at the Design Team and other meetings reported in this book. She served on every specialty team, too, and said little. She had enough confidence in herself and the people she worked with to trust them to bring up the issues, fuss with the factors, and make good decisions. The results didn't always match the specific outcomes she had in mind, but they were always appropriate. She sometimes sat with her hands clasped to keep from raising them to make a point, trusting instead that someone else would make that point, and perhaps better than she could. When she saw that the conversation wasn't going the way it should, she did say something, usually in the form of a gentle question, such as "What would happen if we . . . ?"

She wasn't perfect, especially for staff members who wanted to be told what to do, rather than figure it out through untidy group processes.

She also had confidence that she could leave GHMS and the PLC would continue its good work. There were too many people across the grade levels, curriculum, and roles who cared about it. She had worked with Human Resources and the superintendent to ensure the Design Team's prominent role in the hiring process. And she had already thought through how she would help the new principal: mentoring, inviting him or her to be part of a principals' support group, working collegially as the district circled wagons around the dismal graduation rate.

Thinking back on her career as principal of GHMS, Josie realized that she had instinctively staged her work as a principal, mirroring a framework that Ben Fenton, founder of New Leaders for New Schools, recommended for urban principals wanting to improve their schools (n.d., pp. 1–2):

Stage	Description
Stage 0	"Environment is chaotic and low-achieving; a successful turnaround effort has either not yet begun or is in its earliest phases. Few instructional strategies or cultural practices . . . are shared across the school" (p. 1).
Stage 1	"Practices include building a shared approach to school culture among all the adults in the building. . . . Also the principal gets to know each teacher well enough to address the most urgent development needs for individual teachers and across the faculty. The principal also identifies emerging leaders—strong performers who can serve on the instructional leadership team" (pp. 1–2).
Stage 2	"Stage 1 practices are deepened and supplemented by creating clear, personalized learning plans for every student's academic growth and each teacher's professional development. A principal also strengthens the school's systems for academic intervention and support and broadens the base of instructional leadership through the faculty" (p. 2).
Stage 3	"At this stage, a high functioning leadership team drives a school's culture and learning program as it nears its goal of preparing every student to reach college and career readiness. The principal's ongoing investment in finding and supporting teacher leaders is paying off through distributive leadership" (p. 2).

Let's look more closely at some other aspects of being a principal in an innovating school.

PRINCIPAL TURNOVER RATE

The longevity of a principal is short, especially in innovative schools. Although there are no data about principal turnover nationally, a number of states have studied how many principals leave schools and why they depart as well as the effects of their departure on their schools. According to *Education Week*, October 28, 2009, "data available from a handful of states suggest that only about half of beginning principals remain in the same job five years later, and that many leave the principalship altogether when they go."

A study by the Rand Corporation (2004) revealed that principal turnover rates in "Illinois and North Carolina were 14 and 18 percent per year, respectively, from 1987 to 2001." Researchers discovered that "schools with a larger proportion of minority students had higher rates of principal turnover" (p. 3). They also discovered that "principals at middle and high schools were found to be more likely than principals at elementary schools to change schools" (p. 3).

In a study of principal turnover in Texas, researchers Ed J. Fuller and Michelle D. Young "analyzed employment data from 1995 to 2008 for more than 16,500 public school principals. The average tenure over that time was 4.96 years for elementary school principals, 4.48 years for middle school principals, and 3.38 years for high school principals" (*Education Week*, October 26, 2009).

Researchers in a study of innovative New York City schools over a 10-year period discovered that only 16% of founding principals stayed in their schools. (A founding principal is one who starts an innovative school. In a sense, Josie could be considered a "founding" principal because of her effort to innovate at GHMS.) During that 10-year period, 48% of the schools experienced one change in leadership and 36% experienced two or more changes. Moreover, "47% had their first principal changes within the first four years of opening" (Weinstein et al., 2009, p. 2). They found that "the average tenure for principals in [their] sample is 3.4 and average tenure [in other schools] remains under 4.7 years during our study period" (Weinstein et al., 2009, p. 11).

WHY PRINCIPALS LEAVE

Principals leave because they

- make a career move (usually into district administration);
- abandon education, switching careers;
- are being reassigned within the district; or
- are being released from their principalships (fired or demoted).

Reasons for making a career move or switching careers are many and varied:

- Constant public scrutiny, a 24-7 job
- The frenetic nature of a typical school day
- Day-to-day problems that distract them from focusing on learning
- Poor working conditions
- Having to work within a culture they may not have helped to create
- Little support from other principals

- Few formal support mechanisms from the district
- Being overwhelmed by managerial responsibilities
- Having to "navigate the multifaceted job of principal" (Weinstein et al., 2009, p. 3)
- Finding that being an assistant principal does not prepare a person to be a principal
- "Incredible complicated, and sometimes hostile, transitions to principalship" (Weinstein et al., 2009, p. 12)—example: a midyear transition
- Number of principals preceding current one in a certain number of years (the higher the number in the fewest number of years, the worse the situation, usually)
- Politics and power dynamics in the district
- "This too shall pass" attitude of the staff toward the principal
- Turbulence elsewhere in the district, especially at the district level
- Turbulence in the community and/or school board
- Tensions between old role (sometimes teacher) and new role
- Figuring out how to be a leader in a shared-decision-making culture; learning to lead
- Dealing with teachers who are not meeting expectations

There's some speculation that principal turnover will increase as principals are held more accountable than ever for student achievement results. In fact, as Gerald Leader comments in the blog of Harvard Education Publishing in "No Principal Left Behind," most principals in the past "were not held accountable for their schools' performances" because there were no "accepted measures of student academic performance." In fact, schools were viewed as "assemblages of classrooms linked by corridors. Principals had no direct role in mediating student achievement" (Leader, 2010, p. 1).

SCHOOL REACTIONS TO LOSING A PRINCIPAL

What usually happens when a principal leaves a school? Teachers sometimes leave too, not necessarily to follow their principals but simply because their leaders have left. "High principal turnover [is] correlated with high teacher turnover," related to "decreased teacher satisfaction" (Weinstein et al., 2009, p. 7). The resulting churn of staff can threaten a school's culture. It becomes unstable and unpredictable.

The "best" teachers might leave. "Principals with strong education backgrounds tend to attract and hire teachers with similar qualification" (Viadero, *Education Week*, October 26, 2009). When those principals leave, they draw, like powerful magnets, the best teachers to their new schools.

Student achievement sometimes decreases . . . although some researchers speculate that achievement might have started to slide in the last year or so of the principal's tenure at a school, resulting in principal reassignment or replacement.

New principals may find themselves in a distrustful school community and may want to "reverse previous accomplishments" (Weinstein et al., 2009, p. 6). Indeed, new principals sometimes blockade improvements made BNP (before new principal) and may allow the school to revert "to previous patterns of inefficiency" (Weinstein et al., 2009, p. 7). According to an *Education Week* article (Viadero, October 26, 2009), Brenda J. Turnbull of Policy Studies Associates found that teachers who have developed a certain amount of independence and collegiality amongst themselves might be "making a lot of the decisions themselves. . . . It isn't easy to wrestle some of that power back." Instituting new reforms also becomes more difficult . . . as teachers get used to the constant turnover in the principal's office" (*Education Week*, October 26, 2009).

LEARNING LEADERS

The kind of leader who can ease the turnover trauma is the leader Douglas Reeves (2006) calls the *learning leader*. Reeves establishes four quadrants of leadership: lucky, losing, learning, and leading. He characterizes these types of leaders according to what he calls "antecedents of excellence": "those observable qualities in leadership, teaching, curriculum, parental engagement, and other indicators that assist in understanding how results are achieved" (p. xix).

<table>
<tr><td rowspan="4" style="vertical-align:middle">Achievement
of Results</td><td>**Lucky**

High results, low understanding of antecedents.

Replication of success unlikely.</td><td>**Leading**

High results, high understanding of antecedents

Replication of success likely.</td></tr>
<tr><td>**Losing**

Low results, low understanding of antecedents.

Replication of failure likely</td><td>**Learning**

Low results, high understanding of antecedents. Replication of success likely.</td></tr>
</table>

Antecedents of Excellence

Reeves, D. (2006). *The learning leader: How to focus school improvement for better results.* Alexandria, VA: ASCD, p. xx. Used by Permission from ASCD.

The "lucky" leader just happens to have the easiest-to-teach students and staff who are just fine with results that are just fine (but probably not earthshaking and definitely not attributable to anything the leader did). The "loser" leader probably couldn't do much, if anything, to improve teaching and learning because he or she just keeps "doing the same thing and expecting different results" (Reeves, 2006, p. xx). This person is all about change as long as it doesn't affect certain concrete specifics related to school: time and space, bus and lunch schedules, habits of veteran teachers, cement-bound policies and practices, and so forth. The "learning" leader, in the lower right hand square, may be learning but is not yet applying new knowledge, skills, understanding, or wisdom in any way that makes a difference. The leader who makes a difference as a learner (upper right hand square) applies learning so that the school culture changes significantly, and so do teaching and learning.

The learning leader understands that "leadership decision-making is more accurate and less risky when entrusted to a diverse group than to a single individual, even when that individual has significant expertise," according to Reeves, who replicated an experiment contrasting individuals' predictions of the distance from earth to moon with the group's average, which was closer to the real distance than most of the individual guesses (Reeves, 2006, p. 25).

The learning leader understands that "leadership is not a heroic and solitary enterprise" (Reeves, 2006, p. 16). The learning leader also knows that many types of leadership are needed for an organization to thrive and is content to let others take on some of those roles. You encountered these as "leadership assets" in Chapter 1 (Resource 1.11).

Learning leaders need to remember that the words go together: learning = leading. The "learning" part specifies a certain amount of vulnerability and risk-taking. The "learning" part keeps principals humble. The "leading" part means that something meaningful will happen in a school; it bespeaks confidence and persistence.

Tony Wagner and his coauthors assert in *Change Leadership: A Practical Guide for Transforming Our Schools* (2006), "We need leaders whose expertise is more invested in helping a group create the shared knowledge necessary for sustained improvement than in being the certain source of the answers and solution" (p. 209). They implore readers to realize,

> We can quickly agree that our schools and districts are not going to improve because of the heroic service of a charismatic leader working alone—that we must build teams (and build them not simply so there will be an army to follow our orders and pursue the plans we have masterfully created ourselves). (p. 210)

More than anything else, the principal who has "orchestrated a culture of team-based learning, where teachers relish working interdependently in the service of heightened student performance results" can ease the turnover trauma, according to Gerald Leader, who writes a blog for Harvard Education Publishing. Leader maintains, "Intrinsic to continuous improvement in student learning are teachers who create and execute a student performance assessment feedback loop" (2010, p. 2).

Principal Howard McMackin (responding to Leader's blog) commented on his own school, Rolling Meadows High School in Illinois:

> The work is enormous! Every day, it is more and more clear that our teacher leadership corps is the real heart of our system. No principal and his or her assistant principals can manage it. The typical principal and two assistants with part-time department heads can never find the time to invent and pilot new innovative systems, track and analyze data, train and develop team capacity, and facilitate and supervise everyone that needs to be involved. (Leader, 2010, p. 3)

McMackin suggests that educators consider medical or military systems that have officers and non-commissioned officers, sergeants, and corporals. "We need to rethink leadership roles in education. If we keep to the concept that only administrators are leaders, we will never have the manpower to address all the problems that interfere with causing all students to achieve." Business tends to have one leader or supervisor for every seven staff members. Low-poverty high schools sometimes have one for every 30 teachers, but "many supervisors must oversee more than a hundred people. Teachers laugh darkly about how little they interact with their supervisor" (Leader, 2010, p. 2).

Speaking as a practicing principal, McMackin reveals, "All our new hires must demonstrate leadership abilities," and he's not talking about principal hires; he's talking about instructional staff. "An improving school needs a depth of leadership organized around a set of procedures and protocols that define professional work. We can confirm that our most difficult problem for implementing new effective designs is leadership, not just principal leadership, but teacher leadership" (Leader, 2010, p. 3).

LEARNING LEADERS AND DISTRIBUTED/SHARED LEADERSHIP

What Leader and McMackin are talking about, of course, is shared or distributed leadership. According to Meryle Weinstein and others in *New Schools New Leaders: A Study of Principal Turnover and Academic Achievement at New High Schools in New York City* (2009), "One of the advantages of a model of distributive leadership is that it will minimize the impact of a principal's succession on the school if various parts of the role are shared among the faculty and staff" (p. 2).

Shared leadership is not the only way to save an improving school when a principal leaves. District culture, rules, and procedures are important. The fit of the replacement principal—and the process that was used to select this person—are important. The new principal's openness to shared leadership and ability to honor what has already improved the school are also important.

DISTRIBUTED LEADERSHIP

Richard Elmore (2000) characterized learning leadership that is shared as "distributed leadership." His is the classic definition:

> Distributed leadership, then, means multiple sources of guidance and direction, following the contours of expertise in an organization, made coherent through a common culture. It is the "glue" of a common task or goal—improvement of instruction—and a common frame of values for how to approach that task—culture—that keeps distributed leadership from becoming another version of loose coupling. Distributed leadership does not mean that no one is responsible for the overall performance of the organization. It means, rather, that the job of administrative leaders is primarily about enhancing the skills and knowledge of people in the organization, creating a common culture of expectations around the use of those skills and knowledge, holding the various pieces of the organization together in a productive relationship with each other, and holding individuals accountable for their contributions to the collective result. (p. 15)

DISTRIBUTED LEADERSHIP AS A CONCEPT

Distributed leadership can be used as a theoretical lens for examining leadership practices in a school (Mayrowetz, 2008). James D. Spillane sees the concept of "shared leadership *practice*" as the central and anchoring concern of schools (2006, p. 1).

Distributed leadership can also be examined in terms of democracy and achieving efficiency, efficacy, and building capacity (Mayrowetz, 2008).

"Distributing leadership, in a practical sense, means a shift away from the traditional, hierarchical, 'top-down' model of leadership to a form of leadership that is collaborative and shared," according to Donald Hackmann of the University of Illinois. "It means a departure from the view that leadership resides in one person to a more complex notion of leadership where developing broad based leadership capacity is central to organizational change and development" (n.d., p. 12). Spillane continues this line of thought:

> A distributed perspective on leadership involves more than identifying and counting those who take responsibility for leadership in a school. It also involves more than matching particular leaders with particular leadership functions and activities, though that is an important initial step. A distributed perspective on leadership presses us to examine how leadership practice gets defined in the interactions among leaders, followers, and key aspects of the situation; it urges us to examine the interdependencies among these three defining elements. In doing so, we explore whether and how things like better designed tools, new or reworked organizational structures, different combinations of leaders on particular leadership activities might transform the interactions and thereby potentially improve leadership practice. In this way, distributed leadership is a diagnostic tool that principals and others can use to think about the work of leadership and a set of ideas that can guide efforts to revise leadership practice. It is not, however, a blueprint. (2006, pp. 9–10)

SOME ASSUMPTIONS RELATED TO DISTRIBUTED LEADERSHIP

Distributed leadership is based on five key principles as identified by Elmore (2000):

- "The purpose of leadership is the improvement of instructional practice and performance, regardless of role" (p. 20).
- "Instructional improvement requires continuous learning" (p. 20).
- "Learning requires modeling" (p. 21).
- "The roles and activities of leadership flow from the expertise required for learning and improvement, not from the formal dictates of the institution" (p. 21).
- "The exercise of authority requires reciprocity of accountability and capacity" (p. 21).

One way to think about these assumptions, as they relate to GHMS, is to turn them into essay questions:

1. To what extent did GHMS see the purpose of their work, no matter who they were in the system, as improvement of instructional practice and performance, regardless of role. Give examples.

2. How did PLC work convey the belief that instructional improvement requires continuous learning? Give examples.

3. Who among Glen Haven's staff modeled learning? How?

4. To what extent did the roles and activities of leadership flow from the expertise required for learning and improvement, not from the formal dictates of the institution? Give examples.

5. Were there examples of reciprocity and capacity building? Explain in detail.

GETTING MORE CONCRETE ABOUT DISTRIBUTED LEADERSHIP

Spillane (2006) is interested in two, more concrete, elements of distributed leadership:

- "A distributed perspective on leadership argues that school leadership *practice* is *distributed* in the interactions of school *leaders, followers*, and their *situation*" (p. 2).
- "Key aspects of the situation in interaction with *leaders* and *followers* define leadership practice" (p. 7).

The situation can be "organizational routines and structures, material artifacts, and tools" (Spillane, 2006, p 7).

Don't be misled by Spillane's (2006) use of the words *leaders* and *followers*: "Leadership is typically thought of as something that is done to followers. From a distributed perspective, this is problematic because followers coproduce leadership practice in interaction with leaders" (p. 5). Spillane asserts, "While individual leaders act, they do so in a situation that is defined in part by the actions of others—their actions are interdependent—and it is in these interactions leadership practice takes shape" (p. 5). In other words, "leadership practice is *not* a function of what a leader knows and does. From a distributed perspective, leadership practice takes shape in the *interactions* of people and their situation, rather than from the *actions* of an individual leader" (p. 2).

Spillane (2006) likens distributed leadership to a dance such as the "Texas Two-Step" or a square dance. The individuals each execute certain steps, sometimes mirroring each other, sometimes in tandem. But neither the "Texas Two-Step" nor a square dance can be reduced to its steps, which would be interesting, but not particularly meaningful alone. "The dance is *in-between* the two partners," he says. (p. 2). The successful dance merges from the interaction of the two (or more—think of line dancing) dancers—and from the situation, such as a great band, floor space, and whatever else helps people dance well.

TYPES OF DISTRIBUTED LEADERSHIP

Sometimes distributed leadership is "stretched over leaders and followers. We term this *collaborated distribution* to underscore the reciprocal relationship between the actions of the leaders and followers that gives rise to leadership practice" (Spillane, 2006, pp. 5–6). "Reciprocal interdependencies involve individuals playing off one another, with the practice of person A enabling the practice of person B and vice-versa" (Spillane, 2006, p. 6). Recall the Texas Two-Step, a good example of reciprocity. *Collaboration distribution* seems to describe how the principal, the Design Team, the specialty teams, and the PLC operated at Glen Haven. In fact, at Glen Haven there seemed to be sophisticated (and providential) ways for one group to "cut in" on another or one group to "hand off" a task to another.

There are two other types of distribution: "*coordinated distribution* and *collective distribution*. In a 'coordinated distribution' situation leaders work separately or together on different leadership tasks that are arranged sequentially" (Spillane, 2006, p. 6). Think, for example, of the Glen Haven decision to go with Tier 1 and Tier 2 groups. Think, also, of the coordinated work of the Interview, Focus Group, and Shadowing specialty teams. Spillane describes this cycle as involving

> a number of interdependent sequential steps—student test data and other information has to be analyzed before instructional needs and priorities can be defined. In this situation, the leadership practice is stretched over the different activities that must be performed in a particular sequence for leadership practice. (2006, p. 6)

The third type of distributed leadership can be called *collective distribution* because "practice is stretched over the practice of two or more leaders who work separately but interdependently. The actions of two or more leaders working separately generate leadership practice" (Spillane, 2006, p. 6). Glen Haven did not encounter this type of distributed leadership model but could have, for example, if Stephanie Hodges at the district level had become more involved in the work. The two would have had to work with the Design Team to coordinate their efforts.

Another way to think about types of distributed leadership is through this hierarchy (in terms of impact, the first is highest; the last is lowest):

- **Distribution as cultural:** practicing leadership as a reflection of the school's culture, ethos, and traditions
- **Distribution as opportunistic:** capable teachers willingly extending their roles to school-wide leadership because they are pre-disposed to taking initiative to lead
- **Distribution as incremental:** devolving greater responsibility as people demonstrate their capacity to lead
- **Distribution as strategic:** based on planned appointment of individuals to contribute positively to the development of leadership throughout the school
- **Distribution as pragmatic:** through necessity; often ad hoc delegation of workload
- **Distribution formally:** through designated roles/job description (MacBeath, 2005, pp. 349–366).

Where would you put GHMS based on its first year as a PLC?

DISTRIBUTED LEADERSHIP IN REAL LIFE

In real life, distributed leadership can be understood through a number of different lenses. First, distributed leadership may be *formal* or *informal*. Most schools have some kind of formal distributed leadership:

- Principals and Assistant Principals
- School Improvement Team

- Data Analysis Team
- Student Support Team
- Standards Teams
- Grade-Level Teams
- Subject Area Teams
- Cross-Disciplinary Teams
- Department Heads
- Professional Learning Team
- Peer Coaching Team
- Mentoring Team (Hackmann, n.d., p. 16)

At the beginning of the year, GHMS certainly had its formal leadership structures: principal and assistant principal and instructional coach. It also had department heads who did not actually do as much as they might, although they called meetings periodically to look at curriculum and instructional materials. It had a sixth-grade core team. As the year progressed, Glen Haven relied on leadership from the Design Team and various specialty teams, as well as the whole-faculty PLC. Glen Haven augmented formal leadership through informal means; these people stepped forward as volunteers.

Distributed leadership can be restricted to those who are selected and named—a formal approach—or open, the way Glen Haven's process worked. You may remember how the Investigative Team tackled the structure of the Design Team in Chapter 1. They debated issues such as appointed versus volunteer members; members who are representative or not; exclusive versus inclusive membership; leadership; and how the design team would get its work done. They opted for volunteer, nonrepresentative, open membership and welcoming people who brought a variety of leadership assets to the Design Team. They decided that Design Team members, all volunteer, had to commit to 3 months on the team, that they could quit after that period, and that anyone could join at any time, as long as the new team member was willing to serve for a minimum of 3 months. Think how the culture of the change process might have been different if the Design Team consisted of appointed, representative members who were to serve "in perpetuity."

WHO ARE THE LEADERS?

In distributed or shared leadership, every school staff member is considered a leader. Principals and assistant principals have formal leadership roles that are usually not distributed; that is, they are administrators of a site. They manage what happens at that site. Sometimes teachers have formal leadership roles; they may be Teachers on Special Assignment (TOSAs), coaches, mentors, department chairs, team leaders, or managers of special projects.

Strong administrative leadership emerged as one of the elements of effective schools in the 1970s, but in today's schools, that role must be complemented by teacher leadership, a powerful but informal (that is, not titled) role that helps an entire school focus on student learning. That said, it's important not to distinguish among administrators, certificated, and noncertificated staff in terms of school improvement. Each can bring needed leadership qualities to reform efforts. According to

Charlotte Danielson (2006), leaders from the classroom share certain perspectives. They are engaged in

- "Using evidence and data in decision making" (pp. 29–30);
- "Recognizing an opportunity and taking initiative" (30);
- "Mobilizing people around a common purpose" (pp. 30–31);
- "Marshaling resources and taking action" (pp. 31–33);
- "Monitoring progress and adjusting the approach as conditions change" (pp. 33–34);
- "Sustaining the commitment of others and anticipating negativity" (pp. 34–35); and
- "Contributing to a learning organization" (pp. 35–36).

Pate and his coauthors from Valdosta State University (2005) see teacher leaders as "a catalyst for instructional leadership" (p. 2). They suggest that "fusing teacher leadership into the culture of schools can result in stronger instructional programs and improved student learning" (p. 2). The result "in schools with a high capacity for leadership," they say, is that "learning and instructional leadership become fused into professional practice" (p. 4). They describe specific attributes that teacher leaders bring to school improvement:

- They communicate well, especially in terms of listening to and respecting the ideas of their colleagues.
- They "are credible experts" (p. 5). They have the trust of the community and public.
- They can be persuasive, especially if they share stories of learning or failing to learn.
- They are advocates for improved teaching and learning.
- They "tend to be risk-oriented" (p. 5).
- They are "role models for students" and "they are also models for other teachers" (p. 6).
- "Teacher leaders offer hope and encouragement to others" (p. 6).
- They have a positive effect on the morale of other teachers and staff.

Danielson (2006) catalogues some personal characteristics of teachers that help them serve in leadership roles. Teacher leaders

- Have a "deep commitment to student learning" (pp. 36–37);
- Are "optimistic and enthusiastic" (p. 37);
- Display "open-mindedness and humility" (pp. 37–38);
- Have "courage" and are willing "to take risks" (p. 38);
- Demonstrate "confidence and decisiveness" (pp. 38–39);
- Have "tolerance for ambiguity" (p. 39);
- Demonstrate "creativity and flexibility" (pp. 39–40);
- Persevere; and
- Show a "willingness to work hard" (p. 40).

As I think about the leaders at GHMS, I am struck by how members of the Design Team, the Data Specialty Team, the other specialty teams, and the PLC as a whole demonstrate Danielson's dimensions of teacher leadership.

SIX KEY FUNCTIONS OF SHARED LEADERSHIP GROUPS

Think about the following key functions of shared leadership teams in terms of what GHMS did:

Distributed Leadership Function	What the GHMS PLC Did
"Crafting a vision, delineating expectations for teacher leadership in the school"	Determined the structure of the Design Team
"Identifying and selecting teacher leaders, linking them to leadership opportunities"	Enticed faculty to volunteer
"Legitimizing the work of teacher leaders"	Expected, shared, and celebrated the work that the specialty teams did
"Providing direct support"	The fact that Josie and members of the Design Team participated on each specialty team; getting district support
"Developing leadership skill sets"	Through protocols and practices, such as the opening and closing of meetings, meeting design, the norms
"Managing the teacher leadership process"	Meetings of the Design Team; communication strategies; feedback strategies

Murphy, J. (2005). *Connecting teacher leadership and school improvement.* Thousand Oaks, CA: Corwin. Used by permission from Corwin.

PROBLEMS AND CHALLENGES OF DISTRIBUTED LEADERSHIP

At this point, GHMS does not seem to be facing any particular barriers, but you might be able to predict that one or more of the barriers Hackman (n.d.) describes will arise as Glen Haven moves into its second year of implementation:

- Community (and possibly the district office's) expectation that the principal is in charge of every leadership activity
- Changing a school's culture, when teachers are accustomed to being followers
- Time: For developing leadership skills, releasing teachers to engage in leadership activities
- Union resistance to teachers performing duties perceived to be administrative (such as involvement in teacher supervision or evaluation)
- Administrators' willingness to 'let go' when they ultimately are accountable

- Can create 'winners' and 'losers'; teachers who traditionally have been in leadership roles may perceive a loss of power
- Teachers with leadership skills may be pulled from the classroom by district administrators, to train others throughout the district. They may be recruited by other schools/districts for employment (p. 21).

A DEVELOPMENTAL PROCESS FOR SHARED LEADERSHIP

Speaking of implementation, MacBeath (2005) describes a three-phase process for enacting a distributed leadership model. As you read this, think about how Josie and the Design Team followed this model.

- Phase I: *Treading cautiously*

Principal strategically identifies leadership needs of school, identifies people who have the requisite capacities, and assigns responsibilities to them.

- Phase II: *Widening the scope of leadership*

Creation of a culture that offers teachers an opportunity to learn from one another's practice. Principal works to create an enabling environment, which encourages innovative ideas from all members of the school (teachers, pupils, staff, parents).

- Phase III: *Standing back*

Maintaining the dynamic by supporting others; culture is characterized by mutual trust and self-confidence (p. 364).

This developmental approach fits what Mayrowetz says about distributed leadership: We need a kind of team that can . . . share the work of deciding, assessing, and revising on a path to improvement that is almost never a straight line" (2008, p. 424).

SHARED OR DISTRIBUTED?

According to Spillane, the terms are often used interchangeably, "raising the question as to whether there is really anything new about distributed leadership. Is distributed leadership simply a re-labeling of familiar phenomena? At least in my understanding," he says, "there is much that is new about taking a distributed leadership perspective" (Spillane, 2006, p. 1).

Distributed implies to me an intentionality, a conscious decision at the level about "who" can do "what" and "when" and "where." *Shared* is a little more informal to me. Glen Haven is somewhere in the middle. Although Josie consciously chose three teacher leaders who had already shown potential to go to the summer conference on professional learning communities, other leaders emerged as volunteers for particular tasks.

A WORD ON LEADERSHIP TRAINING

None of the GHMS staff attended leadership training. Certainly, leadership training is available, even training related to distributed or shared leadership. The adventurous can even attend "boot camps" on leadership where they'll assist each other through a web of ropes tied between two trees or fall back from a height into the willing and able arms of colleagues in order to experience trust. The more sedate can sit in hotel conference rooms and learn about leadership from PowerPoints®.

Although it doesn't hurt to have background on leadership, especially the differences between traditional and distributed leadership, leadership is essentially experiential. The best way to learn it is to engage in it and to reflect on and debrief the experience afterwards with a group of trusted colleagues. The best way to learn it is to plan an experience collaboratively and then learn with others how well the experience worked. The best way to learn leadership is to have a constant and reliable feedback loop to provide data on how well the leadership experiences worked.

Before accepting the principalship at E. M. Ross Middle School in Glen Haven School District, Josie asked to attend a PLC meeting. It was held in the multipurpose room after school. Teachers arrayed themselves on the tiny seats that projected from the long lunchroom tables, spider bodies with legs that didn't quite touch the ground. They wiggled around a bit to find some measure of comfort, often with their backs against the table, legs splayed out, rather than facing the table. The principal, Dr. Oscarsson, took up a position at a podium that had been wheeled into the multipurpose room. Acoustics were terrible; even with a microphone, he could hardly be heard over the electronic feedback. Josie found a table toward the back, as had a number of teachers, and scooted around on the tiny seat herself. No position was particularly comfortable.

Dr. Oscarsson hrmmphed into the microphone and tapped it as he apparently did at every PLC meeting: dum-duh-duh-dum-dum. A couple of staff members completed the melodic phrase: dum-dum. He got the attention of the teachers and staff and asked someone close to him to distribute the agenda. Here's what was distributed:

PLC Meeting
April 7, 2XXX
3:00–5:00 PM

1. *Welcome*
2. *News and Announcements*
3. *Parent Conferences—May 6 and 7*
4. *Summer School*
5. *Next Year's Enrollment and Class Size Changes*
6. *News for the Community Newsletter*
7. *Reading*
8. *Last Minute Announcements*

Dr. Oscarsson flipped on the overhead projector and put on his first slide. Unfortunately, no one had lowered the screen on the stage above him, but after a moment of hesitation, a staff member rose, climbed the stairs at the side, and lowered it by hand. Still, the slide was dim—either the afternoon sunlight stirring up the dust motes around the high windows was too bright or the wattage of the projector bulb was too small. The slide featured "WELCOME" in a huge font and a smiley face.

In a genial manner, Dr. Oscarsson welcomed them. He announced the countdown to the end of school by days, hours, and minutes, and everyone cheered (no one knew he had a special reason for knowing so specifically the minute school ended). "Let's begin with announcements," he said. "Who has the first announcement?" A line started to form near the podium and, one by one, teachers and staff broadcast their announcements.

Josie wiggled on the hard, round, plastic seat, understanding for the first time how students felt at lunch—25 minutes was beyond endurance for anyone sitting on such a device. She thought to herself, "Maybe we should cut lunch by 10 minutes just so we can cut damage to the glutes." There were, perhaps, 15 announcements, none of them under a minute in length, and then people who had not yet gotten up to share some news or make an announcement apparently began to worry that they should have done so. They stood up and slowly—it seemed to Josie—made their way to the podium. "Perhaps," Josie thought, "they just need to get their voices in the room."

Just as one more person was rising, Dr. Oscarsson called an end to the news and announcements but promised that there would be time at the end of the PLC for additional podium patter. He then introduced one of the counselors, who had put together a set of transparencies about parent conferences. These were helpful: How to schedule conferences. How to greet parents. How to deal with problems. How to follow up on conferences. The faculty and staff had no questions about this agenda item.

The other counselor rose to talk about summer school, but without a set of transparencies. She listed the possible topics for summer school—math, reading, and language arts at all grade levels. She mentioned that teachers could teach summer school for additional pay, and she asked if there were any questions. Someone had stood up, perhaps in response to bodily agony, and she called on him. "Oh," he said, "I didn't have any questions . . . well, yes, come to think of it, I do have a question. What about a summer school class related to study skills?" "What do the rest of you think?" the counselor asked, and several people responded or raised the possibility of other summer school courses.

"We've got to move on," Dr. Oscarsson said, "or we won't get through this agenda. If you have suggestions for summer school, put them in Mrs. Duran's box. Moving right along," he said as he replaced his transparency with one full of numbers and charts that could hardly be discerned from the first row of tables. "I'll put this in everyone's mailboxes, but I wanted you to see projected enrollment figures and what they'll mean in terms of class sizes for some subjects." He proceeded to trace enrollment patterns for the last 5 years, overall, according to gender, and according to ethnicities. He then showed other slides that provided a 5-year history of class sizes in each subject. "These graphs show small increases every year, with another small increase next year. Any questions?"

His query brought a flurry of questions and comments about hiring practices in the middle school. Josie recalled one in particular: "I know we have to get kindergarten classroom numbers down, but I think that middle school students are just as fragile as 5-year-olds. We need to get class sizes down for sixth, seventh, and eighth grades, too." Several people nodded, but no one seemed surprised at this comment; apparently this subject had been tilled many times over.

Looking at his watch, Dr. Oscarsson said, "Time's flying. We've got to move on. I'd like nominations for stories for the next community letter, the last one this year. Ideas, people?" And, as he wrote suggestions down on a blank transparency on the overhead projector, people called out story ideas—25 of them. Apparently writing the newsletter rotated among departments because Dr. Oscarsson said, "OK, science department, here's the list" and whipped the transparency off the overhead, leaving a huge, white, pulsing square in the center of the screen. Perhaps it was Josie's head that was pulsing; the room had actually gotten darker. It was now 4:30.

"Finally," Dr. Oscarsson said, "we're going to get to the article I gave you to read. Has everybody read it?" Josie could almost hear him chuckling, he-he-he. People looked around and nodded yes. "Well, let's discuss it. What do you think of Steinke's ideas about intramurals?"

The room was noticeably quiet. Josie wondered if anyone cared, especially that late in the day, after a full day of teaching. Finally, someone stood up and said, "It's a great idea, I think." "What's a great idea?" another person shouted to make herself heard. "Having intramurals," the first person responded. "What's great about it?" the second person responded. The first person gave an example, the second person countered, the first person gave another example, the second person parried. "We already do intramurals," another person called out, interrupting the joust. "But," Dr. Oscarsson said, "we could certainly improve them, right?" "Sure," someone else said. "Let's put together a committee on intramurals," Dr. Oscarsson said. "Who'd like to be on this committee?" A few people raised hands, and Dr. Oscarsson wrote down their names.

"Thanks," he said, "that's the only way we can get better, thinking about new ideas and working on them. I wish we had more time for that, actually. Any last announcements?"

And there were, to Josie's amazement. Other people who, perhaps, just wanted to be heard or to be seen as someone important enough to make the PLC meeting last 5 excruciating minutes beyond its ending time. As people were extricating themselves from the torturous disks that served as chairs around the lunchroom tables, a few people called out announcements that were beyond "last," things like "Don't forget to bring pizza on Friday!" Or, "Remember we're doing a canned foods drive next week."

REMEMBERING WHAT A PLC IS AND WHAT IT IS NOT

No wonder educators have disparaged PLCs as one more fad that will pass . . . the flavor of the month or year. "Why would anyone want to attend a meeting like this one?" Josie thought. Even though it was called a PLC meeting, nearly all of the agenda items could have been shared through technology, and the learning related to the article on intramurals could hardly be described as learning. Josie got back to her office and made two lists. She labeled one side "What PLCs Are" and "What PLCs Are Not." You can see this list as Resource 8.1.

ALL ABOARD, NOT

Some of the members of the Design Team were dismayed that people were transferring from GHMS. They were still registering disappointment about the person who told Josie that he or she disliked the direction GHMS was taking and who claimed to be speaking for others. Can a school ever get everybody on board all at the same time so that a school change effort has unanimous support?

No.

Claes Janssen (in Weisbord, 1992, p. 101) provided an image of energy related to change. He proposed a four-room apartment:

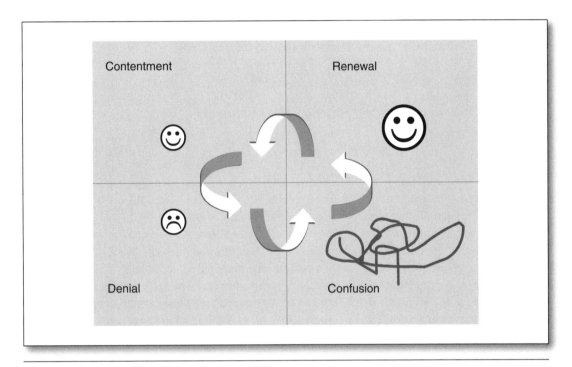

Some people may want to stay in the contentment room; others want to stay in the denial room; still others in the confusion room. In a school improvement initiative, you want everyone to go with you into the renewal room . . . but they might not stay there forever with you. They might, for example, go back into contentment, having made some superficial changes. They might go into denial when the going gets tough. They might choose to remain confused, rather than go back into renewal.

You might recall the discussion in Chapter 6 about the stages of change. One way to look at stages of change is through CBAM (Concerns-Based Adoption Model). You can also characterize people engaged in change according to when they begin to embrace change—some are early adopters or scouts on the frontier. Others are laggards. The Four-Room Apartment is just another way to understand how people go through change . . . and since change is what school improvement is all about, it's useful to have another model.

It's all right if some people (say 10% to 15%) stay in their own rooms and don't come out. In fact, several reform networks say that 80% "buy-in" is about right to initiate and sustain a school improvement effort (Coalition of Essential Schools, n.d.). The Design Team may want a higher percentage, but it'll never have 100%.

Also, it may not be productive to focus on the 10% to 15% who won't come out to play. It is far more productive to focus on helping the 25% to 79% move from room to room, ending up in Renewal.

The room was quiet after Josie made her announcement at the last faculty meeting of the year. Then, spontaneously, people stood up and applauded heartily. "Ahhhh," Josie said when the clapping had died down, "you are glad to see me leave!" Protests broke out, but Josie waved her hand for silence. "In the next week or so I will have a chance to talk to each of you individually. I don't see our conversation as a farewell, at all. I'll be just around the corner. I want to honor your feelings and mine when we have these conversations." She turned away for a moment, perhaps to check tears that were gathering at the corners of her eyes. Others had lowered their heads, perhaps to do the same thing.

She turned to face her faculty again. "I want you all to hear some things at the same time, the same words. First, I am terribly proud of you, not just this year but over the last few years. You have stepped forward, outside the security of your classrooms. You have taken risks. You have helped us get a clearer picture of Glen Haven Middle School, painful as it might have been. You are taking action to make Glen Haven a better school for all of us . . . all of us learners.

"Second, I have learned from you. You have been my teachers these past 4 years. I am not the same person as that new principal who walked through the front doors 4 years ago. I will never be that person again. I hope that whatever I am now will be enough for Ross and the needs of its learners. I also hope to learn from Ross's teachers and students. Four more years—and you won't recognize me!

"Third," she said, "I'm going to need you. You have plenty to do at Glen Haven Middle School, no doubt, but I'm going to want to consult you, to invite you to visit, to interact with Ross teachers and students. Why shouldn't we get together on this challenging task we've taken on, this job of making our middle schools more habitable and humane for young people and the adults who want to work with them?

"Fourth," she said, "the district needs you. You got the stats last month. They're not good. We're losing too many of our kids. We need to learn how to engage them in learning, keep them in school and graduate them prepared to do good work for this world. You've already started the process of figuring out how to do that.

"Fifth," she said, looking around the room, making contact with each individual, "you can do it. You can do what you set out to do this year. You've already taken the first steps, the hardest steps, facing reality, analyzing and interpreting it and deciding that current reality is not good enough for our students or for you. Huge steps! Gigantic, mother-may-I steps! What you do this summer and next year will knock your socks off . . . and mine . . . and the community's." She laughed. "Sorry, I just have this image of all of us going around barefooted in the middle of the winter!

"Finally, I will still be here for you, perhaps not in the way you're used to. But, we're only an e-mail away. Just as I draw on you to move forward at Ross, I hope you'll draw on me to keep moving forward here."

She paused long enough for a few hands to go up. Again, she held up her hands, asking for some more time to speak. "You're probably wondering who is going to re. . . ."

"No one can replace you!" someone shouted.

"Who's going to be the next principal of Glen Haven, then. I can't tell you that. All I can tell you is that several people have applied—all of them worthy candidates—and the process will be based here at the school, rather than at the district office. The Design Team—and anyone else who is interested, including students, parents, and community members—gets to interview the most likely candidates first. You'll want to decide what kind of person you want, so you might want to form a committee—oh, dear, another committee—to decide on the characteristics you desire. The HR Department will help you at some point in the process."

Then she said, "I'm not the only one leaving. You probably know that Myrna is retiring—let's have a cheer for her. And, we have two people transferring to the high school: Frank and Eva. A round of applause for them. We have only one more thing to talk about—actually, you get to talk about this thing—and then we have cake and ice cream and a serenade from the middle school choir.

"As you have read in my e-mails and as we discussed when we did the taking stock and future search, we have some extra money this summer. It has to be spoken for by July 1, so we've got to act quickly. In fact, in some cases, it needs to be spent by July 1, so we've got to act even quicker. We're not going to spend this money just to be spending it, however. We have a year of data and a set of goals that has been refined as a result of better and better data. So, we know what we want to do. We'll spend this money well. We'll use it to build on what we've done this year. K. D. and Anita are participating in the state's Writing project. Tell us more, please, K. D. and Anita."

The two English teachers got to their feet and stood together. K. D. began, "You know how literacy has emerged again and again from our data as a key goal. Well, the high school English teacher who helped us with the writing assessment and the tuning protocol told us about the National Writing Project. There's a version of it held right here in the state."

Anita took over, "And we're going to it for 4 weeks. Actually, we were lucky to be selected. There are over 3,000 teachers selected to participate in the projects at 200 sites around the country and Puerto Rico and the Virgin Islands. Alas [dramatic sigh] . . . we're not going to PR or the Virgin Islands!"

K. D. added, "We spend 4 weeks writing ourselves, discussing our writing, and then learning about how to help students become better writers. At the end of the 4 weeks, we are expected to return to our schools to share what we've learned. I've heard it's grueling . . . but a lot of fun."

"And, I've heard that it makes a huge difference to a faculty to have someone who has graduated from a writing project on the staff," Anita said. "So, we're really looking forward to the experience."

"I'll have my first novel ready to be autographed by September 20," K. D. added and bowed several times. Applause. (For more information on the National Writing Project, see Resource 8.2.)

"Money well spent," Josie said. "I had five people apply for the 2-week lesson study institute offered at the university. All five can go in July: Kelly, Tasha, Forrest, Sue , and Pam. Hooray. From what I know about lesson study, it'll help with both our culture-related goal and our literacy-related goal. What did you learn from the packet I sent you?"

Forrest stood up. "Well," he said, "it looks like it's about a lot more than lessons. It's about everything that happens in the classroom—from classroom culture and management to curriculum and instruction. Formative assessment and cooperative learning. Everything."

Sue Tanaka joined him, "It's a process, like a protocol. It starts with looking at data and setting goals for the year. Not just academic goals, by the way, but character development, too, so that fits in with our interest in culture and self-directed students. Then, the lesson study team chooses a unit related to the academic goal and a lesson that has "soft spots" in it, a lesson that has given students and teachers difficulty. Or any lesson. The team studies the lesson and improves on it as much as they can. Then, they try it out with students, with one of them teaching it and the rest collecting data about what the students do."

"It's not about the teacher," Forrest stated. "It's about what happens with kids. The focus is on the students; anyone in the lesson study group can be the teacher of the lesson the team has agreed upon."

"Then, they have a colloquium and share what they observed during the lesson. They reflect on what they learned and decide whether or not to work on the lesson again or move on to another lesson."

"They might do this cycle—maybe not the first step, actually—but the other three steps—three or four times a year."

"But," Alice asked, "how can you learn much from a single lesson? What difference does a single lesson make?"

Sue responded, "It's not really about that lesson as such. The goal is not to create a bank of 'good' lessons. It's about the professional conversation that the team has in refining the lesson, what they learn from each other. It's about data collection and analysis. It's about understanding how students learn. Most people who take part in lesson study naturally go back to their own lessons to rethink them, based on what they learned from one lesson."

Carol spoke up, "It's not about watching someone else teach? That makes me so nervous. I know we'll have to do that sometime, but I'm uncomfortable having other people in my classroom."

Forrest took on this question. "It's not really about the teacher. In fact, the teacher is only teaching what the whole team has agreed upon. Sure, we all have our little tricks of the trade, our own person-alities, but essentially the teacher has agreed to teach the lesson pretty much as is. . . ."

"And," continued Sue, "if she discovers that something isn't working and has to be changed, that's a point of discussion in the colloquium: What were students doing that resulted in a change in the plan? What did the teacher change? What were the results in terms of the students?"

"So, Josie won't be there to do evaluations?" Carol asked.

"Well," started Josie, "I wouldn't be there, of course, but your new principal would be there only if he or she is a part of a lesson study team, a peer."

"No gotcha?" Carol pursued her thought.

"No gotcha!" Forrest said. "Because it's not about the teacher."

"Actually," Carol said, "I'd like to go, too. Do we have enough money for one more?"

"Let's talk," Josie said. (For more on Lesson Study, see Resource 8.3.)

"We have one more group. Lan, would you like to speak for this group?" Josie said.

Lan He Bin stood up and asked Lorena and Burt to join her. "We've been thinking a lot about culture. It seems to us that schools can change everything they want to but, if they don't attend to culture, none of the changes will make much difference. Josie talked to us about doing some action research on the effect of culture on middle schools, especially those that serve struggling students. Take it over, Lorena."

Lorena said, "We're going to follow a pretty typical action research project structure." She held up a sheaf of papers. "According to what I read, we will first identify a need. Well, I think we've done that through the surveys, the interviews, and the focus groups. We'll probably need to get more specific, come up with a hypothesis for change, for example. Maybe something about belonging, students feel-ing like they belong in a middle school somewhere. We might do some research to narrow our focus, you know typical research. We might want to shadow in other middle schools next fall, interview students in more depth, whatever. Take it, Burt."

Burt spoke up, "So then we think of something that might make a difference in terms of our focus. We might say something like this: 'If we did this, the culture at Glen Haven Middle School will be like this.' Maybe we decide to change the schedule, have longer block periods so we can get to know stu-dents better. . . ."

Groans all around.

"I know, I know, changing the schedule is not a popular thing to do, but maybe that's what we discover makes a difference. Maybe something else. Anyway, we try out this strategy on a limited basis and collect data before and after the change. If the change has positive results, we might look at implementing it schoolwide."

"So," Lan said, "anyone else want to join us? We'll be meeting four times during the summer, four full days, and we have a bit of travel money and money to purchase books and materials."

Several people raised their hands, and Lan took down names. The interest was greater than she expected. (For more about action research, see Resource 8.4.)

"We have one more person who is doing some summer work," Josie said. "Roz, why don't you let us know what you're doing."

Roz stood up, "You know I was asked to be a TOSA this year—a Teacher on Special Assignment—but I had no idea what that meant or what I would do. When I talked with Stephanie Hodges at the district office, she said that it's really up to the school to decide. Last week, Stephanie and I invited the other TOSAs to meet with us, and we decided that we could be of most help to our schools if we learned something about coaching, so we are going as a team to a special summer coaching session in Colorado. I know, I know, it's tough to go to Colorado in the summer, but someone has to do it."

"The key to coaching is that you'll help us implement what we—you—decide to do next year," Josie said. "Let's draw this faculty meeting to a close by handing out awards and having cake and ice cream to celebrate Myrna's long career as a teacher—she's actually going to work while we celebrate because her choir will be serenading us. Let's wish Frank and Eva the best at the high school! And, above all, let's celebrate learning, our own and our colleagues' and our students'. Here's to learning!" And they

all raised their water bottles and headed toward a table sagging under the weight of four sheet cakes and several gallons of ice cream.

YOUR TURN: WHAT ARE YOU LEARNING?

Superintendent Ethan Redding said without hesitation, "I've learned from Glen Haven Middle School that you cannot mandate something and expect it to succeed. There are two sides to the equation. Instead of mandate, you can suggest, nudge, recommend, advocate, entice. . . . On the other side, you can expect. You can support, provide backing for, provide for, care for, fend for, and look after."

What have you learned from this chapter?

SO WHAT?

"It's important that I not back away from high expectations. Even if I don't mandate, I must make clear that our work is to make schools better for both adult and student learners."

What is important to you in terms of your learning in this chapter?

NOW WHAT?

"I see myself as purpose-driven. My job is to engage others in worthwhile purposes in terms of learning. I intend to understand why we must do something before we decide what to do."

How will you use your learning?

RESOURCES FOR CHAPTER 8

8.1 What A PLC Is and Is Not

8.2 More About the National Writing Project (NWP)

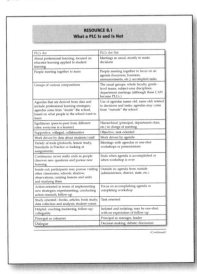

8.3 More About Lesson Study

RESOURCE 8.3
More About Lesson Study

(Excerpt from Lewis, Catherine. [2008]. Lesson study. In L. B. Easton [Ed.], *Powerful designs for professional learning*. Oxford, OH: NSDC.)

Note: Lewis describes a lesson study cycle she did with California teachers called "How Many Seats?" You can find out about this lesson in *Powerful Designs* or in other references at the end of this handout. You can find a 30-minute video of this lesson by going to www.lessonresearch.net.

Overview

Originating in Japan, lesson study is a cycle of instructional improvement focused on planning, observing, and discussing research lessons and drawing out their implications for teaching and learning more broadly. Research lessons are classroom lessons that provide an opportunity for teachers to (1) bring to life their ideas about effective teaching, and (2) carefully record student learning and behavior and give each other feedback on the research lesson, the students, and on teaching and learning. In lesson study, teachers work together to:

- Form goals for student learning and long-term development. Teachers study existing curricula and standards and discuss the qualities they would like students to have five to 10 years later.
- Collaboratively plan a lesson designed to bring to life both immediate and long-term goals.
- Teach the lesson, with one team member teaching and others gathering evidence on student learning and development.
- Discuss the evidence they gather during the lesson, using it to improve the lesson, the unit, and overall instruction.
- Teach the revised lesson in another classroom, if they desire, and study and improve it again (Lewis, 2002a, b).

Through this cycle, teachers deepen their knowledge of content, pedagogy, and student thinking, and increase their access to knowledgeable colleagues. . . . Closely examining student learning and behavior during research lessons helps teachers find effective ways to teach particular subject matter, and also yields broader lessons about teaching and learning. As one team member commented, "I learned that a worksheet can be a dangerous thing." Another noted, "I learned that students need to do the work, not the teacher."

Observations during the research lesson also reveal the student qualities and habits of mind that support or undermine student learning in one's own setting. For example, teachers may discover that students who focus on filling out the worksheet may not be attending to the mathematical content. This discovery may deepen their

8.4 More About Action Research

RESOURCE 8.4
More About Action Research

(Excerpt from Caro-Bruce, Cathy. Action research. In L. B. Easton [Ed.], *Powerful designs for professional learning*. Oxford, OH: NSDC, pp. 63–70)

Picture a spiral going around and around. Or a long mobile, spinning slowly in the breeze. Or a rare shell whose design conveys circular motions evolving over time. Or even a Mobius Strip. These are all images of action research. Action research is far from a linear, lockstep, formulaic process. While traditional researchers sometimes criticize the openness and flexibility of action research, its circular nature is what makes the process so valuable to teachers.

Action researchers clearly follow steps based on good research techniques, but the process invites the researchers to cycle through earlier phases, as they construct new meaning based on what they find in their data or as their questions change to address what has evolved as most central to them in improving their instruction. Action research continually challenges the researcher to reflect on the process to determine what needs to happen next in the researcher's learning and in the learning process of those who will benefit from the research.

Rationale

Action research is a process through which participants examine their own educational practice, systematically and carefully, using research techniques (Watts, 1985). This professional development experience is different from others because of its foundational principles and how it is implemented.

In contrast to some traditional types of professional development that diminish teacher efficacy by viewing them as empty receptacles to be filled with knowledge and skills, action research recognizes that teachers can identify topics important to their teaching, can examine their own work using research techniques, and can explore how to become more effective instructional leaders. Teachers are at the center of this work—their thinking, their questions, their desire to improve.

- Action research is seen as a different genre of research because it is grounded in the real world of the classroom. It balances a classroom culture that is personal, contextual, open-ended, and ever-changing with a research culture that is rigorous, structured, and systematic.
- Action research is an evolving form of inquiry that affects the researchers and the contexts in which they work. While teachers may start with a specific question, as they collect and analyze data and learn from their analysis, the question may evolve into one that is more aligned with classroom/school issues and the researchers' needs.

9

Looking Ahead; Facing Challenges (June–August)

I n which several staff members engage in invigorating professional learning, and the Design Team works with the district to identify a new principal and participates in hiring new staff members. In which the Design Team learns from the interview process and considers some challenges for the next year, including de-privatizing their classrooms, raising the level of intensity to an epidemic, and seeking deeper discussion.

Blue and gold locker doors yawned widely on both sides of the hallways, each locker mostly empty. The hallways were dark—no slightly blue fluorescent glow from the parade of fixtures. No buzzing either. No exuberant shouts, teenage squeals or shared whispers. No footsteps reverberating on the tile at different tempos. Chairs roosted on tables in classrooms shaded against summer sun, the walls bare, books at attention on the shelves. The school smelled different—dusty and meaningless.

The administrative office area was still well lit and, best of all, cool, so that's where the Design Team met the first week after school had ended for students. Josie decided not to be part of the group for this meeting, its main purpose to consider finding a new principal. In the conference room, around the oval table, Design Team members could hear her next door, perhaps packing things up. Jackie, the school office administrative assistant, provided them with coffee, iced tea and remnants of a cake from one of Josie's farewell parties.

"This is really strange," Ariel said.

"I always feel like this right after students have gone home for summer," Aaron volunteered.

Summer Design Team

Kelly Bosco, Science, Seventh and Eighth Grades

Tasha Peart, Fitness and Health, Seventh and Eighth Grades

Aaron Dobroski, Language Arts, Seventh and Eighth Grades

Dottie Gibbon, Aide

Forrest Long, Counselor

Roz Best, School Coach

Andy Mevoli, Mathematics, Sixth-Grade Core, Seventh and Eighth Grades

Robbie Beckel, Language Arts, Seventh and Eighth Grades

Ariel Aboud, Social Studies, Seventh and Eighth Grades

"Actually, that's not what I mean," Ariel said. "It's not having Josie here that's strange for me."

Members of the Design team nodded their heads, and Dottie reached over to pat Ariel on the arm. The door to the conference room opened and Robert Miller came in, apologizing for his lateness. "I couldn't get away. You know how the district offices are. There should be more secret entrances . . . and exits."

Robert, the head of Human Resources, was there to help the Design Team go through the process of choosing a new principal. A few introductions, and then Andy said, "Here's our agenda."

Agenda Item/ Activity	Why Important	Details	Action Expected
Welcome & opening activity	Getting everyone's voice into room; focus	Quote and storytelling	Focus Fun
Norm & agenda check	Enhances work together as a team	Andy sent by e-mail; people will check computers	Agreement to or change of either document
Principal search	Duh?	Robert Miller will help us	A process we agree upon
New teachers search	Duh, take two?	Robert Miller will help us	A process we agree upon
Summer work	Need to support those engaged in summer work and keep the energy up for others	An e-mail system?	Agreement on process and who will initiate, maintain
Sustaining summer work	The work can't just die on August 31	Roz will lead us in the thinking	Rough plan for next year
Learning: This year and next year	Need to capture and think about next year in terms of our learning this year	Dottie will lead us in the taking stock and thinking ahead	List of learnings and implications
Design team changes	Who's staying? Who's coming in? How shall we change?	Forrest will lead us in this process	Parameters for design team and membership
Evaluation of meeting and closure	How did we do in terms of norms? Closure—to-do list	Andy will do	Self-evaluation re. norms To-do list

"Pretty impressive," Robert said. "Actually, we should do something like this for district meetings, which tend to be, uh, very lengthy and meandering." He leaned over to view the agenda on the screen of Kelly's computer. "No paper, huh?"

"No paper," Andy said. "We had to sort of train ourselves to rely on electronics, but I brought an agenda and the norms on paper for you."

"So," Andy continued, "I have a challenge for you as we begin this meeting. We're going to send a telegram to the superintendent about our hopes for Glen Haven Middle School next year. Now, some of you don't know what telegrams are. They are. . . ." He was interrupted by a bit of a boo and then continued, "OK, OK, so you've seen movies that feature telegrams. You have $10; at a dollar per word, that means 10 words. Separate sentences with the word 'Stop.' Go." After looking a bit confused, the Design Team applied themselves to the work. You can read some of their telegrams in the box.

The group considered the norms and agreed to them. Forrest commented on the agenda: "Thanks for doing such a thorough job of the agenda. We've had a variety of agendas this year, but I like this one best."

"Thank you," Andy said. "Robert, what do we need to do?"

Robert distributed a summary of the typical process for hiring new principals and the generic job description for principals, which had been published and had already attracted some candidates. The Design Team immediately wanted to revise the job description and brainstormed a list of characteristics that Robert wrote on the white board:

> ### Telegrams
>
> No principal STOP No problem STOP Strong faculty, strong school STOP Success STOP
>
> Progress is work of all STOP We'll continue to move forward STOP
>
> Next year, new staff STOP New ideas and old combined STOP Learning STOP
>
> We'll do the district proud STOP Making strides for students STOP Everyday STOP
>
> Summer STOP Fall STOP Winter STOP Spring STOP Another year of success STOP Students Staff STOP
>
> PLCs make a difference STOP We'll continue good work STOP Next year STOP

OUR NEW PRINCIPAL MUST

- *Be like Josie*
- *Have confidence enough to let others lead*
- *Understand learning*
- *Know students*
- *Know people, in general, how they work and what they need*
- *Know about and respect the power of professional learning and Professional Learning Communities (PLCs)*
- *Not be afraid of change*
- *Work with a variety of people, with different backgrounds and points of view*
- *Sometimes conflicting points of view*
- *Know what it's like to teach and otherwise work in a school*
- *Know what it's like to work with middle school students*
- *Have respect for others' opinions, ideas, and processes*
- *Be comfortable with shared or distributed leadership*
- *Have a sense of humor*
- *Know how to work with district administrators*
- *Be energetic*
- *Know technology*
- *Be current on recent developments in curriculum, instruction, and assessment*
- *"Buy in" to our Design Team and PLC strategy*
- *Know how to keep the school functioning*

- *Be visionary . . . shared vision*
- *Understand the importance of school culture*

Robert ran out of room on the whiteboard, but Roz caught the next five on her computer.

- *Understand the importance of educator learning (as well as student learning)*
- *Know how to work with teams*
- *Have problem-solving skills*
- *Be a good listener*
- *Be a good speaker and writer*

"Who can do all that?" Andy asked. "We're talking superwoman or superman here."

"A little like Josie," Roz commented. It was going to take awhile for the Design Team—and, probably, the entire faculty—to get beyond their feelings about Josie leaving. "I don't think we realized how great we had it. . . ." Robert agreed to revise the job description and submit it to the Design Team online.

They turned to the hiring process that Robert had outlined and added a few personal touches:

- *We want an interview group composed of volunteers from the faculty and staff, students, parents, community members, and district personnel.*
- *If we have too many volunteers, we will have an oversight team and a smaller team that reports to the oversight team. The smaller team will be involved with every candidate from paper screening to the on-site interviews. The smaller team will be in constant communication with the oversight team.*
- *The on-site interviews should have many components, including these, if possible:*
  - *A tour with students and a subsequent meeting*
  - *A meeting with parents and community members*
  - *An opportunity to plan professional learning with the Design Team*
  - *An opportunity to plan and lead a meeting*
  - *Oral review of a videotape of a teaching episode*
  - *A lesson the candidate teaches to summer school students*
- *The oversight team will recommend a candidate to the Head of Human Resources, who will recommend this person to the superintendent and the Board of Education.*

They ran out of steam at this point and turned the details over to Robert, Andy, and Dottie to refine.

"I never thought this was so important," Tasha said, "but now I understand how important it is to get the right person. Pretty scary, actually." They added one more item:

- *The Design Team and the district Head of HR will arrange for the new principal to be mentored by students and staff for the first year; also involve a district person in the mentoring.*

A quick break, and the Design Team reconvened. Although Robert, Andy, and Dottie would design most of the activities candidates would experience during their phone and day-long, site-based interviews, Kelly suggested that the team think of what they wanted to do during candidates' time with them.

"We can certainly ask them questions, like 'What does professional learning mean to you?' or 'What would you do in terms of professional learning if you were principal?'" Aaron said.

"Actually," Tasha said, "I'd like to focus on what we've done so far and ask each candidate what he or she would do next. I think we could learn a lot from each candidate—rather than generalities, they'd have to respond with specifics."

"We'd need to be able to describe what we've done so far," Robbie said.

"A telegram: 10 words or fewer!" Andy said.

"How about 250 words or fewer?" Tasha said. "I'll work with you, Robbie. And, we can ask follow-up questions, Aaron, if we don't get what we need from our description."

The Design Team returned to the rest of the agenda, deciding that they wanted to keep their summer work "on the front burner" using e-mail. "Perhaps," Kelly said, "we can have those of us who are doing summer work pledge to give everybody an update through e-mail every other day or once a week."

Robbie rationalized the suggestion, "Actually, it'll be good for them—us, actually—to reflect on what we are doing and learning. Perhaps the e-mails can become learning journals and be put into our PLC portfolio." Kelly, the keeper, nodded his approval.

"I'll send out an e-mail about the . . . e-mails," Andy said. "Next?"

"I think the e-mails will help a lot, but we don't want the typical 'I-went-to-a conference-and-here's-what-I-learned' kind of presentation in the fall."

"We didn't do that," said Kelly, remembering The Investigative Team.

"Exactly. I'm thinking that the first PLC meeting in the fall will be all about what we learned this summer. We'll need to let the—what shall we call them? The Summer Investigators?—know that they are expected to plan and facilitate our first meeting in the fall."

"Sounds like they're investigating summer. How about we call us the 'Summer Squads'?" Robbie said.

"OK, the Summer Squads. We ask them to plan the first meeting so that we're all 'on the same page' as we go into the fall. Maybe, we do rounds or some kind of protocol."

"I know the Writing Project people," Robbie said, "of which I am one, will want to do more with writing across the curriculum."

"The Lesson Study Squad, of which I am one, will want to do lesson study," Forrest said. "Aren't most of us on the Lesson Study Squad?" He looked around the room; indeed, four of the seven LSS members were on the Design Team.

"I'll want to get us involved in peer coaching," Roz said.

"We don't know what we're going to want to do," Dottie said. "We have to wait to see what our action research project will focus on—culture probably. But, we won't have a 'to-do' list until at least the fall. . . ."

"See, that's the problem," Roz admitted. "We'll come back from our summer work wanting to implement a whole bunch of things."

"No we won't," Dottie said. "Our work this summer is to explore some possibilities for improving what we do, as adults, so we can help students succeed, especially those who are struggling. It's for the kids."

"You're right!" Aaron said. "We're getting too close to IT." He waved his hands in front of his face as if to ward off an enemy. "We need to keep the focus on what we have learned about students and what they need."

"Our goals and purposes," Robbie said. "We would be like any other school if we just DID all of these things, because they're exciting to us and we think they would be cool to do."

Dottie held up her hand, "Speaking of goals, I noticed that our Future Search goals were a little off; they didn't exactly match our February 12 goals, the ones we generated from the sentence strips based on our new ideas. I did a matrix for us that may capture all of the goals we've developed over the year. We've been saying basically the same thing, just in different ways." She distributed a handout, Figure 9.1, to the rest of her team.

"Dottie, I could get down on bended knee, and bless you, again and again and again," Aaron said. "I was kind of worried about our different 'takes' on the goals. This helps me."

"I subsumed a few things. There are only two categories: School Culture and Classroom Culture. I put the parent and community involvement pieces in School Culture because I think parents and community members make important contributions to the well-being of all of the students here. Also, I didn't separate what we were saying about students and adults. What's good for students is good for the adults."

Figure 9.1 Purposes/Goals From Year One

	Possibilities	Focus #1	Focus #2	Focus #3	Focus #4
School Culture	Parents and community Safety "Core" in seventh and eighth (belonging) Personal and social growth Surviving middle school	The well-being (including physical and emotional safety) of all students and adults	Learning is engaging for students and adults; it is challenging but supported	Students see important roles for themselves in the future and understand how learning can help them succeed in those roles	Students are literate across the curriculum
Classroom Culture	Personalization Engagement "Fun" Support Rigor Challenge Risk-taking Expectations	The well-being (including physical and emotional safety) of all students and adults	Learning is engaging for students and adults; it is challenging but supported	Students see important roles for themselves in the future and understand how learning can help them succeed in those roles	

"I don't think we are finished with these," Dottie ventured. "There are so many ways of representing purposes and goals, but doing this made me feel better."

"Let's hang onto it, Dottie. We can share a history of our goal- and purpose-setting experiences (see Resource 7.6) with the PLC sometime this fall, and I'll bet we'll create still another version. But, all of these discussions of goals and purposes keep us focused on them and flexible as our data and needs change," Robbie said.

THE 279-WORD STATEMENT

They couldn't do it in 250 words, but here is what Robbie and Tasha drafted about the Glen Haven Middle School (GHMS) PLC for the principal candidate interviews. Tasha later commented, "We tried to be matter-of-fact and straight-forward. I wanted to give some clues about why we did things the way we did—like how we structured the Design Team—but I didn't want to give anything away."

The principal and three teachers decided that GHMS students and staff would benefit if the staff participated in a PLC. There was nothing drastically wrong at GHMS, but a lot of things could have been better for both students and staff. The principal and teachers formed an Investigative Team to see whether or not people were interested and, with others, formed a Design Team to propose a structure for the collaborative work.

At GHMS everyone is part of a single PLC that is coordinated by the Design Team, and individuals participate beyond the PLC in specialty teams as needs arise. The first thing the faculty decided is that it needed more and better information, which was gathered by four specialty teams and analyzed by the whole faculty, yielding several goals. Even after analysis of those data, faculty wanted more information, so four additional specialty teams conducted interviews and focus groups, shadowed students at several schools, and gathered information about district resources. This activity yielded another round of goals.

In the meantime, the English Department decided that the school needed to engage in a writing assessment, which yielded still more data, and the English Department learned how to examine student work using protocols. Individuals began to change what they were doing in classrooms; departments were talking about the data; and the school itself began to have a different feel to it.

Along the way, the faculty learned about themselves individually and as a group. They learned about change and how to work together. They learned a lot about students, including how the district's graduation rates had decreased. They made summer plans for more learning.

After candidates had read the statement, the interviewers asked them, "What would you do next in terms of the PLC if you were principal at Glen Haven Middle School?"

WHAT THEY HEARD DURING THE INTERVIEWS

Here is a summary of answers to the question "What would you do next?" from the seven candidates who were interviewed by phone. Some candidates offered more than one response.

- "I would interview each of the Design Team members, including the former principal, so that I could understand the role the Design Team plays in the PLC."
- "I'm wondering if teachers at Glen Haven are ready to begin to open up their classrooms, to de-privatize. That's going to be their biggest challenge in the next year."
- "It doesn't seem to me as if they've done anything yet, so I would talk with the superintendent and the assistant superintendent for curriculum to see what the district goals are, and I would meet with the PLC to discuss how to implement those goals at GHMS."
- "The state Department of Education has a set of requirements for PLCs. I would get a copy of those requirements and discuss how well the Glen Haven PLC is doing in terms of them."
- "The PLC needs to investigate best practices. There are a whole lot of books written about what works in schools. The school needs to decide what to adopt and then implement it with fidelity."
- "I'm glad the PLC didn't settle on one thing to implement from the start. Their first job was to get a deep understanding about what is going on at the school in terms of learning. I think they need to continue their conversations—in fact, deepen them—before they settle on any one thing (or more) to do."
- "We would draft a mission and vision statement that is aligned with the district's mission and vision."
- "I'm a little worried that the PLC concept is closely held by a small group of people—the Design Team. I'm wondering how it can spread and grow and be so compelling that everyone in the school is motivated by the goals and purposes."

- "The principal as an instructional leader needs to be very active from the beginning of the year in terms of helping teachers make changes in their classrooms."
- "I would want to link with other schools in terms of their professional learning. GHMS needs partners in learning."
- "I'm wondering if there are coaches in the school—peer coaches—and if anyone has asked coaches to help them improve what is happening in classrooms. Coaches are the key to implementing change. Without them, change exists as an idea, a possibility, a hope, a dream. With them, students start to thrive because of the changes being made in their learning environments."
- "It sounds as if GHMS is still kind of coasting along. I'm wondering if anyone there is feeling some urgency about making changes. Is anything propelling them through the data and into action in their classrooms?"
- "It would be a good idea for the whole PLC to do a book study about change and innovation, so they're all on the same page."
- "The new principal needs to take the first 6 months to listen and learn—trusting the Design Team to keep the momentum going—before he or she steps in with new ideas."

The Design Team was stunned by the comments the principal candidates made. The scenario had helped the Design Team learn what good ideas the candidates had. It had also helped them discern among the candidates. Some responses fit with the philosophy of professional learning at GHMS, and some challenged it.

Meanwhile, back at the Design Team meeting, Forrest said, "Let's put these two things together. We have our goals or purposes." He held up one hand. "We have all of this summer learning. What are we going to do next year? Hey, I'd be happy to know what we're going to do next fall." He held up both hands.

"What I understand is that we don't know exactly what we will be doing next year," Tasha said, "but goals + experiences = what we'll do."

"Any surprise there?" Kelly interjected.

"So we have to plan for something . . . but we won't know until the end of this summer exactly what."

"My point exactly," Roz said. "I think we should plan that we will be doing something different, and that means talking to someone about next year's schedule right away."

"Ah, I get where you're going with this," Tasha said.

"We need to co-opt the district PD days. We need to be sure we have Design Team days. We need to be sure we have specialty team days, like for the Summer Squads. And, then we need to be sure we have days to engage in the writing process or lesson study or follow-up on the action research project related to culture . . . or. . . . And, we need to keep collecting and analyzing data," Roz finished.

Dottie spoke up, "Don't forget: We have three new staff members and a principal joining us."

"Mentoring," Andy said.

Roz said, "One more thing. If we're going to do anything around lesson study or looking at student work in writing and other subjects, we need to get accustomed to going into each other's classrooms. We need to be comfortable about sharing our work and sharing our students' work. Eventually, we need to expand coaching so I'm not the only one doing it."

"No problem, next item!" Forrest said, trying to inject some humor into the discussion.

Tasha resisted his invitation to move on: "I think we should contact Stephanie right away about the schedule. I'll do that. We need to lay this all out for her and ask her how to proceed."

"Andrew has not been involved yet. I think he should be involved in this," Roz said. "He has not applied for Josie's job, and I think he likes his management responsibilities, but he needs to help us work toward what we want." She was speaking of the assistant principal, Andrew Loyer, who was on the Action Research Summer Squad.

"I'd like to think about mentoring the new staff and the new principal," Kelly said. "Anyone want to work with me?" A couple of hands went up, and he said, "I'll put out an e-mail asking if any other staff members want to join our work. I think we need something in place ASAP."

"I don't want to be the only one thinking about opening up our classrooms next year," Roz said, "but I'll take the lead. I have this vision that we'll all be coaches of one kind or another. Anyone want to join me?" Only Aaron raised his hand, and Roz echoed Kelly's decision to put out an e-mail to other staff members.

"So, four things in terms of sustaining summer work," Roz said after a pause. "One: Internet contact for the WHAT. Time set aside for more WHAT with the whole school in late August. We'll look at SO WHAT and NOW WHAT at that first PLC meeting by looking at our goals one more time. Two: Scheduling professional learning time—Andrew Loyer, Tasha and Stephanie. Three: Mentoring—Kelly and others. Four: Opening up our classrooms and coaching—Aaron and me and others."

OPENING UP THE CLASSROOM

One of the principal candidates and Roz brought up one of the most important steps for a PLC to take: de-privatization of classrooms. De-privatization is often the last aspect of innovation to be addressed . . . if it is addressed at all.

Reformers will change just about anything before they will get into what happens in the classroom between teachers and students, where the "rubber meets the road." De-privatization goes against the history and culture of education. It flies in the face of "my classroom is my kingdom" thinking. It erases one of the reasons some adults enter the profession: autonomy. Conscientious teachers may sense that their individuality and creativity are being threatened by de-privatization. Even those who don't feel threatened professionally risk personal embarrassment when they are called upon to share their own work and that of their students. It's hard for teachers to separate their personal and professional lives.

Yet without addressing what happens in the classroom, true school improvement will remain hazy, hoped-for, a partially realized possibility. Individual teachers may make significant change in their own classrooms, but most students experience school beyond individual classrooms. Even in self-contained classrooms, students experience school before and after the bell rings, at lunch, on the playground or athletic field, and on the bus.

For students in secondary schools, the process of going from one classroom environment to another every 53 minutes is excruciating. Adjusting to the styles, personalities, policies, and procedures of six to seven teachers a day is an ordeal that few adults truly understand (unless they shadow students!). Although one of a student's six teachers might have created a humane classroom for student learning, the others may not have done so, and the work of one teacher may have little effect on how students experience school, generally. There may be little or no change in the culture of the whole school.

So, school improvement is necessarily about a whole school and all of the teachers (and everyone else) in that school. School improvement is not about defending the status quo. Remember that, if school really worked for most or all students, educators and policy makers would not be engaged in improvement. But we do have data that show nationally, regionally, and locally, even in Glen Haven School District, school is not working for many young people. Educators and policy makers could engage in insanity rather than improvement—that is, "doing the same thing over and over again and expecting different results"—or they could substantively change what they are doing. Thanks, Einstein.

Tinkering around the edges of school improvement is insufficient. A fix here, a band-aid there, a silver bullet for that program, adoption of a new program there. These won't do the job. The key of real change is to have an effect on what happens in all classrooms, what happens between and among students and their teachers and what happens between and among teachers and their administrators.

So many researchers and practitioners have described the single quality that most affects student learning—the teacher in the classroom. So, school reformers must get to the level of what happens in classrooms, and that requires getting teachers into each other's classrooms and having teachers share their own and their students' work with the goal of improving both. Did anyone say "de-privatization"?

Glen Haven PLC's goals and summer work may on the surface not appear to require de-privatization, but if staff who participated in the Writing Project or lesson study want to implement much of anything, they'll want to be in each other's classrooms and sharing student work. If Roz has any say, staff will be serving as peer coaches in each other's classrooms.

How does de-privatization happen? Well, it doesn't happen by mandate (or, if so, only in terms of compliance, not learning). It doesn't happen the day after the announcement that it will happen. It takes time and is about as bumpy as roads in the early days of the automobile (to continue the "rubber meets the road" metaphor). Muddy, too.

Like PLCs, it happens because a few teachers are interested in what other teachers are doing. It happens because a few teachers want some feedback, other than the twice-yearly (if that!) supervisory visits from the principal. It happens gradually and partially, and then it suddenly spreads because, as Malcolm Gladwell (2002) says in *The Tipping Point*, it becomes an epidemic, a good one.

GO FOR THE EPIDEMIC

In a book rich with examples and details, Gladwell (2002) makes the case that

> Epidemics are, at their root about . . . transformation. When we are trying to make an idea or attitude or product tip, we're trying to change our audience in some small yet critical respect: we're trying to infect them, sweep them up in our epidemic, convert them from hostility to acceptance. (p. 166)

His examples range from epidemics that are destructive (such as crime in New York subways in the 1980s) to those that try to counteract destructive epidemics (such as curtailing the epidemic of teenage smoking) to those that are benevolent (such as using beauty salons to disburse information about breast cancer). Some are huge (such as Baltimore's syphilis epidemic in the 1990s), some are fun (such as the proliferation of book clubs that made some books instant best-sellers), and some are sad (such as the rise in teenage suicides in Micronesia). Some examples relate to education, such as the innovations in television programming for preschoolers, which led to *Sesame Street* and *Blue's Clues*.

Gladwell's book is essentially an analysis of how epidemics of both the good and bad sort happened, but he speculates that perhaps we can do things deliberately "to start and control positive epidemics of our own" (p. 14). That's the approach we're going to take to de-privatization—we can start a good epidemic of our own. In search of a way to start the de-privatization epidemic, we'll consider as our major example how the PLC epidemic started at GHMS.

THREE RULES FOR EPIDEMICS

Gladwell says that epidemics are influenced by three factors: (1) "The Law of the Few"; (2) "The Stickiness Factor"; and (3) "The Power of Context" (p. 166). Let's take these factors one at a time, applied to scaling up (to use another term for the epidemic phenomenon) de-privatization.

1. "The Law of the Few" It takes just a few special people to start an epidemic, but they must possess "particular and rare social gifts" (p. 33). There needs to be a Maven, the person who sees the potential and goes to work on its behalf. Mavens seek to know everything they can, generally or about a specific subject, and they "want to tell you about it too" (p. 62).

Glen Haven's own PLC development process can be used as an example here. The Investigative Team—Josie, Kelly, Tasha, and Aaron—can be said to be Mavens. Josie was first. As a learning principal, Josie made it her responsibility to know everything she could about school improvement. She discovered the power of professional learning and PLCs. She found people who were similarly curious and sent them to a conference about PLCs. They returned, as she hoped they would, enthusiastic about PLCs and ready to do something about them. They continued their Maven roles throughout the year and were joined by others, such as Robbie, who was bent on learning more about writing and writing assessment and doing something about her learning.

In terms of Mavens who will focus on de-privatization at Glen Haven, chances are they are going to be the Design Team plus any number of other teachers who see the value of learning from other teachers and getting feedback on their own work. In terms of the epidemic that needs to happen at Glen Haven Middle School—and most schools in the country—it will be the ones who "desire to be of service and influence" who will make the radical change from isolation in the classroom to collaboration in the school (p. 67). Gladwell says that the Mavens

> know things that the rest of us don't. They read more magazines than the rest of us, more newspapers, and they may be the only people who read junk mail. . . . [They] have the knowledge and social skills to start word-of-the mouth epidemics . . . [and] they want to help. (p. 67)

Interestingly enough, Gladwell maintains that "to be a Maven is to be a teacher. But it is also, even more emphatically, to be a student" (p. 69).

Another key role in terms of starting and pursuing an innovation is the Connector. These provide the "social glue" (p. 70). They "know lots of people" (p. 38). They are part of not just one group in an organization but a variety of groups. They take an idea and chat it up with all of their colleagues, and suddenly everyone is talking about it. The first Design Team, including the four on the Investigative Team, were Connectors. Although they were not representative of disciplines or grade levels, they provided linkages with a number of subgroups at Glen Haven. Andy, for example, was a sixth-grade core and seventh- and eighth-grade mathematics teacher. He was a soccer coach. He sponsored the chess club. He was the father of one of the students at Glen Haven, and he had worked on a variety of committees and task forces that put him into contact with almost all the staff at Glen Haven. Dottie was a perfect Connector. She had been at Glen Haven the longest among the Design Team; she knew the history and the people. She had worked in classrooms across the curriculum. She knew the district administration inside and out. She "had an extraordinary knack of making friends and acquaintances," a key quality for Connectors (p. 41).

The third type of person needed to launch an epidemic is the Salesman. The word *salesman* often conjures someone who exerts high pressure on others, often forcing them to do something they might otherwise not do. The stereotype is the foot in the door, the closer who comes in to seal a deal at the car dealership, the phone solicitor who must make her quota. Actually, most of us are salespersons of one kind or another. As teachers, we are in the job of selling kids on learning. As school administrators, we may focus on selling parents on sending their children to school on time. As district administrators, we want policy makers to fund our schools adequately . . . or better. So, Salesman (besides being sexist) is not such a bad thing to be as an educator, despite the stereotypes.

Salesmen are good at persuasion. They know how to make a case. They can take an idea that the Maven has formed and that the Connector has communicated, and help it spread, loft it to epidemic proportions. The Salesman's natural tendencies are to "read" the audience—the verbal and subtle nonverbal clues—and help others see how an idea fits them. Sometimes they engage in what Gladwell and others call "interactional synchrony," a conversational "dance," a micromovement of "faces and shoulders and hands and bodies to the same rhythm" (p. 82). Some of us can't do what some Salesmen can: have their "volume and pitch fall into balance . . . their speech rate" equalized with others (p. 82).

Salesmen may be seen in the malevolent sense as manipulative . . . in the more positive sense, they are simply good at helping people understand the benefit of an idea or thing. They are necessary to good epidemics, such as de-privatization. In the PLC example, the Design Team is certainly composed of Salespersons. Tasha is probably most oriented to sales, but Robbie becomes so, and so does Roz at the end of the year. Josie is a behind-the-scenes Salesperson. One way to think about her is to consider what she might have done if the Investigative Team had come back from the PLC workshop not the least bit impressed, unwilling to proceed and, certainly, unwilling to try to persuade others to engage.

One question is whether or not someone appoints or recruits these people in a purposeful epidemic. Josie recruited the Investigative Team, but she let the Design

Team form by itself and create its own job description, and she let others choose to join the specialty teams. She was mindful, however, of the requirement—never quite stated as such and not challenged until three quarters of the year had passed—that everyone participate in the all-faculty PLC meetings. She made time and created a place for them, strong indications that PLCs were important to her.

2. "The Stickiness Factor" Having Mavens, Connectors, and Salesmen on the team to create an epidemic is not enough. According to Gladwell, the virus needs a certain amount of stickiness, which "means that a message makes an impact" (p. 25). It must not only make a difference but be memorable: "Is it so memorable, in fact, that it can create change, that it can spur someone to action" (p. 92). What is it about the reform (or the virus, if you prefer) that makes it sticky?

In this era of a "surfeit of information," which Gladwell calls "clutter," messages need to stick (p. 99). The same is true of school innovations; that's why some of them are called "flavor of the month." How is one to distinguish a really important innovation from one that, too, shall pass? Gladwell suggests, "There may be simple ways to enhance stickiness and systematically engineer stickiness into a message. This fact is of obvious importance to marketers, teachers and managers" (p. 99). In fact, Gladwell uses the effort the producers of *Sesame Street* and *Blues' Clues* used to make their educational programs stick to preschoolers as his chief example of this concept. He describes their stickiness in terms of this "single, breakthrough insight: that if you can hold the attention of children, you educate them" (p. 100). The producers found that "kids stopped watching . . . if they couldn't make sense of what they were looking at" (p. 101). When children looked away—were distracted—it was because they were confused. Researchers linked the times they looked away to what was going on in the program and, little by little, refined episodes until they weren't confusing. Sometimes they tested episodes with children in a room full of delightful toys. Episodes had to be compelling . . . and understandable . . . in order to keep children's attention on them, and not the fascinating toys.

In terms of de-privatization, any of the following may make it sticky:

- Disappointing data about current student success;

- Knowing that the history of education is a history of privatization, which may once have worked but may not work now and in the future;

- Knowledge that teachers in other schools are opening up their classrooms, their work as professionals, and their students' work;

- Understanding the function of corporate research and development departments;

- Understanding that the process will be gradual and begin with the willing;

- Understanding that feedback will be observational rather than judgmental;

- Knowing (and believing) that de-privatization is not about supervision and evaluation but about learning;

- Seeing who participates in de-privatization (including a principal who might invite her peers to give feedback about a faculty meeting);

- Presentation of de-privatization as one way a whole school can be a learning organization;

- Knowing that whole school improvement cannot be accomplished unless teachers understand that it requires all teachers to care about the learning of all students; and

- The story of a school that opened up its practices for everyone in the school and began to make improvements that helped all students succeed.

Doubtless, there are other elements of de-privatization that could help it stick in a school. Unfortunately, there is no one right element of stickiness for every person who is to be infected. Indeed, some infections stick for reasons that no one discerns, perhaps because of someone's powerful personal experience.

Sometimes, as the producers of *Sesame Street* and *Blue's Clues* discovered, the stickiness factors are counterintuitive. Gladwell says, "Here was a show [*Sesame Street*] that eschewed what turns out to be the most important of all ways of reaching young children" (p. 121). Gladwell issues a warning: "The lesson of stickiness is the same. There is a simple way to package information that, under the right circumstances, can make it irresistible. All you have to do is find it" (p. 132).

The Glen Haven Design Team found stickiness for PLCs in student data and the desire for more data. They found it by giving people lots of choices. They found it by dedicating time and space for work related to the PLC. They found it through honoring the professionalism of staff. They found it by saying, in not-so-subtle ways, "We have the answers within us" and "We can do this" and "We know where we can find help." They found it by recognizing the importance of counteracting isolation through collaboration. They found that PLCs stuck because they were active and interactive—not the time for lectures and convoys of PowerPoint® slides. And PLCs might have stuck for some Glen Haven staff for reasons that, even today, are unknown. For some reason, PLCs did not stick for at least two teachers who requested transfers. That's to be expected; there will always be some who resist, perhaps for their own good reasons, any change in the status quo.

3. "The Power of Context" The last of Gladwell's recommendations for creating a good epidemic has to do with the environment. Gladwell's chief example is the "conditions and circumstances" that led Bernie Goetz to shoot four youths on a subway in New York City in 1984 (p. 133). Gladwell describes the conditions of the NYC subway system at the time: "Underground, on the subways, conditions could only be described as chaotic" with "dimly lit platform[s], surrounded on all sides by dark, damp and graffiti-covered walls" (p. 136). Late trains, fires in the system, derailments and slow trains because the tracks needed repair. All these in a city that was "in the grip of one of the worst crime epidemics in its history" (p. 137).

Then, Gladwell relates, "Suddenly and without warning, the epidemic tipped. From a high in 1990, the crime rate went into a precipitous decline. Murders dropped by two-thirds. Felonies were cut in half" (p. 137). What caused the sudden shift in the status quo? The solution has become part of popular lore—the Broken Windows theory, which said "that crime is contagious . . . that it can start with a broken window and spread to an entire community" (p. 141). Cleaned up, the environment in NYC was not as compelling to criminals.

The environment for PLCs and de-privatization is important. Here's a guide to positive or negative environments according to Gayle H. Gregory and Lin Kuzmich (2007, p. 2):

Positive	*Negative*
Encouraging atmosphere	Toxic culture
Providing choices and variety	Unnecessary pressure
Providing appropriate time	Unrealistic timeframes
Offering constructive feedback	Little or no feedback
Ensuring safety	Inappropriate challenges
Ensuring "relaxed alertness"	Uneasiness related to expectations
Offering helpful support and encouragement	Critical and judgmental environment
Honoring personality styles	Individual needs ignored

You can find a survey related to your school and team culture, developed by Gregory and Kuzmich, as Resource 9.1.

A toxic culture is one in which "teacher relations are often conflictual, the staff doesn't believe in the ability of the students to succeed, and a generally negative attitude" prevails, according to Terence E. Deal and Kent D. Peterson in *Shaping School Culture: The Heart of Leadership* (1999).

Glen Haven has already experienced some of the positive conditions that make de-privatization possible, just in the way the PLC functioned:

- Making the effort a whole-school PLC
- Encouraging the actual work to take place in smaller groups, based on participant interest
- Protecting time for the Design Team and the PLCs
- Using given time (district professional development time, other) for PLC purposes, as much as possible
- Finding time and resources for specialty teams and the Summer Squads
- Trusting the Design Team and other teams to make decisions
- Mutual accountability among Design Team and specialty team members
- District approval and assistance
- Very few absolutes in the process; lots of choices
- Lots of ways to gain and give feedback

In terms of the next step, de-privatization, Glen Haven may want to focus on these elements of the environment or context:

- A culture of trust
- Collegial effort to design the purposes and processes of de-privatization
- Full transparency about the purposes and processes of de-privatization
- A clear separation between classroom visits that are for supervisory or evaluation purposes and those that are not

- Visits and examination of work based on teacher goals
- A gradual start-up process, beginning with those who are most interested first
- Protected time to visit classrooms and confer afterwards
- Protected time to look at teacher and student work
- Positive experiences related to giving and getting feedback
- A focus on what and how students are learning
- Working in small groups (three to five people) rather than larger or whole-school groups to visit classrooms, give feedback, and look at teacher and student work

One point that Gladwell (2002) makes about the environment is the importance of small groups; he lauds corporations such as Gore (the company that makes Gore-Tex®) because it keeps its plants and offices at 150 employees or fewer. Bigger than that requires management, which distracts from real work. Gladwell says, "Once we're part of a [small] group, we're all susceptible to peer pressure and social norms and any number of other kinds of influence that can play a critical role in sweeping us up in the beginnings of an epidemic" (p. 171). It's important to have with peers "the kind of relationship that goes with knowing who they are and how they relate to us" (p. 179). He speaks of a kind of peer pressure that means "knowing people well enough that what they think of you matters" (p. 186).

Dottie's role on the PLC speaks to the benefit of small groups. Gladwell describes how "we store information with other people" and call on those people when we need to remember or understand. He calls this a "transactive memory system," and it's certainly true that Design Team members used each other to make sense of what has happened, what is happening, and what will happen (p. 188). He further illuminates this feature of group work: "It's knowing someone well enough to know what they know, and knowing them well enough so that you can trust them to know things in their specialty" (p. 190). Think of how Dottie and Andy were so appreciative of each other's talents in Chapter 3.

Best of all, it is this kind of organization that "makes it far easier for new ideas and information moving around the organization to tip—to go from one person or part of the group to the entire group at once" (p. 191). A mere virus to an epidemic!

Another way of finding the tipping point is through keeping each action relatively small and manageable, yet part of a coherent whole. This is certainly what the PLC did. The PLC was a coherent whole, and the specialty teams, which were relatively small and manageable, were part of the whole, kept that way by a Design Team. That's what needs to happen with de-privatization. The whole school might move to de-privatization, but only one small group at a time and in its own way. As Gladwell says, "In order to create one contagious movement, you often have to create many small movements first" (p. 192). We can certainly think of the work of the many specialty teams as small moves that led to the overall move to PLCs. We can think of small groups engaged in de-privatizing their work as small movements, within the whole.

TEACHER REACTIONS TO DE-PRIVATIZATION

About to welcome a visitor into his classroom, Judd (pseudonymn), stated, "To say that it was emotionally trying is a gross understatement. On the other hand, I would do it again in a heartbeat" (Wasley, 1994, p. xv). In this case, the visitor was researcher and education reformer Patricia A. Wasley, who stayed in each of a variety of classrooms for a week or more. Interested in how teachers undergo change, she researched and then wrote *Stirring the Chalkdust: Tales of Teachers Changing Classroom Practice* (1994). Judd reflected on the week with her as a visiting researcher:

> It is a rare and valuable experience to have someone look at what you do in your life. For most people this never occurs. It opened up windows of self-examination that I never knew existed. The report itself gave me the remarkable opportunity to sit in close proximity to people discussing my work in the most candid way. While some of this was painful initially, most of it was rewarding and supportive. It allowed me to see the strengths and weaknesses of my practice through someone else's eyes. (p. xv)

He recognized how much deeper her observations were than his yearly evaluations:

> This pushed and probed me to think about what I was doing and not doing on a much deeper and clearer level. It reaffirmed my love of children and my sincere belief that all of them can succeed. It brought me to tears. . . . How many teachers ever look at their work with such intensity that it makes them cry? Perhaps more of us should have that opportunity. (p. xv)

Another teacher reflected to Wasley,

> After I got over the initial shock that you were going to ask so many questions, I found it to be a positive experience. It validated me as a teacher. Over the years, I've had very few observers. My administrators have been more interested in management than in content. Besides, they have so many people do that they don't have the time to get into it. (p. xvi)

"Learning about" goes only so far. Think about riding a bicycle. You can learn about bicycles all you want, but at some point, you must get on a bike and try to ride. Riding for the first time—and several subsequent times—is much better if someone who already rides bikes and has fleet feet is running alongside you.

What if you didn't allow anyone to be there for your first or subsequent trials? What if you wanted to privatize your first ride(s)? Based on the number of cuts, bruises, bumps, and fear cycles you went through on your first ride, you might or might not have gotten up on the bike again. Your second ride might have been much the same as your first. Eventually, without feedback and support, you might have given up on bike riding. Think what would have happened if you had de-privatized your bike riding experiences!

"We need to complete this agenda before August," Andy said. "Dottie, you're on."

"I'm going to make it quick," Dottie said. "You get 2 minutes to think, 1 minute to write, 1 minute to explain. That's 4 minutes each. What did you learn this year and what does your learning mean for

next year?" Jaws dropped as they contemplated their task and the time they had for it, but the Design Team got busy writing. Dottie recorded their answers:

Design Team Member	Learning	Implications
Kelly Bosco	Trust people to do their best and they will	We don't need a top-down management structure
Tasha Peart	Have a sense of humor	Apply your sense of humor to yourself
Aaron Dobroski	Communicate, communicate, communicate	We cannot wear out the Internet; let's keep communicating
Dottie Gibson	Everyone has a contribution to make	Continue to involve support staff in the work
Forrest Long	Flexibility, not rigidity	Be ready to change your mind and your actions
Roz Best	Don't rush things	Go slowly; things will work out if there's enough time
Andy Melvoli	Keep a record of what happens	Continue the portfolio, be ready to use its contents to explain the work
Robbie Beckel	There are wonderful people in this building	Trust ourselves—we can do it
Ariel Aboud	It's about the kids, but it's about the adults, too	Keep the focus

"Let's do this when we get back together in the fall, all of us in the PLC," Roz said. "I could have said what each of you said. It's rejuvenating to hear how alike we are, what we look for, and what we learn. Thank you, Dottie."

"Thank YOU," Dottie said and sat down.

Forrest spoke up, "My turn. Who's in? Who's out?" He was speaking of the Design Team membership for the rest of the school year and the beginning of the next school year. Everyone looked around the room, but no one said anything. "I guess we're all in, then. I've heard of a couple of people who want to join the Design Team, but let's wait until we get settled down this summer before we make any decisions."

With that, Andy asked people to evaluate the meeting online, using an online survey form and the group's norms. "For closure," he said, "let's whip around the room. Think of a clock. 1:00 a.m. is early morning, 12:00 p.m. is late evening. Where are we in terms of having a solid, working PLC? And why?" Of the eight members of the design team, four chose 2:00 to 4:00 a.m., two chose 5:00 to 7:00 a.m., one chose 12:00 noon, and the last chose 2:00 p.m. Each had good reasons for his or her choice, and Andy ended the meeting with, "Folks, in terms of hiring a new principal, it's 11:00 p.m. Let's get going!"

COACHING

De-privatization takes a variety of forms: coaching, peer coaching, mentoring, observations, and peer learning walks, for example. All of these forms of de-privatization are part of making change; they help change go from theoretical to practical, from knowing to doing, from planning to implementing. They help educators apply what they are learning to improve student learning.

Roz and several of the principal candidates mentioned the importance of coaching. One of the ways educators open up their practice is through coaching. Formal coaching involves a person whose job title is "coach." This person works with persons who are to be coached. Roz was, in fact, a teacher on special assignment (TOSA) during the past year. She was named "instructional coach," and she was obligated by her contract to specialize in coaching mathematics and language arts teachers. This formal arrangement was awkward for Roz and for the faculty; Roz had been a peer. Suddenly, she was different. She was moved from Instructional Staff on the staff roster to Front Office Staff, along with the principal and assistant principal. She was, thus, an administrator of sorts. Some staff members were afraid that what Roz discovered in their classrooms would get back to Josie, as the principal, and be used to evaluate them and make decisions about whether or not they could continue to work at Glen Haven.

Formally, coaches play a variety of roles in a school (Killion & Harrison, 2006). They may be any of the following:

Resource provider

Data coach

Curriculum specialist

Instructional specialist

Classroom supporter

Mentor

Learning facilitator

School leader

Catalyst for change (p. 1)

And, of course, they should be learners, according to Joellen Killion and Cindy Harrison, who wrote *Taking the Lead: New Roles for Teachers and School-Based Coaches* (2006). You'll find a chapter in their book on each of the coaching functions listed above. You'll also find more about what coaches do (and do not do) on Resource 9.2.

Formal coaching in a district is usually part of a coaching program. People at the district level are involved in selecting and supporting coaches. You'll find Killion's and Harrison's ideas about how districts and schools should support coaches on Resource 9.3. Unfortunately for Roz, there was no selection or support process at the district or school level. Stephanie Rogers would have been the ideal person to have coached the coaches, but she was not given the chance to do so, the district having received funds for coaching shortly before schools opened in the fall. Roz was pulled out of the classroom to coach and given little or no support, except through Josie. And, she was suddenly suspect to a faculty with whom she had been a peer. It was a rough year for Roz . . . and for her colleagues.

Having school-based coaches was a good idea whose time had not yet come in Glen Haven School District. No one was ready for coaching, and there seemed no great purpose for coaching. However, during the year, as data emerged about student achievement (including high school graduation rates) and school culture, so reasons for coaching were becoming apparent. Glen Haven's goals and summer work related to them set in motion the need for coaches. And, Roz's 1-year experience as a coach had helped her and the faculty distinguish what coaches should and should not do. GHMS was ready for a formal school coach.

Sometimes principals are asked to expand their role by becoming coaches. Having principals as coaches is not particularly effective. It is hard for principals to dismantle their role as supervisor and evaluator in order to coach. It is hard for teachers being evaluated by their principals to accept the principal as coach. The roles are essentially incompatible. The principal as supervisor is judgmental: "You are a good teacher" or "You need to improve." The underlying message is fundamental: "Keep doing what you are doing" or "Change in these ways" if you want to stay in this school.

The principal as coach is descriptive: "Three students in the back row were not on the same page as you were during the algebra lesson." The principal as coach invites a teacher to consider what has been described. The principal as supervisor mandates compliance. The messages can be confusing and, ultimately, threatening.

PEER COACHING

Glen Haven has a formal coach, Roz. She'll be helping Glen Haven educators in the next year or two to de-privatize what goes on in their classrooms. Glen Haven staff may also decide to engage others in coaching, peer coaching. Peer coaching may seem the opposite of formal coaching—therefore, *informal* coaching—but peer coaches function in the variety of ways a formal coach might and need just as much support. Peer coaching is hardly informal, in the sense of willy-nilly or lackadaisical. The two types of coaching are not opposites. Peer coaching, however, more directly and speedily helps educators become de-privatized.

Pam Robbins (2004) defines peer coaching as "a confidential process in which two or more professional colleagues work together to reflect on current practices; expand, refine, and build new skills; share ideas; teach one another; conduct classroom research; or solve problems in the workplace" (p. 164). Two of the most important parts of Robbins's definition are (1) the word *confidential* and (2) the mention of two or more people. Please don't imagine that peer coaches just wander into any of their peers' classrooms and out again. Peer coaching requires a very purposeful relationship and a very purposeful process.

Like other ways of de-privatizing practice, peer coaching happens gradually and over a period of time. It is not something that everyone does right away. People who are ready form pairs or triads (never more than a foursome) to share what they do in their classrooms and give each other feedback.

You can consult Resource 9.4 to discover a number of steps that Robbins suggests for implementing a peer coaching program.

DIFFERENTIATED COACHING

One breakthrough in coaching—formal or peer—can be found in the work of Jane Kise. A long-time student of the Myers-Briggs Type Indicator®, she has written a number of books about applying type to teaching and learning. In her chapter on differentiated coaching in *Powerful Designs for Professional Learning* (2008, pp. 143–154), Kise describes four coaching styles as they relate to personality preferences:

Coaching Style	Personality Preferences Related to Information and Decisions
Useful resource	Sensing and thinking preferences
Encouraging sage	Sensing and feeling preferences
Collegial mentor	Intuition and feeling
Expert	Intuition and thinking

Source: Kise (2008, p. 146).

See Resource 9.5 to examine some steps for coaching according to your preferences.

Other ways to open up classrooms for professional learning include mentoring, observations, and peer learning walks. You can read an overview of each of these professional learning strategies in Resourcess 9.6 (mentoring), 9.7 (observations), and 9.8 (peer walk-throughs).

THE VALUE OF TALK ABOUT TEACHING AND LEARNING

Many of the strategies related to professional learning—from protocols to lesson study, from examining student work to analyzing data—are effective in engaging educators in professional conversation. They are effective because their impetus is something concrete: a lesson, a piece of student work, data, the results of a walk-through, an article about teaching. They are grounded in the artifact, not sky-high in an abstraction. Conversations grounded in an artifact are more likely to be professional rather than "bitch-'n'-moan" sessions or gossip. It's not that chit-chat is a bad thing in schools; it's more that, with so little time together, our time as educators needs to be spent on helping all students learn. How disheartening it is, as a facilitator of adult learning, to hear teams descend from something substantive into rumor and hearsay, complaints and peeves.

Thankfully, as Charlotte Danielson observes, "Virtually every educator has experienced the professional rewards that result from rich conversations about practice" (2009, p. 1). "Routinely," she observes, "comments from teachers following a workshop mention that the most positive aspect of the session was the opportunity to engage in dialogue with colleagues" (p. 1). The more educators can talk about their work—dissect it, enlarge it, question it, improve it—and their students' learning, the more certain it is that conditions will improve for both adult and student learning.

Although there may be other purposes to a professional discussion—such as creating a rubric—the professional discussion or dialogue itself is essential. And a powerful artifact helps conversations be professional. Artifacts are hard to ignore, weighty with information and nuance. As much as possible, adult meetings should be founded on artifacts of student and teacher learning and teaching.

A Partial Guide to E-Mail Lingo

☺ = happy

☹ = not happy

BTW = by the way

X-(= brain dead

? = question

(((NAME))) = hugs

BFN = bye for now

FYI = for your information

FYA = for your amusement

IMHO = in my humble opinion

IMNSHO = in my not so humble opinion

JMO = just my opinion

LY = love ya

CIO = check it out

L8R = later

LOL=laughing out loud

"YOU HAVE MAIL!" The e-mails began to sail back and forth across the Internet. Here is the first one, from K. D. Weg to the Staff and Faculty:

Man, it's crazy times here at the Writing Project. I'm glad I'm staying near campus. Thought I could drive to/from home. LOL. We write every morning. My hand is usually shaking by the time we finish. We read our writing aloud and learn to get and give feedback. A lot like a tuning protocol: warm and cool. Then, in the afternoon we delve into teaching writing: curriculum, instruction, and assessment. We usually have homework! The group is fun, a lot of teachers from other content areas, actually. Next year, we're gonna get you here, Libby! Good conversations about students and teaching and learning. BTW, Robbie is turning into real writer. I hope she'll share some of her writing with you.

Later, from Anita:

The good news is I'm having a great time. ☺ The bad news is I'm having a great time. ☹ I want to continue to do this, write and talk about writing, teach and learn about writing. I'll never be the same. I have a ? for you all. Are you ready to help students write in your own content areas? You had better get used to the idea—that's one way to get students to think! I'm X-(. Good night.

Still later, from Robbie:

I had no idea I'd love writing so much. Why have I been teaching all the grammar and usage? I need to get kids to WRITE for an AUDIENCE and PURPOSE (and then we might have some reason for learning usage, at least). BFN
(((Everybody)))

One from Kelly about lesson study:

I had no idea it would be like this. We got right into lesson study, no foolin' around. It's not about us, personally, as teachers. Really! It's about lessons, which we construct together (or we use given lessons). It's about what happens to students when we try out those lessons. It's really about us as professionals sharing our experiences, skills, knowledge, whatever. JMO, it's great.

From Tasha

We have a great process for selecting the new principal . . . and some great applicants. We're involving students in the process—all the way from reading the apps to recommending the hire. Can you believe it? Serena is one of the students! She blows me away. I wish more of you could be involved, but a committee of 7 is probably OK; we have one parent, one community member, and a district administrator in addition to us. IMHO, lesson study is a blast. I think a bunch of us are going to want to do it regularly. It takes time—and we'll have to figure out how to get that—but we're already working with the district to capture some. LY!

From Lan on action research:

Oh, my, there's so much we can do about school culture. Our first task is just to narrow down all the possibilities. Then we're going to look for resources and do a book study with protocols. What do you think are the most beneficial and the most harmful aspects of our culture? Respond ASAP.

Forrest on lesson study:

I'm not sure what lesson study is NOT about. It's certainly not about just this one lesson we've been working on. It's about curriculum, instruction, assessment, classroom management, culture, learning styles and differences. At first I thought, why bother with only a few lessons. What difference would these make? But, now, I can't imagine designing a lesson the old way, which for me LOL was pretty laissez-faire.

Lorena on action research:

Thanks for getting back to us. Lots of you said that "safety" and "risk" were important aspects of culture here. Safety like feeling safe to be yourself. Risk like taking chances on learning new things. We'll follow up.

Andy:

CIO: Well, folks, we're down to two candidates. Either one would be great! Our students are contributing a LOT to the discussion—they have taken each candidate on a tour of the school and have learned a lot more than we have about them through our interviews and watching them teach. The students are unbelievable.

Pam on lesson study:

I wish I had learned this in college ☹! We actually think through lessons in terms of how students might "receive" them. What they might misunderstand or mistakes they might make. I never thought the word *per* was so important until going through this algebra lesson. We argue and argue about how to construct or improve a lesson but, eventually, we just have to go try it out on students and they let us know what works and what doesn't ☺. I'm also learning a lot about collecting data by observing what goes on with students. It's not about the teachers; it's about how well what the TEAM planned for the students really helps them learn.

Robbie:

I'm still writing. The Writing Project was over 4 weeks ago, and I can't stop. Help.

Kelly:

Drum roll, please. We have a principal. Do you remember the high school English teacher who helped us out with writing assessment and examining student writing? Well, she applied and she has accepted the job. It will be her first time as a principal, but she's really looking forward to working with us and she really understands PLCs. Let's welcome Victoria Brant to Glen Haven Middle School. Actually, she goes by the name Vick. . . . L8R

From Forrest:

I've decided to return to school to get my doctorate in professional development! I never thought that what we've done this year with PLCs could have such an influence on anyone, and I sure resisted a lot. LOL. I don't think I can manage counseling and grad work and the Design Team (actually, they are truly unmanageable), so I'm going to have to resign the DT. Anyone want to join up?

From Dinh: Count me in! I'd really like to be on the Design Team.

From Tiffany: Can you accept another aide on the Design Team?

Tasha: You bet! Dinh and Tiffany, you're in!

From Carl: Does someone else have to resign for me to join the Design Team?

From Andy: No, you're in, Carl, but I may want to take a break from the team. Three months, that's all. Would that be OK?

Robbie: We'll miss you, Andy, but welcome Tiffany, Dinh, and Carl. And, who wants to help with hiring new teachers in choir, social studies, and math/ science? Besides people in those departments, I mean.

Burt on action research: We know you are all so busy, but could you take time to read this article on middle schools and students at risk. We're thinking it gives us some direction in terms of an action research project.

Josie: Thanks for copying me on all the emails. You guys are doing great! I'm proud to know you!

YOUR TURN: WHAT ARE YOU LEARNING?

Vicky Brant said, "I'm so glad you asked me what I have learned from my work with Glen Haven Middle School. They reinforce for me how powerful teachers are, how much they know, how much they care. Principals and teachers do not have to be oppositional; they are 'in the game' of learning with each other. The most important word in our lexicon will be 'we' or 'us' not 'I' or 'me' or 'you.'"

What have you learned through reading and thinking about the content in this chapter?

SO WHAT?

"I am like most people. When I'm in a new situation and feeling insecure, I revert to old behavior. I'm worried I will revert to the old concept of principal as THE LEADER, the only one who knows what to do. Even though I've never been a principal, that's the image that's imprinted in my head and I need to trust people around me so that I don't go there."

Why is what you have learned important to you and to your colleagues?

NOW WHAT?

"It will take awhile, but I intend to sit with each and every person and ask this question 'What's important to you?' or 'What matters?' I will listen intensely to their answers and share my own answer to this question. I'm looking forward to learning from the incredible staff at GHMS."

You've finished this book! Congratulations. What (besides taking a well-deserve break) will you do related to what you have learned alongside Glen Haven Middle School faculty, staff and students?

RESOURCES FOR CHAPTER 9

9.1 School Culture Survey

9.2 A Coach Is, a Coach Is Not

9.3 District and School Support for School-Based Formal Coaches

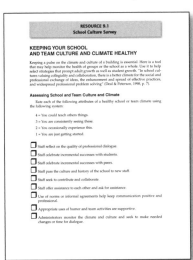

9.4 Resources Related to Peer Coaching

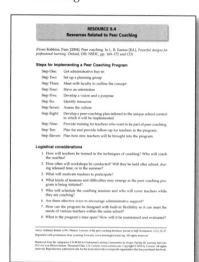

9.5 Personality Preferences

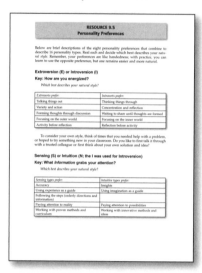

9.6 Resources Related to Mentoring

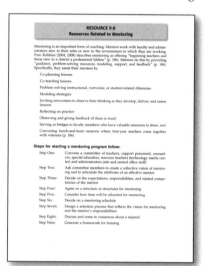

9.7 Resources Related to Observations

9.8 Peer Walk-Throughs

References

Aarons, D. I. (2010, June 10). Data in action: Schools innovate to keep students on graduation track. *Education Week Diplomas Count, 29*(13), 6.

Ackland, R. (1991, Winter). A review of the peer coaching literature. *Journal of Staff Development, 12*(1), 23–27.

Alloway, E., & Conlan, G. (1984, December). Direct versus indirect writing assessment (Summary). *Notes from the National Testing Network in Writing, IV*, 2.

Atlee, T. (2007). *The power of story—The story paradigm.* Retrieved from http://www.co-intel ligence.org/I-powerofstory.html

Bailey, S., & Easton, L. B. (2008). Visual dialogue. In L. B. Easton (Ed.), *Powerful designs for professional learning* (2nd ed.). Oxford, OH: National Staff Development Council.

Bernhardt, V. (2004). *Data analysis for comprehensive schoolwide improvement.* Larchmont, NY: Eye on Education.

Bernhardt, V. (2008). Data analysis. In L. B. Easton (Ed.), *Powerful designs for professional learning* (2nd ed.). Oxford, OH: National Staff Development Council.

Bill and Melinda Gates Foundation. (n.d.). Retrieved from http://www.gatesfoundation .org/united-states/Pages/measures-of-effective-teaching-fact-sheet.aspx

Blankstein, A. (2004). *Failure is not an option: Six principles that guide student achievement in high-performing schools.* Thousand Oaks, CA: Corwin and the HOPE Foundation.

Bridges, W. (2001). *The way of transition: Embracing life's most difficult moments.* Cambridge, MA: DaCapo Press, Perseus Books.

Bridges, W. (2004). *Transitions: Making sense of life's changes* (2nd ed.). Cambridge, MA: DaCapo Press, Perseus Books.

Bridges, W. (2009). *Managing transitions: Making the most of change* (3rd ed.). Cambridge, MA: DaCapo Press, Perseus Books.

Brown, A. L., & Campione, J. C. (1998). Designing a community of young learners: Theoretical and practical lessons. In N. M. Lambert & B. L. McCombs (Eds.), *How students learn: Reforming schools through learner-centered education.* Washington, DC: American Psychological Association.

Caro-Bruce, C. (2008). Action research. In L. B. Easton (Ed.), *Powerful designs for professional learning* (2nd ed.). Oxford, OH: National Staff Development Council.

Chadwick, R. (2002). *Beyond conflict to consensus.* Retrieved from http://www.managing wholes.com/—consensus.htm

City, E. A., Elmore, R. F., Fiarman, S. E., & Teitel, L. (2009). *Instructional rounds in education: A network approach to improving teaching and learning.* Cambridge, MA: Harvard Education Press.

Clinton, W. (1998, September). *Promising practices: New ways to improve teacher quality.* Retrieved from http://www2.ed.gov/pubs/PromPractice/index.html

Coalition of Essential Schools. (n.d.). Retrieved from http://www.essentialschools.org/cs/ resources/view/ces_res/137

Cooper, C. R. (1997). Holistic evaluation of writing. In C. R. Cooper & L. Odell (Eds.), *Evaluating writing: Describing, measuring, judging.* Urbana, IL: National Council of Teachers of English.

Covey, S. R. (1989/2004). *The 7 habits of highly effective people: Restoring the character ethic.* New York: Free Press.

Covey, S. R. (1991). *Principle-centered leadership.* New York: Summit Books.

Danielson, C. (1996). *Enhancing professional practice: A framework for teaching.* Alexandria, VA: Association for Supervision and Curriculum Development.

Danielson, C. (2006). *Teacher leadership that strengthens professional practice.* Alexandria, VA: Association for Supervision and Curriculum Development.

Danielson, C. (2009). *Talk about teaching! Leading professional conversations.* Thousand Oaks, CA: Corwin (with NASSP and NSDC).

Darling-Hammond, L., Wei, R. C., Andree, A., Richardson, N., & Orphanos, S. (Stanford School Design Network). (2009). Professional learning in the learning profession: A status report on teacher development in the United States and abroad. Oxford, OH: National Staff Development Council. (See also the related technical report.)

Deal, T. E., & Peterson, K.D. (1999). *Shaping school culture: The heart of leadership.* San Francisco: Jossey-Bass.

Delehant, A. M. (with von Frank, V.). (2007). *Making meetings work: How to get started, get going, and get it done.* Thousand Oaks, CA: Corwin and National Staff Development Council.

Deming, W. E. (1986). *Out of the crisis.* Cambridge, MA: MIT Press.

Deming, W. E. (2000). *The new economics for industry, government, education* (2nd ed.). Cambridge, MA: MIT Press Center for Advanced Education Services.

Downey, C. J., Steffy, B. E., English, F. W., Frase, L. F., & Poston, W. K., Jr. (2004). *The three-minute classroom walk-through: Changing school supervisory practice one teacher at a time.* Thousand Oaks, CA: Corwin.

DuFour, R., & Eaker, R. (1998). *Professional learning communities at work: Best practices for enhancing student achievement.* Bloomington, IN: Solution Tree.

Durant, M. W. (1999). *Managing organizational change.* Retrieved from http://www.crfonline.org/orc/pdf/ref4.pdf

Eagle Rock School and Professional Development Center. (1994). Retrieved from www.eaglerockschool.org

Easton, L. B. (1991). *The Arizona Student Assessment Program (ASAP) as educational policy* (Doctoral dissertation, University of Arizona). Ann Arbor, MI: University Microfilm International. (UMI 5032, Order No. 9210317)

Easton, L. B. (2002). *The other side of curriculum: Lessons from learners.* Portsmouth, NH: Heinemann.

Easton, L. B. (Ed.). (2004). *Powerful designs for professional learning.* Oxford, OH: National Staff Development Council.

Easton, L. B. (2008a). Context. In L. B. Easton (Ed.), *Powerful designs for professional learning.* Oxford, OH: National Staff Development Council.

Easton, L. B. (2008b). *Engaging the disengaged: How schools can help struggling students succeed.* Thousand Oaks, CA: Corwin.

Easton, L. B. (Ed.). (2008c). *Powerful designs for professional learning* (2nd ed.). Oxford, OH: National Staff Development Council.

Easton, L. B. (2008d). Shadowing. In L. B. Easton (Ed.), *Powerful designs for professional learning.* Oxford, OH: National Staff Development Council.

Easton, L. B. (2009). *Protocols for professional learning.* Alexandria, VA: Association for Supervision and Staff Development.

Editorial Projects in Education. (2010, June 10). *Education Week Diplomas Count, 29,* 34.

Elmore, R. (2000). *Building a new structure for school leadership.* Washington, DC: The Albert Shanker Institute.

Feltman, C. (n.d.). *Leadership and the enemies of learning.* Insight Coaching. Retrieved from http://www.insightcoaching.com/downloads/Leadership_and_Enemies_of_Learning.pdf

Fenton, B. (n.d.). New leaders for new schools: Forming aligned instructional leadership teams. *ASCD Express.* Retrieved from http://www.ascd.org/ascd-express/vol5/504-fenton.aspxF

Festinger, L., Riecken, H., & Schacter, S. (1956). *When prophecy fails: A social and psychological study of a modern group that predicted the destruction of the world*. New York: Harper-Torchbooks.

Fullan, M. (1994, September). Coordinating top-down and bottom-up strategies for educational reform. In *Systemic reform: Perspectives on personalizing education*. Retrieved from http://www2.ed.gov/pubs/EdReformStudies/SysReforms/fullan1.html

Gargiulo, T. (2009). *The power of stories in communication and management*. Retrieved from http://www.linkageinc.com/thinking/linkageleader/Documents/Terrance_Gargiulo_The_Power_of_Stories.pdf

Garmston, R., & Wellman, B. (1999). *The adaptive school: A sourcebook for developing collaborative groups*. Norwood, MA: Christopher-Gordon.

Gibbons, M. (2004, February). Pardon me, didn't I just hear a paradigm shift? *Phi Delta Kappan, 85*(6), 461–467.

Ginsberg, M. B. (2003). *Motivation matters: A workbook for school change*. San Francisco: Jossey-Bass.

Ginsberg, M. B. (2004). Classroom walkthroughs. In L. B. Easton (Ed.), *Powerful designs for professional learning*. Oxford, OH: National Staff Development Council.

Ginsberg, M. B. (2008). Using a school improvement focus to examine context. In L. B. Easton (Ed.), *Powerful designs for professional learning* (2nd ed.). Oxford, OH: National Staff Development Council.

Gladwell, M. (2002). *The tipping point: How little things can make a big difference*. New York, NY: Little, Brown.

Goldsmith, M. (n.d.). *Leadership excellence & bad behavior*. Retrieved from http://www.marshall goldsmithlibrary.com/cim/articles_display.php?aid=363

Graybill, O. (2008). Dialogue. In L. B. Easton (Ed.), *Powerful designs for professional learning* (2nd ed.). Oxford, OH: National Staff Development Council.

Gregory, G. H., & Kuzmich, L. (2007). *Teacher teams that get results: 61 strategies for sustaining and renewing professional learning communities*. Thousand Oaks, CA: Corwin.

Hackmann, D. (n.d.). *Distributed leadership* [PowerPoint]. University of Illinois. Retrieved from wvde.state.wv.us/.../FallDay01_Week1_Hackmann- &ie=UTF-8&oe=UTF-8

Hall, G. E., George, A. A., & Rutherford, W. A. (1986). *Measuring stages of concern about the innovation: A manual for the use of the SoCQ questionnaire* (Report No. 3032). Austin: Research and Development Center for Teacher Education, University of Texas at Austin.

Hall, G. E., & Hord, S. (1987). *Change in schools: Facilitating the process*. Albany: State University of New York Press.

Hall, G. E., & Hord, S. M. (2001). *Implementing change: Patterns, principles, and potholes*. Boston, MA: Allyn & Bacon.

Hall, G. E., & Loucks, S. F. (1978). Teacher concerns as a basis for facilitating and personalizing staff development. *Teachers College Record, 80*(1), 36–53.

Hall, G. E., & Loucks, S. F. (1979). *Implementing innovations in schools: A concerns-based approach*. Austin: Research and Development Center for Teacher Education, University of Texas.

Hiebert, J., Gallimore, R., & Stigleruch, J. W. (2002, June/July). A knowledge base for the teaching profession: What would it look like and how can we get one? *Educational Researcher, 31*(5), 3–15.

Hirsh, S. (2003, November). What's next after adopting the standards? *Results*, p. 3.

Hirsh, S., & Hord, S. M. (2008, December). Leader & learner. *Principal Leadership, 9*(4), 26–30.

Hirsh, S., & Killion, J. (2007). *The learning educator: A new era for professional learning*. Oxford, OH: National Staff Development Council.

Hord, S. (1997). *Professional learning communities: Communities of continuous inquiry and improvement*. Southwest Educational Development Laboratory. Retrieved from www.sedl.org/pubs/change34/

Hord, S. M., & Hall, G. E. (2001). *Implementing change: Patterns, principles, and potholes*. Boston: Allyn & Bacon.

Hord, S. M., & Sommers, W. A. (2008). *Leading professional learning communities: Voices from research and practice*. Thousand Oaks, CA: Corwin (a joint publication with NAESP and NSDC).

Hord, S. M, Roussin, J. L., & Sommers, W. A. (2010). *Guiding professional learning communities*. Thousand Oaks, CA: Corwin.

Hord, S. M., Rutherford, W. L., Huling-Austin, L., & Hall, G. E. (1987). *Taking charge of change*. Alexandria, VA: Association for Supervision and Curriculum Development.

Jaquith, A., Mindich, D., Wei, R. C., & Darling-Hammond, L. (Stanford Center for Opportunity Policy in Education). (n.d.). Teacher professional learning in the United States: Case studies of state policies and strategies: Technical report. Oxford, OH: Learning Forward (formerly National Staff Development Council).

Jerald, C. D. (2007, January). *School culture: The hidden curriculum* [Issue Brief]. Learning Point Associates in Partnership with the Southwest Educational Development Laboratory (SEDL) and WestEd. Retrieved from http://www.centerforcsri.org/files/Center_IB_Dec06_C.pdf

Jolly, A. (2008). *Team to teach: A facilitator's guide to professional learning teams*. Oxford, OH: National Staff Development Council.

Killion, J. (2009). *Collaborative professional learning in school and beyond: A tool kit for New Jersey educators*. Trenton, NJ: New Jersey Department of Education.

Killion, J. (2008). *Assessing impact* (2nd ed.). Thousand Oaks, CA: Corwin & National Staff Development Council.

Killion, J., & Harrison, C. (2006). *Taking the lead: New roles for teachers and school-based coaches*. Oxford, OH: National Staff Development Council.

Killion, J., & Harrison, C. (2007). *Innovation configurations* (Vol. 3). Oxford, OH: National Staff Development Council.

Kise, J. (2006). *Differentiated coaching: A framework for helping teachers change*. Thousand Oaks, CA: Corwin.

Kise, J. (2008). Differentiated coaching. In L. B. Easton (Ed.), *Powerful designs for professional learning* (2nd ed.). Oxford, OH: National Staff Development Council.

Kise, J., & Russell, B. (2010). *Creating a coaching culture for professional learning communities*. Bloomington, IN: Solution Tree Press.

Kotter, J. P. (1996). *Leading change*. Cambridge, MA: Harvard Business School Press.

Kotter, J. (2006, April 12). Power of stories. *Forbes*. Retrieved from http://www.forbes.com/2006/04/12/power-of-stories-oped- cx_jk_0412kotter.html

Kruse, S., Seashore Louis, K., & Bryk, A. (1994, Spring). Building professional community in schools. *Issues in Restructuring Schools*, p. 6. Retrieved from the Center for School Organization and Restructuring: www.wcer.wisc.edu/archive/cors/issues%5Fin%5FRestructuring%5FSchools/issues_NO_6_SPRING_1994.pdf.

Kubler-Ross, E. (1969/1989). *On death and dying*. London: Routledge.

Lambert, N. M., & McCombs, B. L. (Eds.). (1998). *How students learn: Reforming schools through learner-centered education*. Washington, DC: American Psychological Association.

Leader, G. (March 3, 2010). *No principal left behind* [Blog]. Harvard Education Publishing. Retrieved from http:www.hepg.org/blog/10

Learning Forward (formerly National Staff Development Council, NSDC). (n.d.). www.learningforward.org (formerly www.nsdc.org).

Lencioni, P. (2002). *The five dysfunctions of a team: A field guide for leaders, managers, and facilitators*. San Francisco: Jossey-Bass.

Lewin, K. (1947). Frontiers in group dynamics: Concept, method and reality in social science. *Human Relations, 1*(5), 41.

Lewis, C. (2008). Lesson study. In L. B. Easton (Ed.), *Powerful designs for professional learning* (2nd ed.). Oxford, OH: National Staff Development Council.

Lieberman, A., & Friedrich, L.D. (2010). *How teachers become leaders*. New York: Teachers College Press.

Lieberman, A., & Miller, L. (Eds.). 2008 *Teachers in professional learning communities: Improving teaching and learning.* New York: Teachers College Press.

Lieberman, A., & Wood, D. R. (2003). *Inside the National Writing Project: Connecting network learning and classroom teaching.* New York: Teachers College Press.

Lipton, L., & Wellman, B. (2004). *Pathways to understanding: Patterns & practices in the learning-focused classroom* (3rd ed.). Sherman, CT: MiraVia, LLC.

MacBeath, J. (2005). Leadership as distributed: A matter of practice. *School Leadership and Management, 25*(4), 349–366.

Mahaffie, J. (2009, April 30). *Story learning—the power of stories in getting through to people.* Retrieved January 14, 2011, from http://foresightculture.com/2009/04/30/story-learning%E2%80%94the-power-of-stories-in-getting-through-to-people

Many, T., & King, D. (2008, Summer). Districts speak with one voice: Clarity and coherence come from professional learning communities. *Journal of Staff Development, 29*(3), 28–32.

Marzano, R. (2003). *What works in schools: Translating research into action.* Alexandria, VA: Association for Supervision and Curriculum Development.

Mass, N. J., & Berkson, B. (1995). Going slow to go fast. *The McKinsey Quarterly, 4,* 18–29.

Mayrowetz, D. (2008). Making sense of distributed leadership: Exploring the multiple usages of the concept in the field. *Educational Administration Quarterly, 44*(3), 424–435.

McKeever, B., & The California School Leadership Academy. (2003). *Nine lessons of successful school leadership teams: Distilling a decade of innovation.* San Francisco: WestEd.

McLaughlin, M. W., & Talbert, J. E. (2006). *Building school-based teacher learning communities: Professional strategies to improve student achievement.* New York: Teachers College Press.

Mezirow, J. (1991). *Transformative dimensions of adult learning.* San Francisco: Jossey-Bass.

Murphy, J. (2005). *Connecting teacher leadership and school improvement.* Thousand Oaks, CA: Corwin.

Murphy, M. (2009). *Tools & talk: Data, conversation, and action for classroom and school improvement.* Oxford, OH: National Staff Development Council.

Myers, I. B., & Briggs, K. (n.d.). *The MBTI® (or Meyers-Briggs Type Inventory®).* Retrieved from http://www.myersbriggs.org/my%2Dmbti%2Dpersonality%2Dtype/mbti%2Dbasics

National Research Council. (2000). *How people learn: Brain, mind, experience, and school.* Washington, DC: National Academies Press.

National School Boards Association. (n.d.). *Taking stock.* Retrieved from http://www.nsba.org/sbot/toolkit/ts.html

National Staff Development Council. (1998, October). Dealing with difficult people. *Tools for Schools.*

National Writing Project. (2010). *Writing Project professional development continues to yield gains in student writing achievement* (No. 2). Berkeley, CA: Author.

Newmann, F., & Wehlage, G. (1995). *Successful school restructuring: A report to the public and educators by the center for restructuring schools.* Madison: University of Wisconsin Press.

Northwest Regional Educational Lab (NWREL, now known as Education Northwest). (n.d.). *The 6+1 Trait® Writing Framework.* Retrieved from http://educationnorthwest.org/traits

Pascale, R., Sternin, J., & Sternin, M. (2010). *The power of positive deviance: How unlikely innovators solve the world's toughest problems.* Cambridge, MA: Harvard Business School Press.

Pate, J. L., James, L., & Leech, D. (2005). *Teacher leaders: A catalyst for instructional leadership.* Retrieved from http://www.eric.ed.gov:80/ERICWebPortal/search/detailmini.jsp?_nfpb=true&_&ERICExtSearch_SearchValue_0=ED491493&ERICExtSearch_SearchType0=no&accno=ED491493

Peters, T. (2010). *The little big things: 163 ways to pursue excellence.* New York: HarperCollins.

Peters, T. J., & Waterman, R. H., Jr. (2004). *In search of excellence: Lessons from America's best-run companies.* NY: HarperCollins Publishers, Inc.

Pfeffer, J., & Sutton, R. (2000). *The knowing-doing gap: How smart companies turn knowledge into action.* Cambridge, MA: Harvard Business School Press.

Public Conversations Project. (n.d.). *A sample set of agreements for dialogue.* Retrieved from http://www.publicconversations.org/

Rand Education. (2004). *The policies of public school administrators: Policy implications from an analysis of state level data.* Retrieved from www.rand.org

Ravitch, D. (2009). *The death and life of the American school system: How testing and choice are undermining education.* New York: Perseus Books.

Reeves, D. B. (2006). *The learning leader: How to focus school improvement for better results.* Alexandria, VA: Association for Supervision and Curriculum Development.

Roberts, C. (2000). "Leading without control: Moving beyond the 'principal do-right' model of educational leadership." In Senge, P., Cambron-McCabe, N., Lucas, T., Smith, B., Dutton, J., & Kleiner, A. *Schools that learn: A fifth discipline fieldbook for educators, parents, and everyone who cares about education.* New York: Doubleday.

Roberts, T. (1998). *The power of Paideia schools: Defining lives through learning.* Alexandria, VA: Association for Supervision and Curriculum Development.

Robertson, H., & Hord, S. (2008). Accessing student voices. In L. B. Easton (Ed.), *Powerful designs for professional learning* (2nd ed.). Oxford, OH: National Staff Development Council.

Robbins, P. (1999, Summer). Mentoring. *Journal of Staff Development, 20*(3), 40–42.

Robbins, P. (2004). Peer coaching. In L. B. Easton (Ed.), *Powerful designs for professional learning.* Oxford, OH: National Staff Development Council.

Rogers, E. (1962/1983). *Diffusion of innovations.* Glencoe, IL: Free Press.

Ross, R., Roberts, C., & Kleiner, A. (2000). Balancing advocacy and inquiry. In P. Senge, N. Cambron-McCabe, T. Lucas, B. Smith, J. Dutton, & A. Kleiner (Eds.), *Schools that learn: A fifth discipline fieldbook for educators, parents, and everyone who cares about education* (pp. 219–222). New York: Currency/Doubleday.

Roy, P. (2007). *User's guide: Innovation configurations for NSDC's Standards for Staff Development.* Oxford, OH: National Staff Development Council.

Roy, P., & Hord, S. M. (2003a). *Innovation configurations* (Vol. 1). Oxford, OH: National Staff Development Council.

Roy, P., & Hord, S. M. (2003b). *Moving NSDC's Staff Development Standards into practice: Innovation configurations* (Vol. 1). Oxford, OH: National Staff Development Council.

Roy, P., & Hord, S. M. (2005a). *Innovation configurations* (Vol. 2). Oxford, OH: National Staff Development Council.

Roy, P., & Hord, S. M. (2005b). *Moving NSDC's Staff Development Standards into practice: Innovation configurations* (Vol. 2). Oxford, OH: National Staff Development Council.

Senge, P. M. (1990). *The fifth discipline: The art and practice of the learning organization.* New York: Doubleday Currency.

Senge, P., Cambron-McCabe, N., Lucas, T., Smith, B., Dutton, J., & Kleiner, A. (2000). *Schools that learn: A fifth discipline fieldbook for educators, parents, and everyone who cares about education.* New York: Doubleday/Currency/Random House.

Shaughnessy, M. (1977). *Errors & expectations: A guide for the teacher of basic writing.* New York: Oxford University Press.

Sinek, S. (2009a, September). *How great leaders inspire action.* TED (Puget Sound). Retrieved from http://www.ted.com/talks/simon_sinek_how_great_leaders_inspire_action.h tml

Sinek, S. (2009b). *Start with why: How great leaders inspire everyone to take action.* New York: Portfolio Books/Penguin.

Sizer, T. R. (1985). *Horace's compromise: The dilemma of the American high school.* Boston: Houghton Mifflin.

Sizer, T. R. (1992). *Horace's school: Redesigning the American high school.* Boston: Houghton Mifflin.

Sizer, T. R. (1996). *Horace's hope: What works for the American high school.* Boston: Houghton Mifflin.

Sizer, T. R., & Sizer, N. S. (1999). *The students are watching: Schools and the moral contract.* Boston: Beacon.

Smith, M. A. (2008). Immersing teachers in practice. In L. B. Easton (Ed.), *Powerful designs for professional learning* (2nd ed.). Oxford, OH: National Staff Development Council.

Smith, M. L., & Glass, G. V. (1987). *Research and evaluation in education and the social sciences.* Englewood Cliffs, NJ: Prentice-Hall.

Sparks, D. (2004a, Winter). The positive deviance approach seeks solutions that already exist. *Journal of Staff Development, 25*(1), 46–47.

Sparks, D. (2004b, March). Take action to bridge the knowing-doing gap. *Results.* Retrieved from http://www.nsdc.org/news/results/res3-04spar.cfm

Sparks, D. (2007). Use genuine dialogue. In *Leading for results: Transforming teaching, learning and relationships in schools* (2nd ed.). Thousand Oaks, CA: Corwin/Oxford, OH: National Staff Development Council.

Spillane, J. P. (2006). *Distributed leadership.* San Francisco: Jossey-Bass. Retrieved from http://www.northwestern.edu/ipr/publications/papers/Spillane_DistribLead.pdfp.2

Stokes, L. (n.d.). The National Writing Project: Anatomy of an improvement infrastructure. In C. Coburn & M.K. Stein (Eds.), *Research and practice in education: Building alliances, bridging the divide* (pp. 147–162). Lanham, MD: Rowman & Littlefield.

Strickland, C. A. (2009). *Professional development for differentiating instruction: An ASCD action tool.* Alexandria, VA: Association for Supervision and Curriculum Development.

Study Circles Resource Center. (1993, Winter). Dialogue and debate. *Focus on Study Circles.* Retrieved from http://www.nextstep.state.mn.us/res_detail.cfm?id=52

Swanson, C. B. (2010, June 10). Progress postponed: Graduation rate continues decline. *Education Week Diplomas Count, 29*(34), 22.

Taylor, K. (2010, April). The learned word. *Phi Delta Kappan, 91*(7), 7.

Tuckman, B. W. (1965). Developmental sequence in small groups. *Psychological Bulletin, 63*(6), 384–399. Retrieved from http://www.managingwholes.com/—consensus.htm

Viadero, D. (2009, October 28). Turnover in principalship focus of research. *Education Week, 29*(9), 1, 14.

von Frank, V. (Ed.). (2008). *Finding time for professional learning.* Oxford, OH: National Staff Development Council.

Wagner, T. (2001, January). Leadership for learning: An action theory of school change. *Phi Delta Kappan, 82*(5), 378–383. Retrieved from http://www.schoolchange.org/articles/leadership_for_learning.html

Wagner, T. (2003, May). School reform that works: Reinventing America's schools. *Phi Delta Kappan, 84*(9), 665–668.

Wagner, T., Kegan, T., Lahey, L. L., Lemons, R. W., Garnier, J., Helsing, D., Howell, A., & Rasmussen, H. T. (2006). *Change leadership: A practical guide for transforming our schools.* San Francisco: Jossey-Bass.

Wasley, P. A. (1994). *Stirring the chalkdust: Tales of teachers changing classroom practice* (The Series on School Reform). New York: Teachers College Press.

Weinstein, M., Jacobwitz, R., Ely, T., Landon, K., & Schwartz, A. E. (Institute for Education and Social Policy). (2009, June). *New schools new leaders: A study of principal turnover and academic achievement at new high schools in New York City: NYU: Condition Report Prepared for the Education Finance Research Consortium.* New York: NYU Steinhardt School of Culture, Education, and Human Development. Retrieved from http://www.albany.edu/edfin/

Weisbord, M. R. (1987). *Productive workplaces: Dignity, meaning, and community in the 21st century.* San Francisco: Jossey-Bass.

Weisbord, M. R. (1992). *Discovering common ground: How Future Search Conferences bring people together to achieve breakthrough innovation, empowerment, shared vision, and collaborative action.* San Francisco: Berrett-Koehler.

Weiser, C. (2004, July 14). Young people answer call of political action, run for office. *USA Today*. Retrieved from http://www.usatoday.com/news/politicselections/nation/2004–07–14-young-pols_x.htm

Wheatley, M. (1992/1994). *Leadership and the new science: Learning about organization from an orderly universe*. San Francisco: Berrett-Koehler.

Wheatley, M. J., & Kellner-Rogers, M. K. (1996). *A simpler way*. San Francisco: Berrett-Koelher.

Wurtzel, J. (2007, Fall). The professional, personified. *Journal of Staff Development, 28*(4), 30–35.

Young Women's Leadership Charter School. (n.d.). http://www.ywlcs.org

Index

CORWIN

A SAGE Company

The Corwin logo—a raven striding across an open book—represents the union of courage and learning. Corwin is committed to improving education for all learners by publishing books and other professional development resources for those serving the field of PreK–12 education. By providing practical, hands-on materials, Corwin continues to carry out the promise of its motto: **"Helping Educators Do Their Work Better."**

Advancing professional learning for student success

Learning Forward (formerly National Staff Development Council) is an international association of learning educators committed to one purpose in K–12 education: Every educator engages in effective professional learning every day so every student achieves.